2002

Encyclopedia
of
Movie Special Effects

by Patricia D. Netzley

Oryx Press
2000

The rare Arabian Oryx is believed to have inspired the myth of the unicorn. This desert antelope became virtually extinct in the early 1960s. At that time, several groups of international conservationists arranged to have nine animals sent to the Phoenix Zoo to be the nucleus of a captive breeding herd. Today, the Oryx population is over 1,000, and over 500 have been returned to the Middle East.

Published simultaneously in Canada
Printed and bound in the United States of America

∞ The paper used in this publication meets the minimum requirements of American National Standard for Information Science—Permanence of Paper for Printed Library Materials, ANSI Z39.48, 1984.

Library of Congress Cataloging-in-Publication Data

Netzley, Patricia D.
   The encyclopedia of movie special effects / by Patricia D. Netzley.
      p. cm.
   Includes bibliographical references and index.
   ISBN 1-57356-167-3 (alk. paper)
   1. Cinematography—special effects—Encyclopedias.   I. Title.
TR858.N48 2000
778.5'345'03—dc21   99-047733
                                                                            CIP

CONTENTS

PREFACE

Special effects are techniques employed to make the staged events of a movie seem real. These techniques fall into three basic categories: visual effects, mechanical effects, and makeup effects—each with several subcategories. What was once a fourth category, sound effects, is now generally considered separate from the definition of "special effects."

Visual effects are manipulations of the visual images of a movie, either in-camera during photography or using the film negative during postproduction. In the earliest years of filmmaking, all visual effects were in-camera. For instance, a cameraman in 1910 might use a flat object called a matte to block the left side of the film from exposure, photograph an actress sitting on the right side of the scene, rewind the film, move the matte to the right side, and photograph the actress sitting on the left. Upon subsequent viewing, the movie would appear to show the actress sitting next to her identical twin.

The same illusion can be created today in postproduction using two shots of the actress filmed at different times. With a device called an optical printer, the filmmaker can project the two images side by side and then rephotograph them together in one frame of film. Alternatively, the filmmaker might scan the two images into a computer and use software tools to position them in the same frame before transferring them back onto film. In either case, the movie audience would see a scene that never actually existed.

While visual effects experts work with images, mechanical effects experts work with machinery, tools, incendiary devices, and other equipment to manipulate physical events during live-action filming. For example, they might make an elaborate set break apart to simulate an earthquake, or simply cause branches to rustle as though someone were shaking them. Often these effects are combined with visual effects during postproduction. In *Jurasic Park* (1993), for example, mechanical effects experts made branches rustle so that computer experts could later add a browsing dinosaur into the scene. *Jurassic Park* blended mechanical and digital effects in several scenes; the movie won an Academy Award for its visual effects. Academy Awards are also given to movies that create illusions using makeup effects. For example, *Men in Black* (1997) won an Academy Award for combining mechanical effects with makeup to produce a variety of unusual space aliens, including a person who seemed able to stretch his own facial skin.

The *Encyclopedia of Movie Special Effects* provides information about every movie to win a special effects Academy Award, as well as about movies that are responsible for significant advances in the field of special effects. Movies that did not win an Academy Award or provide new technology or techniques are excluded, except for those few that illustrate important aspects of the special effects industry. For example, while *Flubber* (1997) featured advanced digital effects, the movie did not win an Academy Award or contribute new technology to the field, so it has been excluded. The *Star Trek* movies also failed to win Academy Awards for their special effects, and only one of them—*Star Trek II: The Wrath of Khan* (1982)—used a new type of special effects technique, yet they are all discussed in one entry, because doing so illustrates how studios make decisions regarding what kind of effects to employ.

Each movie entry provides information about the basic techniques used to film the movie's special effects scenes, and whenever possible offers details about specific effects. However, although today's filmmakers are extremely forthcoming about their methods, prior to the 1970s filmmakers often did not keep records about how they created certain illusions, much as early magicians did not tell the general public how they performed certain tricks. Therefore details about a specific effect are not always available for pre-1970s films.

General information about such effects can be found, however, in entries on special effects terms, techniques, equipment, and devices. These entries also provide information about special effects films that did not merit their own entries. Consequently if the reader's favorite movie is not in the topical list of entries, it might be found through the subject index.

The *Encyclopedia* covers special effects films released as of June 1999, a total of 366 entries, arranged in an A-to-Z format. All entries have been written for the layperson rather than the special effects professional. No prior knowledge of special effects is necessary to understand the discussions, and the reader need not have seen the films being discussed—although, of course, watching the movies will give greater insights into the material.

The *Encyclopedia* also provides biographical information (including birth and death dates when known) about the best-known mechanical, visual, and makeup effects experts throughout the history of filmmaking, including stuntpeople and directors who have contributed to the field of special effects. In addition, the book discusses some of the early cinematographers who discovered new photographic techniques. However, while the basics of photographic effects are explained, they are not given the same attention as postproduction special effects techniques. Appendixes offer lists of special effects houses and magazines as well as movies that have won, or have been nominated for, Academy Awards for special effects. An extensive bibliography follows the appndixes; in addition, entries provide suggestions for further reading. A subject index completes the book.

This *Encyclopedia*'s emphasis is on the modern era, when the term "trick photography" gave way to "special effects." After reading the book's movie entries and using the extensive cross-references to find further information about various special effects terms, techniques, companies, and experts, the reader will have a thorough understanding of how moviemakers turn illusions into reality.

Acknowledgments

The author wishes to thank Matthew Netzley for his explanations of computer software; Jim Jarrard of Cinenet for providing valuable information about photography and special effects; and George Faber, formerly of Viacom International, for acting as a liaison between the author and various experts in the movie industry.

TOPICAL INDEX

People in the Special Effects Industry

Makeup Artists/Creature Designers

Directors/Producers

Stuntmen and Stuntwomen/Actors

Abbott, L.B. (1908–1985)

Lenwood Ballard Abbott, commonly known as L.B., was a cameraman who became known for his "trick shots" and discovered new types of photographic special effects. For example, while working on the 1970 movie *Tora! Tora! Tora!*, he learned that by filming the explosion of miniatures at an extremely fast speed, the size and power of the display appeared to be magnified.

Abbott won an Academy Award for his work on *Tora! Tora! Tora!*, as well as for work on *Dr. Doolittle* (1967), *The Poseidon Adventure* (1972), and *Logan's Run* (1976). He was also nominated for his work on *Journey to the Center of the Earth* (1959). His other films include *Voyage to the Bottom of the Sea* (1961), *Cleopatra* (1963), *The Sound of Music* (1965), *Fantastic Voyage* (1966), *Planet of the Apes* (1968), *The Towering Inferno* (1974), and *Butch Cassidy and the Sundance Kid* (1969). Abbott also worked on such television series as *Voyage to the Bottom of the Sea* and *Lost in Space*.

Born in 1908, Abbott was the son of a silent-film cinematographer and began his own career as a cameraman when he was only 18. In 1957 he became head of special effects at 20th Century Fox studios, where he remained until his retirement. Abbott died in 1985. *See also* CLEOPATRA; FANTASTIC VOYAGE; PLANET OF THE APES; THE POSEIDON ADVENTURE; TORA! TORA! TORA!; THE TOWERING INFERNO; 20TH CENTURY FOX.

Further Reading

Abbott, L.B. *Special Effects: Wire, Tape, and Rubber Band Style*. Hollywood: ASC Press, 1984.

The Abyss

Directed by James Cameron, the 1989 movie *The Abyss* won an Academy Award for Best Visual Special Effects. Nine special effects houses worked on the film, including Industrial Light & Magic (ILM). Special effects work at this facility at the time was under the supervision of special effects expert Dennis Muren.

ILM provided the most difficult special effect in the film, a water creature that communicated by forming the face of characters in the movie. To accomplish this effect, actors' faces were scanned with a laser, digitized in a computer, and used to shape the face of the computer-generated creature. For this effect, ILM had to develop new software to create realistic water and improve a morphing program that was used to make the transition from one image to the next. Although this sequence was on screen for only 75 seconds and was comprised of just 20 special effects shots, it took eight months to create because of its complexities.

In addition to computer graphics, *The Abyss* employed elaborate props and miniatures. Deep-sea submersibles, for example, were built as both full-sized mockups and miniatures. For a scene in which the submersibles pass over a nuclear submarine, the miniatures were mounted on an overhead gantry. Controlled with wires like marionette puppets, they were then maneuvered over a 60-foot model of the submarine. The film's director, James Cameron, later considered using this same method in making *Titanic* (1997) for a scene in which two submersibles pass over the wreck of the Titanic, but eventually decided on an alternate technique. *See also* ACADEMY AWARDS; CAMERON, JAMES; INDUSTRIAL LIGHT & MAGIC; *TITANIC*.

Further Reading

Duncan, Jody. "20 Years of Industrial Light & Magic." *Cinefex 65,* March 1996.

Shay, Don. "Mayhem Over Miami." *Cinefex 59,* September 1994.

———. "Ship of Dreams." *Cinefex 72,* December 1997.

Academy Awards

The Academy Awards are bestowed each year by the Academy of Motion Picture Arts and Sciences to recognize excellence in various categories of film work. The prize is a gold-plated statuette known as the Oscar, and the categories include Best Picture, Best Director, and Best Actor/Actress.

Although the first Academy Awards were given in 1927, the category of Best Special Effects did not exist until 1939. In 1962 it was split into two categories: Best Special Visual Effects and Best Sound Effects. In 1972, the Academy decided to stop giving an annual award for Special Visual Effects; any movie recognized for such work was given a Special Achievement Award instead. This occurred from 1972 to 1976 and again in 1978, 1980, 1983, and 1990. In between these years, the Best Special Visual Effects category was again designated an annual competitive award.

The Best Special Visual Effects category was again changed in 1996, when it became an annual award called Best Visual Effects. Similarly, the Best Sound Effects category was considered a Special Achievement Award from 1975 to 1979 and again in 1981, 1984,

and 1987, but in the 1990s became an annual award called Best Sound Effects Editing. The Best Makeup Award was not established until 1981, although in 1983 no award was given.

In honoring special effects work, the Academy generally defines an effect as any image that does not already exist for filming. In other words, if a digital artist makes a perfect representation of a particular mountain, his creation will not be worthy of an Academy Award because a cameraman could simply go out and film that mountain naturally. However, if the same artist turns the mountain into a violently erupting volcano, it is considered an award-worthy effect. Movies that earn Academy Awards for special effects typically do not win because of only one such shot, but because of many. A film is judged on its total body of effects. *See also* APPENDIX A: ACADEMY AWARD WINNERS AND NOMINEES FOR SPECIAL EFFECTS.

Further Reading

Academy Awards Web site. http://www.oscar.com, 1999.

Wiley, Mason, and Damien Bona. *Inside Oscar: The Unofficial History of the Academy.* New York: Ballantine Books, 1993.

Accidents

Accidents are always a concern in special effects work. According to government statistics, an average of seven people are injured during the making of every movie. Most of these injuries are minor, but some can be severe.

In 1920, while working on *The Haunted Spooks,* actor Harold Lloyd blew off one of his fingers and the thumb of his right hand. During the filming of *The Wizard of Oz* (1939), actress Margaret Hamilton was seriously burned in a scene in which her character, an evil witch, was to vanish in a burst of flame. Her stuntwoman was also hospitalized after a smoking broomstick exploded. Similarly, a stuntman was seriously burned during the filming of *War of the Worlds* (1953); he was intentionally set on fire for a scene but the flames were not extinguished quickly enough and his face was burned.

Such accidents were due to the misuse of pyrotechnics; however, fires and explosions do not always cause the most serious injuries on movie sets. Stuntwork is considered the most dangerous activity, whether or not it is accompanied by pyrotechnic effects. Experts estimate that over half of all film-related injuries are due to stuntwork, and there are 2.5 deaths for every 1,000 stunt-related injuries. These injuries can be caused by improper animal handling, blank ammunition use, falls, car or motorcycle chases, and airplane or helicopter stunts.

The latter category has caused the most fatalities. Out of the 37 stunt-related deaths that occurred between 1980 and 1990, 24 involved helicopters. Among these, the most notable occurred in 1982, when actor Vic Morrow and two Vietnamese children, Myca Dinh Lee and Renee Chen, were killed by a helicopter while filming the movie *The Twilight Zone*. This incident triggered the creation of new restrictions regarding the kinds of scenes in which children can perform and also increased concern for health and safety issues in the entertainment industry.

Unfortunately, it often takes a serious accident to make filmmakers pay more attention to safety issues. The first safety regulations were established after an accident occurred on the set of the 1929 movie *Noah's Ark*. Before that time, directors often used untrained extras rather than stuntpeople for some scenes, even if they involved dangerous work. In *Noah's Ark* thousands of extras were placed on a set that had been rigged to be flooded. Only 40 to 50 of the extras were qualified stuntmen, and therefore, they were ill prepared when tons of water slammed onto the soundstage. In the resulting chaos, several people died and many were injured, including one man who lost his leg. After this incident, several new safety regulations and policies were enacted.

The 1980s had a particularly high fatality rate. In addition to the *Twilight Zone* deaths, pilot Art Scholl was killed performing plane stunts for *Top Gun* (1986), cameraman Bruce Ingram while filming a car crash for *The Wraith* (1986), and famed stuntman Dar Robinson while performing a motorcycle stunt for *The Million Dollar Mystery* (1987). In 1989 stuntman Clint Carpenter was killed performing a helicopter stunt for the movie *Hired to Kill* and stuntman Geoff Brewer and four other people were killed in a helicopter crash while working on the movie *Delta Force 2*. Several nonfatal but still serious injuries also occurred during the 1980s. Stuntwoman Heidi Van Beltz was thrown from a car during a crash for the movie *Cannonball II* (1984) and is now a paraplegic, two stuntmen received eye injuries from flying glass in the 1988 movie *Sanctuary*, and stunt coordinator Joel Kramer broke his back while filming an unreleased action movie in 1989.

Because of such incidents, today's directors are well aware of safety issues on the set, and they typically change stunts at the first sign of trouble. For example, while making the 1997 movie *Titanic*, director James Cameron decided not to film any more stunt falls after several injuries occurred on the set; while working on an upended ship one stuntman cracked a rib, another broke his ankle, and a stuntgirl fractured her cheek. Cameron also took elaborate safety precautions while filming scenes with actors, because of the rushing water involved in his movie. During the final scenes of the ship sinking, 30 members of the huge crowd were lifeguards who wore wetsuits under their costumes and took up strategic positions so that no actor was more than 15 feet from a lifeguard. Similarly, special effects experts working on *Jurassic Park* (1993) held several meetings for actors, stuntpeople, and crewmembers specifically devoted to safety issues regarding their 18,000-pound mechanical Tyrannosaurus rex, which stood 20 feet tall and was 40 feet from nose to tail.

But despite such precautions, fatalities still occur. One of the most recent stunt-related deaths was in 1995, when a boat killed stuntwoman Janet Wilder and injured four other people during the filming of *Gone Fishin'*. The boat was supposed to go up a ramp, fly over a strip of land, and come back down into water on the other side. Instead it came off the ramp and flipped into a crowd of actors and stuntpeople.

In addition, there have been several recent accidents involving the improper use of production equipment, two of them fatalities. In 1992 a worker on the movie *The Bodyguard* died after being crushed between two lighting cranes. In 1993 actor Brandon Lee accidentally shot and killed himself while filming *The Crow* after a prop gun was mistakenly loaded with a .44-caliber slug. During filming of the 1998 movie *Mighty Joe Young* a camera crane platform broke and seriously injured two crewmen. Such tragedies highlight the need for continuing awareness on every movie set, no matter what type of equipment or special effects are being used. *See also* ANIMALS; CAMERON, JAMES; *NOAH'S ARK;* PYROTECHNICS; STUNTS; *TITANIC; WAR OF THE WORLDS; THE WIZARD OF OZ.*

Further Reading

Harmetz, Aljean. *The Making of* The Wizard of Oz. New York: Knopf, 1977.

LaBrecque, Ron. *Special Effects: Disaster at* Twilight Zone. New York: Scribner, 1988.

McCann, Michael. "Stunt Safety." *Center for Safety in the Arts,* http://www.tmn.com/Artswire/csa/arthazards/performing/stunts, May 1999.

Stuntmen and Special Effects. New York: Ripley Books, 1982.

Alien Movies

The 1979 movie *Alien* spawned three sequels: *Aliens* (1986), *Alien³* (1992), and *Alien Resurrection* (1997). The first two movies each won an Academy Award for special effects, and *Alien³* was nominated for such an award as well. All of the films featured the same basic effects, including pyrotechnics, miniature photography, mechanical effects, makeup work, creature creation, and elaborate puppetry. However, the technology behind these effects improved from movie to movie.

For example, every *Alien* film used a man in a foam latex suit to portray the main alien, but the suit's design underwent several changes over the years. The original suit, created from an illustration by Swiss artist H.R. Giger, had a transparent head dome that was eliminated for *Aliens* and *Alien³* but reinstated for *Alien Resurrection*. Similarly, the suit in the first two movies had appendages on its back that were deleted for *Alien³* but reinstated for *Alien Resurrection*. In fact, the makers of *Alien Resurrection* located some of the original alien molds and suit pieces and refurbished them for their movie.

In each of the movies, the alien suits had tiny blackscreened holes in the neck to allow the wearer to see, and all used a form-fitted helmet to mount the elaborately sculpted head. By the time the fourth movie was filmed, the head of the suit had become much lighter, with its weight distributed more evenly for the wearer's comfort. This was partly because the silicone molding materials used to make the head improved over the years, as did the head's mechanisms.

For each movie, there were both unmoving, or nonarticulated, heads and moving ones, the latter operated either by cable or radio control. However, whereas in *Aliens* there was a human performer inside of the queen alien, in *Alien Resurrection* the queen was an animatronic figure operated with hydraulics and cables that were later removed from the scene digitally. The queen's baby was also an animatronic figure, 8 feet tall and operated by a combination of hydraulics and puppetry rods.

Advances in animatronics also helped improve the "chest burster" torso featured in the movie series. In each case, a fake shell allowed an alien, which was actually a puppet, to pop out of what seemed to be the actor's chest. However, the torso in the fourth movie had complex mechanisms that were not present in the first; the chest split was rigged to occur automatically when a laser scalpel touched the chest, and the scene was later enhanced digitally to make it seem even more realistic. Similarly, the alien egg puppets featured in the series were highly mechanized in *Alien Resurrection*, allowing them to move in more subtle ways and open more smoothly.

Another special effect technique that improved between *Alien* and *Alien Resurrection* was the way in which alien blood was made to seem acid-like. In the first three movies, this illusion was created by dripping acetone onto Styrofoam made up to look like metal, which then dissolved. However, the fumes resulting from this process were toxic and difficult to control. Therefore in *Alien Resurrection* this method was largely replaced with two other techniques. In some instances a foaming substance was placed on a piece of metal that had been rigged to drop away at a key moment. In others the appearance of an acid eating away at metal was created digitally.

Makeup techniques also improved with each movie, as did miniature photography. For example, whereas *Alien* used basic bluescreen methods during filming, *Alien Resurrection* used a sophisticated redscreen method, which yielded mattes of higher quality. In each process, a miniature is filmed in front of a screen, blue or red respectively, and this background is later replaced. However, because the model spaceships had a blue tone, their edges were more defined when a red background was employed.

In *Alien Resurrection*, the miniatures were more detailed and more sophisticated than in previous *Alien* movies, with working interior lights and moving parts. An "observation room," built in 1/6 scale, had a rotating center operated via motion control. It was 7 feet tall and 30 feet in diameter, and around its perimeter were 14 chambers meant to hold aliens. During filming, orange cards were placed in the chamber windows, and in postproduction, the orange areas were removed so that the creatures could be digitally matted into the scene.

A total of eight spaceship models were featured in *Alien Resurrection*, the largest a craft called the *Auriga*. Built out of steel and urethane at 1/1000 scale, it was 12 feet long and weighed 200 pounds. The docking bay miniature for this craft was 13 feet tall and 18 feet long; it was made to appear even longer with digital matte paintings. Interestingly, the paintings were done in Paris, France, in the studio of Jean-Marie Vives, and transmitted to the filmmakers via the Internet. Scenes with the miniatures had many other elements as well—sometimes as many as 12 layers of images—which required a motion-control camera to make multiple passes.

Alien Resurrection relied on computer work for many of its 205 special effects shots, sometimes even using digital techniques to fix problems that occurred during filming. For example, an underwater scene was first created using the alien suit with a slit in the throat, through which the stuntman could place a breathing device between takes (this was very similar to the filming conditions involved in making 1954 movie *The Creature From the Black Lagoon*). The footage, however, was disappointing, so a computer-generated alien later replaced the live-action one, except for a few closeup shots. For a shot of the alien getting hit underwater with a grenade, a wax dummy filled with fake viscera was substituted.

The *Alien* series reflects changes in special effects technology that occurred between 1979 and 1997. It also demonstrates how budgets affect the quality and quantity of special effects shots. The budget for *Alien Resurrection* was $70 million, which was far more than any previous film in the series. *See also* ANIMATRONICS; BLUESCREEN PROCESS; MAKEUP; MINIATURES AND MODELS; PUPPETS.

Further Reading

Murdock, Andrew, and Rachel Aberly. *The Making of* Alien Resurrection. New York: HarperPrism, 1997.

Norton, Bill. "Cloning Aliens." *Cinefex* 73, March 1998.

Allen, Irwin (1916–1991)

Irwin Allen was a writer, director, and producer best known for his special effects-laden disaster movies of the 1970s, which include *The Poseidon Adventure* (1972) and *The Towering Inferno* (1974). He also created the 1960s television series *Lost in Space*. For many of his movies, Irwin employed the talents of special effects cinematographer L.B. Abbott, who was known for his "trick shots."

Born in 1916, Allen graduated from Columbia University with a journalism degree. He worked as a magazine editor and then a radio producer before becoming a documentary filmmaker. In 1953 he won an Academy Award for producing *The Sea Around Us*, which was based on an environmental book by Rachel Carson. His other films include *Voyage to the Bottom of the Sea* (1961) and *Five Weeks in a Balloon* (1962). Allen died in 1991. *See also* ABBOTT, L.B.; *THE POSEIDON ADVENTURE*; *THE TOWERING INFERNO*.

Anaglyphic Process

Developed in the 1950s, the anaglyphic process is a method by which the eye perceives two-dimensional film images as being three-dimensional, having depth as well as width and height. To create this illusion, an image is superimposed on top of its own likeness, but one is printed in red and the other in blue-green. If the viewer wears glasses with a red filter in one lens and a blue-green one in another, the image appears to be three-dimensional; without the glasses the audience sees no 3-D effect.

Audience viewing a movie through special glasses to perceive its 3-D effects, which were created via the anaglyphic process. *Corbis/Bettmann.*

Examples of movies made with the anaglyphic process include *House of Wax* (1953), *It Came From Outer Space* (1953), and *Creature from the Black Lagoon* (1954). These films are still popular today, but are shown as black-and-white prints without their 3-D enhancements. *See also* 3-D.

Further Reading

Hayes, R.M. *3-D Movies: A History and Filmography of Stereoscopic Cinema*. Jefferson, NC: McFarland & Company, 1998.

Kawin, Bruce F. *How Movies Work*. Berkeley: University of California Press, 1992.

Anamorphic Process

Invented in France in 1927, the anamorphic process is the method whereby a special camera lens is used to compress a widescreen image so that it fits into a standard-sized film frame. The image is restored to its original widescreen size during projection. Two examples of the anamorphic process are the CinemaScope and Panavision widescreen filming systems.

In terms of special effects, the anamorphic process is significant because its squeezing process causes problems in post-production when optical effects are added to a scene. The squeezed anamorphic image must be decompressed before a special effects artist can work with it. Therefore while making *Star Wars* (1977), special effects experts at the Industrial Light & Magic (ILM) studio decided to avoid these problems by filming with a nonanamorphic widescreen 35mm camera system called VistaVision, which had been largely abandoned by that time in favor of Panavision.

VistaVision creates enough space for widescreen images by running standard 35mm film horizontally, rather than by using the anamorphic squeezing process. However, it can be combined with a squeeze, in which case it is called Technirama; the most famous example of a film made with Technirama is *The Music Man* (1962). *See also* CAMERAS, MOTION PICTURE; CINEMASCOPE; EDITING, FILM; NEGATIVE, FILM; VISTAVISION.

Further Reading

Imes, Jack. *Special Visual Effects: A Guide to Special Effects Cinematography*. New York: Van Nostrand Reinhold, 1984.

Kawin, Bruce F. *How Movies Work*. Berkeley: University of California Press, 1992.

Ryan, Rod. *American Cinematographer Manual*. Hollywood: The ASC Press, 1993.

Stecker-Orel, Elinor. *Special Effects Photography Handbook*. Buffalo, NY: Amherst Media, 1998.

Angle, Camera

A camera angle is simply the point of view of the camera lens during filming as defined by the physical position of the camera. For example, a high-angle shot is when the camera is shooting down on the subject from above it, and a low-angle shot is when the camera is shooting up at the subject from below. By varying camera angles, a director can make the film more visually engaging and influence its dramatic thrust.

One director particularly known for employing unusual camera angles was Alfred Hitchcock. In *Vertigo* (1958), for example, he used a camera angle called a bird's-eye-view shot to look down on a man hanging from a rain gutter. This angle emphasized the distance from the hanging man to the ground.

Example of unique camera angles used by Alfred Hitchcock in *Vertigo* (1958). *Photofest.*

Another director who employed a variety of camera angles was Orson Wells. His 1941 movie *Citizen Kane* offers many examples of unique cinematography. For example, in one scene, the camera begins at a small boy's eye level and then tilts upwards to show a man looking down at him. In another scene, the camera pans, or moves slowly in a sweeping motion, across a room to arrive at a mirror before a character does. *See also* CAMERAS, MOTION PICTURE.

Further Reading

Kawin, Bruce F. *How Movies Work*. Berkeley: University of California Press, 1992.
Ryan, Rod. *American Cinematographer Manual*. The ASC Press, 1993.
Stecker-Orel, Elinor. *Special Effects Photography Handbook*. Buffalo, NY: Amherst Media, 1998.

Animals

Animals have been used in stuntwork since the early days of filmmaking. At first, the most prevalent performers were horses. Horses were often treated as living props and used without consideration for their physical safety, which resulted in many equine injuries and deaths. More than 100 horses were killed during the filming of the chariot race scene in *Ben-Hur* (1926). Such events eventually inspired the creation of laws and regulations protecting not only horses but other animal actors as well, which include creatures ranging from the lions, monkeys, and elephants seen in jungle pictures to "movie star" dogs such as Lassie, Rin Tin Tin, and Beethoven.

Modern movie animals appear on the set accompanied by a professional trainer who is well prepared for the acting job at hand. In most cases, the trainer has been given several months to prepare the animal for a desired stunt, and often more than one animal has been trained to play a single part. For example, there were 60 mice used to play the role of one mouse in *Mouse Hunt* (1997); each of them had been trained for six months.

Similarly, dozens of puppies performed for the 1996 movie *101 Dalmatians* and had to be replaced with new ones as they grew older during the six-month shoot. A replacement puppy was made to look like his predecessor by adding, subtracting, or reshaping spots with makeup. In addition, great care was taken to disinfect areas where the puppies would work, because at six to eight weeks of age the puppies would be susceptible to a potentially fatal canine disease known as parvo.

The demands of an animal acting job can be extensive. This is particularly true for movies like *Mouse Hunt* and *101 Dalmatians*, in which the animals were the stars of the film. It is also true for animals involved in special effects scenes, which often have to be filmed several times to provide enough material for subsequent digital work, as was the case for both *Babe* (1995) and *Dr. Doolittle* (1998).

On occasion, however, it is either impractical or impossible to get a live animal to perform a particular special effects stunt. In such cases an animatronic figure or other type of puppet is substituted for the animal. This occurred for some scenes in *Mouse Hunt*, *Babe*, and *Dr. Doolittle*, as well as for scenes in *Free Willy* (1993) and *Star Trek IV: The Voyage Home* (1986) that featured whales. However, creating realistic digital or animatronic animals is not always an easy task.

For *101 Dalmatians*, for example, special effects experts at Industrial Light & Magic (ILM) tried unsuccessfully to input information about live puppies into their computers to create computer-generated puppies. They attempted to scan the shape of the puppies but couldn't get them to hold still long enough for this technique to work. They then put motion-capture sensors on the puppies, but the dogs only chewed them off. Finally they ended up building a maquette, or sculpture, of a puppy, scanning it into the computer, animating it, and adding texture and paint. By varying the spot patterns and slightly altering the puppy's shape, many versions of a puppy were possible.

Once the digital puppies were complete, they were replicated and added to shots as necessary, primarily to fill in backgrounds or puppy groups. In such situations, digital and live puppies often sat side-by-side. This was one of the most difficult aspects of the digital work, because it was important for the audience not to be able to discern a difference between the two types of puppies.

In most closeup scenes, however, animatronics were used whenever a live puppy could not perform a particular action. Jim Henson's Creature Shop provided several such figures for the movie, including 50 puppies, an Airedale dog, three dairy cows, a pig, a horse, a sheep, three raccoons, and some chickens. The puppies, which were constructed of foam latex, urethane, and silicone, were made in several forms; some were operated by remote-control, some by cables and/or puppetry rods, and some by hand. Many had complex mechanisms to provide realistic movements, such as breathing motions. One puppy had a tube and pump system that enabled it to urinate, and the cows had tubes in their udders that provided baby formula to the live puppies sucking on them. Cables, rods, and other puppetry devices were removed from each scene digitally during postproduction.

Digital effects and animatronics have eliminated the need for animals to perform in dangerous situations. However, in closeup live-action work, most viewers can still discern the difference between a real animal and a counterfeit one. Therefore animal "stars" remain a vital part of filmmaking. *See also* ACCIDENTS; ANIMATRONICS; *BABE; DR. DOOLITTLE; MOUSE HUNT;* PUPPETS; *STAR TREK* MOVIES.

Further Reading
Duncan, Jody. "Puppy Proliferation." *Cinefex 69*, 1997.
Fry, Ron, and Pamela Fourzon. *The Saga of Special Effects*. Englewood Cliffs, NJ: Prentice-Hall, 1977.
Shay, Estelle. "*Dr. Doolittle*: Animals with Attitude." *Cinefex 75*, October 1998.
———. "Of Mice and Men." *Cinefex 73*, March 1998.

Animatics

Animatics are a series of animated images used to represent special effects elements during the preproduction or production phases of a movie. Essentially a moving storyboard, animatics can be made with sketches, objects, or computer graphics, and they can appear either by themselves or intercut with filmed material.

Modern animatics are often computer-generated stick figures composited with other such elements as live-action background plates. Early animatics were more primitive. For example, the animatics for the speeder bike scene in *Return of the Jedi* (1983) was a videotape of models moved on sticks. But no matter what technique is used to make an animatic, its basic purpose is to show how a particular special effect will work once the movie is finished. In 1999, the *Star Wars* movie *The Phantom Menace* became the first movie to employ animatics to previsualize every shot in the film. The creation of these animatics was supervised by David Dozoretz, one of the foremost experts in the craft. *See also* ANIMATION, COMPUTER; COMPUTER GRAPHICS; DOZORETZ, DAVID; *STAR WARS* MOVIES; STORYBOARDS.

Further Reading
Duncan, Jody. "The Ghost and Mr. Muren." *Cinefex* 63, September 1995.
Smith, Thomas G. *Industrial Light & Magic: The Art of Special Effects*. New York: Ballantine Books, 1986.

Animation, Cel

Cel animation is a process that animates, or gives life to, a drawn figure. The process begins with an artist drawing and/or painting a figure on a series of translucent celluloid sheets, or cels. This figure is varied only slightly from cel to cel, each of which is placed on a device called an animation stand and photographed one cel per frame of film. When these frames are projected in sequence at the rate of 24 frames per second, which is the standard for motion picture film, the figure seems to move.

The first animated cartoon was made by American filmmaker J. Stuart Blackton in 1906, but he did not expand on this work. The first true animator was Winston McCay, a newspaper cartoonist who made a series of animated cartoons beginning with "Little Nemo" in 1910. McCay's cartoons were made from rice paper mounted on cardboard. Cels were not employed until 1913, when J.R. Bray created what is known as "The Artist's Dream." Bray discovered that several layers of cels could be put together to create one image and subsequently developed several tools and techniques to refine this practice.

In 1917, animator Max Fleischer used Bray's idea to develop the Rotoscope, which was a device used to overlay drawings on live-action film. Fleischer made several cartoons during his career, including the first to in-clude a soundtrack, "Song Car-Tune" (1924). The first sound cartoon to involve dialogue was Walt Disney's "Steamboat Willie" (1928).

Disney also created the first full-length animated movie, *Snow White and the Seven Dwarves* (1937). In fact, Disney was responsible for many innovations related to animation and film technology, including the first color cartoon (*Flowers and Trees*, 1932), the first use of the multiplane camera (*The Old Mill*, 1937), and the first stereophonic sound (*Fantasia*, 1940). Today Disney continues to be at the forefront of cel animation, creating such movies as *The Little Mermaid* (1989), *Beauty and the Beast* (1991), *Aladdin* (1992), and *Mulan* (1998).

Warner Brothers Studios has also offered significant contributions to the field of cel animation, most notably through its "Bugs Bunny" cartoons. A more recent contributor is 20th Century Fox, which created the full-length feature *Anastasia* (1997).

Modern cel animators are increasingly relying on digital techniques to enhance their films. However, 3-D computer animation is considered a separate branch of animation. Notable 3-D animated films include *Toy Story* (1995), *Antz* (1998), and *A Bug's Life* (1998). *See also* ANIMATION, COMPUTER; ANIMATION STAND; DISNEY, WALT; THE WALT DISNEY COMPANY; 20TH CENTURY FOX; WARNER BROTHERS.

Further Reading
Lasseter, John, and Steve Daily. Toy Story: *The Art and Making of the Animated Film*. New York: Hyperion, 1995.
Thomas, Bob. *Disney's Art of Animation: From Mickey Mouse to* Beauty and the Beast. New York: Hyperion, 1991.

Animation, Computer

Computer animation is the process by which a computer-generated figure is animated, or made to move, through time and space. There are two main categories of computer animation: computer-assisted animation and computer-generated animation. Computer-assisted animation typically involves the traditional cel animation process, which uses sequential two-dimensional (2-D) drawings to create the illusion of movement.

The earliest computer animation systems enabled an artist to scan these drawings into a computer one at a time, color them using a paint software program, and then film the computer screen as the computer flipped from one drawing to another. Later systems made it possible to transfer the animated drawings directly from the computer to video and then to film.

The first full-length animated movie to employ computer scanning, painting, and 2-D animation of drawings was *The Little Mermaid* (1989), but only for one scene. The following year, *The Rescuers Down Under* became the first to use the technique for every scene in a movie. Computerized 2-D animation is still used for animated features today, along with three-dimensional (3-D) computer animation, which gives an animated figure depth as well as height and width.

The first use of 3-D computer animation in a full-length animated feature was for *Beauty and the Beast* (1991), for a scene of a couple dancing. The virtual camera representing the audience's viewpoint moved around the dancing couple, showing them from all angles to create the illusion that they were

Title characters in *Beauty and the Beast* (1991), the first full-length animated feature film to employ 3-D animation. ©*The Walt Disney Company/Photofest.*

real 3-D figures instead of just flat drawings on an animation cel. This kind of animation is called computer-generated animation, because the computer and the artist work together to generate, or create, a 3-D figure.

The degree to which the artist drives the animation process varies. Sometimes the animator does most of the work, whereas other times the computer performs the task almost unaided. For example, one artist might outline and color each part of an image by hand, using computer drawing and paint software tools, while another might tell the computer to use a database of images to create and animate a scene automatically, so that no hand-drawing is necessary.

In order to give the digital artist a starting point from which a figure or scene can be created, a device called a scanner is often used to input digital information about a photograph, model, maquette, or body cast of an actor into the computer. Scanning a 2-D image into a computer is a relatively simple process; the image is simply laid on the scanning device and the computer does the rest of the work. Methods for scanning 3-D objects into a computer are more complicated. One of the most common is to lay a grid of lines over the object and press against key points on the grid with a stylus or digital wand from a 3-D scanning apparatus. A digital wand is capable of providing information about more than 3,000 points on an object, creating a complex figure of dots on a corresponding virtual grid. Once all of these dots are in place, they can be digitally connected with lines to create a 3-D wireframe image.

To animate a wireframe figure, an animator can choose from several techniques. One is to animate freehand, manipulating the image frame by frame using software drawing tools. Another is to use a software animation program that makes it possible for the computer to fill in movement in between key frames. In this case, the animator gives instructions regarding how the figure should move in time and space to get from point A in one frame to point B in another. The computer then automatically moves the figure. However, these movements are typically so perfect that they are not realistic, and animators often adjust them later by hand.

Alternatively, an animator can create more lifelike movement with a telemetry or motion-capture system. A telemetry system uses a puppet shaped like the computer-generated figure that is linked to the computer, so that as the puppeteer moves the puppet the computer records those movements and applies them to the computer-generated figure. A motion-capture system also records movement information, but is more typically used with live actors than with puppets. There are several different types of motion-capture systems, but the basic principle is the same for all. Some form of sensor placed at various locations on the person's body "captures" a performance, digitizing it so it can be used to drive a computer-generated figure. Motion capture can create extremely realistic movements. One example of it in use appears in the 1997 movie *Titanic*, which featured lifelike computer-generated people in background scenes.

Computer-animated figures have virtual skeletons that are unseen by the audience but ensure that the final figure will move correctly. The figures also have animation "chains" that perform much like muscles, connecting various points on a figure to make them move in concert. Figures might have hundreds of control points. In the 1995 movie *Jumanji*, for example, the animals were so complex that their animation chains had to be color coded to help artists differentiate them. A chain of red spirals might move a leg, while a chain of blue spirals might control a shoulder.

Moreover, just as a computer can tell one part of a figure's body how to move in relation to another, it can tell an entire object how to move in relation to other objects in a scene. This makes it possible to create a realistic flock or swarm, in which a large group of computer-generated creatures move through time and space without ever bumping into one another. One recent example of a movie that employed this to good advantage is *Starship Troopers* (1997). It used Dynamation software, which animates points or particles, to generate dozens of dots that could be applied to the background plate to represent swarming bugs. Each dot was assigned its own radius, speed, and direction capabilities and then given information about the terrain in the scene, so that once it was

animated it would not hit rocks or other bugs. In this way, the Dynamation software allowed digital experts to create a background filled with moving insects, without having to animate each one individually. Dynamation and other particle animation programs can also be used to create dust, debris, comet tails, galactic clouds, firestorms, and similar digital images, but of course these require less complicated programming parameters than animation involving complex wireframe characters.

Once animation with a wireframe figure is perfected, the figure must be given color, texture, shading, and other features in a process called rendering, which yields the final, high-quality image. Sometimes, however, the figure is rendered before it is animated. But regardless of which approach is used, animators must check the final figure to make sure that surface features are behaving properly. A computer can have difficulty recognizing solidity, which means, for example, that a character's elbow might move straight through a sweeping cape. This happened in the 1996 movie *Mars Attacks!;* animators had to correct the problem by hand.

New animation software programs are continually being devised to solve such problems, as well as to improve the way that computers and artists work together to create realistic computer-generated figures. Some of these programs are available commercially, while others are proprietary to whatever special effects house has developed them. Digital artists are continually adapting commercial software and developing new software to meet the needs of a particular movie project. For example, *The Flintstones* (1994) and *Jumanji* inspired the first software to generate realistic digital hair, *Waterworld* (1995) and *Titanic* (1997) were responsible for the first software to give digital oceans realistic surface movements, and *Jurassic Park* (1993) transformed the process by which 3-D computer animation is combined with live action. Each new movie brings with it the possibility of new computer software and new advances in digital technology. *See also* ANIMATION, CEL; DIGITAL WAND; DYNAMATION; *THE FLINTSTONES;*

JUMANJI; JURASSIC PARK; MARS ATTACKS!; TITANIC; WATERWORLD; WIREFRAME.

Further Reading

Bell, Jon A., and George Maestri. *3-D Studio Special Effects.* Indianapolis: New Riders Publishing, 1994.

Jones, Karen R. Mars Attacks! *The Art of the Movie.* New York: Ballantine Books, 1996.

Robertson, Barbara. "Cyber Movie Stars." *Digital Magic*, January 1996.

———. "*Jumanji*'s Amazing Animals." *Computer Graphics World*, January 1996.

Simak, Steven A. "Cloning the Digital Way." *Digital Magic,* August 1997.

Street, Rita. *Computer Animation: A Whole New World.* Gloucester, MA: Rockport, 1998.

Upstill, Steven. *The Renderman Companion: A Programmers Guide to Realistic Computer Graphics.* Reading, MA: Addison Wesley, 1990.

Animation Stand

An animation stand is a backlit device that holds an animation cel or similar artwork in place for photography. Modern animation stands are controlled by computers, enabling the operator to move, light, and photograph the artwork in a variety of ways and then duplicate those actions as many times as necessary.

One of the earliest computer-controlled animation stands was the "Compsey," short for Computer Operated Motion Picture System. Invented by Douglas Trumbull for his work on *Star Trek: The Motion Picture* (1979), it was used as a compositing tool to add animated images to miniature photography. *See also* ANIMATION, CEL; COMPOSITING; ROTOSCOPING; TRUMBULL, DOUGLAS; *STAR TREK* MOVIES.

Further Reading

Sammon, Paul M. *Future Noir: The Making of Blade Runner.* New York: Harper Collins, 1996.

Animatronics

Animatronics are electronic and mechanical creatures that perform as actors on a live-action shoot. They can represent a nonexistent beast such as a dragon, dinosaur, or space alien or a real animal that is difficult or impossible to film. Sometimes an animatronic is an entire creature, while on other occa-

sions it is only a head worn by a performer in a body costume.

When an animatronic represents the entire body of a creature, it is first made as a sculpture, which is used to make an epoxy or fiberglass mold. The mold is then injected with silicone or foam latex and baked to make skin. Meanwhile the creature's skeleton, or armature, is made out of steel and/or lightweight aluminum. This understructure includes the mechanisms that enable the creature to move, such as hinges, servo connectors, wiring, pneumatics, hydraulics, and a variety of other electronic-, radio-, and cable-controlled devices.

These devices were greatly improved as a result of work done on *Jurassic Park* (1993) and *The Lost World* (1997). The designer of the animatronics in those movies was Stan Winston, who is, to date, considered the foremost expert in the field. For *Jurassic Park*, Winston hired a team of engineers to design a new hydraulics system for one of his animatronic dinosaurs, a Tyrannosaurus rex. As a result, the T-rex was the most sophisticated animatronic that had ever been built. It had 57 different functions, with all but the radio-controlled eyes driven with a hydraulics system in the understructure of its belly. For scenes involving gross body movements, the figure was placed on a hydraulics motion base similar to ones used for flight simulators and amusement park rides such as Disneyland's "Star Tours" and Universal Studio's "Back to the Future" attractions. Such equipment had never before been used on a motion picture shoot.

Another unique feature of Winston's T-rex was the way its hydraulics were controlled. Instead of traditional hand-held devices, such as joysticks, the dinosaur was manipulated via a telemetry device, which was a 1/4-scale aluminum duplicate of its armature. Movements on the armature were transmitted to a computer, which in turn immediately sent an electronic signal to produce corresponding movements on the full-sized T-rex. The computer could also record these movements for repeated playback. This system made it possible for far fewer puppeteers to operate a figure than had previously been the case.

For *The Lost World*, Winston improved this system still further, by combining the telemetry device with cables and placing the hydraulics outside of the figures' bodies. This meant that when a puppeteer manipulated the telemetry device, those movements were transmitted via cables to the hydraulics unit, which in turn transmitted them via cables to the full-sized figure. This system was a revolutionary development, because with the hydraulics outside of the figures there was more room for other devices inside the animatronics. Consequently Winston's dinosaurs were able to perform more complex movements than previous animatronics.

Another technological advance to come out of *The Lost World* involved the manufacture of skin for animatronics. Winston used foam latex for the dinosaur skins in both movies, but for the second one he developed thinner skin that enabled him to make realistic folds. He also added simulated muscles beneath the skin. These muscles were made of foams, elastics, spandex, and other fabrics, while the skin was made of foam latex. In addition, Winston sealed his skins with a weatherproofing silicone coating, because of some rain damage experienced by the T-rex during the filming of *Jurassic Park*. Artists then painted the skins in a realistic fashion. Had the animals required fur, the hair would have been applied as individual strands, punched into the skin by hand after being dipped in adhesive.

Winston also designed a creature for the 1997 movie *Relic*. Because the structure of the suit had to fit the actor exactly, it was made from a lifecast rather than a sculpture. To create the lifecast, the actor had to don a bodysuit and climb onto a special rig. He was then wrapped in plaster bandages, which required several hours to dry. The resulting body and head casts were slit, carefully removed and repaired, and used to create fiberglass forms. Wire was placed over the fiberglass, and clay was sculpted over the wire. Once the clay hardened, it was used to make another mold for foam latex skin pieces.

These pieces were then detailed and applied back over the mold, which formed the core of the creature.

Various mechanisms within the creature were made of aluminum, in order to keep the weight of the suit down to 35 pounds. Although some of the mechanisms were radio-controlled, others were powered by a cable that ran along the actor's back to the underside of the creature's tail and then out of the suit. Combining cable-controlled devices with radio-controlled ones is extremely common in animatronics work, as well as in modern puppetry. In fact, puppets increasingly employ sophisticated devices developed for animatronic creatures, because puppeteers are the ones responsible for manipulating both types of figures during a movie shoot. *See also* ARMATURE; DIGITAL IMAGE DATABASE; LATEX, FOAM; HYDRAULICS; *JURASSIC PARK; THE LOST WORLD;* PUPPETS; TELEMETRY DEVICE; WINSTON, STAN.

Further Reading

Cadigan, Pat. *The Making of* Lost in Space. New York: HarperPrism, 1998.

Cosner, Sharon. *Special Effects in Movies and Television*. New York: J. Messner, 1985.

Culhane, John. *Special Effects in the Movies*. New York: Ballantine, 1981.

Duncan, Jody. *The Making of* The Lost World. New York: Ballantine Books, 1997.

Esseman, Scott. "A Gorilla Named Joe." *Cinefex 76,* January 1999.

Murdock, Andrew. *The Making of* Alien Resurrection. New York: HarperPrism, 1997.

Timpone, Anthony. *Men, Makeup, and Monsters*. New York: St. Martin's Griffin, 1996.

Aperture

The word "aperture" typically refers to the opening in a camera lens. The size of this opening controls the amount of light that reaches the film. Aperture can also refer to the opening that lies behind the lens of a camera or projector; this opening determines the size of a single film frame or of a projected image.

Aperture sizes are commonly expressed in terms of *f-stop*, which is a number that defines the relationship between the focal length of the lens and the width of its opening. Most movie lenses fall into the range of f/2.2 to f/22; an f/2.2 allows far more light to reach the film than an f/22.

The expression "full aperture" refers to film whose entire width is exposed. Before the advent of sound, which requires a soundtrack along the edge of the negative, all 35mm film was full aperture. Today, however, there is only one full-aperture 35mm format; it is sized to use its full width while still providing a soundtrack. Known as Super35, its negative is .980 inches x .73 inches, with an aspect ratio of 1.319. In comparison, the standard aperture, also called the Academy aperture, has a negative of .864 inches x .63 inches and an aspect ratio of 1.37.

The Super35 format is unique in that it creates widescreen movies without using anamorphic lenses, which squeeze an image within a camera and then unsqueeze it during projection. The anamorphic process makes it more difficult to create digital special effects, because a squeezed anamorphic image must be decompressed before an artist can use it to create a visual effect. The Super35 format has been employed for such effects-laden movies as *Terminator 2* (1991), *True Lies* (1994), *The Abyss* (1989), *Apollo 13* (1995), *Dragonheart* (1996), *Independence Day* (1996), *The Fifth Element* (1997), *Titanic* (1997), *Godzilla* (1998), and *The X-Files* (1998). *See also* THE ABYSS; ANAMORPHIC PROCESS; APOLLO 13; DRAGONHEART; GODZILLA; INDEPENDENCE DAY; TERMINATOR 2: JUDGEMENT DAY; TITANIC; THE X-FILES.

Further Reading

Fielding, Raymond. *The Technique of Special Effects Cinematography*. Boston: Focal Press, 1985.

Hutchison, David. *Film Magic: The Art and Science of Special Effects*. New York: Prentice-Hall, 1987.

Imes, Jack. *Special Visual Effects: A Guide to Special Effects Cinematography*. New York: Van Nostrand Reinhold, 1984.

Pincus, Edward, and Steven Ascher. *The Filmmaker's Handbook*. New York: Plume, 1984.

Robertson, J.F. . *The Magic of Film Editing*. Blue Ridge Summit, PA: Tab Books, 1983.

Apogee Inc.

Apogee Inc. was a highly influential special effects house founded in 1978 by several of the special effects experts who had worked on *Star Wars* (1977), including John Dykstra. Dykstra did not want to relocate when Industrial Light & Magic (ILM) moved from Southern to Northern California, and subsequently began his own special effects company. Douglas Trumbull later added his expertise to the group.

For 15 years Apogee was one of the leading special effects houses in the industry, contributing special effects to such films as *Star Trek: The Motion Picture* (1979), *The Last Starfighter* (1984), *She-Devil* (1989), *Invaders from Mars* (1986), and *That Night* (1992) as well as to television shows. The company also won Academy Awards for technical achievements involving the bluescreen process. However, Apogee eventually encountered financial difficulties and went out of business in 1993. *See also* DYKSTRA, JOHN; STAR TREK MOVIES; TRUMBULL, DOUGLAS.

Further Reading

Sammon, Paul M. "The Perigee of Apogee." *Cinefex* 54, May 1993.

Apollo 13

The 1997 movie *Apollo 13* won an Academy Award for its visual effects, which were provided in large part by Digital Domain. The movie's story concerns an historic NASA flight to the moon, and many viewers believed that NASA footage was used in the film. However, director Ron Howard felt that the quality of such footage was irregular and decided instead to create his spaceflight images entirely with special effects.

The Saturn 5 rocket featured in the film was built as a miniature in two scales, one of which yielded a model 5 feet long and the other 18 feet long. The latter needed six 13-foot towers for support. Sometimes these models were photographed in front of a greenscreen, but on most occasions they were lit with a black light and photographed in front of an orange background. First used to film miniature spacecraft for the television show

Star Trek: The Next Generation, this technique minimizes contrast between foreground and background elements.

The *Apollo 13* models were filmed using motion-control photography, and subsequently combined with live action and computer-graphic elements using a compositing system proprietary to Digital Domain. Their digital work included creating condensation, vapors, and ice on the rocket during its launch sequence, adding gas and debris to an in-flight explosion, and generating authentic starfields throughout the spaceflight. Additional ice was added to the launch sequence by filming chunks made of paraffin and stearic acid, and then compositing that footage with the other elements in the scene.

The most complicated compositing took place while preparing the explosion sequence. There were more than 20 individual elements involved with depicting the destruction of the Apollo service module, requiring 10 passes with the motion-control camera. One greenscreen pass was required to put the actors in the window of the command module, and the rest were related to various atmospheric, pyrotechnic, and background elements which were then digitally combined and rephotographed. To create the explosion itself, the filmmakers used a 4/5-scale ply-

wood and steel model of a craft section that was blown out with a pneumatic ram. The rivets and debris were computer-generated, but the gas was real carbon dioxide (CO_2) from a fire extinguisher.

The pyrotechnics for the film required many different techniques. The launch, for example, was created by igniting a mixture of chemical and fuels that had been placed in a firetrench of plywood and plasterboard. CO_2 and propane mortars triggered the blast. The camera filming this scene was protected with a shield and fire-retardant cloth. The fire surrounding the capsule upon reentry was filmed in a similar way, but this time a steel spaceship model was placed within the flames to give them definition. However, the model could only withstand a 16-minute burn, so the footage had to be created in several takes.

The most physically demanding effects in the film, however, were related to the illusion of weightlessness. Director Howard used wires to suspend actors for a few scenes, including a nightmare sequence sucking them out of the ship and into space, but the majority of weightless shots were achieved in a NASA weightlessness simulator. This simulator was actually a KC-135 aircraft, which is a military version of the Boeing 707. Weightlessness is simulated by taking the

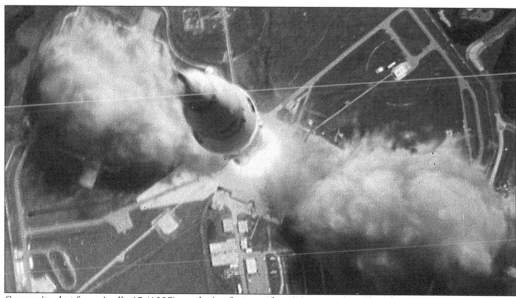

Composite shot from *Apollo 13* (1997) employing footage of a miniature rocket. *Photofest.*

plane to an altitude of 36,000 feet and then dropping it suddenly. Each drop yields 22 seconds of simulated zero gravity, which meant that camera operators only had 22 seconds in which to film the actors' movements before they were slammed back down to the airplane floor. This filming process was extremely demanding, but resulted in amazingly realistic live-action footage. *See also* BLUESCREEN PROCESS; COMPOSITING; DIGITAL DOMAIN; PYROTECHNICS; *STAR TREK* MOVIES; WIREWORK.

Further Reading

Prokop, Tim. "Launching Apollo." *Cinefex 63,* September 1995.

Shay, Don. "In the Digital Domain." *Cinefex 55,* August 1993.

Armageddon

Nominated for an Academy Award for its visual effects, the 1998 Touchstone Pictures movie *Armageddon* is significant because it employed a new pyrotechnics device for miniature photography. Connected to the computer driving the motion-control camera, this device allowed the photographer to program explosions frame by frame, all timed to the millisecond, and could trigger multiple explosions along a model. However, it also required extremely fast film, which meant that while the rest of the movie was shot with the VistaVision film format, the model pyrotechnics were shot with anamorphic 35 mm film, which can shoot hundreds of frames a second.

Although it was not used until *Armageddon,* the motion-control pyrotechnics device was originally invented during the filming of *Dante's Peak* (1997). Many of the same people worked on the models and pyrotechnics for both movies, because Digital Domain provided most of the effects for the two projects.

There were more than 14 other effects companies also involved with *Armageddon,* including Dream Quest Images, Blue Sky/VIFX, The Computer Film Company, Pacific Ocean Post, and Cinesite. The movie required so much support because of the large number of visual effects shots involved. *Armageddon* featured a total of 240 such shots, with an additional 60 digital wire removals related to actors portraying astronauts in zero gravity. In addition, the production crew was allowed to film live action at the real astronaut training and launch facilities of the National Air and Space Administration (NASA).

The film's models, which were shot in studios in front of greenscreens, included an all-terrain drilling vehicle for use on the asteroid surface, several space shuttles, a space station, and an asteroid. The all-terrain vehicle was a radio-controlled, ¼-scale miniature, 6 feet long and 3 feet wide. The model was an exact duplicate of a full-sized version also built specifically for the movie. The space shuttle *Atlantis* was a 4-foot-long urethane model hung 30 feet above the floor and rigged with pyrotechnics, while the space shuttles *Independence* and *Freedom* came in several versions, including a 1/20-scale, 7-foot-long model for motion-control shots, a 1/12-scale, 10-foot-long model for crashes, and a 1/4-scale, 30-foot-long model for runway shots. The crash model flew on a track, propelled to a speed of 30–40 mph using a computer-controlled winch, cables, and electric motor. The space station was built in two versions, a 1/20-scale, highly detailed Plexiglas and styrene model and a 1/12-scale pyrotechnics model made of cardboard and epoxy resins. The asteroid model, which was 25 feet long and 12–15 feet in diameter, had a steel armature covered with sculpted, painted foam. The asteroid's haze and gaseous tail were added with computer graphics, as were many other asteroid effects throughout the movie.

One of the most elaborate digital asteroid effects involved the partial destruction of Paris, France. To create shots of the destruction, pyrotechnics experts first created an explosion at a Southern California rock quarry using 6,000 feet of primacord covered with sand, mulch, fuller's earth, and other natural substances. They also added eight 5-gallon cans of aluminum powder at the horizon line to provide a brief flash. This explosion was then composited with background plates made from aerial photographs of Paris. The same photographs were used to create 3-D digital buildings which would replace the real ones at the impact site. The asteroid was digital as well, but the sky was created from footage of the quarry explosion. Additional materials blown into the air, including some gargoyles, were props filmed in front of a bluescreen as they were fired out of an air cannon. In all, there were more than 50 elements composited into the Paris destruction shots and manipulated by digital artists.

Also notable is a wholly computer-generated shot that occurs in the opening of the movie. Only two minutes long, it depicts an asteroid's impact with Earth eons ago. The filmmakers intentionally made this shot to look like the "Genesis Effect" shot in *Star Trek II: The Wrath of Khan* (1982), which was the first time that computer graphics had been used to create realistic images of that kind.

In addition to its extensive computer graphics, miniatures, and pyrotechnics, *Armageddon* employed a large asteroid set that required filmmakers to cut a hole in a soundstage floor. They then dug down several feet to create subterranean caverns and rigged the asteroid set with various mechanical effects, including a fissure that could open and close. Pyrotechnics were also used on the set, as well as on miniature asteroid sets. For the final scene in which the asteroid is split in two, the steel and foam asteroid model had to be cut in half and pulled apart with a model mover during filming. *See also* ANIMATION, COMPUTER; ANAMORPHIC PROCESS; *APOLLO 13*; BANNED FROM THE RANCH ENTERTAINMENT; BLUE SKY/VIFX; *DANTE'S PEAK*; DIGITAL DOMAIN; COMPUTER GRAPHICS; MECHANICAL EFFECTS; MINIATURES AND MODELS; PYROTECHNICS; *STAR TREK MOVIES*; VISTAVISION.

Further Reading

Silberg, Jon. "*Armageddon.*" *Film & Video*, June 1998.
Simak, Stephen. "Graphics that Sizzle!" *Digital World*, April 1997.
Vaz, Mark Cotta. "Journey to Armageddon." *Cinefex* 75, October 1998.

Armature

An armature is the skeleton of a stop-motion model or puppet or of an animatronic figure. Early stop-motion armatures were made of wire, later ones of steel, and since the 1930s most have included ball-and-socket joints to allow for more realistic poses. The first person to use such joints was modelmaker Marcel Delgado, who sculpted figures for such films as *The Lost World* (1925) and *King Kong* (1933). Armatures for animatronic figures have advanced mechanisms that provide realistic live-action movements, and they are covered not by clay but by simulated musculature made of foams, elastics, spandex, or other fabrics overlaid with a foam latex skin. *See also* ANIMATRONICS; DELGADO, MARCEL; *KING KONG; THE LOST WORLD*; STOP-MOTION MODEL ANIMATION.

Further Reading

Archer, Steve. *Willis O'Brien: Special Effects Genius.* Jefferson, NC: McFarland and Company, 1998.
Duncan, Jody. *The Making of* The Lost World. New York: Ballantine Books, 1997.
Smith, Thomas G. *Industrial Light & Magic: The Art of Special Effects*. New York: Ballantine Books, 1986.

Ashton, Roy (1909–1995)

Australian makeup artist Howard Roy Ashton worked on dozens of horror movies during the 1960s and 1970s, including *The Curse of the Werewolf* (1960), *Brides of Dracula* (1960), *The Curse of the Mummy's Tomb* (1964), *Kiss of the Vampire* (1964), *Plague of the Zombies* (1966), and *Tales of the Crypt* (1971). Ashton originally intended to be a commercial artist, but while a student he began working for a film company and became interested in makeup. His first horror movie was a 1959 color remake of *The Mummy* (1932) for Hammer Pictures.

Ashton continued to work for Hammer for many years, creating a wide variety of monsters. He relied on painstaking research to make his subjects more plausible. For example, before fashioning a werewolf mask, he studied real wolves at a natural history museum. Similarly, he studied snakes while inventing a reptilian monster for the movie

The Reptile (1966), and he enhanced the monster's facial makeup with plastic snakeskin created from a mold of real snakeskin.

Because of his early training as a commercial artist, Ashton was able to make detailed sketches of his creations to aid him in his work. He also proved skillful at designing dental appliances and contact lenses. Working with dentists and opticians, respectively, he created realistic fangs, zombie eyes, and other appliances. He also used blue wool to add veins to his zombies, which had an unusual skin color created with earth, dust, and liquid latex paint.

Gradually, however, Ashton abandoned the horror genre. He worked on *The Pink Panther* (1964) and some of its sequels, and later provided makeup for several Disney movies, including *Candleshoe* (1978) and *Unidentified Flying Oddball* (1979). *See also* HAMMER FILMS; MAKEUP.

Atmospheric Effects

Atmospheric effects are special effects related to elements in the earth's atmosphere. Rain, hail, snow, fog, smoke, and similar effects can all be created on a soundstage or outdoor set with the use of special equipment and materials.

To make rain, special effects experts use manufactured rainstands, which come in various heights and disperse rain over areas from 50x100 feet to 120x200 feet. The size of the raindrops can be adjusted by changing the pressure of the water fed into the rainstand, with the highest pressure creating a fine mist.

In situations in which a rainstand cannot be used because its structure would interfere with the shot, hoses with rainheads or nozzles are substituted. These hoses are typically elevated over the filming location with cables strung between buildings, trees, or other stationary components. Rainheads and nozzles come in many different varieties and disperse drops in different ways.

For scenes shot inside on a sound stage, the floor to be struck by rain is first covered with waterproofing material, typically tar paper coated with tar or a fiberglass pan with

rimmed sides. The surface is then covered with a rain mat, which is a type of rubberized cushion, in order to muffle the noise of the raindrops and improve sound recording. Rain mats are also used in outdoor shoots wherever the rain would be striking a noisy surface. For example, rain mats are often placed in a catch basin beneath a window being pelted with rain. To minimize the noise of the rain on the window itself, the glass is often smeared with liquid soap, because a thin coating of the substance dampens sound.

Rain on a moving car can be created with a special rig attached to the car's roof. Sprayers disperse the water onto the car windows. The water source is typically a pressure tank in the car's trunk, connected to the spraying rig with a hose. Another way to create rain over a moving vehicle is with a rainbar. The vehicle is towed or pulled by a camera car equipped with a water tank and a bar that extends over the vehicle being filmed. This bar delivers water in much the same way as a rainstand would. In fact, a series of roadside rainstands are sometimes used to create rain over a moving car, in situations in which extreme long shots are desired. The water for these rainstands and other outdoor rain devices is supplied by portable water tanks, fire hydrants, fire trucks, or even pumps fed by lakes or rivers.

To create a heavy storm, wind machines are often necessary, and there are several types from which to choose. Some are powered by gasoline engines, some by electricity. One of the most common wind machines is a fan powered by a car engine, and one of the strongest is a hurricane fan, which uses a 13-foot-long airplane blade to create winds up to 120 mph.

In many cases, wind machines are used in concert with wave machines and other mechanical effects. In *The Truman Show* (1998), for example, a scene in which a sailboat is lashed by wind and rain until it turns over was filmed in a lake on the Universal Studios backlot, using a boat rigged with hydraulic mechanisms to make it flip. Wave machines, wind machines made with jet engines, and two 50-foot-tall dump tank towers, each with a 1,200-gallon capacity, accompanied the action.

Wind machines have different attachments to incorporate rain, snow, or smoke effects. Plastic snowflakes are commonly dropped in front of a wooden-bladed fan by hand or automatically, via a machine that shakes the flakes as they are dropped. Foaming agents that simulate snow are dispersed via a foam spinner placed in front of a wind machine. Other substances used to simulate snow are shaved or chopped ice, synthetic cotton matting, salt, aerosol shaving cream, gypsum, and white sawdust; these are not dispersed with fans during filming but are placed on the ground, windowsills, rooftops, or other surfaces before filming. Windows can also be "frosted" with substances like lacquer, freon, or a mixture of Epsom salts and beer applied to the glass with a cotton ball. Puddles are often made to look frozen by coating them with wax. Chunks of snow or hailstones are frequently simulated with rock salt.

Fog is created with foggers or fog machines that use a variety of substances and machinery to deliver fog either along the ground or in the air. The most common substance used to make ground fog is liquid nitrogen, which is heated to convert it to its gaseous state. However, liquid nitrogen is not used for higher levels of fog because breathing this substance is unsafe. Dry ice is a safer material, and can be used either at ground level or higher. Various oils have also been used to create fog, with varying degrees of success and safety.

Oil or oil-based fluids are the ingredients for many smoke machines, which heat the oil and blow the resulting smoke into the atmosphere. Another way to make smoke is with powdered or granulated Spectrasmoke, a commercial product that can be ignited with electricity or a fuse. Long-burning smoke cartridges, smoke pellets, smoke "cookies," smoke grenades, smoke solutions, and similar products are also manufactured to create smoke.

New ways to provide not only smoke but other atmospheric effects continue to be developed, because these effects are such an important part of moviemaking. Recent movies known for their unique or spectacular atmospheric effects include *Twister* (1996) and *Dante's Peak* (1997), and *Godzilla* (1998), which employed an excessively large number of rainstands during live-action filming. In *Godzilla*, for example, the mist and rain on the live-action set were provided by two truck-mounted foggers, a 100-foot rain bar, two 40-foot rain crosses hung from cranes, and 20 30-foot-tall rainstands. For a scene of a taxicab driving through the rain, the vehicle was fitted with a 220-gallon tank and a remote-control pump that propelled water to a rain bar extended over the car. *See also* DANTE'S PEAK; GODZILLA; TWISTER.

Further Reading

Bernard, Wilkie. *Creating Special Effects for TV and Film*. New York: Hastings House, 1977.

Cosner, Sharon. *Special Effects in Movies and Television*. New York: J. Messner, 1985.

Culhane, John. *Special Effects in the Movies: How They Do It*. New York: Ballantine, 1981.

Engel, Volker, and Rachel Aberly. *The Making of Godzilla*. New York: HarperPrism, 1998.

McCarthy, Robert E. *Secrets of Hollywood Special Effects*. Boston: Focal Press, 1992.

Martin, Kevin H. "*The Truman Show:* The Unreal World." *Cinefex* 75, October 1998.

B

Babe

Released by Universal Pictures, *Babe,* which won the 1995 Academy Award for Best Visual Effects, used digital effects to make live farm animals appear to talk. This technique would again be used in the 1998 version of *Dr. Doolittle.*

More than 500 live animals were used to film *Babe.* The animal's digital mouth movements were created using 3-D computer animation by a company called Rhythm & Hues. To begin the animation process, digital artists built wireframe heads of the animals while looking at sculptures, photographs of live animals, and other reference materials. From these wireframes the artists made 3-D digital models that were then joined with their live-action counterparts and manipulated to make the overlay more precise.

As the digital images were refined, certain aspects of the animals' mouths, such as the shape of a tongue, were altered to appear more realistic. Sometimes animators also replaced the eyes of an animal to correct for a squint or a look in the wrong direction. When the computer animation was finished, an art-

From a scene in *Babe* (1995), which created mouth movements on live animals using 3-D computer animation. *Photofest.*

ist either digitally fixed the background areas that were affected by computer-generated changes or hand-painted the background fixes on individual frames of film.

In all, *Babe* had a total of 132 computer-generated shots. The film also contained 150 animatronic shots that were used when it was not possible to film a particular action with a live animal. The animatronic animals were provided by Jim Henson's Creature Shop, which had to build multiple versions of 11 different types of creatures. Babe was one of the first films in which animatronics were used extensively on location, and also one of the first to employ silicone to create lighter weight "skins" for the animatronic figures, as opposed to traditional foam latex.

Both the Creature Shop and Rhythm & Hues also worked on the sequel to *Babe*, *Babe: Pig in the City* (1998), which employed the same basic techniques and technology as its predecessor. However, animatronics were used more extensively in the second film and were driven by a new computer-controlled system called PAC (for Performance Animation Control System). PAC allowed the animatronics' movements to be programmed in advance, in some cases using motion-capture data from a real pig's movements. Software advances also enabled digital effects experts to create more realistic computer-generated 3-D animals for stuntwork. *See also* ANIMALS; ANIMATION, COMPUTER; ANIMATRONICS; *DR. DOOLITTLE;* HENSON, JIM; MOTION CAPTURE.

Further Reading

Kaufman, Debra. "Synergistic Effects." *Digital Magic,* August 1998.

Shay, Estelle. "From the Mouth of Babe." *Cinefex, 64,* December 1995.

Strauss, Bob. "Dogged Path to Making of *Dr. Doolittle." Los Angeles Daily News,* June 27, 1998.

Back to the Future Movies

Two sequels to the 1985 movie *Back to the Future*—*Back to the Future Part II* (1989) and *Back to the Future Part III* (1990)—contributed new techniques and equipment to the field of special effects. *Back to the Future II* was nominated for an Academy Award for its visual effects, which were created by Industrial Light & Magic (ILM) under the supervision of Ken Ralston. All three movies were directed by Robert Zemeckis.

The most advanced special effect in *Back to the Future Part II* involved split-screen photography, which allowed actor Michael J. Fox to play more than one part in the movie. While filming each split-screen scene, two passes were made, one with the actor standing on Side A of the shot with Side B blacked out, and the other with him standing on Side B with Side A blacked out. A motion-control camera was used to make sure that each scene was filmed in exactly the same way, so that the only variable was Fox's movements.

Because this was a challenging task, ILM invented a new motion-control dolly system specifically for *Back to the Future Part II*. The system made the camera's movements virtually silent and included a video playback feature that allowed the actor to see his Side A performance on a monitor while he was acting the Side B part, thereby helping him determine where to look and stand in relation to his other self. ILM's new system would later be perfected and used for the 1996 movie *Multiplicity*, which required one actor to play four parts.

Back to the Future Part II was also one of the first films to take advantage of digital wire removal, whereby a computer is used to erase wires used to "fly" characters or objects. In this case, the object was a miniature car. The car was the same 1/5-scale model used for the time-travel scenes in *Back to the Future*, remodeled so that 15-inch-tall servo-controlled puppets could fit inside. The lighting that hits the car during a storm was added by animators.

Back to the Future Part III was shot immediately after *Back to the Future II*, because the two movies were originally going to be made together as one film. Therefore, both movies share the same basic special effects techniques. In *Back to the Future Part III*, once again, the split-screen process enabled actor Michael J. Fox to play more than one part. For a scene in which he passes a plate of food to his duplicate, a motion-control mechanical arm handed the plate from one side of the split to the other, giving it to the actor while ensuring that the movement was identical for both Side A and Side B filming.

Another unique feature in *Back to the Future Part III* was a train, which was both a real locomotive and a 1/4-scale miniature model. The miniature was capable of going 20 mph on its track, propelled by a pulley system, for a scene in which it had to crash into a ravine. The ravine was part of a miniature set, and the crash was recorded with six high-speed cameras. *See also* BLUESCREEN PROCESS; COMPOSITING; INDUSTRIAL LIGHT & MAGIC; MINIATURES AND MODELS; SPLIT-SCREEN PHOTOGRAPHY; RALSTON, KEN; ZEMECKIS, ROBERT.

Further Reading
Duncan, Jody. "20 Years of Industrial Light & Magic." *Cinefex* 65, March, 1996.
Smith, Thomas G. *Industrial Light & Magic: The Art of Special Effects.* New York: Ballantine Books, 1986.

Background Plate

A background plate is any background image used to make a composited sequence. In other words, it is the environment into which all other elements in a shot—live action, miniature photography, animation, and/or computer-generated images—will be added. The word "plate" is a holdover from the time when background scenery was created by placing still photographs on glass plates. *See also* COMPOSITING; COMPUTER-GENERATED IMAGES; MINIATURES AND MODELS; MOTION-CONTROL CAMERA SYSTEMS.

Further Reading
Fielding, Raymond. *The Technique of Special Effects Cinematography.* Boston: Focal Press, 1985.
McAlister, Michael J. *Language of Visual Effects.* Los Angeles: Lone Eagle Publishing, 1993.

Baker, Rick (1950–)

Rick Baker is one of the foremost makeup artists and creature designers in the special effects industry. He won the first Best Makeup Academy Award when the category was created in 1981, receiving it for his work on *An American Werewolf in London.* He later won another Academy Award for *Harry and the Hendersons* (1987).

Born in New York in 1950, Baker got his first makeup job while still in high school, when he was hired to create makeup and appliances for Art Clokey Productions, which is best known for creating Gumby. In college Baker made a creature for *The Octaman* television show, and shortly after graduation he was hired to make an apelike creature for the movie *Schlock* (1971). The following year he made a two-headed gorilla costume for *The Thing with Two Heads* (1972) and wore this costume in the film. Baker would later wear his own ape costume in *King Kong* (1976) and in several other movies as well.

In 1972, Baker was hired to assist famed makeup artist Dick Smith on *The Exorcist.* A year later, Smith recommended Baker for *Live and Let Die* (1973), a James Bond movie that required Baker to make two special effects heads, one that would be shot and another that would inflate and explode. Around the same period, Baker worked on *It's Alive* (1974), for which he made a monster baby.

Baker's most famous assignment was to create the aliens for the cantina scene in *Star Wars* (1977). He was given the assignment after British makeup artist Steward Freeborn, who designed the Wookie costume for the film, became ill and could not finish the rest of his work. The team that Baker formed to assist him in creating the cantina aliens included Phil Tippett, John Berg, and Rob Bottim, all of whom are now special effects experts in their own right.

After *Star Wars,* Baker went on to provide makeup and/or creatures for *Cocoon* (1985), *Gorillas in the Mist* (1988), *Batman Forever* (1995), *The Nutty Professor* (1996), *Men in Black* (1997), and *Mighty Joe Young* (1998). He also established his own special effects company, Cinovation, which is a leading supplier of creature effects. *See also* BATMAN MOVIES; BOND MOVIES; *COCOON; KING KONG; MEN IN BLACK; THE NUTTY PROFESSOR;* SMITH, DICK; *STAR WARS* MOVIES.

Ballard, Lucien (1908–1988)

Lucien Ballard was a cinematographer and director of photography who developed new lighting techniques for black-and-white interior photography. He also received acclaim for his outdoor photography on Western movies during the 1960s and 1970s. In addition, he worked on trick shots for the 1961 Disney movie *The Parent Trap*, in which actress Hayley Mills played two roles.

Born in 1908, Ballard attended the University of Oklahoma and the University of Pennsylvania. He began his career as a cameraman at Paramount Studios; his first film was *Morocco* (1930). His additional work includes *Crime and Punishment* (1935), *True Grit* (1969), *Nevada Smith* (1966), *Prince Valiant* (1954), *Breakheart Pass* (1976), and *Rabbit Test* (1978). He died in 1988. *See also* MULTIPLE EXPOSURE.

Banned from the Ranch Entertainment

Located in Santa Monica, California, Banned from the Ranch (BFTR) Entertainment is a digital production company that has created visual effects for such major motion pictures as *Congo* (1995), *Twister* (1996), *Dante's Peak* (1997), *Men in Black* (1997), *Starship Troopers* (1997), *Spawn* (1997), *Titanic* (1997), *Deep Rising* (1998), and *Dr. Doolittle* (1998). These effects include digital compositing, wire removal, morphs, and 3-D character animation. The company also creates display graphics that appear on computer screens seen in movies. For example, in *Dante's Peak*, characters look at computer data imagery made by Banned from the Ranch. The name "Banned from the Ranch" refers to Skywalker Ranch in Novato, California, headquarters of George Lucas. Banned from the Ranch founder Casey Cannon once worked as an animator in the computer graphics department of Lucas's special effects company, Industrial Light and Magic (ILM), and watched two talented coworkers become "banned from the ranch" when they ignored a company policy. She decided to create a place where such creative "rebels" could work.

Cannon remains the CEO of Banned from the Ranch Entertainment; the company president is Van Ling, who previously worked for James Cameron to create visual effects for *The Abyss* and *Terminator 2*. *See also* CONGO; DANTE'S PEAK; DR. DOOLITTLE; MEN IN BLACK; STARSHIP TROOPERS; TITANIC; TWISTER.

Further Reading

Banned from the Ranch webstite, http://www.bfr.com

Basevi, James (1890–)

James Basevi was an art director at MGM during the movie studio's silent film era, then with the advent of sound, he became a special effects expert.

Basevi's two most notable films during his time as a special effects expert are *San Francisco* (1936) and *The Hurricane* (1937). The former featured a climatic earthquake sequence and footage of the Golden Gate Bridge under construction, although a reissue of the film eliminated many of the city shots. For *The Hurricane*, Basevi spent $150,000 to build a 600-foot-long full-scale village beside a tropical lagoon. This lagoon was actually a studio water tank. Pistons in the tank churned the water to simulate storm conditions, and at a key moment, 2,000 extra gallons of water were released into the tank to create a giant tidal wave. To this scene he added airplane engines that acted as wind machines, as well as fire hoses that sprayed water on actors. The movie's hurricane scenes took four months to film and cost $400,000.

In 1939 Basevi returned to his career as an art director and in 1943 he won an Academy Award for his work on *The Song of Bernadette*. His other films include *Tobacco Road* (1941), *The Ox-Bow Incident* (1943), *Fort Apache* (1948), and *East of Eden* (1955).

Batman Movies

A series of four movies, *Batman* (1989), *Batman Returns* (1992), *Batman Forever* (1995), and *Batman and Robin* (1997), illustrate the increasing reliance of special effects experts on computer graphics. Each of the *Batman* movies features a crimefighter named Batman and his unique car, the Batmobile. However, the way these images were created on screen changed over time.

In the first movie, Batman's seemingly ordinary car was transformed into the technologically superior Batmobile via hand-drawn cel animation. In other words, a series of drawings filled in the steps from one car to another. By the second movie, however, this transformation was being created via computer animation.

Similarly, in the first two movies, a Batman puppet was used for certain stunts. By the third movie, a completely digital Batman was being used in addition to the puppet. Computers were also being used to generate fake snowfall, to create flying objects such as a whirling umbrella and some bats, and to eliminate bluescreen elements and wirework during postproduction.

A tally of the number of special effects shots in each *Batman* movie reflects the increasing reliance on digital effects. While there were less than 100 special effects shots in the first movie, there were 115 special effects shots in the second, 250 in the third, and 400 in the fourth.

Of course, not all special effects shots included computer graphics. The movies also relied on traditional elements such as matte paintings, pyrotechnics, makeup, miniatures, and puppetry work. But even these types of special effects reflect the advances in technology that occurred over the years the *Batman* series was made.

For example, the second movie included puppetry equipment that was not available for the first. Provided by the Stan Winston Studios, which would later create dinosaurs for *Jurassic Park* (1993), these puppets included 30 animatronic penguins, each with 194 mechanized parts, as well as a Batman puppet controlled by hand with wires and rods. A puppet Batman was also used in *Batman Forever*, for a scene in which it had to be launched through a missile tube.

In another scene in *Batman Forever*, in which Batman falls 600 feet and deploys his

Animatronic penguins from *Batman Returns* (1992). *Warner Bros./Photofest.*

cape like a parachute, the puppet was replaced with a computer-generated Batman. This is one of the first examples of a computer-generated stuntman, another being the lawyer who was eaten by a dinosaur in *Jurassic Park*. To animate the computer-generated Batman, computer programmers used an early form of motion-capture, which provided them with a digital template of a real gymnast's movements. They then used this template to drive the computer-generated Batman. By the time *Batman and Robin* was made, even more sophisticated motion-capture devices were available, and it was possible to capture digital data not just from a single gymnast but from an entire parachuting team. These data provided movements to shots of computer-generated characters performing freefalls and skyboarding.

Another example of the way that technology changed a film element from one movie to another is the Batman distress signal, which is a bat shape projected into the sky. In the first two films, the signal was created by projecting traditional artwork onto fiberfill "clouds." In *Batman Forever*, the sky was computer-generated, as was the signal.

Advances in computer software also changed the way that makeup effects were accomplished in the *Batman* movies. The early films required extensive trial and error, but by the time *Batman Forever* was made, makeup effects were being previsualized with computers, which allowed an artist to consider different "looks" before developing a single appliance. As an example, to create makeup for the character of "Scarface" in *Batman Forever*, special effects expert Rick Baker scanned the actor's face into a computer and used the resulting image to design foam latex appliances that fit the actor perfectly.

Digital previsualization was used more extensively for *Batman and Robin*, as a tool not only for makeup design but also for planning camera moves and miniature sets. For example, before building a miniature Gotham City for *Batman and Robin*, special effects experts made 3-D digital wireframes of its buildings and ran a virtual camera through its streets, experimenting with different configurations. This run-through helped them decide exactly how to construct the set, and also helped determine which shots were best accomplished with miniatures and which would require computer graphics.

A unique feature of *Batman and Robin* is that, unlike its predecessors, its miniature Gotham City extended both horizontally and vertically with computer-generated buildings. Earlier *Batman* movies used 2-D matte paintings to extend real cityscapes, although *Batman Forever* did have one entirely computer-generated cityscape shot.

Even without their digital extensions, however, the miniatures used for *Batman and Robin* were highly advanced. There were approximately 35 1/24-scale-model buildings, each approximately 16–30 feet tall, representing just the upper portion of Gotham City, and all were extremely detailed, with etched brass railings, fire escapes, and roof antennas. The city also included miniature billboards and a motorized elevated train. *See also* ANIMATION, COMPUTER; ANIMATRONICS; BAKER, RICK; COMPUTER-GENERATED IMAGES; COMPUTER GRAPHICS; COSTS, SPECIAL EFFECTS; PREVISUALIZATION; *JURASSIC PARK*; MAKEUP; MINIATURES AND MODELS; MOTION CAPTURE; WINSTON, STAN; WIREFRAMES.

Further Reading

Kaufman, Debra. "Summer's CG Stars." *Digital Magic*, August 1997.

Vaz, Mark Cotta. "Forever and a Knight." *Cinefex 63*, September 1995.

———. "Freeze Frames." *Cinefex 71*, September 1997.

———. "A Knight at the Zoo." *Cinefex 51*, August 1992.

Bau, George (1905–1974), and Gordon Bau (1907–1975)

Born in 1905 and 1907, respectively, George and Gordon Bau made many important contributions to the field of movie makeup, particularly in regard to latex facial prosthetics. In 1937, while both men were working at a rubber company in Torrance, California, they began developing their own business, making rubber products for the movie industry. Shortly thereafter, George invented a new type of sponge rubber that resembled human skin and had thin outer edges for easy application to an actor's face. This material assured the Baus' success, and in 1938 they were hired to work as independent contractors at the Warner Brothers Makeup Department, where they made facial prosthetics for the movie *The Hunchback of Notre Dame* (1939). In addition, George continued to develop new techniques related to his foam latex sponge makeup, including a special foam sponge beater that is still used today.

In World War II, Gordon joined the navy and developed prosthetics for those injured in the fighting. After the war he became director of makeup at RKO Studios. Three years later he became director of makeup at Warner Brothers and developed a line of makeup called Warner Brothers' Cosmetics.

George, meanwhile, continued to invent new makeup devices and techniques. For example, he replaced the traditional rubber bald cap with a rubber latex one, created the first plastic toupee cement, developed new resins for mask-making, and came up with a new way to preserve plaster molds. He also devised a method for inserting foam latex into large casting molds, using extreme pressure to inject the material through a small, drilled hole. He also invented Scarola, a plastic material sold in tubes that could simulate scars.

During the early 1950s, George began a side business called Hollywood Latex Products in order to sell his inventions to the general public. Later he changed the company's name to G.T. Bau Laboratories. In 1954, George's son Robert began working for him, both in this side business and at Warner Brothers, where Gordon remained the director of makeup.

Gordon, George, and Robert worked together on many television series, including *77 Sunset Strip, Maverick,* and *F-Troop.* Robert became head of his father's laboratory in 1970. The following year, George was forced to retire from studio work; he died in 1974. His brother Gordon retired from Warner Brothers in 1972 and died in 1975. *See also* MAKEUP; WARNER BROTHERS.

The Beast from 20,000 Fathoms

Released in 1953, *The Beast from 20,000 Fathoms* was the first film of famous stop-motion animator Ray Harryhausen, and advanced the field of stop-motion animation. The movie's "beast," a dinosaur called a Rhedosaurus, was actually a miniature sculpted in clay. The model had a wire skeleton, or armature, to provide flexibility, and a skin of gray liquid latex, textured scales, and tiny spikes. Harryhausen painstakingly moved the model in tiny increments, filming it in one position and then stopping the camera to move the model before filming it again.

To make the Rhedosaurus model appear more realistic, Harryhausen gave it a shadow using lighting and projection techniques. He also used an optical printer to combine footage of the miniature with footage of live action. For example, in one shot he sandwiched film of the miniature in between film of two live-action scenes, a background of people fleeing the monster and a foreground of cars and building debris. This technique required him to use mattes to block out unnecessary images in each shot and to make sure that the lighting in all three scenes was consistent.

Harryhausen also combined miniature and live-action photography via front-screen and rearscreen projection. He would cut the shape of an object out of cardboard, place the cardboard in front of the Rhedosaurus, and then, with the help of mirrors, project the image of the object onto the cardboard while filming the miniature dinosaur. At the same time, he would project background action scenes behind the Rhedosaurus. He also used rearscreen projection to show a live actor standing in front of the Rhedosaurus by projecting an enlarged image of his monster behind the man. For some of these rearscreen projections, Harryhausen used a hand puppet instead of a miniature, because the puppet offered a more detailed dinosaur head.

A few scenes also required a miniature rollercoaster, which was moved with wires as the beast attacked it, and a full-scale iceberg constructed from 30 tons of plaster, 10 tons of salt, and 500 pounds of corn flakes, over which 40 tons of ice were sprayed. By using simple techniques to create these set elements, Harryhausen was able to limit the cost of his film to $200,000. *See also* ARMATURE; HARRYHAUSEN, RAY; OPTICAL PRINTER, STOP-MOTION MODEL ANIMATION.

Further Reading
Jenson, Paul M. *The Men Who Made the Monsters.* New York: Twayne, 1996.
Johnson, J.J. *Cheap Tricks and Class Acts.* Jefferson, NC: McFarland & Company, 1996.

Bedknobs and Broomsticks

The 1971 Disney movie *Bedknobs and Broomsticks* received an Academy Award for its special effects. Largely a continuation of the work done on the 1964 movie *Mary Poppins*, the film featured no new special effects techniques. However, it did offer filmmakers a chance to improve their ability to blend live action and animation, producing more polished work in this regard than ever before. The movie also included the work of Danny Lee, an expert in mechanical effects. *See also* THE WALT DISNEY COMPANY; *MARY POPPINS.*

Further Reading
Matlin, Leonard. *The Disney Films.* New York: Bonanza Books, 1973.
Smith, Dave. *Disney A-Z.* New York: Hyperion, 1996.

Ben-Hur

The 1959 version of *Ben-Hur* won an Academy Award for its special effects and included the work of A. Arnold Gillespie, who also provided effects for a 1926 version of the film.

The 1959 *Ben-Hur* featured scenes of warring galley ships, which were actually shots of detailed miniatures that were combined in an optical printer with background plates, images of fireballs, and live-action scenes filmed on a soundstage set that reproduced sections of a galley in full size.

The movie also employed elaborate stuntwork. One of its most spectacular scenes was a chariot race in which chariots flip over to spill their drivers onto the ground. These flips were triggered by the stuntman riding the chariots; each vehicle was rigged with hydraulic brakes that could be applied in an instant, and the resulting sudden stop would upset the chariot. At one point, a chariot was supposed to jump over some wreckage rather than flip, but the jump went wrong and the driver, the son of famous stuntman Yakima Canutt, was accidentally thrown from the vehicle. While it appears in the film as though he was seriously injured, in actuality he suffered only minor injuries.

In the 1926 version of *Ben-Hur,* the chariot race was created by Gillespie and another special effects expert, Cedric Gibbons, by combining film of a full-sized set with film of a miniature. The full-sized set represented the racetrack portion of the stadium, and the miniature represented the stands and spectators. In order to make the miniature seem more realistic, groups of tiny seated spectators were mechanically rigged to stand at various points in the race. This created the illusion that the crowd was alive and cheering.

The 1926 movie also featured one of the first travelling mattes, which was used to make it appear as though a building was collapsing on a crowd of people. The building was actually a miniature, rigged to fall apart, and was photographed as it fell. Each frame of this footage was then projected and enlarged so that artists could draw a series of mattes, or silhouettes, of the building. It took thousands of mattes to trace the structure's collapse; these mattes were then used as

Chariot race in the 1959 version of *Ben-Hur. Metro-Goldwyn-Mayer (1959)/Photofest.*

placeholders during the process of combining the miniature photography with live-action footage. *See also* ACCIDENTS; CANUTT, YAKIMA; GIBBONS, CEDRIC; GILLESPIE, A. ARNOLD; STUNTS; TRAVELLING MATTE.

Further Reading

Brosnan, J. *Movie Magic*. New York: St. Martin's Press, 1974.
Fry, Ron, and Pamela Fourzon. *The Saga of Special Effects*. Englewood Cliffs, NJ: Prentice-Hall, 1977.

Bitzer, G.W. (Billy) (1872–1944)

Johann Gottlob Wilhelm Bitzer, who went by the nickname "Billy," was a pioneer of cinematography. In conjunction with director D.W. Griffith, with whom he made most of his films, Bitzer developed many photographic techniques that became standard in the industry, including the closeup shot, the fade, and backlighting. He and Griffith also created the camera dolly. Bitzer's works include *The Birth of a Nation* (1915), *Intolerance* (1916), and *Broken Blossoms* (1919). Many of his films were made for the Biograph Company, and in his later years he documented his experiences there for a New York film library. He died in 1944. *See also* GRIFFITH, D.W.

Blade Runner

Directed by Ridley Scott, the 1982 movie *Blade Runner* was nominated for an Academy Award for its special effects and features the work of two major special effects experts, Douglas Trumbull and Richard Yuricich. Trumbull and Yuricich also worked together on *2001: A Space Odyssey* (1968), *Silent Running* (1971), *Close Encounters of the Third Kind* (1977), and *Star Trek: The Motion Picture* (1979). Shortly before making *Blade Runner* Trumbull and Yuricich founded their own company, the Entertainment Effects Group (EEG). EEG created many unique effects for *Blade Runner*, primarily using motion-controlled miniature photography and mattes.

The opening shot in *Blade Runner* uses one of the company's most impressive miniatures, a futuristic industrial landscape 13 feet deep and 18 feet wide. The miniature's foundation was Plexiglas and cast foam; its buildings were molded from foam as well. The front fourth of the model was detailed with etched brass, while the latter three-fourths were simply brass silhouettes. There were photographic floodlights beneath the Plexiglas foundation to illuminate the model, as well as 7 miles of fiberoptic strands with 2,000 colored light points inserted into various buildings. The brightness of the strands was regulated by the motion-control camera filming the model.

The landscape also had several towers, each approximately 18 inches to 3 feet high, and two pyramids with air-travel warning lights shining from their points. To make the towers appear to flame, the EEG crew front-projected shots of gas explosions onto white foam cards that had been attached to the top of the towers. To create the pyramids, they used still photographs of a model that were made as transparencies, physically mounted to the miniature set, and backlit.

The model itself was used in closeup shots of the pyramids, but even then it was photographed separately and matted in duplicate into the scene. Like the rest of the landscape, the pyramids were detailed with etched brass and filled with fiberoptics. The pyramid model was intended to represent structures approximately 600–900 stories high, which means that at a scale of 1/750, the model was 2 ½ feet high, with a 9-foot base. A companion to the pyramid model, the "Pyramid Insert Model," was a 4-foot-high, 5-foot-wide miniature representing part of the pyramid's interior. The model included an interrogation room, working 3-inch-high elevator cars, revolving ceiling fans, furniture, and other details.

Several more cityscape models were used for other shots, including a police headquarters building and 20 buildings representing a city block. Interestingly, the round roof of the police headquarters was made from the mold for the main spaceship in *Close Encounters of the Third Kind*. Other models were borrowed to fill in buildings in a night cityscape. One was a replica of the *Millenium Falcon* spaceship model used in *Star Wars* (1977), appearing in the mid-foreground of a scene featuring the landing of a "Spinner" police car.

Four different models of this police car were made: a 1-inch, a 3 ½-inch, a 15-inch, and a 45-inch. The latter weighed 65 pounds, cost $50,000, and was both extremely detailed and mechanized. This model included four panels, two side and two rear, that could open and close, as well as two rotating wheel covers, an illuminated dashboard, and two 18-inch-tall puppets with moving heads. The puppet in the driver's seat could also move its arm to simulate steering. A full-sized mockup of the Spinner car was used for live-action filming. Its dashboard, which included a working video monitor, was added into scenes during postproduction.

To complement the miniatures, EEG employed many different matte paintings in their shots. The matte paintings were designed by placing transparent paper over photographs of live-action scenes and painting a rough background in watercolor around the live-action images. The watercolors were then used as a guide to create more detailed paintings on 7x3-foot masonite boards.

The artist who did the final mattes was Matthew Yuricich, Richard Yuricich's brother, who had previously produced matte paintings for *Forbidden Planet* (1956), *Close Encounters of the Third Kind*, *Star Trek: The Motion Picture*, and *Logan's Run* (1976). One example of Matthew Yuricich's work for *Blade Runner* appears in shot of the main character dangling from a tall building. In actuality, the actor was dangling from a rooftop set, and everything below him was a matte painting. Similarly, for a shot of the main character driving up to his apartment building, the first story and balcony of this building was a full-sized set, while everything above the first story was a matte painting. When the character walks onto his balcony, the matte painting and live action are shown composited with a shot of a Spinner car model, some animated effects, lighting effects, and additional elements. This final composited shot was created with an optical printer during postproduction.

EEG found that two of the most difficult elements to composite were smoke and rain, which appear frequently in the movie. To create the latter, EEG suspended rain machines from a height of 40 feet and shot the resulting rain from different distances, so that they had foreground, midground, and background rain shots. In all cases, the rain fell in front of a black background and was backlit with bright lights to make it stand out. The different distances of rain shots were subsequently composited together to make a single shot, which was then used to make a black-and-white print. This print was run through an optical camera with a black-and-white print showing everything else that would appear in the shot, which sometimes included as many as 30 composited elements. The optical camera yielded a film negative that combined the images from both prints. As for the smoke, it was filmed separately, projected onto 4x5-inch screen attached to an area of a model or miniature set, and then filmed again during one of the motion-control passes over the miniature.

Not all of the effects in *Blade Runner* were done with opticals and miniatures, however. A few were the result of expert makeup work, props, and other on-set effects. For example, a character's head is crushed by virtue of a duplicate made by makeup expert Michael Westmore. To create the duplicate, Westmore first created a cast of the actor's head using a type of plastic called dental-alginate. During the hour it took for the alginate to harden, the actor had to breathe through straws inserted in his nostrils. When the cast was done, Westmore split it in half, removed it, and used it as a mold, filling it with a silicone substance that solidified to become the "skull" of the fake head. This skull was covered with a latex liquid rubber "skin" that was then painted. The head also had fake eyebrows, a wig, and glass eyes, behind which Westmore inserted blood bags that popped when the eyes were gouged. The skull included foam and latex brains that splattered, but this image was cut from the American version of the film. (There have been several versions of *Blade Runner,* including a 1993 "Director's Cut" in which the movie's ending has been changed.) *See also* CLOSE ENCOUNTERS OF THE THIRD KIND; COMPOSITING; EDLUND, RICHARD; *LOGAN'S RUN;* MAKEUP; OPTICAL PRINTER; SCOTT, RIDLEY; *STAR TREK* MOVIES; TRUMBULL, DOUGLAS; *2001: A SPACE ODYSSEY;* WESTMORE, MICHAEL.

Further Reading
Sammon, Paul M. *Future Noir: The Making of* Blade Runner. New York: Harper Collins, 1996.

Blau, Fred (1939–)

Fred Blau is a makeup artist who worked with John Chambers in developing the makeup for the 1967 movie *The Planet of the Apes.* Born in 1939, Blau was an actor before he accepted a three-year apprenticeship in the makeup department of Warner Brothers. His first assignment was to provide makeup for the 1967 film *Cool Hand Luke.* His other work includes *Finnian's Rainbow* (1968), *Bite the Bullet* (1975), and *Apocalypse Now* (1979), for which he created realistic war injuries. *See also* CHAMBERS, JOHN; *PLANET OF THE APES;* WARNER BROTHERS.

Blithe Spirit

The 1946 movie *Blithe Spirit* won an Academy Award for its special effects, which were provided by Tom Howard. In telling the story of a ghost who haunts her former husband and his new wife, the film uses invisibility techniques pioneered by John Fulton, including wirework to move props and optical effects to make the ghost appear and disappear. *See also* INVISIBILITY; FULTON, JOHN; HOWARD, TOM.

Blood

Many substances have been used to simulate blood. In the days of black-and-white filming, colored syrups often substituted for blood. Modern filmmakers use corn syrup or gelatin colored with red food coloring, commercial makeup blood, red paint, or chemical mixtures. For alien blood, such as appeared in the 1997 movie *Starship Troopers,* a substance called methocel, tinted green,

is sometimes used. In *The X-Files* (1998), however, colored corn syrup was used for some shots, but more often alien blood was simulated by digital effects.

Commercial makeup blood is manufactured in varying degrees of viscosity; it can appear to be flowing, clotted, or dried. Flowing blood is required for the plastic blood bags, also called squibs, that are used to simulate bullet hits. These squibs are sewn into an actor's clothes or placed against the skin, and when the squib is suddenly punctured, the blood comes rushing out. Puncturing is typically accomplished through a small explosive charge detonated by remote-control; the actor's skin is protected from the explosion by a small metal plate attached to the back of the squib. *See also* STARSHIP TROOPERS; *THE X-FILES.*

Further Reading
McCarthy, Robert E. *Secrets of Hollywood Special Effects.* Boston: Focal Press, 1992.

Blue Sky/VIFX

Blue Sky/VIFX was established in 1997, when VIFX, a special effects company owned by 20th Century Fox, took over another special effects company called Blue Sky Studios. Before they merged, both companies were well regarded for their computer animation and other visual effects, and they continued to contribute work to such movies as *Alien Resurrection* (1997), *Armageddon* (1998), *The X-Files* (1998), and *Star Trek: Insurrection* (1998). For the latter, Blue Sky/VIFX handled digital shots related to scenes that took place on the Ba'ku planet and inside an alien spacecraft, while another effects company, Santa Barbara Studios, handled exterior space scenes.

In March 1999, the VIFX portion of the company was purchased by Rhythm & Hues Studios, another visual effects and animation company. *See also* ALIEN MOVIES; *ARMAGEDDON;* RHYTHM & HUES STUDIOS; *STAR TREK* MOVIES; *THE X-FILES.*

Bluescreen Process

The bluescreen process is a way to create a travelling matte that allows live-action footage to be combined with special effects elements such as background paintings or computer-generated images. The process was originally accomplished chemically using a device called an optical printer, but today it is generally done electronically via a compuer. Bluescreen work that is done on videotape (rather than film) is called chromakey.

To begin the bluescreen process, an actor, miniature, or similar element is filmed against a brightly illuminated blue screen, typically lit with florescent tubes, or against a specially colored blue cloth. After filming, if the optical printer is going to be employed, the camera negative is used to make a positive, which turns the dark areas of the negative light and the light areas of the negative dark. During the creation of the positive, the film is allowed to record only the brilliantly blue areas. Further manipulation of the original negative, duplicate negatives, the original positive, and additional positives combined with various optical printing techniques eventually result in two sets of film: one with the full-color, live-action figure moving against a black background and the other with the live-action figure as a black silhouette moving against a clear background. The latter is a travelling matte, which can be used to prepare the background that will appear in the final version of the film.

When computers are used, the bluescreen process is much simpler, because the computer can be programmed to automatically eliminate bluescreen elements once the filmed images have been digitized. These bluescreen elements not only include large backgrounds but also bluescreen puppetry rods and bluescreen clothing, which can be used to create the illusion that a portion of a person or even a whole person is invisible. Similarly, by cloaking an actor's head in bluescreen, it can later be replaced with someone else's face. This method was used to great advantage in the 1992 movie *Death Becomes Her,* which won an Academy Award for visual effects.

Computers have also made it possible to eliminate colors other than blue. Blue was initially selected for the optical printer because the color is not found in human skin tones,

which made it easier for the optical printer to distinguish between the bluescreen object and the live-action subject's flesh. Computers, however, are sophisticated enough to make more subtle distinctions in color, and the best results are achieved when there is a marked degree of color contrast between the foreground images and the background screen.

Therefore when a scene has a lot of blue in it, the bluescreen is typically replaced with a greenscreen. For example, a greenscreen was used in filming *True Lies* (1994) and *Lost in Space* (1998), because they both featured a vehicle—in the first case a Harrier jet and in the second a spaceship—that was predominantly blue. Greenscreens were also used for *Judge Dredd* (1995), because its miniature buildings were somewhat blue.

Yellow and orange screens, and redscreens can also be used for this process. The latter was selected for much of the special effects work in *Alien Resurrection* (1997) and *Starship Troopers* (1997), because although redscreen work requires slower film processing, it yields higher quality mattes and matte edges. Greenscreens can produce irregularities in matte edges during the compositing process, while bluescreens, although fast, can produce grainy images.

Model photographers working on *Titanic* (1998) chose a fluorescent orange screen lit with ultraviolet light for some of their work. The backlit orange technique was originally developed for the *Star Trek: The Next Generation* television show and has been used in the making of the most recent *Star Trek* movies. It is favored for some types of model photography because it produces soft rather than crisp matte lines. *See also* ALIEN MOVIES; *DEATH BECOMES HER;* INVISIBILITY; *JUDGE DREDD; LOST IN SPACE; STAR TREK* MOVIES; *TITANIC;* TRAVELLING MATTE.

Further Reading

Holsinger, Erik. "Bluescreen Compositing: Tools, Tips, and Tricks." *Digital World,* December 1997.

Stecker-Orel, Elinor. *Special Effects Photography Handbook.* Buffalo, NY: Amherst Media, 1998.

Bond Movies

Some of the most famous stuntwork in the movie industry has been performed for a series of films about a British spy named James Bond. There have been more than 20 Bond movies, beginning in 1962 with *Dr. No*. Only one of the films, however, has won an Academy Award for its special effects: *Thunderball* (1965), which features a climactic underwater battle.

Nonetheless, Bond films continue to rely heavily on stuntwork rather than on computerized special effects. This tradition was established by the effects supervisor for most of the series, Derek Meddings, who did not believe in using computer-generated imagery. Meddings began working on the Bond movies in 1973 with *Live and Let Die;* he died shortly after finishing *GoldenEye* (1995).

Meddings primarily shot his scenes on location or in the Pinewood Studios, where a soundstage known as the "007 Stage" was built for the 1976 Bond movie *The Spy Who Loved Me*. Some shots, however, had to be created with miniatures. For example, *GoldenEye* featured miniatures of a poison gas factory, the Swiss Alps, a radar dish, an airplane, and people. Both the airplane and the people were moved on wires, and, contrary to common practice, these and other wires in the film were not removed digitally, because Meddings did not even believe in using computers for this purpose. Instead he used various effects tricks, including backlighting, to make sure that the wires were "lost" in the background.

Chris Corbold, who was the head of special effects on the first post-Meddings Bond movie, *Tomorrow Never Dies* (1997), continued the tradition of avoiding computer-generated effects. As an example, he created moving backgrounds for a jet chase scene on the set with a series of paintings rather than with digital composites during postproduction. He also adhered to the series' unwritten rule that every movie must contain elaborate mechanical effects and stuntwork. In the case of *Tomorrow Never Dies*, the most significant mechanical effect is a car that ap-

pears to drive itself. The real driver was actually hidden inside the car and used video monitors to see where he was going. The stuntwork on *Tomorrow Never Dies* was equally impressive. However, during one fight sequence a stuntman accidentally cut the lip of Pierce Brosnan, the actor playing Bond. The wound required 17 stitches and delayed filming.

Further Reading

Brosnan, John. *James Bond in the Cinema*. San Diego: AS Barnes & Co., Inc., 1981.

Rogers, Pauline. "Tomorrow Never Dies." *International Photographer*, December 1997.

Waldman, Alan. "Bond on the Run." *Hollywood Reporter*, 19 December 1997.

Williams, David E. "Reintroducing Bond . . . James Bond." *American Cinematographer*, December 1995.

Boss Film Studios

Nominated seven times for Academy Awards, the Boss Film Studios was once one of the most influential special effects houses in the film industry. Boss Film Studios contributed shots to more than 33 movies, including *2010* (1984), *Alien 3* (1992), *Batman Returns* (1992), *Cliffhanger* (1993), *True Lies* (1994), *Waterworld* (1995), *Species* (1995), *Multiplicity* (1996), *Air Force One* (1997), and *Starship Troopers* (1997).

The company was founded by special effects expert Richard Edlund in 1983, when he agreed to take over the facilities and equipment of Douglas Trumbull's special effects house, Entertainment Effects Group. This equipment included a very valuable device, Trumbull's "Compsey" or Computer Operated Motion Picture System. Originally built for effects work related to *Star Trek: The Motion Picture* (1979), the Compsey was a computerized animation stand and camera system. Edlund's staff not only used this system but adapted it for use with matte photography as well as animation, which enabled them to create ghosts for their first movie, *Ghostbusters* (1983).

Over the next several years, Boss was extremely successful, and in 1993 it invested millions of dollars in state-of-the-art digital equipment. This proved to be the company's undoing. Shortly after Boss incurred debt to buy its new equipment, a revolution in digital technology made computers more affordable, and the company was suddenly faced with more competition from smaller special effects houses. Despite Edlund's best efforts to gain additional financing, Boss went out of business in 1997. *See also* ALIEN MOVIES; *BATMAN* MOVIES; *CLIFFHANGER;* EDLUND, RICHARD; *GHOSTBUSTERS*; *MULTIPLICITY; STARSHIP TROOPERS;* TRUMBULL, DOUGLAS; *WATERWORLD*.

Further Reading
Vaz, Mark Cotta. "Boss Film Studios: End of an Era." *Cinefex 73*, March 1998.

Bowie, Les (1913–1979)

Les Bowie was a special effects artist known for his versatility and inventiveness. Born in England in 1913, Bowie began his career as a matte painter, but eventually began working with mechanical effects, pyrotechnics, car stunts, and many other aspects of the special effects industry.

Bowie's first major work was for Hammer Films, which made monster movies during the 1950s. He created many of Hammer's monsters and came up with ingenious techniques to make them appear more realistic. For example, for the 1956 movie *The Creeping Unknown*, Bowie added pieces of real bovine stomach lining, or tripe, to a throbbing blob made out of rubber.

After working for Hammer, Bowie took a job with Pinewood Studios in England, but during the 1950s he decided to become a freelance special effects artist. He was noted especially for being able to create effects on a very low budget. For example, he made the prehistoric world for *One Million Years B.C.* (1966) for only 1,100 British pounds, and he developed a way to save money on modelmaking by blowing up still photographs of buildings instead of miniatures.

Bowie's other films include *The Crawling Eye* (1958), which was originally released in England as *The Trollenberg Terror* (1957); *The Haunted Stranger* (1958); *The Red Shoes* (1948); and *Superman* (1978). Bowie died in 1979. *See also* HAMMER FILMS.

Breakaways

Breakaways are props designed to break apart easily and relatively safely upon impact. The most common type of breakaway is breakaway glass, also called candy glass. Breakaway glass was originally made of sugar, but that substance has not been used for several years; special plastics are now used instead. Like original candy glass, these plastics can be molded into various shapes and sizes, creating such breakaway items as bottles and window panes.

There are some situations, however, when breakaway glass will not work for a window stunt. For example, breakaway glass is difficult to handle in sheets larger than 4x6 feet. It also breaks apart in fairly large chunks, which makes it problematic for use in miniature buildings. When such a building is exploded or otherwise destroyed, its window pieces must look in scale with the rest of the structure. For such situations, real tempered glass is often substituted for breakaway glass.

Tempered glass is commercially manufactured to shatter into extremely small fragments when struck. Nonetheless, it is still solid glass, which means that striking it with the body can cause injury. Therefore in stunts in which a person has to crash through a tempered-glass window, a set of spring-loaded or explosive devices are attached to the glass and triggered to break the sheet right before the stuntperson plunges through it.

There are many other types of breakaways besides glass; any object that needs to be broken during a stunt can be manufactured to come apart easily. Breakaway furniture is typically made of soft balsa wood, and breakaway walls are made of plaster of paris or other relatively soft materials. In addition, the plastics used to make breakaway glass can be molded and colored to create other objects, such as seemingly solid tools. *See also* STUNTS.

Further Reading
McCarthy, Robert E. *Secrets of Hollywood Special Effects*. Boston: Focal Press, 1992.
McKenzie, Alan, and Derek Ware. *Hollywood Tricks of the Trade*. New York: Gallery Books, 1986.
Rovin, Jeff. (1977) *Movie Special Effects*. South Brunswick, NJ: A.S. Barnes, 1977.

Stuntmen and Special Effects. New York: Ripley Books, 1982.

The Bridges at Toko-Ri

The 1955 movie *The Bridges at Toko-Ri* won an Academy Award for its special effects, specifically because of its aerial action sequences. These sequences combined live-action footage filmed on a soundstage with aerial photography via rearscreen projection and other optical effects. *See also* OPTICAL EFFECTS; PROJECTION PROCESSES.

Browning, Ricou (1930–)

Ricou Browning was the underwater stuntman who portrayed the "Creature from the Black Lagoon" in a 1950s film trilogy. He happened upon the role by accident. In 1953, he was the producer of several water shows in Florida when director Jack Arnold asked him to help find a location to film *The Creature from the Black Lagoon* (1954). During this search, Arnold discovered that Browning, a former Olympic swimmer, could hold his breath for five full minutes and hired him to play the monster in water. Browning continued this role in *Revenge of the Creature* (1955) and *The Creature Walks Among Us* (1956). The creature on land was played by other stuntmen, most notably Ben Chapman.

Browning performed this moviework in Florida, but traveled to Hollywood for the construction of his costume. Once the creature films ended, Browning returned to his former life. However, in 1964 he found himself acting again, in the movie *Flipper's New Adventure.* He subsequently became a stunt director, specializing in underwater work. *See also* MAKEUP; STUNTS.

Buck

A buck is a simple metal form shaped like a full-sized or miniature building (or similar object). It is used during pyrotechnics as a placeholder for that object, giving the flames something around which to move. During postproduction the buck is optically or digitally replaced by the object it represents.

The 1998 movie *The X-Files* includes a shot of a man being blown up in a room full of vending machines. The explosion was actually a miniature. During this explosion a 3/16-inch-thick steel buck was used to represent the man and give shape to the flames; it was placed between the camera and the five mortars used to create the explosion. *See also* FIRE; PYROTECHNICS.

Burton, Tim (1960–)

American director Tim Burton has created several movies with significance to the field of special effects, most notably *Batman* (1989), *Batman Returns* (1992), and *Mars Attacks!* (1996). An aficionado of stop-motion model photography, Burton revived interest in the technique by using it to create *The Nightmare Before Christmas* (1993). He originally planned to use the same stop-motion animation to make *Mars Attacks!*, but determined that computer graphics would prove more expedient.

Born in 1960, Burton studied animation at the California Institute of the Arts. He then served an apprenticeship in animation at the Disney Studios. He also began making short animated films, and in 1982 he won an Acad-

Director Tim Burton (left) with actor Vincent Price on the set of *Edward Scissorhands* (1990). *Zade Rosenthal/ 20th Century Fox/Photofest.*

emy Award for one entitled *Vincent*. Eventually his animation work attracted the attention of Warner Brothers, which hired him to direct a live-action film entitled *Pee-Wee's Big Adventure* (1985). When the movie was a commercial success, Burton's career as a director was assured. His other films include *Beetlejuice* (1988), *Edward Scissorhands* (1990), *Ed Wood* (1994) and *James and the Giant Peach* (1996). *See also* BATMAN MOVIES; MARS ATTACKS!

Butler, Lawrence W. (1908–1988)

Lawrence W. Butler had a long career as a special effects technician and won an Academy Award for his work on *The Thief of Bagdad* (1940). Born in 1908, Butler began working in the business when he was only 15. His first employer was his father, who was a special and optical effects director at Warner Brothers. Later Butler went to England to work for Alexander Korda, but during World War II he again worked for Warner Brothers. After the war Butler became the head of the special effects department at Columbia Pictures, a job he held for almost 30 years. In addition to *The Thief of Bagdad*, his films include *Casablanca* (1942), *A Thousand and One Nights* (1945), *Robinson Crusoe on Mars* (1964), *In Harm's Way* (1965), and *The Gospel Road* (1973). Butler died in 1988. *See also* KORDA, SIR ALEXANDER; *THE THIEF OF BAGDAD*.

C

Cameras, Motion Picture

Motion picture cameras have gone through many changes since the inception of filmmaking; however, their basic principle remains the same. Light enters the camera lens through its aperture, striking an area—called a frame—of the film and recording an image there. The camera's shutter then closes to block out light while the film advances to the next frame. A mechanism moves the film through the camera at a controlled speed and coordinates this movement with the opening and closing of the shutter. The standard speed of filming is 24 frames per second.

Early cameras were powered by a hand crank, while modern ones are driven by an electric or battery-powered motor or a spring mechanism. Computerized camera systems allow a filmmaker to operate a camera with great precision, automatically changing the filming speed or other variables at key points during filming. Computers also make it possible for cameras to be operated by remote control—even while attached to the underside of a flying helicopter, for example—and to store information about camera movements and operation for exact repetition later. In fact, computerized motion-control photography is one of the most important tools of special effects work today.

The earliest motion picture cameras were mere wooden boxes. The first was created in 1888 by William Laurie Dickson, working in the laboratory of inventor Thomas A. Edison. Edison's camera was initially used to make movies for viewing by one person at a time. It wasn't until seven years after Edison's camera that a movie was projected for group viewing, by inventors August and Louis Lumiere.

In 1896 American inventor George Eastman created perforated celluloid film, which allowed the camera to hold the film steady as it moved. This enabled Edison to improve both his camera and his projection device. Other improvements in motion picture photography soon followed, not only by Edison but by many others who became interested in the field. By 1920, the wooden box had been replaced by a metal one with far more sophisticated mechanisms.

Then, as now, the standard film size for professional filming was 35mm, but today 70 mm film is also used for widescreen filming. In years past, 16 mm film was used for amateur photography, newsreels, and documentaries; today this narrower film is also used for some special effects shots because some 16 mm cameras are capable of filming at much faster speeds than 35mm ones. When 16 mm film is used, it must be "blown up," or rephotographed, to a 35mm size before it can be shown in a theater. Regardless of its size, film is made of a transparent plastic, usually acetate or a commercial material called Estar. Prior to the 1940s, film was made of nitrate, which is both flammable and difficult to preserve; many old films have been damaged or destroyed because of nitrate deterioration.

Early cameras housed their film within the camera body, but modern ones hold film in a cartridge, or film magazine, atop the camera. Special effects experts typically use bipack cameras, which have two film magazines, to make two strips of film run through the camera simultaneously. One of these pieces of film can hold a traveling matte to facilitate the process of combining live action with other elements such as miniature photography or a matte painting. Mattes or other effects accomplished in this way are called "in-camera effects." Early color systems also used bi-pack cameras. Two or three strips of film were run through the camera at the same time, filtered so that each one picked up a different primary color.

In addition to bi-packs, modern cameras can be fitted with a wide variety of attachments. Different lenses can be used to distort an image in different ways. Zoom lenses allow camera operators to film dangerous explosions from a safe distance. Special harnesses hold a camera steady and allow for greater precision. The "Steadycam," which was created for Stanley Kubrick while he was filming *The Shining* (1980), makes the camera so balanced and weightless than the camera operator can run without shaking the images it is filming. There are also special camera mounts and stands that hold a camera steady during animation, stop-motion, and motion-control photography sessions.

New types of cameras are also being developed for specialized purposes. For example, to enable filmmakers to shoot underwater, cameras have been created that are not only waterproof but completely airtight. The air is pumped out of the camera before submersion, creating a seal so tight that the air must be pumped back in before the camera can be opened and the film removed. Digital still cameras have also been invented to capture nonmoving images, translate them into digital form, and send them directly into a computer, where they can be used as a guide in creating a matte painting or other computer-generated image. Digital

motion picture cameras, however, have yet to be developed. *See also* EDISON, THOMAS A.; LUMIERE, AUGUST, AND LOUIS LUMIERE; MOTION-CONTROL CAMERA SYSTEMS; STOP-MOTION MODEL ANIMATION.

Further Reading

Fielding, Raymond. *The Technique of Special Effects Cinematography*. Boston: Focal Press, 1985.

Hutchison, David. *Film Magic: The Art and Science of Special Effects*. New York: Prentice-Hall, 1987.

Imes, Jack. *Special Visual Effects: A Guide to Special Effects Cinematography*. New York: Van Nostrand Reinhold, 1984.

Kawin, Bruce F. *How Movies Work*. Berkeley: University of California Press, 1992.

Ohanian, Thomas A., and Michael E. Phillips. *Digital Filmmaking*. Boston: Focal Press, 1996.

Smith, Thomas G. *Industrial Light & Magic: The Art of Special Effects*. New York: Ballantine Books, 1986.

Cameron, James (1954–)

American screenwriter and director James Cameron is known for creating movies with award-winning special effects, including *Terminator* (1984) and *Terminator 2* (1991), *Aliens* (1986), *The Abyss* (1989), *True Lies* (1994), and *Titanic* (1997), which is currently the top grossing movie of all time.

Cameron was born in 1954 in Ontario, Canada. As a boy, he made 8 mm films as a hobby and studied art. Later he attended the California State University at Fullerton, where he pursued a major in physics before switching his major to English and then dropping out of school entirely to pursue a screenwriting career. At the same time, he took a series of jobs that included machinist and school bus driver.

In 1977 Cameron saw the movie *Star Wars* and decided to pursue filmmaking more aggressively. He studied information about movies and special effects in the library of the University of Southern California and experimented with his own camera equipment. He subsequently made a 10-minute film featuring models, sets, and mattes, which he used to get a job with New World Pictures, run by filmmaker Roger Corman. His work there led to an assignment directing *Piranha II: The Spawning* (1981).

Cameron had numerous problems with the producers of this film, and determined that he would never again work for someone else. During this time, he devised the idea for *The Terminator* and sold the script on the condition that he would have complete control over its production. The resulting movie, which was made on a budget of $6.5 million, was a financial and critical success, as was Cameron's next movie, *Aliens*.

For his third movie, *The Abyss*, Cameron developed a digital morphing technique that he again used in *Terminator 2*. The enormous potential of this technique led him to create his own special effects company, Digital Domain. His partners in this venture were special effects expert Stan Winston and a corporate sponsor, IBM.

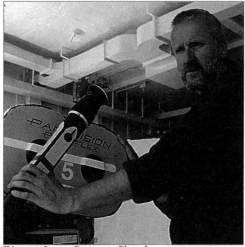

Director James Cameron. *Photofest.*

During the production of *Terminator 2*, Cameron also created his own production company, Lightstorm Entertainment, and immediately signed a three-picture contract with 20th Century Fox. The first two films of this deal were *True Lies* and *Titanic*, the latter of which had a budget of approximately $200 million. Cameron won an Academy Award for Best Director for his work on *Titanic*. *See also* THE ABYSS; ALIEN MOVIES; COST, SPECIAL EFFECTS; DIGITAL DOMAIN; SPECIAL EFFECTS HOUSES; *STAR WARS* MOVIES; *TERMINATOR 2: JUDGEMENT DAY*; *TITANIC*; WINSTON, STAN.

Further Reading

Shay, Don. "In the Digital Domain." *Cinefex 55,* August 1993.

Campbell, Clay (1901–1982)

Makeup artist Clay Campbell supervised makeup on many major motion pictures during the 1940s, 50s, and 60s, but he began his career as a maker of wax figures. Born in 1901, Campbell's first job was at the Oates Wax Factory in Los Angeles. He worked there from 1922 to 1932, when the factory placed him in charge of maintaining the wax figures used for the Warner Brothers movie *The Mystery of the Wax Museum* (1933). A makeup artist at Warner convinced him to try the makeup profession himself, and that same year Campbell went to work for Warner. He remained there until 1938, when he became head of the makeup department at 20th Century Fox. Two years later, dissatisfied with Fox, he returned to Warner, but in 1941 he left again, this time to become head of the makeup department at Columbia Pictures. He retired from Columbia in 1966 and became an independent consultant.

Throughout his career Campbell remained an expert wax maker. He oversaw the production of wax manikins for *Charlie Chan at the Wax Museum* (1939), for example, and made a wax head to represent a melting Dracula in *The Return of the Vampire* (1943). He made a realistic head of John the Baptist for the movie *Salome* (1953). He also worked in latex. His space alien costumes for *Earth Versus the Flying Saucers* (1953) were latex, and although they appear heavy, they weighed only 20 pounds. *See also* EARTH VERSUS THE FLYING SAUCERS; MAKEUP.

Canutt, Yakima (1895–1986)

Enos Edward "Yakima" Canutt was an actor, stuntman, and director who became famous for his horse-related stunts. Canutt fell dramatically from horseback, rode horses off cliffs, leaped from the ground to a galloping horse, and allowed himself to be dragged or trampled by horses and coaches. He also was the first person to perform the horse transfer, which was a jump from a galloping horse onto a moving object such as another horse, a stagecoach, or a wagon.

In two movies, *Riders of the Dawn* (1938) and *Sunset in El Dorado* (1943), Canutt not only transferred onto the horses of a moving stagecoach but "fell" between the team's traces, whereupon he went under the coach, grabbed its rear axle, and climbed back up on the coach from the back. He was well-padded for this stunt, which scraped him along the ground, and the scene was shown at a faster speed to make it look as though the horses were traveling more rapidly than they really were. Nonetheless, it was a dangerous trick.

Born in Colfax, Washington, on November 29, 1895, Canutt developed his horseback skills in childhood. He worked as a ranch hand while growing up, and at age 17 he joined a Wild West show. Later he became a rodeo world's champion. When a newspaper reporter dubbed him "the Cowboy from Yakima," Washington, the nickname "Yakima" stuck.

Canutt first became involved in filmmaking during the silent-film era of the 1920s. Because of his rodeo fame, Hollywood producers asked him to perform stunts in Western movies. After a time, he began acting and was soon given starring roles. His movies during this period include *Romance and the Rustlers* (1924), *Ridin' Mad* (1924), *The Riding Comet* (1925), *White Thunder* (1925), *The Human Tornado* (1925), and *The Outlaw Breaker* (1926).

Stuntman Yakima Canutt (right), famous for performing leaps from galloping horses. *Photofest.*

When silent films became "talkies," Canutt's career as a cowboy star ended because his voice proved unsuitable for movies. Consequently he returned to stuntwork and became a double for other cowboy stars like John Wayne and Roy Rogers, performing stunts in such famous movies as *Stagecoach* (1939), *Gone With the Wind* (1939), and *The Great Train Robbery* (1941).

Eventually Canutt was recognized as an expert in stunts and became a second-unit director, a position that required him to stage action scenes. In this capacity he worked on such major films as *Ben-Hur* (1959), *Spartacus* (1960), and *How the West Was Won* (1962). He was also second-unit director for several Disney Studios live-action films during the 1950s and 1960s. In addition, Canutt developed many safety devices and procedures for the stunt business, including the roll bar and the first air bags. He received a special Academy Award for his stuntwork in 1966. Canutt died in Colfax, Washington, in 1986. *See also* BEN-HUR; THE WALT DISNEY COMPANY; STUNTS.

Casper

Released in 1995 by Universal Pictures and Steven Spielberg's Amblin Entertainment, *Casper* features a variety of special effects, but it is particularly significant in that it featured computer-generated characters in more scenes than any previous movie had. Casper the ghost and his uncles are on screen for a total of more than 40 minutes, in contrast with the digital dinosaurs in *Jurassic Park*, which were on screen for a total of only six and a half minutes. Moreover, unlike *Jurassic*'s dinosaurs, the characters in *Casper* were required to talk. This meant that Industrial Light & Magic, (ILM), which provided digital effects for the movie, had to create lip-sync software that would convert filmed live-action mouth movements into digital lip movements.

Casper's computer-generated characters were first sculpted as 10-inch maquettes, or small clay sculptures, by special effects experts at ILM under the supervision of Dennis Muren. The maquettes were scanned into a computer, which converted them into wireframe skeletons. These skeletons were used to build the characters and animate them—a demanding process, because digital animators had to create a 3-D ghost that would still resemble the 2-D ghost of the original *Casper* cartoons on which the movie was based. The artists also had to achieve the correct degrees of smoothness and transparency for the ghosts, which would not receive their glow and shadows until the final stages of the work.

An additional challenge was the fact that digital artists had to make Casper's face expressive, something that was not required for the *Jurassic Park* dinosaurs. To aid them in their work, the artists used a motion-capture system to transfer information about live actors' facial movements into the computer and develop a library of facial expressions that could be used on the ghost characters as needed. The capture system was also used to create lip movements. But even working from filmed images, it still took special effects experts from two weeks to two months to animate a single shot.

Another problem was the fact that the ghosts often changed shape. To create a changing image with traditional 2-D cel animation, as was used for the original cartoon, an animator merely draws a new shape. With the computer, however, the animator must build an entirely new model.

Moreover, once the animation phase was complete, the computer-generated characters still had to be composited with other scene elements. Their placement was assisted by animatics made during live-action filming. Drawn on the set, these rough sketches were combined with a video recording of the live action, and the resulting videotape was played back so the actors and technicians could get an idea of the ghosts' positions.

In all, approximately 25 animators worked on the film, with additional support personnel. Postproduction required approximately nine months to complete, and *Casper* ultimately employed about 360 computer-generated shots. *See also* ANIMATICS; ANIMATION, COMPUTER; COMPUTER-GENERATED IMAGES; MAQUETTE; MOTION CAPTURE; MUREN, DENNIS; SPIELBERG, STEVEN; UNIVERSAL STUDIOS; WIREFRAME.

Further Reading

Duncan, Jody. "The Ghost and Mr. Muren." *Cinefex* 63, September 1995.

———. "20 Years of Industrial Light & Magic." *Cinefex* 65, March 1996.

Magid, Ron. "Transparent Effects Make *Casper* a Landmark." *American Cinematographer*, December 1995.

Chambers, John (1923–)

John Chambers is a makeup expert best known for his work on the 1968 movie *Planet of the Apes*, which earned him a special Academy Award.

Chambers's task for *Planet of the Apes* was to turn human actors into apes, but he quickly discovered that conventional rubber facial appliances were so thick that they muffled the actors' voices and so stiff that they did not allow the ape lips to move as the actors spoke. Working with chemists, Chambers developed a new type of rubber compound for his ape appliances, along with new adhesives, glues, and paints. These substances were porous, so that the actors' skin could breathe and sweat through the appliances, and some of these appliances could be reused, which reduced makeup costs to approximately $700 to $800 per day. Chambers also streamlined the makeup application and removal process, using a large staff and teamwork to cut the time from approximately 10 hours to four and a half.

Chambers first began working with facial appliances during World War II. The army had trained him as a dental technician, but later assigned him the task of creating artificial noses, ears, and other body parts to be used for reconstructive surgery on wounded soldiers. After the war Chambers continued to make prosthetics for various hospitals, but in the early 1950s he decided to apply his skills to television makeup. He took a job with NBC, where he worked for six years on such shows as *I Spy, Mission Impossible, Star Trek*, and *Lost in Space*. He then joined the makeup department at Universal Studios, where he gained fame as a movie makeup artist after working on *The List of Adrian Messenger* (1963), in which many major Hollywood stars appeared in disguise. His other films include *The Island of Dr. Moreau* (1977) and *A Man Called Horse* (1970). For the latter, he had to create a false chest for a scene in which a man's skin appears to be torn by hooks.

Chambers eventually opened his own commercial makeup laboratory, John Chambers Studio, where he trains many young makeup artists. He also acts as a consultant to hospitals developing prosthetics. He has received awards for both types of work. *See also* MAKEUP; *PLANET OF THE APES*.

Further Reading
Essman, Scott. "John Chambers: Maestro of Makeup." *Cinefex 71,* September 1997.

Chan, Jackie (1954–)

Jackie Chan is an Asian actor known for performing his own spectacular stunts, which are primarily related to the martial arts and include flying kicks and falls. He has made more than 100 movies, including *Rumble in the Bronx* (1996), *Mr. Nice Guy* (1997), and *Rush Hour* (1998).

Actor/stuntman Jackie Chan, an expert in martial arts. *Photofest.*

Chan was born in Hong Kong, China, in 1954. From the ages of six to 16 Chan was indentured to the Chinese Opera Research Institute, where he learned martial arts, acrobatics, dancing, singing, and acting. At the age of 17 Chan got his first film work as a stuntman in Bruce Lee's *Fist of Fury,* during which he performed a spectacular high fall. As a result of this, Chan's career grew steadily, from small bit parts to more significant roles in Asian movies, many of which featured martial arts. Chan's first American film was *Big Brawl* (1980).

In the 1990s, Chan created his own stuntman association, his own talent agency, and his own production company; nonetheless, he continues to perform his own stunts. His stuntwork has resulted in severe injuries; he has broken many bones and permanently damaged his skull. Other stuntmen have also been injured working with Chan, particularly during the making of Chan's 1985 movie, *Police Story. See also* LEE, BRUCE; STUNTS.

Chaney, Lon Sr. (1883–1930)

Silent-film actor Lon Chaney Sr. became so famous for his makeup that he was often called "The Man of a Thousand Faces." Chaney created his own disguises, and he acted in more than 150 movies. Two of his most notable roles were Quasimodo in the 1923 movie *The Hunchback of Notre Dame* and the phantom in the 1925 movie *The Phantom of the Opera*. For Quasimodo, Chaney wore a 40-pound hump with a 30-pound harness.

Born in 1883, Chaney first began working in the theater as a stagehand for a Colorado Springs, Colorado, opera house. Soon he began acting as well, and he moved to Hollywood in 1912 to make movies. In 1915 he began directing films for Universal Studios. Chaney died of cancer in 1930 after acting in his first sound movie, *The Unholy Three*. His son, Lon Chaney Jr. (1906–1973), also became an actor and portrayed many horror-film monsters during the 1940s. *See also* MAKEUP; UNIVERSAL STUDIOS.

Chase, Ken

Ken Chase is a makeup artist who is an expert on making movie and television actors appear to age. Chase learned his trade from two of the most prominent makeup artists in modern film history, John Chambers and Dick Smith, and he started his own company, Ken Chase Studio, in 1977. Chase's works include *Jeremiah Johnson* (1972), *Day of the Locust* (1977), and the television series *Wild, Wild West*. *See also* CHAMBERS, JOHN; MAKEUP; SMITH, DICK.

Cinderella

Cinderella was one of the first movies made by George Melies, one of the pioneers of filmmaking and special effects. Released in 1899, *Cinderella* used photographic tricks that were innovative at the time. The movie featured some of the earliest stop-motion photography, which was used to transform a pumpkin into a coach, an ordinary dress into a ball gown, and similar illusions. The movie also used fast and reverse action to add humor, as well as slow motion to enhance a dancing scene. In addition, some of the movie's black-and-white frames were colored by hand. *See also* MELIES, GEORGE; STOP-MOTION MODEL ANIMATION.

Further Reading
Fry, Ron, and Pamela Fourzon. *The Saga of Special Effects*. Englewood Cliffs, NJ: Prentice-Hall, 1977.

CinemaScope

The first major 35 mm anamorphic process, CinemaScope was first used to film the 1953 movie *The Robe* and is proprietary to 20th Century-Fox Studios. CinemaScope uses a special lens that forces an extra-wide image to fit onto a standard-sized frame of film during photography, and then restores it to its full width during projection, thereby creating a widescreen movie. The aspect, or width-to-height, ratio of this projected frame is 2.35 to 1 when photographed on 35 mm film and 2.2 to 1 when photographed on 70 mm film; in contrast, standard film usually has a ratio of 1.33 to 1. *See also* ANAMORPHIC PROCESS; APERTURE.

Further Reading
Kawin, Bruce F. *How Movies Work*. Berkeley: University of California Press, 1992.

Cinematographer

Also called the director of photography or the first cameraman, the cinematographer oversees camera operation. In the early days of filmmaking, cinematography involved the running of the camera itself, but today's cinematographer does not actually operate a camera. Instead that job is done by the camera operator, also called the second cameraman. The cinematographer selects the appropriate type of film for the camera, determines how many cameras will be needed for a shoot, and helps ascertain the correct lighting for a set on location, while working closely with the film's director to decide camera angles, lenses, and many other technical details involved with photographing and printing the movie. *See also* ANGLE, CAMERA; CAMERAS, MOTION PICTURE.

Cinerama

Cinerama is a widescreen filming process that employs 70 mm film and a single camera lens. Originally, however, it was created with three camera lenses. Each scene was filmed from three different perspectives—centered, right, and left—and then run side-by-side during projection to make a single movie. This movie had to be shown on a specially curved screen, which is still required today.

Invented in the late 1930s by special effects expert Fred Walla, Cinerama was first used in a feature film, *How the West Was Won*, in 1962. Prior to that it was used in a short film called *Metropolitan Opera of the Movies*, which debuted in 1952. Although Cinerama was only popular for about 10 years, it inspired the creation of many other widescreen formats, including CinemaScope, VistaVision, and Panavision. *See also* ANAMORPHIC PROCESS; CINEMASCOPE; VISTAVISION.

Cleopatra

Released by 20th Century Fox Studios, the 1963 version of *Cleopatra* won an Academy

Award for its special effects and was the most expensive movie made up until that decade.

The costs incurred were largely because of *Cleopatra*'s lavish sets. Cleopatra's barge, which cost approximately $250,000 to build, was full-sized, and Egypt's Nile River was recreated as a 360-foot-long tank (which was used again in the movie *Tora! Tora! Tora!*). The city of Alexandria, Egypt, was partially recreated in full size on 20 acres of land on location in Italy and was constructed with 142 miles of tubular steel, 20,000 cubic feet of lumber, 7 tons of nails, 26,000 gallons of paint, and several California palm trees transported at great expense to the Italian site. Because of such extravagance, the total cost of the 1963 *Cleopatra* was $32–$40 million.

In contrast, a 1934 version of *Cleopatra*, made during the Depression, created its special effects on a tight budget. To save money on the movie, the special effects supervisor, Gordon Jennings, used only two miniatures to represent more than 35 galley ships. He multiplied these two models several times, using a mirror system and split-screen double exposures, so that there appeared to be enough ships for two different fleets. Similarly, for his land battles, Gordon decided to save money by using battle footage from an earlier movie, *The Ten Commandments* (1920).

Gordon also created Cleopatra's barge economically. The barge was a mechanized model about the size of a rowboat, with 300 miniature oars powered by an electric motor. The barge's wake and spray were not caused by the relatively lightweight model, but by compressed air being shot into the water through underwater tubes. *See also* JENNINGS, GORDON; *THE TEN COMMANDMENTS; TORA! TORA! TORA!; WAR OF THE WORLDS.*

Further Reading

Fry, Ron, and Pamela Fourzon. *The Saga of Special Effects.* Englewood Cliffs, NJ: Prentice-Hall, 1977.

McKenzie, Alan, and Derek Ware. *Hollywood Tricks of the Trade.* New York: Gallery Books, 1986.

Cliffhanger

Nominated for an Academy Award for its special effects in 1993, *Cliffhanger* used new techniques in miniature photography and featured several spectacular stunts.

Much of the stuntwork for *Cliffhanger* was performed in the Italian Alps using doubles for the actors, who performed correspond-

Full-size barge built for the 1963 version of *Cleopatra. Cleopatra (1963), 20th Century Fox/Photofest.*

ing scenes either on a soundstage or outdoor set representing various portions of a cliff. Soundstage sets were filmed in front of a bluescreen or in combination with front and rear projection of Italian Alps footage. Stunts involving a DC-9 airplane were filmed using a fuselage mockup in front of a bluescreen. In both cases, safety rigs used by stuntpeople were removed digitally during postproduction. Falling snow and gray skies were created digitally as well.

The DC-9 and another plane, a JetStar, were also built as miniatures. The DC-9 was made as a 1/6-scale miniature and rigged with primer cord, naphthalene, and kerosene for a shot of it exploding. The JetStar miniature was "crashed" into a mountain using a 140-foot-long, highly detailed mountain set covered with biodegradable paper confetti "snow." A dolly on a hidden track pulled the plane along the landscape via cables attached to a pickup truck. This system enabled the model plane to achieve a speed of 40 mph. A full-sized JetStar was used for closeups; it ran on the same kind of dolly-and-track system but could only reach a speed of 25 mph.

A more complicated rig was a motion-control camera elevator used to film live-action, on-location mountain scenes. The elevator was mounted at the top of one cliff and at the bottom of another, so that downward and upward shots of both cliffs could later be combined to make it appear as though the footage was taken at one location. In this way, the filmmakers created a sheer cliff face of more than 600 feet. The elevator rig was also used to shoot an actor on an outdoor set representing a cliff ledge; the motion-control camera allowed filmmakers to duplicate the camera angles employed earlier for the background footage. A matte painting filled in the scenery around the cliff ledge for this shot and others.

Several other cliff sets were constructed for the film. One was built horizontally rather than vertically, so that the actors could be pulled safely along its face but seem as though they were sliding down the cliff. Two other sets were miniatures, one in 1/48 scale and the other in 1/6 scale. The former was made

of hard foam, the latter of wood, chickenwire, muslin, and urethane foam. The 1/6-scale model was built in sections because of its size, which was 60 feet wide, 50 feet high, and 30 feet deep. The model was placed in a parking lot in front of a painted backdrop of the Colorado Rockies, where the movie was supposed to be taking place.

For a scene of a helicopter dangling from the cliff and crashing to its base, each miniature cliff model was filmed with an appropriately sized miniature helicopter and puppet figures. Three 1/6-scale remote-controlled puppets were built to represent one of the characters in the scene, who is seen kicking and twisting as he hangs precariously over the cliff. A simpler puppet, with springs and wires inside to make it move only slightly, was built to represent the helicopter pilot. To make the helicopter explode as it fell, the models were rigged with remote-controlled black smoke cartridges and primer cord detonators. Throughout this scene, miniature photography was intercut with live-action shots, some of which were done on location with stuntmen and a full-sized stunt helicopter. A total of six special effects houses worked on the film, with most of the work handled by Richard Edlund's Boss Film Studios. *See also* BLUESCREEN PROCESS; BOSS FILM STUDIOS; EDLUND, RICHARD; MINIATURES AND MODELS; PYROTECHNICS; STUNTS.

Further Reading
Kaufman, Debra. "Effects in the Vertical Realm." *Cinefex 54,* May 1993.

Close Encounters of the Third Kind

Nominated for an Academy Award for its special effects, the 1977 movie *Close Encounters of the Third Kind* featured the work of noted director Stephen Spielberg and special effects expert Douglas Trumbull.

Trumbull developed new special effects techniques for the film. For example, the lead alien in the movie, which was considered advanced technology at the time, was a mechanical puppet operated by 15 crewmembers using levers and wires to manipulate its latex surface from within its head, thereby creating realistic facial movements.

The alien was filmed interacting with live actors on a special landing-site set constructed in an abandoned dirigible hanger on an Alabama Army Air Corps base. The set's surrounding rocky terrain was made of fiberglass, and matte paintings were used to show more distant scenery. Matte paintings were also used elsewhere in the movie, such as to depict a night horizon. One of Trumbull's assistants, Scott Squires, invented a new method of making clouds for this horizon—he filmed white paint moving through a tank of water. The cloud tank remains a significant part of special effects work today.

Another invention was developed to ensure that live-action and miniature elements of the movie would fit together well. Spielberg used matte cameras for both types of photography, and Trumbull created a system whereby camera movements during live-action filming could be recorded and replayed during work with miniatures.

The chief modelmaker charged with building the movie's miniatures was Greg Jein, who is considered one of the foremost experts in the field. In addition to a miniature version of the landing site, he built several spaceships, including a fiberglass mothership that was approximately 4 feet high by 5 feet wide. Photographed through smoke, the ship's surface was enhanced with metal parts, including aluminum cylinders and brass rods. The ship also featured dozens of lights created with neon tubes and other incandescent and fiberoptic materials wired from inside the ship. Additional light shimmers were created by projecting rotating dots onto the ship's underside. In the original version of the film, the audience does not see the inside of this mothership, but in a 1980 revised "Special Edition" version, additional footage was added of the ship's interior. *See also* CLOUD TANK; MATTE; MINIATURES AND MODELS; SPIELBERG, STEVEN; SQUIRES, SCOTT; TRUMBULL, DOUGLAS.

Further Reading
Shay, Don. "A Close Encounter with Steven Spielberg." *Cinefex 53*, February 1993.

Closeup

A closeup is a camera shot with a very narrow view of a subject, so that the subject fills the frame and consequently seems very close to the camera lens. In some cases the camera truly is in close physical proximity to the subject; however, most of the time the shot is achieved from a normal or even extended distance, using a closeup or zoom lens. In other words, a closeup on an actor's face or even part of a face might be shot from 100 yards away with a telephoto lens. One example of an extreme closeup occurs in *Citizen Kane* (1941), in a scene of a man typing. The camera frame is filled with just his typing fingers. *See also* ANGLE, CAMERA; CAMERAS, MOTION PICTURE.

Further Reading
Kawin, Bruce F. *How Movies Work*. Berkeley: University of California Press, 1992.

Cloud Tank

The cloud tank effect was created by Scott Squires, under the supervision of Douglas Trumbull, for the 1977 movie *Close Encounters of the Third Kind*, which featured unusual clouds that formed whenever a particular spaceship appeared.

A cloud tank is simply a water tank into which paint, colored gels, or other substances are released to create cloud-like formations. Layers of fresh and salt water are employed to alter the way these substances move. For example, using thin celluloid divider sheets that are carefully removed before filming, salt water might be placed in the bottom half of the tank and fresh water in the top half. If paint is then injected at the bottom of the tank, it will rise, being lighter than the salt water, then spread out when it reaches the fresh water.

This salt/fresh water technique was used to make volcanic clouds for the 1997 movie *Volcano*. The filmmakers filled a 2,100-gallon tank halfway with salt water, set a thin cover of polyurethane sheeting on the surface, and filled the tank the rest of the way with fresh water. They then carefully removed the sheeting and injected tempura paint in mixtures of black, white, and gray into the tank through a tube at the tank's bottom. Because the paint was lighter than the salt water, it traveled upwards until it reached the fresh water, then fanned out across the surface. This created a realistic cauliflower-shaped plume.

Cloud tanks have also been used to make clouds or similar swirling images for such movies as *Raiders of the Lost Ark* (1981), *Independence Day* (1996), and *Contact* (1997). By varying the viscosity of water in the tank, many different formations can be created. Different types of lighting projected through the glass, as well as different camera angles, can also alter the overall appearance of the shot. In addition, sometimes imitation clouds made of kapok, a material used to stuff cushions, are added to the tank. Miniature spaceships, ghost figures, or other objects can also be filmed in the tank. In many cases, computer graphics are now used to enhance cloud tank effects during postproduction, which was the case for the cloud tank footage used in *Independence Day. See also* CLOSE ENCOUNTERS OF THE THIRD KIND; CONTACT; INDEPENDENCE DAY; INDIANA JONES MOVIES; SQUIRES, SCOTT; TRUMBULL, DOUGLAS; *VOLCANO*.

Further Reading
Street, Rita. "Toasting the Coast." *Cinefex 71*, September 1997.

Cocoon

Released in 1985, *Cocoon* won an Academy Award for its visual effects, which were under the supervision of Ken Ralston at Industrial Light & Magic (ILM).

Most of *Cocoon's* effects were accomplished with miniatures, makeup, and puppets. The alien spaceship, for example, was a 3-foot diameter model with moving lights filmed with a motion-control camera. A boat that lifts into the air was also a model, manned by puppets and filmed with stop-motion photography. The live-action aliens were actors in makeup that had been created by Greg Cannom Creations. The aliens were shot in front of a bluescreen, and their unusual glow was adding during postproduction using optical tricks and animation.

A 1988 sequel to the movie, *Cocoon II*, used a more complicated but also more effective method to create this glow. By then a new type of camera had been invented that allowed the filmmaker to add the optical effect while filming the actor in front of a bluescreen using multiple passes. A far simpler technique was used to create the alien spaceship for *Cocoon II;* the filmmaker merely used footage from *Cocoon. See also* BLUESCREEN PROCESS; INDUSTRIAL LIGHT & MAGIC; RALSTON, KEN.

Further Reading
Duncan, Jody. "20 Years of Industrial Light & Magic." *Cinefex 65*, March 1996.

Cohl, Emile (1857–1938)

Emile Cohl was one of the pioneers of animation, both cel and stop-motion. Originally a political cartoonist, he made more than 100 animated films between 1907 and 1918 using his own drawings. At the same time, he experimented with stop-motion photography, and in 1908 he created *The Animated Matches*, a brief public-service announcement that was perhaps the first film to employ stop-motion puppet animation. At one time his cartoons were extremely popular, but by 1918 his work was considered outdated. Unable to find a job, he lived in poverty for the remainder of his life. *See also* STOP-MOTION MODEL ANIMATION.

Columbia Pictures

Columbia Pictures is responsible for such important special effects movies as *Close Encounters of the Third Kind* (1977) and *Ghostbusters* (1984). Founded in 1920 by two brothers, Harry and Jack Cohn, and a friend, Joe Brandt, Columbia became a major motion picture company during the 1930s and 1940s. In the 1950s it created a subsidiary, Screen Gems, to develop television projects.

In 1982 Columbia Pictures was purchased by the Coca-Cola Company for $750 million, and that same year it cofounded TriStar Pictures, which is responsible for such major special effects films as *Terminator 2* (1991) and *Jumanji* (1995). In 1989, the Sony Corporation bought Columbia Pictures for $3.4 billion. It also purchased TriStar, placing both companies under the control of Sony Pictures Entertainment as the Columbia TriStar Motion Pictures Companies. *See also* CLOSE ENCOUNTERS OF THE THIRD KIND; COLUMBIA PICTURES; *JUMANJI;* TERMINATOR 2: JUDGEMENT DAY; TRISTAR PICTURES.

Compositing

Compositing is the layering of two or more elements, which have been created separately, into the same shot. An element is a single photographic, digital, or artistic image. Special effects artists generally speak in terms of a shot being "comped" when it has all of its layers in place and is in final form. The compositing process typically takes place during postproduction, after all of the live action has been filmed.

Prior to the 1980s, the most important tool for postproduction compositing was the optical printer, a device that uses projection techniques and a camera to rephotograph several pieces of film as one. It allows, for example, a frame of film showing an actor to be composited with a frame of film showing an animated character or a hand-drawn bolt of lightening. Each "pass" of the film through the optical printer can add a new layer of elements, sometimes as many as 30 in one shot. This was the case for the 1982 movie *Blade Runner*, where shots of matte paintings, miniatures, rain, live action, and many other elements were added using an optical printer during postproduction.

However, beginning in 1989 with the movie *Indiana Jones and the Last Crusade*, computers have increasingly replaced optical printers as the main compositing tool. Digital compositing involves scanning filmed images into a computer, combining and altering them, and scanning the final product back out of the computer onto film. Digital compositing has made it possible to create computer-generated movie characters who realistically interact with live-action film elements. In the 1997 movie *Godzilla,* for example, almost all images of the monster were

computer-generated, as was much of the debris that he created, while most of the buildings and cars he interacted with were either real or miniatures. All of these elements were later digitally composited.

An important tool in such compositing is the bluescreen process, which makes it easier to isolate shot elements and add them to background plates. When an actor, for example, is filmed in front of a bluescreen, a computer or optical printer can later extract the blue area from the scene and automatically replace it with some other background. *See also* BLADE RUNNER; BLUESCREEN PROCESS; COMPUTER GRAPHICS; *GODZILLA; INDIANA JONES* MOVIES; OPTICAL PRINTER; POSTPRODUCTION.

Further Reading
Holsinger, Erik. "Bluescreen Compositing: Tools, Tips, and Tricks." *Digital World,* December 1997.
Kawin, Bruce F. *How Movies Work*. Berkeley: University of California Press, 1992.
Sammon, Paul M. *Future Noir: The Making of* Blade Runner. New York: Harper Collins, 1996.
Ohanian, Thomas A., and Michael E. Phillips, *Digital Filmmaking*. Boston: Focal Press, 1996.

Computer-Generated Images

Computer-generated images, or CGIs, have become a major part of modern special effects work. Creating a CGI begins with either an existing image that has been scanned into a computer or with the process of drawing an image within the computer environment using software tools. Scanned images can be derived from drawings, photographs, clay sculptures called maquettes, or real objects such as a person's face. Two-dimensional objects are scanned using traditional flatbed scanners, while three-dimensional ones are scanned with tools such as a digital wand, which is touched to the object at various points to orient them on a digital grid. Once all of these points are transferred into the computer, they are connected to create a wireframe image of the object.

Wireframe objects are the skeletons of 3-D computer characters. A digital effects artist can work with a wireframe to adjust it, perfect it, and animate it. Generally after the wireframe is animated (though sometimes before), the character's "skin" is added, along with textures, colors, lighting effects, and other details that make the creation look realistic. The process by which the computer adds these details is called rendering

In cases where computer-generated characters are intended to perform entirely in a computer-generated setting, such as in the fully computer-animated features *Toy Story* (1995), *Antz* (1998), and *A Bug's Life* (1998), the background is developed digitally in the same way as the character, through drawing or scanning, perfecting wireframes, providing the computer with texture and color information, and going through the rendering process. Many times, however, the computer-generated character is intended to accompany live action, which means that a person called a "match-mover" must precisely place the computer-generated figure in each live-action background plate and make sure that the movements of the virtual camera are identical to those on the live-action shoot. In other words, the computer-generated character must be viewed from the same angles as the live-action ones, so that both types of characters will appear to have been filmed together.

To create this illusion, the match-mover uses measurements taken on the live-action set, along with wireframe duplicates of the objects on that set, which will appear only in the computer and not in the final film. Once match-moving is complete and all other desired elements, such as miniature photography or pyrotechnics effects, have been composited with the computer-generated character and the live action, each shot is scanned back out onto film. *See also* ANIMATION, COMPUTER; COMPOSITING; COMPUTER GRAPHICS; DIGITAL WAND; MATCH-MOVER; MINIATURES AND MODELS; PYROTECHNICS; RENDERING; SCANNING; WIREFRAME.

Further Reading

De Leeuw, Ben. *Digital Cinematography*. Boston: AP Professional, 1997.

Street, Rita. *Computer Animation: A Whole New World*. Gloucester, MA: Rockport, 1998.

Computer Graphics

Computer graphics are a major part of modern special effects work. The first computer graphics were simple geometric shapes created by a computer programmer. The first computer drawing system was invented in 1959 through a joint effort of General Motors, an automobile manufacturer, and IBM, a computer corporation; however, it was used privately and was not unveiled to the public until 1964. There were also crude computer shapes produced by the Bell Laboratories in the 1950s, but again, knowledge of this work was not widespread.

The first computer drawing to gain public attention was that of Ivan Sutherland, a Ph.D. student at the Massachusetts Institute of Technology (MIT). In 1962 Sutherland invented a computer program called Sketchpad, which allowed people to draw lines directly on a cathode ray tube (CTR) screen. Two years later, Sutherland joined with Dr. David Evan at the University of Utah to create the first university department devoted to research in computer graphics. During the 1960s and 70s, many important advances came out of this department, and other institutions began studying computer graphics as well.

The most prestigious work in this field came out of the New York Institute of Technology (NYIT) computer graphics laboratory, which lured away many researchers from the University of Utah. After a start-up cost of $2 million for computer equipment and staff, NYIT immediately began developing the tools to create a computer-animated movie. Meanwhile, Ivan Sutherland and David Evan founded their own company, Evans and Sutherland (E&S), to produce computer graphics tools, and in 1969 they released the first CAD (Computer Animated Drawing) wireframe graphics machine system, called LDS-1 (Line Drawing System-1). Other companies sprung up to develop their own systems, and commercially manufactured computer games began to appear, including PONG in 1972.

At this time filmmakers began to realize the advantages that computer graphics held for their work. In 1976, *Futureworld* became the first full-length movie to employ computer graphics, after American International Pictures hired Dr. Edwin Catmull, the head of

NYIT's computer graphics lab, to make a wireframe, computer-generated hand for a single shot. The following year, George Lucas featured a computer-generated Death Star simulation in his movie *Star Wars*. The image was created using a computer graphics system designed at the University of Illinois. In 1978, Lucas hired Dr. Catmull to head his newly established Lucasfilm Computer Development Division, which was devoted to finding new ways to use computer graphics in filmmaking.

Meanwhile, Disney Studios was exploring computer graphics, and in 1979 they used a computer-generated grid and black hole simulation in *The Black Hole*. The television industry also began using computer graphics for advertising logos and shots within commercials. However, the computer-generated images of this period were, by later standards, crude, and the hardware required to make them was expensive and not very powerful.

In the early 1980s, this situation began to change. Many advances in computer hardware and software occurred, and tools such as the computer-assisted animation stand were invented. As a result, in 1982 the first sequence of realistic images created entirely from computer graphics appeared in a feature film. Created by the Lucasfilm Computer Division and known as "The Genesis Effect," this image was a 60-second shot in the 1982 movie *Star Trek II: The Wrath of Khan* depicting the rapid transformation of a "dead" planet into first a fiery world and then a green paradise. That same year, *Tron* featured the first extensive use of 3-D computer animation in a movie; it had 15 minutes of shots made entirely of computer animation, plus 25 minutes of shots of computer animation composited with other film elements. This compositing was done with an optical printer, but in 1983 the first digital compositing for a motion picture was used in an animated feature called *Where the Wild Things Are*.

Both *Tron* and *Where the Wild Things Are* were released by Disney Studios, and the computer work for both films was done by Information International Inc. (III) and Mathematical Applications Group Inc.

(MAGI). *Tron* also required the services of computer experts at Robert Abel & Associates and Digital Effects. Along with the Lucasfilm Computer Division, these four computer graphics studios were the largest in the business at that time. In 1986, they were joined by Pixar, a computer animation studio established by Steve Jobs, the creator of Apple Computers, and four of the founders of the Lucasfilm Computer Division: Edwin Catmull, John Lasseter, Ralph Guggenheim, and Bill Reeves. Lasseter also worked for MAGI during the making of *Where the Wild Things Are*. Pixar created the first entirely computer-generated animated feature, *Toy Story*, in 1995, and today it is the premier computer animation company in the business, having recently released *A Bug's Life* (1998).

Another company formed in the 1980s was Digital Productions, established by John Whitney and computer programmer Gary Demmos. Digital Productions is noted for creating the first lengthy, detailed, computer-generated space scenes, which appeared in the 1984 science fiction movie *The Last Starfighter*. The movie initially had 30 minutes of such scenes, but 10 minutes were cut during editing.

That same year, the movie *Dune* featured 3-D body armor, the first serious attempt to re-create a human form with computer graphics. In 1985, the first fully computer-generated character appeared in a feature film, a stained-glass knight who comes to life in *Young Sherlock Holmes*. This character was also the first to be applied directly onto the film negative with a computer-guided laser. However, the knight was not intended to look like a real-life figure, whereas computer-generated women in the 1985 movie *Looker* were intended to be fairly realistic. *Looker* features the first full-body digital representations of people; the movie's plot centers around a corporate executive who makes computerized women to be used in television advertisements.

Other significant advances during the 1980s include the first use of digital morphing technology (for the 1988 movie *Willow*), the first all-digital composite for a live-action feature film (for the 1989 movie *Indiana Jones and the Last Crusade*), and the first digital water (for the 1989 movie *The Abyss*). The 1990s saw several more important advances, including the first digitally manipulated matte painting (for the 1990 movie *Die Hard 2: Die Harder*), the development of motion capture to create realistic human movements for a computer-generated character (for the 1991 movie *Terminator 2: Judgement Day*), and the creation of software to make realistic computer-generated human skin (for the 1992 movie *Death Becomes Her*) and hair (for the 1994 movie *The Flintstones*, with further improvements for the 1995 movie *Jumanji*). The 1990s also brought the invention of Cari facial animation software (for the 1996 movie *Dragonheart*), the first use of realistic digital water (for the 1995 movie *Waterworld*, with further improvements for the 1997 movie *Titanic*), and the creation of lifelike 3-D dinosaurs (for the 1993 movie *Jurassic Park* and its 1997 sequel *The Lost World*).

In addition, throughout the 1990s computer hardware became more affordable, as did the work provided by computer graphics studios. Therefore filmmakers began to rely on a larger number of digital effects. For example, the 1995 movie *Casper* used more than 400 computer-generated shots, and *Titanic* (1997) featured 150. The latter created large crowds of digital extras and filled in missing portions of a ship set with computer-generated images. The makers of *Titanic* also relied on computers to composite scenes and remove technical equipment, such as wires and safety harnesses, from shots, which is a common use of computers today. Whereas optical printers were once essential for combining film elements and removing unwanted images, now they are gradually being replaced by computer equipment. *See also* THE ABYSS; CASPER; COMPUTER HARDWARE AND SOFTWARE; DEATH BECOMES HER; DRAGONHEART; DUNE; THE FLINTSTONES; INDIANA JONES MOVIES; JUMANJI; JURASSIC PARK; THE LOST WORLD; STAR TREK MOVIES; STAR WARS MOVIES; TERMINATOR 2: JUDGEMENT DAY; TITANIC; WATERWORLD; YOUNG SHERLOCK HOLMES.

Further Reading

Duncan, Jody. "20 Years of Industrial Light & Magic." *Cinefex* 65, March 1996.

Street, Rita. *Computer Animation: A Whole New World*. Gloucester, MA: Rockport, 1998.

Vaz, Mark Cotta, and Patricia Rose Duignan. *Industrial Light & Magic: Into the Digital Realm*. New York: Del Rey, 1996.

Computer Hardware and Software

At the largest special effects houses, the standard equipment for digital special effects is a computer workstation, which is a computer system designed for graphics professionals who need high-quality performance and the fastest computer processors available. Approximately 80 percent of all workstations sold in the United States today are manufactured by three companies: Hewlett Packard, Sun Microsystems, and Silicon Graphics Inc., which uses a UNIX operating system. Each of these vendors offers different models of their workstations, with different levels of processing power. Full-service effects houses like Industrial Light & Magic (ILM) typically choose the most powerful version of the Silicon Graphics workstation, which costs thousands of dollars.

Recently, however, special effects houses have begun to recognize that relatively inexpensive personal computers (PCs) can also produce excellent digital effects, providing they have high-speed processors and the Microsoft Windows NT operating system. For example, Digital Domain used PCs, Windows NT, and software called LightWave 3D to create a digital ship for a long shot in *Titanic* (1997). The rest of the effects for *Titanic*, however, were created with a workstation.

Consequently, workstations offer a wider variety of professional visual effects software. The most common 3-D animation tools are Softimage, RenderMan, and several products made by Alias/Wavefront, which is owned by Silicon Graphics. There are many other commercial programs as well, along with proprietary software developed by individual special effects houses and used exclusively by them.

Commercial Software Used for Special Effects Production

Vendor	Title	Used For
Alias/Wavefront	Animator	3-D animation
	Composer	Compositing
	Dynamation	3-D particle animation
Discreet Logic	Flame	2-D Animation and Compositing Systems
	Flint	2-D Animation and Compositing Systems
	Inferno	2-D Animation and Compositing Systems
Electric Image	Electric Image	3-D graphics and animation (for Macintosh computers)
Interactive Effects	Amazon	Paint program
Kinetex	3D Studio MAX R2	3-D animation
Microsoft	Softimage	3-D graphics and animation
NewTek	LightWave 3D	3-D graphics and animation
Phototron	Primatte	Bluescreen work
Pixar	Renderman	Rendering
Quantel	Domino	Image compositing
Side Effects	Houdini	3-D graphics and animation
	Prisms	3-D graphics and animation
Ultimatte	Ultimate	Bluescreen work

Further Reading

"Digital Tools." *VFX/HQ.* http://vfxhq.com/tools/index.html, April 1999.

Maestri, George. "Something for Everyone." *Digital World,* September 1997.

Wagstaff, Sean. "Buyer's Guide: After Effects Plug-Ins." *Digital World,* September 1997.

White, Charlie. "It's a Horserace! The Workstation Derby." *Digital Magic,* October 1997.

Congo

The 1995 movie *Congo* employed new equipment and techniques related to animatronics and the creation of lava effects. The movie's animatronics were used to create a realistic ape named Amy and a group of mutant apes called the Grays. Amy was played by two actresses who provided the face and body casts used to design their animatronic costumes.

The ape's body was made of a new kind of silicone that was extremely soft and yet still able to retain its shape. Beneath it the actresses wore a "muscle suit" to provide padding to various areas of the body, and beneath the muscle suit they wore a garment designed to absorb sweat from their skin. The stomach of the suit held a battery pack used to power the animatronic head, which had a carbon fiber understructure with 23 servo motors that drove its radio-controlled movements. Three puppeteers worked the controls, one of them wearing a telemetry device on his head that transmitted his own jaw movements to the animatronic jaw.

The Amy head was far more sophisticated than prior animatronic heads because the filmmakers wanted to use it for most of the shoot. This was the first time that an animatronic head had been required to perform a full range of expression. Previously, a costume would have several animatronic heads, each performing only one or two movements. In contrast, the only movement the Amy head was unable to perform was a scream, which was accomplished with a substitute head. Three stunt heads were also used for action sequences, two incapable of movement and one with limited movement.

Another advanced feature of the Amy head was its eyes. Designed by Jon Dawe, who also created the eyes for the dinosaurs in *Jurassic Park* (1993), they were cast out of resin, painted, and then covered with a polyester material to simulate the lens. Right before filming, the eyes were brushed with a window cleaning solution to make them look wet, but their construction made it impossible for anyone to see through them. This meant that the actresses had to look through a fiberoptic peephole installed in one nostril of the head. Even with this arrangement, it was difficult to see, so the performers had to count their steps and memorize them for each scene.

The actors playing the Grays, however, had no such difficulty, because their ape costumes relied on the performers' eyes rather than mechanized ones. Otherwise the Gray costumes were made in the same way as the Amy ones, using casts of the actors' bodies as a design tool. Both types of costumes were covered with various shades of yak hair that had been dipped in an adhesive and hand-punched into the silicone skin. There were a total of 12 Gray costumes, all with moving facial features. Of these, eight were very expressive while four had only limited motion. Ten performers wore the suits, which were operated by 16 puppeteers, and additional Grays were added by compositing extra shots of them into a scene during postproduction.

In addition to the animatronic apes, the movie featured a robot hippopotamus. Built by Stan Winston Studios, it was a complex mechanism powered by hydraulics and air compression along a 25-foot track submerged in a water tank. This aspect of the creature was designed by special effects supervisor Michael Lantieri, who also worked on the dinosaur effects for *Jurassic Park* and *The Lost World* (1997). Like the ape costumes, the hippopotamus's skin was silicone, but instead of hair it had painted surface features.

Congo's lava effects were also unique. Originally the filmmakers planned to use simulated lava on full-sized sets, but they realized that this would be too difficult. Therefore they decided to employ miniature sets that had been painted in a bluescreen color, so that photographs of the lava could be removed from the background and added to live action via a bluescreen process. There was a separate miniature set for each camera angle needed for a lava scene. Each set was carved in 1/6 scale from urethane foam and sprayed with a hard urethane substance to waterproof it so it could be sprayed with warm water after each filming session.

The lava was made of a liquid material called methocel, with Styrofoam beads added for thickness. Its surface crust was black paint mixed with polysorb, a substance typically used to absorb excess moisture in soil or to soak up chemical spills. The lava itself was white; its color and heat glow were added later using computer graphics. This was very different from the way that methocel was later colored for *Volcano* (1997). That movie added red ultraviolet-sensitive paint to the methocel and then lit it from underneath with an ultraviolet light to create a realistic lava color and glow. For *Congo,* because color and glow were added during postproduction, some of the lava scenes could be done with water instead of methocel. This made it easier to create shots of it spewing into the air. *See also* ANIMATRONICS; *JURASSIC PARK;* LANTIERI, MICHAEL; *THE LOST WORLD;* MECHANICAL EFFECTS; *VOLCANO;* WINSTON, STAN.

Further Reading
Duncan, Jody. "Gorilla Warfare." *Cinefex 62,* June 1995.

Contact

Released by Warner Brothers in 1997, *Contact* offers an example of how digital previsualization has affected modern moviemaking. The film features an alien transport machine, which was originally going to be made as a miniature. To this end, a computer-generated version was created as a previsualization tool to enable director Robert Zemeckis to view different configurations for the machine and determine which one he preferred before any full-sized set or miniature was built. However, the computer-generated image proved so realistic that Zemeckis eventually decided to use it for the final film, even for a shot of it exploding apart. The explosion shot was particularly difficult to create, because each flying piece of the machine had to be animated individually.

Miniatures were still used for a few shots of the machine's pod, which was a small globe within the larger structure. This pod was built in both 1/16 and 1/4 scale. For shots of it dropping into water, the pod was either photographed on a model mover or dropped into a tank of water.

A full-sized, 38-foot-high set representing the interior of the pod, which filled an entire soundstage, was also used. The floor of this full-sized pod was a bluescreen, because in one shot it had to turn into a swirling cloud. This cloud was created using a cloud tank, with a technique similar to that used for the movie *Volcano* (1997). The walls of the pod were altered digitally during postproduction so that they appeared to shift and vibrate, and a lightshow similar to the one in *Stargate* (1994) was used to suggest that the pod was travelling through space at a rapid rate.

Another interesting special effect in the movie is related to a scene on an alien beach. The beach background plate was photographed in Fiji, then digitally altered to have strange textures, colors, and motions. The actors in the scene were filmed in front of a bluescreen. Their images were later composited onto the background to created a multilayered 3-D computer-generated effect. *See also* COMPUTER-GENERATED IMAGES; CLOUD TANK; *STARGATE; VOLCANO;* ZEMECKIS, ROBERT.

Further Reading

"*Contact*: A New Space Odyssey." *Preview Magazine,* July-August 1997

Martin, Kevin H. "Close *Contact." Cinefex 71,* September 1997.

Coppola, Francis Ford (1939–)

Director Francis Ford Coppola has made many movies that feature realistic special effects. However, his most important role in terms of the effects industry was to serve as a mentor to George Lucas, who created *Star Wars* (1977).

Coppola was born in 1939 and began making amateur films as a boy. He studied filmmaking at the University of California at Los Angeles (UCLA), where he made a mildly pornographic movie that led to an apprenticeship with producer-director Roger Corman. Under Corman's guidance, Coppola made his directorial debut with the horror movie *Dementia 13* (1963). His next film, *You're a Big Boy Now* (1967), was also his master's thesis for the UCLA fine arts program. Coppola's first major movie was *Finian's Rainbow* (1968), a Warner Brothers musical.

In 1969 Coppola established his own production facility, American Zoetrope, with financial backing from Warner Brothers. By this time he had met George Lucas, who had won a Warner Brothers scholarship to observe the making of *Finian's Rainbow* and who worked on Coppola's next film, *The Rain People* (1969). Coppola made Lucas the vice president of American Zoetrope and gave him the chance to direct the studio's first film, *THX-1138,* which was an expanded version of a short film Lucas had made as a student. Warner Brothers so hated the movie that the company pulled its financing from American Zoetrope.

Coppola was able to keep the company afloat, however, thanks to successes such as *Patton* (1971), which earned him an Academy Award for Best Screenplay; *The Godfather* (1972) and its sequels; *American Graffiti* (1973), which he produced and Lucas directed; *Apocalypse Now* (1979); *Peggy Sue Got Married* (1986); and *Bram Stoker's Dracula* (1992). However, he also produced box-office failures, including *One From the Heart* (1982), *The Outsiders* (1983), and *The Cotton Club* (1984). Eventually the losses exceeded the profits and American Zoetrope filed for bankruptcy. The company still exists today, but offers production support to other filmmakers besides Coppola. *See also* LUCAS, GEORGE.

Further Reading

Johnson, Robert K. *Francis Ford Coppola.* Boston: Twayne, 1977.

Costs, Special Effects

In 1908 the average film cost only $200–$500 to make. By the early 1920s, that cost had risen to $100,000–500,000, largely be-

The 10 Most Expensive Special Effects Movies of 1997 by Cost of Special Effects
(approximate dollar amounts in millions)

Movie	U.S. Box Office	Production Cost	Special Effects Cost and % of Budget
Starship Troopers	$52.9	$110	$50–45%
Titanic	$600+	$200	$42–21%
Batman & Robin	$107.3	$120+	$30–25%
Dante's Peak	$67.1	$100+	$25–25%
Contact	$100.8	$85	$23–27%
Volcano	$63.5	$90	$22–24%
The Lost World	$248.8	$75	$21–28%
Men in Black	$229.1	$90	$20–22%
Alien Resurrection	$36.7	$75	$15–20%
Spawn	$54.8	$45	$13–29%

cause the standard length of a movie had expanded from only eight minutes to about 90 minutes. As time passed, however, the average length of a movie held at around two hours, yet costs continued to escalate. This was due in large part to the rising demand for special effects, which can be a significant part of a film's budget. For example, for the 1953 movie *War of the Worlds*, which won an Academy Award for its special effects, the cost of live-action filming was $600,000, while the cost of special effects was $1,400,000.

Today a single visual effects shot can cost $700,000, so special effects movies often have budgets of several million dollars. However, such budgets are not always recouped at the box office. Some of the most expensive special effects movies, such as *Waterworld* (1995) and *Batman and Robin* (1997), did not make a profit, while others that were more modest in cost, such as *The Lost World* (1997) and *Men in Black* (1997), did phenomenally well.

Recently, filmmakers have become more careful about keeping costs down. In particular, they now realize that it is more expensive to fix a shot during postproduction than to shoot it right in the first place. For a time, many filmmakers believed that most mistakes could be repaired in postproduction via digital effects and that extra time spent in postproduction would be less expensive than time spent on a location shoot, where the average cost can be several hundred thousand dollars a day. However, records indicate that an overreliance on digital tools can double a postproduction budget.

Further Reading

DiOrio, Carl. "The After-Effect: Slowing Down Follows the FX Explosion." *Hollywood Reporter,* 10 December 1997.

Karon, Paul. "Filmmakers Pay a High Price for Techno Tricks." *Variety,* 28 September–4 October, 1998.

Street, Rita. "Independents Day: The State of the State-of-the-Art in Visual Effects." *Film & Video,* May 1999.

Crash Dive

Released by 20th Century Fox in 1943, *Crash Dive* won an Academy Award for its special effects. The movie's plot concerns a conflict between two submarine officers, and many of the effects produced underwater action sequences. Ocean scenes were filmed at Fox Studios in a large tank, which was eventually named after the film's special effects supervisor, Fred Sersen.

Cyclorama

A cyclorama is a curved backdrop, typically a painting on cloth, used to represent the scenery behind a shot. The cyclorama was extremely popular in the 1950s, when it was used in such movies as *Forbidden Planet*

(1956) but fell out of favor with the development of the bluescreen process and other forms of sophisticated matte work. The cyclorama is still used on occasion, however. In the 1994 movie *The Flintstones* a cyclorama was used to depict volcanic terrain behind a "Stone-Age" nightclub, and in the 1999 movie *My Favorite Martian*, a cyclorama served as the backdrop for a set representing the surface of Mars. The Mars cyclorama measured 19x125 feet and included both painted scenery and greenscreens the latter of which were used to add computer-generated elements during postproduction. *See also* BLUESCREEN PROCESS; *THE FLINTSTONES; FORBIDDEN PLANET; MY FAVORITE MARTIAN.*

Further Reading

Duncan, Jody. "The Making of a Rockbuster." *Cinefex* 58, June 1994.

Kawin, Bruce F. *How Movies Work*. Berkeley: University of California Press, 1992.

Martin, Kevin. "Martian Chronicles. *Cinefex* 77, April 1999.

D

Danforth, Jim (c. 1940–)

Jim Danforth is an expert in stop-motion model animation. He first began working in the field at age 18, when he was employed by Art Clokey Productions to provide animation for television shows. Danforth then began doing movie animation for Project Unlimited, a company formed by special effects men.

However, Project Unlimited gave Danforth no screen credits, so he left there to work for Film Effects of Hollywood, where he did animation for his first major film, *It's a Mad, Mad, Mad, Mad World* (1963). This movie featured a scene in which several people were flung, one by one, from a wildly swinging ladder. To create this scene, Danforth used three scales of miniatures: 1/4-inch scale for long shots, 1-inch for stop-motion, and 2-inch for high-speed shots of the figures flying from the ladder.

Danforth's other films include *The Seven Faces of Dr. Lao* (1964), for which he sculpted and animated a Loch Ness monster; *Around the World Under the Sea* (1965); and *When Dinosaurs Ruled the Earth* (1971). His animation work for the latter took more than 17 months. *See also* THE SEVEN FACES OF DR. LAO; STOP-MOTION MODEL ANIMATION.

Dante's Peak

The 1997 Universal Pictures movie *Dante's Peak* is responsible for the creation of new digital compositing software, as well as new techniques for creating lava effects. The film also employed more miniature photography than almost any other film to date. Several special effects companies worked on the film, including Digital Domain, which also contributed to *Waterworld* (1995) and *Apollo 13* (1995); and Banned from the Ranch, which provided scientific instruments, graphics, and similar effects for *Twister* (1997).

The plot of *Dante's Peak* concerns a volcanic eruption and the destructive force of its lava flow. After production began, the filmmakers learned that a rival studio, 20th Century Fox, was working on a similar project, *Volcano* (1997). However, whereas the lava in *Volcano* was created primarily with a material called methocel, the lava in *Dante's Peak* was accomplished with 3-D computer graphics, combined with live action, miniature photography, and practical effects filmed on location in Wallace, Idaho.

In Wallace, mechanical effects experts built false buildings rigged for demolition by hydraulic pumps and other equipment. A false church steeple was destroyed with pyrotechnics. The town was also covered with false ash, which was made of pieces of gray paper mache. The ash was distributed throughout the town with insulation blowers, snow blowers, and air mortars. Additional ash was added digitally during postproduction.

Careful planning allowed the filmmakers to build sets that would interact with digital lava that would be added later. For example, in one scene the lava had to push in the wall of a cabin. Set designers therefore built the cabin set so that the wall could be removed. During live-action scenes with the cabin intact, the wall remained in place. For shots in which the wall was being destroyed, they replaced the wall with a greenscreen, and the actors performed on the set as though the lava were there instead. At the same time, special effects experts rigged a full-sized duplicate of part of the cabin, which included some of its furniture, for repeated pyrotechnics and burning. One of its walls had a hydraulic mechanism that could push it into the room. Shots of the intact cabin, the greenscreen cabin, and the pyrotechnics cabin were later combined to achieve the final effect.

To create the computer-generated lava, digital artists first made simple tubular geometric shapes, which were then animated to represent the moving mass. Details such as shading, texture, and color were not added until the final rendering process. Of these, color was the most difficult, because the digital artists not only had to create a realistic appearance for the lava but maintain consistency from shot to shot. In addition, they used customized software to create the lava's crust and crevices and to integrate its edges with live-action background plates. Of vital importance in their work were surveys of the live-action locations, providing them with exact details regarding the surface terrain. This information allowed the artists to build a digital duplicate of the live-action environment, which in turn helped them determine how the lava would move over the landscape and interact with various scene elements.

Most interactions between lava and objects, however, were accomplished with miniatures. In fact, *Dante's Peak* employed some of the most detailed miniature sets ever constructed for a major film, perhaps in part because its visual effects supervisor, Patrick McClung, had once been a modelmaker. One of the most impressive sets was built to shoot a mud flow destroying a bridge and a dam. These two structures were built at a scale of 1/3.5 and shared a steel framework 100 feet long and 35 feet high; they were constructed side by side to take advantage of the same miniature riverbed and accompanying water system. A large elevated tank at one end of the sloped river flooded the set with 650,000 gallons of colored water, to which three cups of petroleum had been added to reduce its foaminess, and at the other end a recapture tank recycled the water back to its starting point. The water was released at a rate of 150,000 gallons per minute, with an additional 5,000 gallons of water per minute provided by a supplemental system of eight water pumps placed along the banks of the riverbed. The entire event was over in only four minutes, and each miniature structure had to be photographed separately. This meant that the set had to be restored time and time again to get the necessary shots.

Another impressive miniature was a volcano model, designed from topographical maps of Mount St. Helen's in Washington State. Thirty feet tall and 110 feet at its base, it was built inside an airport hanger but sat on a wooden platform with wheels so it could be moved outdoors for filming. This was a unique feature, as was the way the model was constructed. Miniature mountains are typically made of several layers, the first a wooden frame, the second wire, the third a screening material shaped in the desired topography, and the fourth a covering of foam or gunnite that is then sculpted to create the final appearance. The *Dante's Peak* mountain, however, had only two layers, the wooden frame and the foam, in the form of stacked blocks.

Because of the eliminated layers, the mountain was constructed much more quickly than usual, but without the screening material to shape it, the foam required extensive sculpting. Modelmakers carved the structure from the bottom up, and to reach the upper part of the mountain they had to be lowered on ropes from the hanger ceiling. Once the carving was complete, the modelmakers made a mold of the mountain's top and used it to make four identical 9-foot-tall mountaintop models to be used for pyrotechnics effects. Both the mountaintop and full mountain models were finished with spray paint, with additional paint added by hand to provide shading and shadows.

To create the mountaintop pyrotechnics, the model was built with a layer of detonator cord beneath its plaster exterior, and air mortar cannons were placed beneath it, within the steel framework supporting the model. These mortars were filled with dry, powdered driller's mud which simulated ash. The mortars were timed to go off immediately after the detonator cord exploded, thereby blowing off the top of the mountain and spewing the ashlike material.

In all, there were 209 special effects shots in the film, the majority of them involving miniatures. Of these, 80 were multiple-layer shots, with up to 45 different elements being composited together onto one background plate. Much of this work was completed in only three weeks of postproduction, due to competition with the makers of *Volcano,* and new computer software had to be written to speed up the digital compositing. Filmmakers also added extra personnel, not just during postproduction but also during filming, to get it finished before *Volcano*. As a result, *Dante's Peak* had as many as 400 to 600 people working on the movie at one time. *See also* APOLLO 13; BANNED FROM THE RANCH ENTERTAINMENT; DIGITAL DOMAIN; MECHANICAL EFFECTS; MINIATURES AND MODELS; PYROTECHNICS; *TWISTER;* UNIVERSAL STUDIOS; *VOLCANO;* WATERWORLD.

Further Reading

Simak, Steven A. "Graphics That Sizzle!" *Digital World,* April 1997.

Street, Rita. "Dante's Inferno." *Cinefex 69,* March 1997.

Dawn, Jack (1889–c. 1978), and Bob Dawn (c. 1919–1988)

Makeup artist Jack Dawn developed many new makeup techniques. Born in Kentucky in 1889, at age 16 Dawn ran away to Hollywood, where he found work first as a movie extra and later as a Keystone Kop. After a stint in the Canadian Army during World War I, Dawn returned to acting. He also took up sculpting as a hobby, and this led him to become interested in facial makeup as a form

of movie special effects. Eventually he completely abandoned acting in favor of makeup work and was named director of makeup at Fox Studios. After a short time he left Fox and went first to 20th Century Pictures and then to MGM, where he became director of makeup in the mid-1930s.

Dawn's specialty was making non-Asians appear Asian in such movies as *The Good Earth* (1937) and *Lost Horizon* (1937). He also did the makeup for the character of Scrooge in the 1938 version of *The Christmas Carol*. In addition, while designing the makeup for *The Wizard of Oz* (1939), he solved a key makeup problem by discovering that adding laundry bluing to silver makeup made it look like metal.

Jack Dawn retired from the business in 1954, but his son Bob carried on in his profession. Bob Dawn was a fighter pilot in World War II, and after his return to California in 1944 he studied aviation engineering at the University of California at Los Angeles (UCLA). He changed his career goals after receiving an apprenticeship at MGM's makeup department, where he worked for his father. After finishing his apprenticeship in 1951, he continued working for MGM until 1954, when he became a freelance makeup artist. His works include *The Creature from the Black Lagoon* (1954), *The King and I* (1956), *Psycho* (1960), and television shows like *Star Trek* and *Mission Impossible. See also* MAKEUP; METRO-GOLDWYN-MAYER; 20TH CENTURY FOX

Dawn, Norman O. (1886–1975)

Producer and special effects artist Norman O. Dawn was one of the first filmmakers to use a glass shot in a motion picture. He employed the technique in a 1907 film entitled *Missions of California,* when he filmed a mission with a damaged roof through a piece of glass onto which an undamaged roof had been painted. In this way, he was able to make an old building appear new.

Born in 1886, Dawn was an artist and still photographer when he met filmmakers George Melies and the Lumiere Brothers in Paris in 1906. Fascinated with their work, he bought his own camera and began making films himself, traveling around the world to create documentaries. In 1911, he settled in California to work for various movie studios as a special effects expert. However, he found it difficult to work under the control of others, and consequently decided to become an independent producer.

Dawn's first film was a Western entitled *The Drifter* (1913), which was also the first motion picture to use rear projection in creating a scene. His subsequent films, which include the Keystone comedy *Oriental Love*, featured more and more special effects, particularly the in-camera matte. The popularity of the films inspired other filmmakers to use these techniques as well. *See also* GLASS SHOT; LUMIERE, AUGUST, AND LOUIS LUMIERE; MATTE; MELIES, GEORGE.

Death Becomes Her

Directed by Robert Zemeckis, the 1992 movie *Death Becomes Her* won an Academy Award for its visual effects, which featured many innovative special effects techniques created under the supervision of Ken Ralston at Industrial Light & Magic (ILM). The movie also inspired the creation of a new computer system that coordinated the camera's filming speed with its aperture, so that changes in speed could be made instantly. This enabled the camera operators to go from slow motion to normal speed in a single shot; on one occasion, they went from a filming speed of 48 frames a second to 18 frames a second. This ability was an important advance in the field of special effects cinematography.

The plot of *Death Becomes Her* involves two rivals, Madeline and Helen, who become younger and more beautiful after taking a magical elixir, then maim one another out of jealousy and discover they cannot die despite their horrific injuries. This situation inspires the movie's most impressive special effects.

Of primary importance was the work of makeup supervisor Dick Smith, who made the actresses playing the two women appear to change from old to young. He aged actress Meryl Streep, who portrayed Madeline,

from age 35 to age 50 using a combination of traditional makeup and foam latex appliances. For both the makeup and the appliances, Smith had to experiment with various materials and application techniques because Streep was extremely allergic to his usual products.

Because Madeline's transformation occurs onscreen, computer-graphics work was needed to morph her body from one form to another. Two shots, one with the aging makeup and one without, were scanned into a computer, where morphing software provided the necessary shifting of images.

This was not necessary for the character of Helen, played by Goldie Hawn, because she changes shape offscreen. However, the actress still had to wear aging makeup for scenes before her transformation, and she had to appear to be extremely fat before using the elixir. To create the illusion of extra weight, Smith had to construct a "fat suit" for the actress. In areas of the suit that required more density, such as the seat, Smith incorporated a relatively new substance called flabbercast, a plasticized urethane that feels and moves like gelatin. This substance is extremely heavy, which meant that the actress could wear the suit no more than an hour at a time. Her makeup took more than four hours to apply, because in addition to the fat suit she needed foam latex appliances for the face, neck, and arms.

For the violent damage caused to both women's body parts, ILM combined Smith's makeup with computer graphics and animatronic puppets. One example of such work is a scene in which the character of Madeline falls down the stairs, staggers to her feet, and discovers that her neck has been twisted completely around. The Madeline lying at the bottom of the stairs was a puppet operated with rods. As she struggles to stand, her image is blocked for two frames by the elbow of another character. At this point the puppet was replaced with the live actress, who appears to have her head on backwards.

For this illusion, the actress was first filmed wearing a bluescreen hood as she performed the scene. Her face was then filmed in front of a bluescreen. Finally, the twisted neck was sculpted by the makeup team and photographed in front of a bluescreen as well. (Streep was originally going to wear the neck appliance herself, but she was allergic to the material.) These three images—a headless body, a twisted neck, and Streep's face—were all scanned into a computer, where they were put together using a digital bluescreen process.

A similar technique was used for the moment when Madeline twists her head back to its normal position. The actress sat in a revolving chair, and her head was filmed turning around. This footage was then added to that of a headless body and untwisting neck, although in this case the torso and neck belonged to a life-sized animatronic puppet.

There were a total of eight Madeline puppets used in the film, two for the scene involving her fall down the stairs and the rest elsewhere. A puppet was also used to depict Helen in a scene where she is shot through the stomach. A full-sized dummy with a pyrotechnic charge in its midsection was used to depict the moment of the shooting, and a stuntwoman performed her subsequent fall backwards into a fountain. At this point, the stuntwoman was replaced with a cable-operated headless puppet that had a hose inside to run water through its gaping hole as it rose from the water. This image was later combined with a bluescreen image of the actress's head. Subsequent shots of Helen with her gaping hole were created either digitally or with traditional mattes using an optical printer. There were a total of 28 shots with the body hole, 10 done digitally and 18 optically.

Additional bluescreen heads were used elsewhere in the movie, and the work on such shots was made easier by a new computer program called the "digital pinblock program." Invented for the movie *Hook* (1991), this program is a tool for aligning various elements of a composited shot, such as foreground images, background images, and bluescreen heads. Animatronic heads and fake torsos were also used for several other scenes involving Madeline's damaged head. At one point, for example, her head flops backwards

so that it hangs upside-down behind her. To create this illusion, a stuntwoman wore a bluescreen bag over her own head, and an animatronic head attached to her back. The bluescreen element was later removed digitally.

Meryl Streep portraying a damaged Madeline in *Death Becomes Her* (1992). *Universal City Studios/ Photofest.*

In addition to its elaborate puppetry, makeup, and bluescreen work, the film required many miniatures, including a mansion that was 14 feet tall and 6 feet wide and sat on a 12-foot-wide table. Built in 13 wooden sections, the mansion's surface was a vacuform plastic that had been detailed. The model's base was fully landscaped with a variety of substances, including a sculpturing material for the trees and lichen for the grass, and there was a miniature car parked out front. It took eight ILM modelmakers a total of nine weeks to make the mansion and car, which were filmed several times with a motion-control camera so that rain, lightning flashes, and car headlights could subsequently be added to the scene using an optical printer.

The miniature theater that appeared in the beginning of the film featured a marquee with 3,500 lights too hot to leave on for very long.

The filmmakers therefore connected their power to the motion-control camera, so that the lights would automatically blink off whenever the camera's shutter was closed. In designing the marquee, as well as the other miniatures in the film, the ILM model shop used computer software that allowed them to previsualize a structure before it was built. *See also* APERTURE; BLUESCREEN PROCESS; FILMING SPEED; *HOOK;* INDUSTRIAL LIGHT & MAGIC; MOTION-CONTROL CAMERA SYSTEMS; OPTICAL PRINTER; PREVISUALIZATION; RALSTON, KEN; SMITH, DICK; ZEMECKIS, ROBERT.

Further Reading
Martin, Kevin H. "Life Neverlasting." *Cinefex 52,* November 1992.

Deep Focus

Deep focus involves the expansion of a camera's depth of field, so that objects in the extreme foreground and distant background appear equally sharp. The ability to achieve deep focus did not occur until new film stock, lighting equipment, camera lenses, and camera lens coatings became available in the late 1930s. The technique was subsequently developed by cinematographer Gregg Toland, who used it while filming such movies as *Citizen Kane* (1941) and *The Best Years of Our Lives* (1946). *See also* TOLAND, GREGG.

Delgado, Marcel (1898–1977)

Sculptor Marcel Delgado was one of the first artists to make models for use in stop-motion animation. His first movie was *The Lost World* (1925), which required more than 40 rubber models of dinosaurs with air pumps to provide the illusion of breathing. The movie's animator, Willis O'Brien, discovered Delgado at the Otis Art Institute in Los Angeles.

Delgado worked with O'Brien again on *King Kong* (1933). For this film he made six 18-inch models of a gorilla that were the most advanced of their time. Each model had a metal framework, or armature, with ball-and-socket joints, a feature that had never before been used for movie modelwork. This framework was covered by rubber overlaid with rabbit fur. Delgado subsequently worked on

Mighty Joe Young (1949) with Ray Harryhausen, who became one of the most famous model animators in filmmaking history and on *The War of the Worlds* (1953), which won an Academy Award for its special effects. His last filmwork was an uncredited contribution to the miniatures in *Fantastic Voyage* (1966). *See also* ARMATURE; *FANTASTIC VOYAGE;* HARRYHAUSEN, RAY; *KING KONG; THE LOST WORLD;* STOP-MOTION MODEL ANIMATION; *WAR OF THE WORLDS.*

Further Reading
Archer, Steve. *Willis O'Brien: Special Effects Genius.* Jefferson, NC: McFarland & Company, 1998.

Demille, Cecil B. (1881–1959)

American director-producer Cecil B. DeMille was a driving force in the development of new special effects techniques, because many of his films required complicated stagings and stunts. Born in 1881, Demille studied drama and performed in his first Broadway play when he was only19. His mother ran a theatrical company, and DeMille eventually became its manager. In 1913, he and two friends formed their own motion picture company, which later became known as Paramount Pictures, and DeMille began directing films.

His first film, *The Squaw Man* (1914), was a huge success, as were most of his subsequent efforts. He specialized in "spectaculars"—large productions on subjects of epic proportions. In terms of special effects, perhaps the most notable of these are *The Ten Commandments* (1923; remade in 1956) and *Cleopatra* (1934). His other films include *Adam's Rib* (1923), *The Buccaneer* (1938), *Samson and Delilah* (1949), and *The Greatest Show on Earth* (1952).

In the 1920s, DeMille left Paramount for MGM, then became a freelance director. From 1936 to 1945, he also had a own radio show. He died in 1959, shortly before his autobiography was published. *See also* CLEOPATRA; THE TEN COMMANDMENTS.

Destination Moon

The 1950 movie *Destination Moon*, which won an Academy Award for its special effects, was the first film of special effects pioneer George Pal. Pal wanted the movie to be as scientifically accurate as possible given the knowledge of the time. Therefore he hired rocketry expert Hermann Oberth to act as a consultant on the film, along with Robert Heinlein, who wrote the 1947 novel *Rocketship Galileo* on which the movie was based. Pal also hired a noted astronomical artist, Chesley Bonestell, to create matte paintings for the movie's backgrounds, and he placed Lee Zavitz, the special effects expert who had burned the city of Atlanta for the 1939 movie *Gone With The Wind*, in charge of mechanical effects.

The special effects in *Destination Moon* are concentrated around three sequential events: a rocket launch, a flight to the Moon, and a period of exploration on the Moon. For the time just prior to the launch, a full-sized spaceship was built in a California desert, but a miniature was used for the launch itself. As the rocket takes off, the actors are shown suffering from the effects of Earth's gravitational pull. To create this illusion, their seats were equipped with air bladders that were deflated in unison. At the same time, the skin on their faces was pulled back via extremely thin membranes that had been attached to their skin with special glue.

For scenes when the rocket is supposed to be in flight, the crew is made to appear weightless through the use of wires suspending them from an unseen crane above their heads. More elaborate were the effects that made them appear to walk on the walls of the spaceship once they put on "magnetized" boots. To accomplish this, the set of the rocketship's control room was built to rotate both vertically and horizontally, and the movie camera was placed on a giant boom that could rotate a full 360 degrees.

Shortly after this scene, the characters leave the ship to repair a piece of equipment, and one of them accidentally floats away from the ship. To make this character and his rescuer appear to float, the actors were again attached to wires strung from a device similar to ones used to manipulate marionette puppets. Puppeteers manipulated this device, which was attached to a traveling crane, in order to move the men. There were 36 separate strands of wire on each actor, and each of those strands had to be painted to minimize reflection during filming. This paint frequently wore off, so a crew member was assigned the job of regularly touching up each one using a long pole and a sponge dabbed in paint. The same process was also used to make the characters appear weightless on the

Soundstage set in *Destination Moon* (1950) recreating the moon's surface. *Photofest.*

moon as they hopped from one spot to another.

The moon's surface was recreated in a soundstage, using photographs of the real Moon as a guide. The most difficult part of this recreation was not the ground but the atmosphere of the Moon, which is absolutely clear. Dust and smoke therefore had to be kept from the set. This necessitated the use of special exhaust and ventilation equipment, which was kept in operation during filming and required that the soundstage doors be kept open. Because of the noise involved with this situation, the actor's dialogue had to be dubbed into the film's soundtrack later.

Another problematic part of recreating the Moon's surface is the fact that light appears harsh there. To simulate this environment, huge arc lights were used to illuminate the set, but they made it almost impossible to see the regular light bulbs used to represent stars in the dark sky. After much experimentation, special effects experts replaced these bulbs with automobile headlight bulbs, which remained visible under the glare of the arc lights. More than 2,000 headlight bulbs were used on the set, linked together with more than 70,000 feet of wiring. The bulbs were covered with a green gelatine screen, also called a gel, to minimize the slight red glow they produced on film, but the gels were melted by the heat of the bulbs and had to be replaced several times a day. *See also* PAL, GEORGE; WIREWORK.

Further Reading

Brosnan, John. *Movie Magic*. New York: St. Martin's Press, 1974.

Fry, Ron, and Fourzon, Pamela. *The Saga of Special Effects*. Englewood Cliffs, New Jersey: Prentice-Hall, 1977.

Johnson, John. *Cheap Tricks and Class Acts*. Jefferson, NC: McFarland & Company, 1996.

O'Conner, Jane. *Magic in the Movies*. Garden City, NY: Doubleday, 1980.

Digital Domain

Digital Domain is one of the premier special effects houses in the motion picture industry. Located in Venice, California, Digital Domain was co-founded in 1993 by James Cameron, Stan Winston, and Scott Ross after Cameron realized the potential of computer-generated images. Cameron is a director whose movie, *Titanic* (1997), won an Academy Award for visual effects; Winston is an expert in animatronics and puppetry who also runs the Stan Winston Studios; and Ross is currently president and CEO of the company. The company employs more than 225 people and has provided visual effects for such films as *True Lies* (1994), *Apollo 13* (1995), *Dante's Peak* (1997), *The Fifth Element* (1997), *Titanic* (1997), and *Armageddon* (1998). While working on *Apollo 13*, Digital Domain set a record for the number of elements it combined in a single shot: 42. The company bested this record while working on *The Fifth Element*, when its digital effects experts combined 84 elements into one shot. Digital Domain provided a total of 223 effects shots for *The Fifth Element*, many of which included digital matte paintings. *See also* APOLLO 13; ARMAGEDDON; CAMERON, JAMES; DANTE'S PEAK; THE FIFTH ELEMENT; TITANIC; WINSTON, STAN.

Further Reading

Shay, Don. "In the Digital Domain." *Cinefex 55*, August 1993.

Digital Effects *See* ANIMATION, COMPUTER; COMPUTER-GENERATED IMAGES; COMPUTER GRAPHICS; MATCH-MOVER; ROTOSCOPING; WIRE REMOVAL, DIGITAL.

Digital Image Database

Digital image databases are collections of computer images that can be used in creating a digital environment. For example, if a computer artist needs to include a skyscraper in a computer-generated (CG) city or an ice-skating trophy in a CG bedroom, there is no need to draw the skyscraper or trophy from scratch. Instead the building or prop can simply be copied from the database. Many film studios and special effects houses have their own digital image databases, but there are also companies dedicated to maintaining such libraries and providing images to customers. *See also* COMPUTER-GENERATED IMAGES; COMPUTER GRAPHICS.

Further Reading
Ohanian, Thomas A., and Michael E. Phillips. *Digital Filmmaking*. Boston: Focal Press, 1996.

Digital Input Device (DID)

The Digital Input Device (DID) was developed by Craig Hayes and Phil Tippett for *Jurassic Park* (1993) to allow stop-motion model animators inexperienced with computers to create computer animation.

In essence, the DID is a metal puppet armature with electronic sensors. These sensors are linked to a computer that contains a wireframe image of the puppet. When the DID is manipulated, the digital image responds accordingly, and those movements are stored in the computer.

The DID used for *Jurassic Park* was relatively crude, but the device was advanced significantly during the making of *Starship Troopers* (1997) to improve response time and maneuverability. Nonetheless, it is rarely used in modern filmmaking because most computer animators are now skilled in animating computer-generated images without an intermediary, stop-motion tool. *See also* COMPUTER-GENERATED IMAGES; COMPUTER GRAPHICS; INDUSTRIAL LIGHT & MAGIC; *JURASSIC PARK; STARSHIP TROOPERS;* TIPPETT, PHIL.

Further Reading
Duncan, Jody. "The Beauty in the Beasts." *Cinefex 55,* August 1993.
Sammon, Paul M. "Bug Bytes." *Cinefex 73,* March 1998.

Digital Wand

A digital wand is a tool for transferring the image of a model or other object into a computer. Each time the wand is pressed onto the model, it registers a point in space. When enough points are established—sometimes as many as 3,000—the computer has created an image map of the model's shape, which digital artists can then enhance. *See also* SCANNING.

Disney, Walt (1901–1966)

Walt Disney was an animator and producer who created one of the largest entertainment companies in America, the Walt Disney Company. He won 30 Academy Awards during his lifetime and was responsible for many advances in animation. Born in 1901, Disney

Walt Disney with Donald Duck, one of his most famous animated characters. ©*Walt Disney Company/Photofest*

began studying art when he was 14 years old. Four years later he got a job with a commercial art studio, where he met fellow employee Ub Iwerks. Together the two men founded an animation company in Kansas City, Disney's birthplace.

After that business failed, Iwerks went to work elsewhere while Disney started a new animation company, this time in Hollywood, with his brother Roy. The brothers then hired Iwerks to work for them. Disney and Iwerks created a cartoon series, *Oswald the Rabbit,* and developed the character that would make them famous: Mickey Mouse. Mickey appeared in two silent shorts before being featured in a sound cartoon, *Steamboat Willie* (1928). More Mickey cartoons soon followed, as did cartoons with other animal characters.

The Walt Disney Company made its first full-length animated movie, *Snow White and the Seven Dwarves,* in 1937. Subsequent animated features include *Dumbo* (1941), *Peter Pan* (1953), and *101 Dalmatians* (1961). In the 1950s, the company also began making live-action movies, many of which featured elaborate special effects. These include *20,000 Leagues Under the Sea* (1954), *The Absent-Minded Professor* (1961), *The Parent Trap* (1961), *The Shaggy Dog* (1959), and *Son of Flubber* (1963). In 1954, Walt Disney began hosting a television show, and in 1955 he opened an amusement park, Disneyland. He died in 1966. *See also* THE WALT DISNEY COMPANY; IWERKS, UB; *20,000 LEAGUES UNDER THE SEA.*

Further Reading

Smith, Dave. *Disney A-Z.* New York: Hyperion, 1996.
Thomas, Bob. *Walt Disney: An American Original.* New York: Pocket Books, 1976.

The Walt Disney Company

The Walt Disney Company is one of the most successful entertainment companies in America. Established by Walt Disney and his brother Roy in 1923, the company began as an animation studio. Its early work includes *Steamboat Willy* (1928), which was the first cartoon with audible dialogue; and *Snow White* (1937), which was the first feature-length cartoon. The Walt Disney studios began making live-action films during the 1950s, as well as both live and animated television programs. In 1955 the company opened an amusement park, Disneyland; a similar park in Orlando, Florida, followed in 1971; another in Tokyo, Japan, in 1983; and another in France in 1992.

After Walt Disney died in 1966, the Walt Disney Company underwent some turmoil, and for a time it appeared as though it would go bankrupt. In 1984, however, the company again began to prosper, due to its creation of a production division called Touchstone Pictures. The concept behind this decision was that Touchstone would focus on making films for adults, while the original production company, Walt Disney Studios, would continue to produce films for all ages. However, Touchstone's first film, *Splash* (1984), actually appealed to a wide age range. It was a tremendous success, as were many subsequent live-action films produced by Touchstone.

Meanwhile, the chairman and CEO of the Walt Disney Company, Michael Eisner, and the executive in charge of Walt Disney Studios, Jeffrey Katzenberg, were working to revitalize the Disney animation department. The result was such popular films as *The Little Mermaid* (1989), *Beauty and the Beast* (1991), and *Aladdin* (1992). In 1995, Katzenberg left Disney to found his own studio, DreamWorks SKG, with Steven Spielberg and David Geffin.

Nonetheless, the Walt Disney Company continues to prosper. In addition to its movie and animation studios and amusement parks, it owns a television network and cable channel, a publishing company, a series of stores selling Disney merchandise and videos, and a chain of activity centers for young children. It also produces theatrical shows based on its movies. *See also* DISNEY, WALT; DREAMWORKS SKG; SPIELBERG, STEVEN.

Further Reading

Thomas, Bob. *Disney's Art of Animation: From Mickey Mouse to* Beauty and the Beast. New York: Hyperion, 1991.

Dissolve

A dissolve is an optical effect whereby one scene fades from the screen as another one gradually emerges to take its place. This effect was originally created in-camera with double exposures, but is now made by manipulating fade-ins and fade-outs in a device called an optical printer.

Filmmakers have historically used the length of the dissolve to indicate how much time is supposed to have passed between two scenes in a movie. A long "melting" of one scene into another means that a great deal of time has passed, whereas a short transition suggested a brief interlude between scenes. In the 1941 film *Citizen Kane,* for example, a series of dissolves show stages in the completion of a jigsaw puzzle to suggest time passing.

Another use of the dissolve is to show a figure disappearing. For example, in the 1921 movie *Nosferatu,* a dissolve is used to make a vampire fade away when daylight comes. *See also* FADES; MULTIPLE EXPOSURE; OPTICAL PRINTER.

Further Reading
Kawin, Bruce F. *How Movies Work*. Berkeley: University of California Press, 1992.
Pincus, Edward, and Steven Ascher. *The Filmmaker's Handbook*. New York: Plume, 1984.

Dr. Cyclops

Released by Paramount Pictures in 1940, *Dr. Cyclops* was nominated for an Academy Award for its innovative special effects, which featured a new use of rearscreen projection. The movie was directed by Ernest B. Schoedsack, who codirected *King Kong* (1933), and featured the work of special effects expert Farciot Edouart.

Edouart employed rearscreen projection to create the illusion that characters in the film had been drastically reduced in size in relation to their surroundings. But rather than rely on standard screens, as previous filmmakers had done, he used extremely large and extremely small ones as well.

Edouart also used transparencies, double exposures, split screens, glass shots, and other optical tricks to make it seem as though five people had been shrunk to a height of 5 inches. Extremely high camera booms were set up to shoot down on the actors to enhance the illusion, and many large props were designed to make the actors seem small in comparison. *See also* EDOUART, FARCIOT; *KING KONG;* MULTIPLE EXPOSURE; PROJECTION PROCESSES; PROPS; SCHOEDSACK, ERNEST B.

Further Reading
Fry, Ron, and Pamela Fourzon. *The Saga of Special Effects*. Englewood Cliffs, NJ: Prentice-Hall, 1977.

Dr. Doolittle

The 1967 version of *Dr. Doolittle* won an Academy Award for its special effects, which included the work of noted expert L.B. Abbott. The movie featured an animatronic fox, advanced for its time, and used detailed miniatures to depict a boat caught in a storm and an island pushed by a whale. However, although the plot of *Dr. Doolittle* concerns a man who can understand animal language, the filmmakers made no attempt to make the animals appear to be speaking English. Instead the animals made their regular noises, and the actor playing Dr. Doolittle merely translated their sounds for the audience.

In contrast, in a 1998 version of *Dr. Doolittle*, the audience heard the animals speak, and their mouths seemed to be moving. As in the 1995 movie *Babe* which also featured talking animals, this effect was created using a combination of live animals and birds, animatronic puppets, and digital elements added during postproduction. But because, unlike the animals in *Babe*, the animals in *Dr. Doolittle* had to interact with a live actor in almost every talking scene, the movie had to develop new techniques for filming the animals in preparation for postproduction manipulation.

There were more than 100 live creatures on the set of the 1998 *Dr. Doolittle,* most provided by a company called Birds & Animals Unlimited. The majority of these animals had to be filmed in the presence of a trainer, with different species requiring different professionals. These trainers had to be eliminated from final shots. Therefore photographers used a sophisticated system of motion-tracking cameras combined with on-set digital video monitors similar to those used for *The Nutty Professor* (1996). This system made it easy for the director to create a split-screen during the filming of a live animal. The animal was positioned on one side of the split and the trainer on the other, with the latter blocked out of the shot. The motion-tracking cameras then duplicated the shot later with the title character, Eddie Murphy, placed in the position once occupied by the animal trainer. This time the animal was missing from the scene, but Murphy had to act as though he were conversing with it. To help him know where to look, a tennis ball marked the position of the animal's eyes; the ball was on a wire connected to a motion-control device that had been programmed with the animal's movements, so that it would change position as the scene progressed.

Sometimes, however, it was either not practical or not possible to use a live animal for a scene. In these cases, just as in the 1967 *Dr. Doolittle,* an animatronic figure was substituted. There were approximately 75 to 100 such shots in the 1998 film, using animatronics made by Jim Henson's Creature Shop. One of the most frequently used figures was a dog named Lucky. The animal was built in three different poses, one sitting, one crouching, and one walking. There were

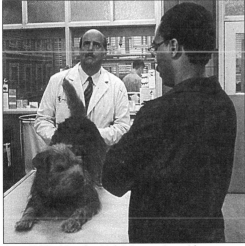

Actor Eddie Murphy (right) interacting with an animatronic dog in *Dr. Doolittle* (1998). *Photofest.*

also two tigers built for the movie, one that could be posed to sit or recline and one that stood, as well as two guinea pigs, several rats, and two pigeons. One of the guinea pigs was in a cage, which Murphy was required to carry. The animatronic was therefore operated by radio control, so there would be no cables to interfere with the scene. The rest of the animals were cable-controlled.

There were a total of approximately 300 animal shots in the movie, 59 of which required moving mouths. This footage was given to digital effects experts at Rhythm & Hues, which also worked on *Babe,* for transformation into the final product. But whereas in the case of *Babe,* mouth movements were added using a 3-D digital technique, for *Dr. Doolittle* the digital artists primarily used a 2-D technique. Using the 3-D method, artists replace the image of the animal's mouth, muzzle, jaw, beak, and/or entire head with an animated 3-D version. With the 2-D method, they simply manipulate photographs of the live animal, frame by frame, in a way similar to cel animation, making it appear as though the animal's own mouth is moving. However, the 2-D approach requires a shot of the animal with its mouth open as well as closed. When one of these shots was not available, the 3-D approach had to be used instead. In several cases, both approaches were required to complete a scene, and sometimes a 2-D approach would be used for the mouth while a 3-D approach was used for the tongue and teeth.

Another assignment given to digital artists was the removal of unwanted elements in a scene. Sometimes these elements were cables or other equipment. Other times it was a live-animal training tool. The guinea pig, for example, danced with the help of a rod between its paws, and this rod later had to be removed digitally. The same was true for the food used to make the rats sit up, and for the long stick holding meat to attract the tiger's attention. Digital experts also had to remove food and chewing motions from the rats' mouths, and eliminate the tiger's tongue whenever he licked himself in the middle of a scene. *See also* ABBOTT, L.B.; *BABE; THE NUTTY PROFESSOR.*

Further Reading

Shay, Estelle. *"Dr. Doolittle:* Animals with Attitude." *Cinefex 75,* October 1998.

Strauss, Bob. "Dogged Path to Making of *Dr. Doolittle." Los Angeles Daily News*, 27 June 1998.

Double Exposure *See* MULTIPLE EXPOSURE.

Dozoretz, David (1971–)

Animator and artist David Dozoretz is a specialist in creating animatics, which are digital moving storyboards used to previsualize special effects shots. As an assistant art director at Industrial Light & Magic (ILM) in 1993, he became the first person to create an animatic for an entire movie sequence as opposed to just a few isolated special effects shots. This animatic, which employed approximately 100 low-resolution shots with very basic 3-D figures, depicted a helicopter-train chase sequence for the 1996 movie *Mission: Impossible,* and in the end the sequence was shot on film almost exactly as it appeared in the animatic.

For the 1999 *Star Wars* movie *The Phantom Menace,* Dozoretz created an animatic for every shot in the movie, the first time this had ever been done. He had originally intended to provide animatics for only the most complex shots; his decision to expand his work ultimately proved a great help to director George Lucas, who referred to the animatics on the set during filming.

Dozoretz also provided animatics for some of the added shots in *Star Wars: Special Edition* (1997) and rendered computer-generated elements for *Forrest Gump* (1994), *Star Trek: Generations* (1994), and *Dragonheart* (1996). *See also* ANIMATICS; DRAGONHEART; FORREST GUMP; INDUSTRIAL LIGHT & MAGIC; LUCAS, GEORGE; *STAR TREK* MOVIES; *STAR WARS* MOVIES.

Dragonheart

The 1996 movie *Dragonheart* is extremely important in the history of computer animation, because it inspired the creation of a new software program called Cari, which makes it possible to animate a rendered figure. Rendered figures have color, texture, and depth,

Helicopter chase scene in *Mission Impossible* (1996), which was previsualized via an animatic by David Dozoretz. *Photofest.*

in contrast to wireframe figures, which are skeletons of lines.

Prior to *Dragonheart*, digital artists could only animate wireframes, and they had difficulty envisioning the final, rendered product. But while working on *Dragonheart* at Industrial Light & Magic (ILM), visual effects expert Cary Phillips realized that he needed better software to create the character of Draco the Dragon and developed Cari.

Cari not only animates a rendered figure but gives that figure more complex facial and muscle movements. As a result, the digital Draco is four times more detailed than the computer-generated dinosaurs of *Jurassic Park* (1993). The digital model for the latter's Tyrannosaurus rex, for example, had 37,173 control vertices, or key points where angles in the wireframe intersected, and its geometry used 1.03 megabytes (MB) of space within the computer. In contrast, the digital model for Draco had 261,000 control vertices and used 5.68 MB. Consequently Draco exhibits far more emotion in his face than previous computer characters.

Draco's body structure was designed with the help of a 5-foot-long maquette (a preliminary model) sculpted by Phil Tippett, who had also sculpted the dragon for *Dragonslayer*. Tippett's maquette of Draco was so detailed that it took five months for

ILM's digital artists to make a 3-D digital version of it. They worked on parts of the figure separately, scanning images of sculpture sections into the computer and using them to make templates they could adjust.

Tippett's maquette was also used to design full-sized dragon parts, such as a claw used to hold down Draco's friend Bowen, played by actor Dennis Quaid. Another scene in which Draco holds Bowen in his mouth required a mechanical jaw and teeth. Hydraulic pistons controlled the action of the mouth as well as the motions of the tongue. Quaid performed the scene within this mouth, although a computer-generated Bowen was used for the moment when Draco first grabs him. A computer-generated Bowen was also used for the scene with the giant claw, after the live-action footage proved disappointing.

Whenever mechanical parts were used, the rest of the dragon was computer generated. The same was true for scenes in which Bowen hung from a rope beneath the dragon. Quaid was actually "flown" by a harness and crane that were digitally removed later, to be replaced by a computer-generated rope and dragon. Many backgrounds in the movie were also digital, first created as matte paintings and then scanned into the computer and refined. *See also* COMPUTER GRAPHICS;

The characters of Draco the Dragon and Bowen (Dennis Quaid) in *Dragonheart* (1996). *Industrial Light & Magic/ Photofest.*

DRAGONSLAYER; INDUSTRIAL LIGHT & MAGIC; JURASSIC PARK; MATTE PAINTINGS; TIPPETT, PHIL.

Further Reading

Duncan, Jody. "Heart and Soul." *Cinefex 66,* June 1996.

Robertson, Barbara. "A Draconian Effort." *Digital Magic,* August 1996.

Dragonslayer

The 1981 movie *Dragonslayer,* which won an Academy Award for its visual effects, marks the first use of the Go-Motion Device. Developed by Phil Tippet of Industrial Light & Magic (ILM), this device creates a link between a puppet and a computer, allowing the movements of the puppet to be programmed into the computer. Once this process is complete, the computer can then use the recorded movements to drive the puppet for repeated camera shots.

Tippett created Go-Motion in order to make the dragon in *Dragonslayer* more realistic. Prior to the computer link, the puppet would have been filmed with stop-motion photography, with Tippett changing the position of the figure in between each shot. This stop-and-start process makes the movement jerky rather than smooth. In contrast, with Go-Motion, the computer moves the puppet as the camera films, making it appear realistic.

The puppet was attached to the computer via motor-powered rods. After filming was complete, these rods were hidden by travelling mattes. To create the mattes, an animator traced the shape of the rods from each frame of film and used these tracings to paint black rod shapes on a series of animation cels. The cels were then photographed in sequence, and the resulting travelling matte was sent to the optical printer to be composited with live action and background footage. This process replaced the "holes" made by the matted rods with other images.

There was actually more than one dragon puppet used with the Go-Motion Device; one type of puppet was used for walking and another for flying, and not all were the same scale. The smallest versions were used for long shots. For extreme closeups, a hand puppet of the dragon's head was used rather than a full-figure Go-Motion puppet. A few shots also employed a full-sized mechanical dragon. *See also* GO-MOTION; INDUSTRIAL LIGHT & MAGIC; PUPPETS; TIPPETT, PHIL; TRAVELLING MATTE.

Further Reading

Smith, Thomas G. *Industrial Light & Magic: The Art of Special Effects.* New York: Ballantine Books, 1986.

Dream Quest Images

Currently owned by the Walt Disney Company, Dream Quest Images is a full-service visual effects and animation facility located in Simi Valley, California. The company recently earned Academy Award nominations for its special effects work on *Armageddon* (1998) and *Mighty Joe Young* (1998). For *Armageddon,* Dream Quest perfected a new motion-control pyrotechics device for miniature photography, which the company had invented for a previous film, *Dante's Peak* (1997), but never used. For *Mighty Joe Young,* Dream Quest developed advanced survey techniques to gather details about each location filmed for background plates. Company engineers also built a new motion-control system specifically for location filming; its rig was more compact than previous versions. In addition, Dream Quest contributed special effects shots to *Flubber* (1997) and *Total Recall* (1990), the latter of which won a Special Achievement Academy Award for its visual effects. *See also* ARMAGEDDON; MIGHTY JOE YOUNG; TOTAL RECALL.

The Dreams of a Rarebit Fiend

The Dreams of a Rarebit Fiend is an early example of the work of Edwin Porter, one of the pioneers of special effects. Made in 1906, this short film depicts the nightmare of a man who ate rarebit right before bed. He dreams that his possessions leave his room of their own accord, whereupon his bed dances and leaves as well, with him in it. Together the man and the bed fly over New York City, returning to the room through the ceiling.

To create this flight over the city, Porter used an in-camera matte shot. First he filmed New York City while blocking off the upper part of the camera frame with a matte card. This card was opaque on the top and clear on the bottom, so that the camera recorded the city's buildings and not the sky. Then he covered the camera lens entirely, cranked the film back to its starting point, removed the matte card, and replaced it with a counter-matte, which was opaque on the bottom and clear on the top. Porter then filmed the bed and the man, both of whom were suspended from wires against a black background.

To create the illusion of movement, while filming the city Porter moved the camera in a sweeping motion, or pan, but while filming the bed and man he kept the camera steady. When the two images were combined, it appeared as though the ground were rushing beneath the bed at a rapid rate. *See also* MATTE; PORTER, EDWIN S.

Further Reading

Fry, Ron, and Pamela Fourzon. *The Saga of Special Effects.* Englewood Cliffs, NJ: Prentice-Hall, 1977.

DreamWorks SKG

Founded in 1994, DreamWorks SKG is a major multimedia entertainment studio in Southern California, which has divisions for live-action and animated feature films, television programming, music and sound projects, and interactive software.

The company's first feature film was *The Peacemaker* (1997), followed by *Amistad* (1997) and *Mouse Hunt* (1997). In addition, the studio sometimes produces films in conjunction with other studios. These include *Deep Impact* (1998) and *Saving Private Ryan* (1998), both of which DreamWorks made with Viacom/Paramount Pictures, and *Small Soldiers* (1998), which it made with Universal. The "SKG" stands for the studio's creators: filmmaker Steven Spielberg and industry executives Jeffrey Katzenberg and David Geffen. *See also* MOUSE HUNT; SPIELBERG, STEVEN.

Dune

The 1984 science fiction movie *Dune* featured the first serious attempt to re-create a human form with computer graphics. The image was a holographic 3-D body armor, which the main character in the film dons while training for a battle. However, the rest of the film did not include any computer work at all. Although there were more than 1,000 different effects elements that had to be composited during postproduction, with some shots having as many as 10 elements in one frame of film, all compositing was done with an electronic optical printer. Similarly, although the crew had motion-control cameras, they did not have computers to guide them, so all camera instructions had to be carefully calculated and input by hand.

In addition to optical effects, *Dune* included both mechanical models and miniatures. The largest mechanical model was a full-sized, 15-foot-long creature called the Third-Stage Guild Navigator, which appears to be in a gas-filled tank. In reality, the gas was smoke, pumped into the tank area from a rear section that concealed 22 puppeteers. These puppeteers also operated levers and other devices manually to create forty different movements for the creature, which was made of a rubber "skin" over a structure made of aluminum and other metals. Also made of rubber and aluminum were the sandworms, another type of *Dune* creature. There were 16 mechanical models used to represent thousands of sandworms, each with several complicated movements, and again they were operated manually.

The movie also used 42 spaceship and building miniatures, including a 29x13-foot palace, which was later composited with live-action shots of soldiers in front of full-sized palace doors. The miniature had an empty space where these doors, as well as the full-sized stairs leading to them, would be composited into the shot. The largest spaceship model was 60x40 feet, representing the craft of the emperor. A 28x19-foot spaceship appears on a 54x36-foot landing field with thousands of miniature soldiers. Other miniature sets included a 32x16-foot desert rock cavern, a 16x13-foot desert landscape, and a 6-foot-tall castle on a hill, below which was a 75-foot-wide pool. Miniature sets were primarily made of resins, plasters, and wood, and most had electrical wiring for night shots. Many also had working parts, such as pumps that created steam.

Dune's physical effects were supervised by Kit West, who won an Academy Award for similar work on *Raiders of the Lost Ark* (1981). Much of his work for *Dune* involved advanced pyrotechnics. As an example, in one scene a wall explodes after being hit with sound waves from a futuristic weapon. The wall was actually made of packed Styrofoam, into which holes were bored. Explosives placed in these holes were triggered by remote-control.

Another explosion scene was created without explosives, by using air rams and wires to pull a wall off the set. In this scene, a character was sucked outside of a room into an airless environment, so the actor had to perform on a wire rig in front of a bluescreen. Wires were also used on a floating character called the Baron; the actor wore a body harness attached to wires suspended from a track above the set. For close-up shots where the wires would show, the actor was attached to a trolley that held him around the waist. *See also* INDIANA JONES MOVIES; MINIATURES AND MODELS; WIREWORK.

Further Reading
Naha, Ed. *The Making of Dune*. New York: Berkley, 1984.

Dunn, Linwood (1904–1994)

In 1981, Linwood Dunn received a special Academy Award in technological achievement for inventing the Acme-Dunn special effects optical printer, which quickly became the standard in the industry. He won another Academy Award for his contributions to filmmaking in 1984.

Born in 1904, Dunn's first film-related job was in 1923 as a projectionist. From 1928 to 1956 he was head of the photographic effects department at RKO studios, where he worked on such notable movies as *King Kong* (1933) and *Citizen Kane* (1941). During World War II he also worked with Eastman Kodak and the U.S. Armed Forces designing special effects photographic equipment. In 1946 he founded an optical effects house, Film Effects of Hollywood, and remained its president until 1980. He died in 1998 at the age of 94. *See also* KING KONG; OPTICAL PRINTER.

Dykstra, John (1947–)

John Dykstra is one of the foremost special effects artists in the business and the recipient of numerous achievement awards. Born in 1947, Dykstra attended a Southern California design school and earned money as a still photographer before entering the film industry. One of his first jobs was working for special effects artist Douglas Trumbull on the 1972 movie *Silent Running*.

The following year Dykstra was hired by the Institute of Urban and Regional Development (IURD) in Berkeley, California, which was making a movie about urban development. Dykstra's job was to make miniature buildings look like real buildings on film. To accomplish this, he and two associates, Al Miller and Jerry Jeffress, developed some new filming techniques, most significantly the use of a computer to control camera movements.

In 1975, after the IURD project shut down for lack of funds, Dykstra returned to Los Angeles to work for Douglas Trumbull again. When Trumbull turned down the chance to contribute special effects to George Lucas's movie *Star Wars* (1977), Dykstra offered his services to Lucas instead. His first task was to help set up Lucas's special effects studio, Industrial Light & Magic (ILM). In doing so, Dykstra decided to save money by purchasing old VistaVision camera equipment and adapting it to his needs, using his experience as part of the IURD project to develop the first sophisticated motion-control camera system.

This system, which became known as Dykstraflex, revolutionized the special effects industry, in part because camera movements could be perfectly duplicated as many times as necessary during a shoot. In 1978 Dykstra won an Academy Award for his invention, as well as one for his special effects work on *Star Wars*. That same year he formed his own company, Apogee. Apogee went out of business in 1993, but Dykstra continues to provide special effects for major films, most recently *Batman and Robin* (1997). *See also* APOGEE INC.; *BATMAN* MOVIES; INDUSTRIAL LIGHT & MAGIC; MOTION-CONTROL CAMERA SYSTEMS; *STAR TREK* MOVIES; *STAR WARS* MOVIES; TRUMBULL, DOUGLAS.

Dynamation

Dynamation was the term created by stop-motion model animator Ray Harryhausen to define a process of three-dimensional (3-D) animation, which employed stop-motion models, as opposed to two-dimensional (2-D) animation, or cartoons. The process involved sandwiching an animation model between a background plate and a foreground plate, both of which featured superimposed live-action footage, so that the model would truly seem part of the live-action setting. Harryhausen called this technique Dynamation, for Dynamic Animation.

The word Dynamation is still sometimes used to refer to 3-D stop-motion model animation, but now it more frequently refers to a software program developed by Alias/Wavefront for use with Silicon Graphics computers. Dynamation software creates 3-D animation by setting points or particles in motion. In the 1997 movie *Starship Troopers,* Dynamation software was used to generate dozens of dots representing swarming bugs. Each dot was assigned its own radius, speed, and direction capabilities, and given information about the terrain in the scene, so that once it was animated it would not hit other bugs or rocks in the live-action background. In this way, the Dynamation software allowed digital experts to create thousands of moving insects without them having to animate each one individually. Dynamation software is also used to generate smoke clouds, jet exhaust, debris within tornadoes, and similar images. *See also* ANIMATION, COMPUTER; COMPUTER-GENERATED IMAGES; COMPUTER GRAPHICS; COMPUTER HARDWARE AND SOFTWARE; HARRYHAUSEN, RAY; STOP-MOTION MODEL ANIMATION.

E

Earth Versus the Flying Saucers

Released in 1956 by Columbia Pictures, *Earth Versus the Flying Saucers* advanced the field of stop-motion model animation through the work of Ray Harryhausen, one of the pioneers of the field. The film's producer was Harryhausen's longtime associate Charles Schneer.

The movie features several miniature spaceships, six of which were the first examples of miniatures being constructed to achieve a pyrotechnic effect. These miniatures were built out of plaster of paris and rigged with black powder charges. Three other spaceships were machined out of aluminum, and a fourth was carved out of wood. The aluminum ships were used for long shots, and one of them had a base that could be replaced with a "death ray" attachment. The wooden ship, which measured 12 inches in diameter, was used for closeup shots; its death ray attachment was permanent and could be extended or retracted. The wooden ship also had a revolving section, painted with parallel lines to made the revolutions noticeable. All of the model spaceships were held in a flying position by an aerial brace, which is a stand with a bar to which wires can be attached. The ship's humming sound was actually made using a recording of underground motors at a sewage disposal plant.

In several scenes, the spaceships destroy landmark buildings, which were also detailed miniatures. Harryhausen did not have enough money to blow up his miniatures with explosives while filming the scene at high speed, so instead he used stop-motion photography, changing the buildings slightly between each frame of film so that they appeared to crumble. Pieces of debris were suspended by wires to simulate falling, and dust was superimposed onto the scene during postproduction. *See also* HARRYHAUSEN, RAY; PYROTECHNICS; STOP-MOTION MODEL ANIMATION.

Further Reading

Brosnan, John. *Movie Magic*. New York: St. Martin's Press, 1974.
Fry, Ron, and Pamela Fourzon. *The Saga of Special Effects*. Englewood Cliffs, NJ: Prentice-Hall, 1977.
Jenson, Paul M. *The Men Who Made the Monsters*. New York: Twayne, 1996.

Earthquake

Released in 1974, *Earthquake* won a Special Achievement Academy Award for its visual effects. The movie had a $7.5 million budget and featured some of the most spectacular mechanical effects of its decade. *Earthquake*'s mechanical effects supervisor was Glen Robinson, who also worked on such successful movies as *Forbidden Planet* (1956) and the 1956 version of *Ben-Hur*.

More than 100 special effects experts worked on all aspects of the film, as well as 141 stuntpeople. The latter were frequently seen running from debris, which was made of Styrofoam with steel inside of it for weight.

In some cases, real concrete chunks were dropped near stuntpeople; such scenes required careful timing to prevent injuries. Stuntpeople and actors also had to be careful while performing on the shaking sets. These sets had hydraulic equipment under the floor designed to lift and tilt the structure.

Earthquake also employed elaborate miniatures and matte paintings to make it seem as though the city of Los Angeles was being destroyed. As an example, a Hollywood dam was recreated as a miniature in the hills behind Universal Studios. The scale of this miniature was 1:16, which means that it was 16 times smaller than life-sized; whereas the real dam is 880 feet across, the miniature was 54 feet across. A large storm drain was then constructed to funnel water from a lake into the dam, using gravity and mechanical devices to propel the flow. The water would strike the model at a force of 360,000 gallons per minute, and a 300-foot-long flume was built to carry the water away from the model after it struck. The dam model was designed to break apart upon impact, but several back-up measures were taken to make sure that this happened. These back-ups included trip wires, hydraulic rams, and explosives. However, the water did indeed break the model apart in a realistic fashion.

The backgrounds for such miniature scenes were matte paintings done by Albert

Dam bursting in *Earthquake* (1974), filmed with miniatures. *Universal Pictures/Photofest.*

Whitlock, then one of the foremost artists in the field. Whitlock produced 22 2x3-foot paintings for approximately 40 scenes of destruction, leaving black the area where live action would be matted in. He won an Academy Award for his work on this film, as did Glen Robinson.

Earthquake also contributed two advances to the field of special effects. The first advance was the camera shaker movement, which was the concept that shaking could be re-created on film by jiggling the camera horizontally and vertically in varying intensity. The second advance was Sensurround, a system that enabled the movie audience to experience the shaking of an earthquake while viewing the film. Sensurround adds a fourth channel to the soundtrack of a movie, which is translated by special theater speakers into sound pressures that vibrate the theater air and give the illusion of physical shaking. *See also* MINIATURES AND MODELS; SENSURROUND; STUNTS; WHITLOCK, ALBERT.

Further Reading

Brosnan, John. *Movie Magic*. New York: St. Martin's Press, 1974.
Fry, Ron, and Fourzon, Pamela. *The Saga of Special Effects*. Englewood Cliffs, NJ: Prentice-Hall, 1977.
O'Conner, Jane. *Magic in the Movies*. Garden City, NY: Doubleday, 1980.
Stuntmen and Special Effects. New York: Ripley Books, 1982.

Edison, Thomas A. (1847–1931)

Thomas Alva Edison is one of the most famous inventors in American history, and some of his work affected the film industry. In 1889 Edison developed the Kinetophonograph, or Kinetophone, and its derivative, the Kinetoscope. These devices displayed moving pictures to a single viewer; the Kinetophone's films were accompanied by sounds from a phonograph record. Edison also created the first movie studio, the Black Maria, in 1893. Three years later he acquired the rights to a movie projection device that would enable more than one viewer to see his movies at one time, and shortly thereafter he began showing his films in a New York music hall.

Inventor Thomas Edison, who briefly dominated the film industry. *Corbis/Bettmann.*

Born in 1847, Edison began working as a telegraph operator when he was only 15 years old. When he was 21 he invented the stock ticker. Several more telegraph-related inventions followed. In 1876 he set up his own research laboratory, where he invented the microphone, phonograph, and light bulb. Edison's interest in the film industry began in the late 1880s and lasted until 1917. By this time, Edison so dominated the business of film production and exhibition that the government charged him with violating antitrust laws. Edison consequently ended his association with the movie industry, turning his inventive genius to other types of products. Edison died in 1931. *See also* KINETOSCOPE.

Further Reading

Israel, Paul. *Edison: A Life of Invention.* NY: John Wiley & Sons, 1998.

Editing, Film

Film editing is the process by which shots and scenes are put together and rearranged to create the final film. This process has gone through many changes since moviemaking began, and new advances in film editing technology continue to develop.

During the early years of filmmaking, editors worked with the original film negative, physically cutting it apart and splicing pieces of it together to change the sequence of images. (The film that comes from a camera is called a negative because it reverses the color and density of the images it has recorded; when the negative is printed, the colors and density of the images reverse back.) Optical effects were created by projecting and rephotographing elements together in order to acquire a new negative that could be used during this physical editing process.

Today some film editors continue to work with negatives; however, they do not use the original print but a duplicate called a workprint. Once they have finished rearranging shots in the workprint, they deliver it and the original negative to a negative cutter, usually along with written instructions regarding how the scenes are to be put together. The cutter then physically alters the original negative to create what is known as the "final cut."

With the advent of video technology, many film editors stopped using a workprint and instead began editing on videotape. Film images can be converted into video images using a machine called a telecine device; video recording equipment allows shots to be erased or copied and moved to create the final version of the movie. Once this process is complete, the videotape is given to the negative cutter, who can then use it like a workprint as a reference for cutting the original negative.

During the 1980s, however, most film editors gradually converted to a digital editing system, also called nonlinear editing, whereby film images were transferred to videotape and then converted into digital images that could be cut, pasted, and combined with digital effects shots using editing software. As technology advanced, the process of converting filmed images into digital ones became more sophisticated, as did the process of transferring the digital images back out of the computer and onto film. Scanning devices now bring images into the computer, and laser film recorders put digital data onto film, so that the physical cutting of an original negative is no longer necessary.

The first nonlinear editing system, called Editdroid, was invented in 1980 and sold to Avid Technology Inc., in the early 1990s. Today, Avid's digital editing equipment is the industry standard, used by such prominent special effects houses as Industrial Light & Magic (ILM). In 1998 the company won an Academy Award for its development of the Avid Film Composer, a digital, nonlinear editing machine that can store, recall, manipulate, and play back shots instantaneously.

There are more than 45 other digital editing systems in existence. In the near future, these systems will no longer incorporate devices that transfer film into a digital format, because filmmakers have begun experimenting with high-definition digital videotape, which they use in place of film. Director George Lucas, in making the 1999 *Star Wars* movie *The Phantom Menace,* used digital videotape for approximately 20 shots to test whether there was a difference in quality between digital videotape and film. When he could detect no difference, Lucas announced that all future *Star Wars* movies would be shot entirely with digital videotape.

Digital-video projectors are currently being developed for movie theaters to take advantage of this new technology. Digital projection guarantees a perfect print, free of scratches and irregularities in brightness, focus, and color, regardless of how many times a movie is shown or how many copies of that movie are made. In June 1999 *The Phantom Menace* became the first feature film to be digitally projected for moviegoers. Considered a milestone in cinematic history, this event took place on two screens in Los Angeles and two screens in New York City. *See also* COMPUTER GRAPHICS; MATTE; MATTE PAINTINGS; NEGATIVE, FILM; OPTICAL PRINTER.

Further Reading

Bouzereau, Laurent, and Jody Duncan. Star Wars: *The Making of* Episode I: The Phantom Menace. New York: Ballantine, 1999.

Ohanian, Thomas A., and Michael E. Phillips *Digital Filmmaking.* Boston: Focal Press, 1996.

Pincus, Edward, and Steven Ascher. *The Filmmaker's Handbook.* New York: Plume, 1984.

Robertson, Joseph F. *The Magic of Film Editing.* Blue Ridge Summit, PA: Tab Books, 1983.

Edlund, Richard (1940–)

Richard Edlund is a special effects artist who has shared Academy Awards for his work on *Star Wars* (1977), *The Empire Strikes Back* (1980), *Return of the Jedi* (1983), and *Raiders of the Lost Ark* (1981). *Star Wars* was Edlund's first project. Not only was he the first cameraman for the movie's special effects unit, but he also helped assemble and maintain the camera equipment used by Industrial Light & Magic (ILM), the studio where the special effects were made.

Edlund learned camera repair and photography in the U.S. Navy. Born in 1940, he entered the service upon graduating from high school. After leaving the military a few years later, he attended the University of Southern California (USC) Film School. As a student he submitted his resume to the California Office of Human Resources in Hollywood, which resulted in his receiving a job at an optical effects company. Edlund remained there for four years, lettering movie title cards, repairing and building electronic equipment, and photographing insert shots for television shows and feature films. He then became a photographer of rock musicians and made his own experimental films before getting a job at a small special effects studio. There he met special effects expert John Dykstra, who hired him to work on *Star Wars*.

Edlund was employed by ILM for several years, but in 1983 he formed his own special effects company, Boss Film Studios. This company provided the special effects for films such as *Ghostbusters* (1984), *2010* (1984), *Starship Troopers* (1997), and *The Parent Trap* (1998). Nonetheless, it went out of business in 1998. Edlund later reported that it cost him $1 million per month to keep his effects equipment in operation and maintain a staff of 90 people. *See also* DYKSTRA, JOHN; *INDIANA JONES* MOVIES; *STAR WARS* MOVIES; *STARSHIP TROOPERS*.

Further Reading

Huffstutter, P.J. "Visual Effects Pioneer Tells How Digital Showed His Studio Who Was Boss." *Los Angeles Times,* 20 October 1997.

Smith, Thomas G. *Industrial Light & Magic: The Art of Special Effects.* New York: Ballantine Books, 1986.

Vaz, Mark Cotta. "Boss Film Studios: End of an Era." *Cinefex 73,* March 1998.

Edouart, Farciot (1897–1980)

Special effects expert Farciot Edouart was one of the pioneers of the film industry and advanced numerous optical effects, including travelling matte techniques. He was particularly famous for his rearscreen work, in part because he developed a new device for rearscreen projection that used three projectors to intensify the background image.

Born in 1897, Edouart became head of the special effects department at Paramount Pictures during the 1920s. He remained there for several years, earning an Academy Award for his work on *Spawn of the North* (1938), *I Wanted Wings* (1941), and *Reap the Wild Wind* (1942). Edouart's other films include *Dr. Cyclops* (1940), *A Connecticut Yankee in King Arthur's Court* (1949), *Sunset Boulevard* (1950), *To Catch a Thief* (1955), *Vertigo* (1958), *It's a Mad, Mad, Mad, Mad World* (1963), and *Rosemary's Baby* (1968). He died in 1980. *See also* DR. CYCLOPS; *I*

WANTED WINGS; PARAMOUNT PICTURES; PROJECTION PROCESSES; *REAP THE WILD WIND; SPAWN OF THE NORTH;* TRAVELLING MATTE.

Element

An element is a single image, created through photography, computer graphics, animation, or 2-D or 3-D painting, which can be joined, or composited, with others to create a complete visual effects shot. *See also* COMPOSITING.

Ellenshaw, Peter (1913–)

British special effects artist Peter Ellenshaw earned an Academy Award for his work on the 1964 Disney movie *Mary Poppins*. Born in London in 1913, he learned matte painting from W. Percy Day, who was one of the earliest artists working in the field. He then found employment with director-producer Alexander Korda doing matte paintings for such films as *The Thief of Bagdad* (1940). After a short stint as a freelance artist, Ellenshaw joined Disney as a matte artist and special effects expert in 1948. Ellenshaw remained with the company until his retirement in 1979. His first major work for Disney was for *Treasure Island* (1950). His other films include *Robin Hood* (1952), *The Sword and the Rose* (1953), *20,000 Leagues Under the Sea* (1954), *Old Yeller* (1957), *Kidnapped* (1960), *The Absent-Minded Professor* (1961), *Mary Poppins* (1964), and *The Black Hole* (1979). *See also* THE WALT DISNEY COMPANY; KORDA, SIR ALEXANDER; MATTE PAINTINGS; *THE THIEF OF BAGDAD; 20,000 LEAGUES UNDER THE SEA*.

Emmerich, Roland (1955–)

Director Roland Emmerich created two extremely popular movies known for their special effects, *Stargate* (1994) and *Independence Day* (1996). Emmerich also owns his own production company, Centropolis Entertainment, and special effects facility, Centropolis Effects. Emmerich was born in 1955 in Stuttgart, West Germany, where he attended the Munich Film and Television School. His early films were created in Europe; *Stargate* was his first American directing assignment. His other films include *Joey, The Noah's Ark Principle* (1985), *Ghost Chase* (1988), *Moon 44* (1990), and *Universal Soldier* (1992). *See also* INDEPENDENCE DAY; STARGATE.

The Enemy Below

Released by 20ᵗʰ Century Fox in 1957, *The Enemy Below* won an Academy Award for its special effects. The award was given in this case to the individual responsible for the movie's sound effects, Walter Rossi, who had to create sounds related to an underwater submarine chase and conversations between crew members on an American submarine and those on a German submarine.

The Epper Family

The Epper family encompasses several generations of stunt people. Patriarch John Epper Sr. was an accomplished rider who began performing horse stunts in the 1920s. He had three sons and three daughters, all of whom took up stuntwork themselves. Five of John Epper's grandchildren subsequently joined the profession and continue to work in the business today. They include stuntwomen Eurlyne Epper and Jeannie Epper, who is also a stunt coordinator. While the Eppers are not as well known outside of the stunt world, they have appeared in hundreds of films performing a wide variety of stuntwork. *See also* STUNTS.

ET: The Extraterrestrial

Directed by Stephen Spielberg, the 1982 movie *ET: The Extraterrestrial* won an Academy Award for its visual effects, which were created at Industrial Light & Magic under the supervision of Dennis Muren. However, the movie is particularly significant because it was responsible for several new advances in the field of special effects.

For example, *ET* was the first movie to employ a technique known as latent image matte painting. This technique is a double-exposure process whereby a matte painting is combined with unexposed film rather than with a live-action scene that has already been developed. The technique was used for the scene in which the character of Elliott encounters ET in a backyard. The actor was shot in the studio, and a matte of a night sky, with a moon over a cornfield, was subsequently added via latent image matte painting.

ET: The Extraterrestrial also features an early variation on Go-Motion, a technique developed for the 1996 movie *Dragonheart*. It was used for the scene in which children fly on bicycles across the night sky. The front and back wheels of the bicycle were rotated by a computer-controlled motor rather than manually by an animator, automatically moving the legs of the puppets representing the children.

In addition, special effects experts developed new equipment while making *ET,* creating a smaller version of the Dykstraflex camera involved with motion control photography, as well as a new kind of boom rig that could suspend objects for moving bluescreen elements. This rig made it possible to shoot a scene of objects moving in the air as live action rather than animation; it was used to create the illusion that ET was moving objects in a bedroom in order to show his planet's position in the universe.

Miniature and photographic techniques also advanced during the making of *ET*. The movie featured elaborate miniatures of forests, a neighborhood of houses, and an alien spaceship. It also marks the first time that Industrial Light & Magic did not use the widescreen format while filming live action; standard 35 mm film was used instead. *See also* DRAGONHEART; DYKSTRA, JOHN; GO-MOTION; INDUSTRIAL LIGHT & MAGIC; MATTE; MATTE PAINTINGS; MULTIPLE EXPOSURE; SPIELBERG, STEVEN; VISTAVISION.

Further Reading

Duncan, Jody. "20 Years of Industrial Light & Magic." *Cinefex 65,* March 1996.

Smith, Thomas G. *Industrial Light & Magic: The Art of Special Effects*. New York: Ballantine Books, 1986.

F

Factor, Max (1872–1938)

Max Factor (originally Faktor) provided makeup to the earliest movie stars in Hollywood. At first Factor merely imported cosmetics from Europe and distributed them, but after two of his customers, Charlie Chaplin and Tom Mix, complained that his clay-based foundation cracked, Factor started experimenting with his own products. In 1914 he invented the first cream-based makeup for movie use, and two years later he developed a version for street use. In 1919 he created the first false eyelashes.

By 1925 Factor's makeup had become an industry standard. That year, just one production, *Ben-Hur*, used more than 600 gallons of Factor's Liquid Body Makeup. The substance was mixed in various colors to represent different ethnicities and sprayed with a hose onto more than 3,000 extras. This production marked the largest use of cosmetics in any movie to date.

In addition to his skill with makeup, Factor was an experienced wig-maker; as a child he sewed wigs for the Russian Imperial Ballet. Born in Lodz, Poland, in 1872, he immigrated to the United States in 1904 and began his own wig business. His first work for the film industry was providing wigs and toupees to actors, but eventually he accepted more creative assignments; for example, he made tail enhancements for movie horses and fur underpants for chimpanzees acting in Tarzan movies. He also developed and manufactured a shampoo to kill head lice.

By the time Factor died in 1938, his makeup business was worth millions. The company remained in the family until 1973, when it was sold for $480 million. *See also* BEN-HUR; MAKEUP; MIX, TOM.

Fades

A fade is an optical effect created by gradually changing a film's exposure to light, either in-camera or with an optical printer. The result of this process is either a fade-in, in which a scene moves from complete blackness to normal brightness, or a fade-out, in which a scene slowly goes dark. A fade-out followed by a fade-in is often used in shifting from one scene location to another or to indicate that time has passed in the same scene. Overlapping fade-ins and fade-outs can create a dissolve. *See also* DISSOLVE; OPTICAL PRINTER.

Further Reading
Kawin, Bruce F. *How Movies Work*. Berkeley: University of California Press, 1992.

Fairbanks, Douglas Sr. (1883–1939)

Actor Douglas Fairbanks Sr. was one of the most popular screen heroes of the 1910s and 1920s, and he performed many of his own stunts. His best known movies include *The Mark of Zorro* (1920), *The Thief of Bagdad*

Actor Douglas Fairbanks (right), who performed most of his own stunts, in *The Black Pirate* (1926). *Photofest.*

(1924), and *The Black Pirate* (1926), the latter of which featured Fairbanks's most famous stunt. In a shipboard scene, he climbs to the top of a mast, plunges his knife into the sail, then slides down the canvas, cutting it as he goes.

Fairbanks was born in Denver, Colorado, in 1883. He began performing in local theater when he was only 12 years old and appeared in his first Broadway play at age 19. His movie career began in 1915, when he made three films for the Triangle film corporation: *The Martyrs of the Alamo*, *The Lamb*, and *Double Trouble*. In 1919 he and his second wife, actress Mary Pickford, went into partnership with actor Charlie Chaplin and producer D.W. Griffith to form their own film company, United Artists. Fairbanks divorced Pickford in 1936, remarried, and shortly thereafter retired from acting. He died in 1939. By this time his son, Douglas Fairbanks Jr., had become a well-known movie actor himself. *See also* GRIFFITH, D.W.; *THE THIEF OF BAGDAD*.

Falls *See* STUNTS.

Fantastic Voyage

The 1966 20th Century Fox film *Fantastic Voyage,* which won an Academy Award for its special effects, had some of the largest and most expensive sets made for a movie until that time. The movie's budget was $6.5 million, which was then an astronomical amount, and its special effects were supervised by noted special effects expert L.B. Abbott. *Fantastic Voyage* took more than two years to make, only five months of which were spent on live-action filming; the sets took more than a year to build.

One of the most costly sets was that of a military complex where, in the movie's plot, a submarine called the *Proteus* was shrunk and inserted into a man who needs microscopic surgery. The laboratory of the complex was a 100x300-foot interior set that cost $1.25 million. The *Proteus* set, which was built full-sized at 23x42 feet, weighed more than 8,000 pounds and cost $100,000.

All of the sets representing areas inside the man's body were built large enough for the submarine set to fit inside of them. The brain set was 100 feet high, 100 feet long, and 35 feet high; the pulmonary artery set was 8 feet in diameter and 40 feet long; the lymph node set was 14 feet high and 25 feet in diameter; the eye set was 17 feet long and 5 feet high; and the heart set was 130 feet wide and 30 feet high. All body parts were made as medically accurate as possible, given the materials and knowledge of the time. The heart, which was rubber and latex, was rigged to "pump" in a realistic fashion. The lung sac was also rigged to "breathe." The lung sac contained 300,000 cubic feet of surface area and was made of resin, fiberglass, and other ingredients.

The capillary into which the *Proteus* was first injected was a set 50 feet wide and 100 feet long, made of flexible resin and fiberglass. It was lit with soft amber lights and had rotating spots of violet and pink light to represent moving cells. The idea that a set could be "painted" with light was a new concept in filmmaking. Another art technique, the matte painting, was made to make the capillary look even longer than the distance represented by the set.

Matte paintings were similarly used elsewhere in the film. However, the red blood cells that appeared as big blobs in the movie were not paintings but real drops of Vaseline and clear oil, blended together and colored. They were dripped into a glass tank, filmed through the glass, and then composited into the scene with the live actors later via an optical printer. An optical printer was also used to make the *Proteus* seem to shrink, by superimposing matte paintings of increasingly smaller submarines onto a laboratory background.

Scenes with the actors "swimming" through the bloodstream were accomplished by hanging the actors on wires attached to their bodies via suspension harnesses. Filming was done at three times the normal rate, so that when the film was replayed at regular speed it seemed as though the actors were moving slowly because of the water resistance. Wires and a photographic trick were also used to make "antibodies" attack one of the film characters. The antibodies, which were made of plastic strips, were attached to the actress and pulled off with wires. The film was then played in reverse, to make it seem as though the antibodies were moving onto the woman instead of off of her. *See also* ABBOTT, L.B.; MATTE PAINTINGS; PROPS; WIREWORK.

Further Reading

Brosnan, John. *Movie Magic*. New York: St. Martin's Press, 1974.
Fry, Ron, and Pamela Fourzon. *The Saga of Special Effects*. Englewood Cliffs, NJ: Prentice-Hall, 1977.
McKenzie, Alan, and Ware, Derek. *Hollywood Tricks of the Trade*. New York: Gallery Books, 1986.

The Fifth Element

The 1997 movie *The Fifth Element* features some of the most extensive use of digital matte paintings in recent years, as well as a record number of special effects elements in a single shot. The movie contained a total of 223 special effects shots, all provided by Digital Domain. This special effects company had previously set the record of having 42 elements in a single shot, for the movie *Apollo 13* (1995); *The Fifth Element* had 84 elements in a single shot. These elements not only included digital matte paintings but computer-generated images, live action, and miniature photography.

The miniatures used in *The Fifth Element* were particularly detailed, and some were reused in *Godzilla* (1998). It took five months to construct a New York cityscape of approximately 25 futuristic skyscrapers. Built in 1/24 scale, some were more than 20 feet tall. Buildings were made of steel, wood, plastic sheeting, acrylic, and foamed styrene and included miniature fire escapes. Behind some of the windows in the buildings were lightboxes showing pictures of room interiors. This helped give the miniature additional depth and realism.

Computer-generated buildings or building parts were used for some scenes, as when a flying car falls past the structures at a rate and angle too difficult to film with miniatures.

But an entire city of computer-generated buildings would have been impossible to create, because such work is not only extremely time-consuming but requires massive computer space and processing power. However, computers proved valuable for planning miniature construction, particularly when developing the movie's intricate flying-car chase through the city. Wireframe buildings were placed and moved in order to help a director previsualize the miniature set and plan camera moves, allowing for changes before a single model was constructed.

The miniature vehicles in the chase scene were built both in 1/24 and in 1/6 scales. To create them, modelmakers first carved patterns from an African wood called jelutong. These patterns were used in a vacuform process that resulted in styrene models, which were then detailed and employed as models to create the final fiberglass cars. One 1/6-scale taxicab was made in three versions, one intact and two damaged, because it becomes battered and bullet-ridden during the chase. Cars that appear in the background, when not the 1/24 models, were computer-generated. Trains were motorized fiberglass miniatures, one in 1/24 and another in 1/8 scale.

The populace of the city was created by photographing some extras in front of a greenscreen, then reducing their images and compositing them into shots. The photography was done with videotape rather than film because it was less expensive. Moreover, because the images of the people were so small, the difference in quality between videotape and film would not be noticeable.

A flying restaurant used for one shot was a full-sized set attached to a rotating, hydraulically powered motion base. The engine was beneath its hull was computer-generated, the buildings around it were miniatures, and the ones in the distance were part of a digital matte painting. Digital matte paintings were also used in spaceship scenes, along with shots of spaceship models.

A more unique effects sequence involves a woman being constructed from a fragment of DNA. To generate this image, digital effects experts used information from a scientific endeavor called the Visible Human Data (VHD) project. VHD researchers planed tiny slices from a human cadaver, then scanned their images into a computer. The result was a detailed database of photographs and statistics related to the human body. Digital Domain used this material to make the woman appear to be assembled piece by piece in a special tank. *See also* APOLLO 13; DIGITAL DOMAIN; *GODZILLA;* MINIATURES AND MODELS.

Further Reading
Elrick, Ted. "Elemental Images." *Cinefex 70,* June 1970.
Laski, Beth. "High Five." *Cinescape,* May/June 1997.

Filming Speed

The term "filming" refers to the photographic process whereby moving images are recorded on the film of a motion picture camera. During this process, the film typically runs through the camera at a speed of 24 frames per second; therefore a standard movie theater projector shows films at a speed of 24 frames per second. Modern motion picture cameras are capable of changing this speed, but even if they do, the theater projector still runs the film at 24 frames per second. This makes it possible to create certain effects by varying film speed.

For example, a scene shot at a fast speed, such as 48 frames per second, will appear to be moving in slow motion when it is projected at the reduced speed of 24 frames per second. Slow motion is very common in special effects work involving miniatures, because filming a miniature vehicle such as a spaceship at a very fast speed makes it appear to be slow and heavy upon projection. Similarly, filming a miniature explosion at fast speed makes it appear larger and more forceful than it really was. *See also* MINIATURES AND MODELS; SHOT.

Further Reading
Kawin, Bruce F. *How Movies Work*. Berkeley: University of California Press, 1992.

Fink, Michael (c. 1947–)

Michael Fink is a visual effects supervisor and an expert at filming miniatures in front of a bluescreen. Fink began his career as an artist, but in 1977 he took a job creating effects for the movie *The China Syndrome*. As a result of this work, Fink developed the first computer-controlled movie set, which represented the control room of a nuclear power plant; he wired the set so that a computer would make its controls respond to an actor's touch.

Fink subsequently went to work for a visual effects facility, Universal Hartland, established by Universal Studios, but he left there in 1979 when Douglas Trumbull offered him a job working on *Star Trek: The Motion Picture*. Fink later worked on *Batman Returns* (1992), *Braveheart* (1995), and several other movies as a freelance visual effects supervisor. He was nominated for an Academy Award for his work on *Batman Returns,* for helping to create the first animals realized completely through 3-D computer graphics (bats and penguins). In 1995 Fink joined Warner Digital Studios as a senior visual effects supervisor. *See also* BATMAN MOVIES; STAR TREK MOVIES; TRUMBULL, DOUGLAS; UNIVERSAL STUDIOS.

Further Reading
Shay, Estelle. "Michael Fink: From Fine Arts to Filmmaking." *Cinefex 66,* June 1996.

Fire

Fire effects such as fire, fireworks, and explosions can be added to a scene in postproduction, using computer graphics or an optical printer. However, fire effects are still created live on the set during filming. This work is extremely dangerous, but pyrotechnics experts are skilled and are able to create fire effects with great care.

Flames are typically ignited and contained in special fire bars or pans, which are commercially manufactured specifically for special effects work. A fire bar is a black iron pipe with holes drilled in it. A gas hose is attached to one end of the pipe, and the flames spout up through the holes, which come in different sizes and are spaced at different distances depending on the type of flame effect desired. Fire bars also come in different lengths and widths. A fire pan is a similar device but disperses the flame over a wider area. Both the bar and the pan can be ignited from a safe distance using a fire ribbon, which is a flammable substance that comes in a tube. Fire ribbons are used to start fires for other types of special effects as well.

Sometimes a door or wall needs to be set ablaze. This is typically done by painting the wood with several coats of rubber cement, which is highly flammable. A firebar is often put at the base of the painted object and then ignited, which in turn ignites the door or wall.

On other occasions it is a human being that must be set ablaze. To accomplish this stunt, which is called a body burn, the stuntperson is first coated with stunt gel, a protective fire-retardant substance that keeps the skin cool. He or she is then dressed in fireproof underwear, a fireproof suit, fireproof headgear, and a fireproof headpiece with a breathing tube connected to a three- to nine-minute supply of oxygen. After being donned, the clothing is coated with rubber cement or with a special substance called a pyro gel. When bare arms must appear on screen, the actor dons fake, fire-retardant arms to cover his or her real ones. Similarly, a fire-retardant mask is sometimes used to represent the actor's face.

Once the costume is complete, the suit is ignited and the scene filmed. As soon as the stuntperson gives the signal—which is universally a face-down fall—the fire is extinguished by crew members with fire extinguishers and/or special blankets.

Another type of fire effect is the fireball. This effect is increasingly being added in postproduction, but when created on the set an air mortar is used to shoot a streak of flaming propane gas. However, because a mortar explosion is involved, the fireball is often classified as a pyrotechnic effect rather than a fire effect. *See also* ACCIDENTS; MINIATURES AND MODELS; PYROTECHNICS; STUNTS.

Further Reading
Finch, Christopher. *Special Effects.* New York: Abbeville Press, 1984.
McCarthy, Robert E. *Secrets of Hollywood Special Effects.* Boston: Focal Press, 1992.
McKenzie, Alan, and Derek Ware. *Hollywood Tricks of the Trade.* New York: Gallery Books 1986.

First Men in the Moon

Released by Columbia Pictures in 1964, *First Men in the Moon* was one of the first movies to rely entirely on miniatures for its sets. Live action was added later through the use of travelling mattes. One of its scenes, a landing capsule separating from a spaceship, was later shown on television by news reporters explaining what would take place during a real Apollo space mission. This scene and others involving miniature work were created by Ray Harryhausen, one of the pioneers of stop-motion model animation, in association with producer Charles Schneer. *See also* HARRYHAUSEN, RAY; MINIATURES AND MODELS; STOP-MOTION MODEL ANIMATION; TRAVELLING MATTE.

Further Reading
Jenson, Paul M. *The Men Who Made the Monsters.* New York: Twayne, 1996.

Fleischer, Richard O. (1916–)

Richard O. Fleischer had a long career as a film director, and five of his movies won Academy Awards for their special effects: *20,000 Leagues Under the Sea* (1954), *Fantastic Voyage* (1966), *Dr. Doolittle* (1967), and *Tora! Tora! Tora!* (1970). All employed advanced miniature work and mechanical effects.

Born in Brooklyn, New York, in 1916, Fleischer was the son of Max Fleischer, who made animated cartoons during the 1920s, 1930s, and early 1940s. Richard Fleischer studied drama as a young man, and in 1942 he took a job at RKO Studios editing newsreels. He soon advanced to directing. His later work includes *Soylent Green* (1974), *Amityville 3-D* (1983), and *Conan the Destroyer* (1984). *See also* DR. DOOLITTLE; FANTASTIC VOYAGE; TORA! TORA! TORA; 20,000 LEAGUES UNDER THE SEA.

The Flintstones

The 1994 movie *The Flintstones* features sophisticated animatronics from Jim Henson's Creature Shop and mechanical, visual, and digital effects by Michael Lantieri and Industrial Light & Magic. However, it is particularly significant for being the first movie to have a computer-generated character with realistic fur.

Before *The Flintstones,* no digital artist had been able to make realistic digital animal hairs. Digital artists had to create fur for a saber-toothed tiger named Kitty. The character was first built as a maquette (clay model), which was photographed from a variety of angles. These photographs were then scanned into the computer and traced to provide animators with a basic wireframe they could animate and render. As soon as the model was ready for its fur, it was turned over to a special team at Industrial Light & Magic (ILM). Although they already had experience creating realistic dinosaur skin for *Jurassic Park* (1993), the experts still had difficulty figuring out how to make digital fur. Whereas for skin the computer only has to be told how to texture—i.e., raise and lower—a flat surface, for hair it must also determine the direction of individual 3-D hairs. Moreover, fur lays in different directions depending on the features beneath it. This made the process of creating computer-generated fur even more difficult.

It took the ILM team two months to develop computer software that could grow hair on sections of skin using instructions regarding hair length and color as well as skin texture. However, the artists' first efforts looked mangy, then wet. Eventually the team discovered that the fur software alone was not enough to create realistic fur. It required adjustments made with other types of software, including those involved with modeling, animating, painting, and rendering a character. After a great deal of work and patience, they managed to make Kitty's fur fairly realistic. They further advanced the technique while making *Jumanji* (1995), and relied on it extensively while creating computer-generated puppies and other animals for *101 Dalmatians* (1996). *See also* INDUSTRIAL LIGHT & MAGIC; JUMANJI; JURASSIC PARK; LANTIERI, MICHAEL.

Further Reading
Duncan, Jody. "The Making of a Rockbuster." *Cinefex 58,* June 1994.
———. "Puppy Proliferation." *Cinefex 69,* 1997.

Flowers, A.D.

A.D. Flowers was once one of the foremost experts in mechanical special effects and pyrotechnics. He began his career as a propman in charge of foliage, then worked with other types of props before becoming involved with pyrotechnics. He created explosions for war movies, Westerns, and television series such as *Combat* and *Gunsmoke*. His films include *The Forbidden Planet* (1956), which earned Flowers an Academy Award nomination, and *The Poseidon Adventure* (1972), and *Tora! Tora! Tora!* (1970), both of which won Academy Awards for their special effects. He also provided mechanical effects for the *Towering Inferno* (1974), *The Godfather* (1972), and *The Godfather Part II* (1974), the latter two of which involved the use of hundreds of squibs (plastic blood bags with detonators) to simulate bullet hits. *See also* FORBIDDEN PLANET; THE POSEIDON ADVENTURE; TORA! TORA! TORA!

Flying *See* WIREWORK.

Foley Artist

A foley artist is a person who watches a scene and re-creates many of the sound effects that the scene requires, such as a series of footsteps, a door opening, or the jangling of keys. All kinds of tools, devices, and equipment, even foodstuffs, are used to produce sound. Crunching celery might be used to make the sound of a crunching bone, and footsteps are created by stepping into troughs called Foley pits, which are rectangular areas filled or covered with a variety of materials, such as dirt, sand, carpet, grass, or wood. Different types of shoes are used according to the type of footsteps desired.

Foley artists are specialists within the field of sound effects. Other sound effects experts specialize in making recordings of environmental noises to create appropriate movie sounds. For example, the crowd sounds for the podracing sequence in the 1999 *Star Wars* movie *The Phantom Menace* were recorded at a San Francisco 49ers football game. In *Earth Versus the Flying Saucers* (1956), the sound of a spaceship was actually the underground motors at a sewage disposal plant.

Sound effects can also be created by manipulating recordings via electronic equipment. For example, in the movie *One Million B.C.* (1940), the dinosaurs' roar was created by combining sped-up sounds of lions, dogs, and elephants; this sound effect became a standard of dinosaur movies for many years. In *The Phantom Menace,* submarine sounds were an electronically created combination of various small motor sounds, while the sea monster sounds were a blend of marine and mammal noises. Sound effects also come from special sound effects libraries, where sound editors pay to use standard movie sounds, or are recorded as part of live-action filming.

Forbidden Planet

When it was released by MGM Studios in 1956, *Forbidden Planet* featured the most elaborate robot ever built for a film production. "Robby" the robot had many moving parts and flashing lights, all of which were

Robby the Robot making his film debut in *Forbidden Planet* (1956). *Photofest.*

powered via more than 2,600 feet of electrical wiring. He was so expensive that MGM kept him and used him for another film, *The Invisible Boy* (1957), and several television shows. But despite his elaborate movements, Robby was still nothing more than a costume, with a man inside to walk and move his arms.

Forbidden Planet also used expensive, elaborate models and miniature sets. For example, MGM spent $1 million on a miniature set of a laboratory. The set had more than 50,000 feet of electrical wiring and had to be operated by 15 electricians. Three models of a spaceship, one 20 inches, one 44 inches, and one 88 inches in diameter, cost $20,000. There was also a full-sized mock-up of a spaceship. However, only the bottom portion and mechanical stairway were reproduced, with a curved painted canvas, called a cyclorama, placed behind it to depict scenery. The upper part of the ship was added in postproduction using two matte paintings. Similarly, a 20-mile-wide underground power plant was built as a 30-foot-high, 10-foot-wide model, and its missing parts were added with a matte painting. Matte paintings were also used for two long shots, one of a scientist's house and another of a graveyard.

The movie also included something revolutionary in the field of sound effects: the first electronic synthesizer music ever heard in a motion picture, which was used to represent the sound of a musical instrument created by space aliens. *See also* CYCLORAMA; MATTE; MATTE PAINTINGS; METRO-GOLDWYN-MAYER; MINIATURES.

Further Reading
Johnson, John. *Cheap Tricks and Class Acts*. Jefferson, NC: McFarland & Company, 1996.
Kawin, Bruce F. *How Movies Work*. Berkeley: University of California Press, 1992

Forrest Gump

Directed by Robert Zemeckis, the 1994 movie *Forrest Gump* won an Academy Award for its visual effects. The film featured footage of its main character interacting with real historic figures, an effect created on computers by special effects experts at Industrial Light & Magic.

To accomplish this effect, the actor was first photographed in front of a bluescreen, and this bluescreen footage was scanned into the computer. Digital artists removed the blue background and replaced it with historical documentary footage, taking care to make the new shots of the actor look as grainy as the old footage. Care was also taken in planning the actor's movements prior to filming, so that he would appear to be truly interacting with the documentary setting. To this end, digital artists used computer software to change some of the mouth movements of the documentary figures. Computers also added extra characters to crowd scenes and eliminated the legs of an actor playing an amputee. The actor wore bluescreen stockings on his legs to make it easier for his legs to be digitally removed; digital artists then replaced the "hole" they left with appropriate background images. *See also* ANIMATION, COMPUTER; BLUESCREEN PROCESS; COMPUTER GRAPHICS; ZEMECKIS, ROBERT.

Further Reading
Duncan, Jody. "20 Years of Industrial Light & Magic." *Cinefex 65,* March 1996.

Freund, Karl (1890–1969)

German cinematographer Karl Freund was in charge of photography on dozens of films, both in Europe and in the United States. During the 1930s, he strenuously objected to the establishment of separate special effects departments, believing that cinematographers should have complete control over all photography in a movie, even trick photography.

Born in 1890 in what is now the Czech Republic, Freund became a cameraman when he was 17 years old. He had a distinguished career in Germany before settling in the United States in 1929, where he worked on Hollywood films such as *Camille* (1937), *Dracula* (1931), *Air Mail* (1932), *Tortilla Flat* (1942), and *Key Largo* (1948). Freund won an Academy Award for his cinematography on *The Good Earth* (1937), and in his later years he worked in the television industry. He died in 1969.

Fulton, John P. (1902–1966)

American special effects artist John P. Fulton was famous for his trick photography, particularly as it related to making a character seem to be invisible. His best-known work in this regard is the 1933 film *The Invisible Man* and its sequels, which include *The Invisible Man Returns* (1940), *The Invisible Woman* (1941), *The Invisible Agent* (1942), and *The Invisible Man's Revenge* (1944), as well as *Topper* (1937) and *Wonder Man* (1945), the latter of which won an Academy Award for its special effects.

Fulton's invisibility techniques were varied, and included mechanical effects to manipulate props (making it appear as though an invisible hand were moving them) as well as optical effects that allowed an invisible man to wear clothes. For the latter trick, a stuntman was dressed entirely in black velvet; even his face was covered. Over the velvet he wore clothing in light colors. He was then filmed in front of a black background, and this footage was used to create travelling mattes that would later add the moving clothing to background footage.

Born in 1902, Fulton worked as a surveyor before convincing a movie cameraman to teach him the trade. He was an assistant cameraman on several projects and a cinematographer on two films, *Hell's Harbour* (1929) and *Eyes of the World* (1930), before getting a job in a special effects laboratory. He was subsequently named head of the special effects department at Universal Studios, where he primarily worked on horror films such as *Frankenstein* (1931), *The Mummy* (1932), and *The Werewolf of London* (1935). He also made a John Ford film, *Air Mail* (1932).

Air Mail earned Fulton a great deal of acclaim. The movie featured spectacular flying scenes, with background footage filmed by Fulton himself. He used rearscreen projection to combine this footage with live action; actors sat in a replica of an airplane cockpit that was rocked by propmen and buffeted by wind machines. In addition, Fulton constructed realistic miniature airplanes that could be suspended on fine wires in front of the projection screen. He spent five months filming scenes with these miniatures.

In 1945, Universal Studios loaned Fulton to Goldwyn Studios, which needed his trick photography skills for the movie *Wonder Man*. This film features a man being haunted by the ghost of his murdered brother, and one actor played both parts. After finishing the project, Fulton decided to accept a permanent position at Goldwyn. However, he was unhappy there and soon left to become a freelance special effects artist. In 1953 he abandoned freelancing to become head of the special effects department at Paramount Pictures. His most famous work at this studio was for the 1956 version of *The Ten Commandments,* which required him to part the Red Sea.

Fulton remained at Paramount until the 1960s, when he again became a freelancer. He took ill while working on the effects for *The Battle of Britain* (1968) and died in 1966. *See also* INVISIBILITY; *THE TEN COMMANDMENTS;* UNIVERSAL STUDIOS; WIREWORK; *WONDER MAN.*

FX

"FX" is an abbreviation used to refer to any kind of effect, but it most commonly refers to a visual special effect or a sound effect. It was first written as a code, "f.x.," in the margins of movie scripts to indicate when a special effect was necessary. Now the term is used not only by screenwriters and by filmmakers but by moviegoers as well, sometimes to indicate all effects in a movie or even the entire field of special effects.

G

Gawley, Steve

Steve Gawley is one of the foremost modelmakers in the film industry. In 1975, shortly after graduating from California State University at Long Beach, he went to work at Industrial Light & Magic (ILM), which was working on the movie *Star Wars* (1977). He subsequently supervised the modelmaking on many other ILM movies, including *The Empire Strikes Back* (1980), *Return of the Jedi* (1983), *Raiders of the Lost Ark* (1981), *Back to the Future* (1985), *Star Trek II: The Wrath of Khan* (1982), *Star Trek III: The Search for Spock* (1984), and *Star Wars: The Phantom Menace* (1999). *See also* INDUSTRIAL LIGHT & MAGIC; *STAR TREK* MOVIES; *STAR WARS* MOVIES.

Ghostbusters

Released by Columbia Pictures in 1984, *Ghostbusters* inspired the creation of new special effects equipment. The movie also represents the first special effects created by Boss Film Studios, whose founder, Richard Edlund, won Academy Awards for his work on *The Empire Strikes Back* (1980), *Raiders of the Lost Ark* (1981), and *Return of the Jedi* (1983). Edlund was nominated for an Academy Award for his work on *Ghostbusters*.

In establishing his new company, Edlund took over the facilities and equipment of the Entertainment Effects Group (EEG), a special effects house founded by Douglas Trumbull. This equipment included Trumbull's "Compsey," or Computer Operated Motion Picture System. Originally built for effects work related to *Star Trek: The Motion Picture* (1979), the Compsey was a computerized animation stand and camera system. Edlund's staff adapted it for use with matte photography as well as animation, thereby making it possible to create realistic rather than cartoonish ghosts. With the Compsey, they could take still photographs of a puppet or an actor in a ghost costume posing against a black background, and then combine the images with background plates as though they were animation cels rather than photographs.

Boss Film Studios also created new cameras and optical printers for *Ghostbusters*, including the Super Printer and the Zoom Aerial Printer, both of which had 70mm telecentric lenses. Telecentric lenses can focus an image without changing its size, whereas traditional still-camera lenses change the size of an image as it is focused. *See also* BOSS FILM STUDIOS; EDLUND, RICHARD; *INDIANA JONES* MOVIES; *STAR WARS* MOVIES; TRUMBULL, DOUGLAS.

Further Reading

Vaz, Mark Cotta. "Boss Film Studios: End of an Era." *Cinefex* 73, March 1998.

Gibbons, Cedric (1893–1960)

Cedric Gibbons was an art director and special effects expert who worked on more than 1,000 films, including *Ben-Hur* (1926), *Mutiny on the Bounty* (1935), *Captains Courageous* (1937), and *The Postman Always Rings Twice* (1946). He won 11 Academy Awards for the films *The Bridge of San Luis Rey* (1929), *The Merry Widow* (1934), *Pride and Prejudice* (1940), *Blossoms in the Dust* (1941), *Gaslight* (1944), *The Yearling* (1946), *Little Women* (1949), *An American in Paris* (1951), *The Bad and the Beautiful* (1952), *Julius Caesar* (1953), and *Somebody Up There Likes Me* (1956). He was also the designer of the Academy Award statuette, which is known as the Oscar. Born in 1893, Gibbons started his film career in 1915, working at the Edison Studios as the assistant to a set painter and designer. In 1918 he went to the Goldwyn Studios, and six years later to MGM, where he remained until 1956. He died in 1960. *See also* BEN-HUR.

Art director and special effects expert Cedric Gibbons. *Photofest.*

Gillard, Nick (1958–)

Nick Gillard was stunt coordinator for the 1999 *Star Wars* movie *The Phantom Menace*. Gillard choreographed the movie's fight sequences, including a climactic lightsaber duel that involved leaps and swordplay. Gillard planned such sequences in advance using 3-D stunt modeling software.

Gillard has performed stunts himself in more than 35 movies. He played the Alien Queen in *Aliens* (1986), appeared in the boat and tank battle sequences in *Indiana Jones and the Last Crusade* (1989), doubled for actor Tom Cruise in *Interview with the Vampire* (1994), and exhibited his swordplay in *Henry V* (1989), *Robin Hood: Prince of Thieves* (1991), *The Three Musketeers* (1993), and *1492: Conquest of Paradise* (1992). He has been set on fire for stunts more than 100 times.

Gillard also holds two unofficial world records related to his stuntwork. For the movie *Amsterdammed* (1988), he jumped a powerboat 200 feet over two bridges, and for the movie *Alien 3* (1992) he performed a full-body burn without an oxygen supply for more than two minutes. He did not breathe during the fire stunt, because inhaling during a full burn can cause the air in a person's lungs to ignite.

Gillard began performing stunts when he was 16 years old. By that time, he was already an experienced horseman, having performed riding tricks for the Moscow State Circus. He ran away from a military school to join the circus when he was 12. His first movie stuntwork was for *The Thief of Bagdad* (1978). *See also* ALIEN MOVIES; INDIANA JONES MOVIES; STAR WARS MOVIES; STUNTS.

Gillespie, A. Arnold (1899–1978)

A. Arnold Gillespie worked as an art director at MGM Studios from 1924 to 1936, whereupon he became the head of the company's special effects department. He worked on all types of effects but was particularly skilled at special mechanical effects. His films include *Adam's Rib* (1923), *Ben-Hur* (1926), *The Good Earth* (1937), *The Wizard of Oz*

(1939), *Forbidden Planet* (1936), *North by Northwest* (1959), *How the West Was Won* (1962), and *The Greatest Story Ever Told* (1965). He won Academy Awards for his special effects work on *The Plymouth Adventure* (1952), *Ben-Hur* (1959), *Thirty Seconds Over Tokyo* (1944), and *Green Dolphin Street* (1947). Gillespie died in 1978 at the age of 79. See also BEN-HUR; METRO-GOLDWYN-MAYER; THE WIZARD OF OZ.

Glass Shot

A glass shot is created by placing a piece of glass in front of a stationary camera. An artist then paints background scenery on the glass, leaving certain areas clear for live-action filming. When the camera films through the glass, it appears as though the action is taking place amidst the painted scenery.

Two of the first filmmakers to use the glass shot were G.A. Smith and Norman Dawn. Dawn used the technique while filming *Missions of California* (1907) in order to repair roof damage on an historic building. He filmed live action in front of a real mission through a piece of glass onto which a perfect roof had been painted. In this way he made a crumbling structure look brand new. *See also* DAWN, NORMAN O.; SMITH, GEORGE ALBERT.

Godzilla

The 1998 version of *Godzilla* is significant because, unlike previous movies that featured realistic computer-generated characters such as *Jurassic Park* (1993) and *The Lost World* (1997), it avoided the use of animatronics. Only 24 shots of the Godzilla monster and its offspring involved animatronics, which included a 1/24-scale animatronic head and body, a 1/6-scale animatronic head and shoulders, nine 1/24-scale radio-controlled "baby Godzilla" heads, a full-sized jaw and head used to hold a taxicab, and a 1/6-scale tail with a 25-foot-long mechanism to pivot, raise, and lower the figure. The remainder of the Godzilla shots, totaling 155, were created entirely with computer graphics. There were an additional 587 digital effects in the film, and in one sequence in which Godzilla

is trapped in the cables of a suspension bridge, 98 percent of everything seen on screen is computer generated—not only Godzilla but also the bridge, cables, cars, and water.

The movie also used sophisticated mechanical effects to make it seem as though the computer-generated Godzilla was really present on the live-action set. For example, a full-sized fishing boat was submerged in a tank with a hydraulic mechanism, making it seem as though Godzilla were pulling it under the water. In city scenes, 20 "car-thumpers" used automobile jacks with foot-long pneumatic cylinders to jiggle cars up and down, as though the monster's heavy footsteps were shaking them. Other cars were crunched on cue using steel plates dropped from cranes; the cars had no engines and their tires had been altered to make them flatten easily. In addition, two 20x20-foot drop units, hung from cranes, deposited debris on the set to make it seem as though Godzilla had damaged the surrounding buildings.

Similar devices were used in conjunction with miniature sets. For example, modelmakers built a miniature Brooklyn Bridge in 1/24 scale and broke it apart by ramming it with a 1/24-scale greenscreen shape of Godzilla; the greenscreen Godzilla

Computer-generated monster added to images of miniature buildings in *Godzilla* (1998). *Photofest.*

was subsequently replaced with a computer-generated, realistic Godzilla. Additional miniatures used in the film included a 1/6-scale remote-control taxicab, several 1/8-scale helicopters, and a miniature city set that incorporated many of the buildings from *The Fifth Element* (1997).

Special effects for *Godzilla* were created by Centropolis Effects, a company co-owned by the movie's director, Roland Emmerlich. Centropolis was working with the cooperation of Toho Studios, which created the Godzilla character for a series of Japanese science fiction movies in the 1950s.

The first of these films, entitled *Gojira,* was released as *Godzilla* in the United States in 1954. Its effects were under the supervision of Eiji Tsuburuya, who originally intended to use stop-motion model animation to create the monster; however, his budget would not allow for this technique. Consequently he used a man in a monster costume to portray the monster instead, surrounding him with miniature buildings to make it seem as though he was 400 feet tall. *See also* AT-MOSPHERIC EFFECTS; BLUESCREEN PROCESS; *JURASSIC PARK; THE LOST WORLD;* MINIATURES AND MODELS; TSUBURUYA, EIJI.

Further Reading
Kaufman, Debra. "Synergistic Effects." *Digital Magic,* August 1998.
Robertson, Barbara. "Gadzooks! It's *Godzilla.*" *Computer Graphics World,* July 1998.
Rogers, Pauline. "Godzilla." *International Photographer,* May 1998.
Street, Rita. "The Communication of Monster-Sized Ideas through Digital Tools." *Film & Video,* May 1998.

Go-Motion

Go-Motion is a system whereby a puppet or similar object is moved with computer-controlled rods during filming. It was developed by Phil Tippett and other special effects experts at Industrial Light & Magic (ILM) for the 1981 movie *Dragonslayer* but has since been used for many other films.

Go-Motion's forerunner was stop-motion model animation, in which a puppet is moved by hand, frame by frame, with the camera stopped intermittently to prevent the puppeteer from being caught on film. Because a stop-motion puppet is not moving continuously, its filmed image lacks a subtle quality called motion blur and can therefore look jerky. In contrast, Go-Motion creates smooth, realistic animation because the puppet, controlled by a computer, moves just as a live-action character would during filming.

The only drawback with Go-Motion is that the rods must be removed from shots during postproduction through a technique called rotoscoping. To make this removal process easier, the rods are typically made out of bluescreen material and the puppet is shot in front of a bluescreen. A computer is then used to eliminate the bluescreen background. *See also* BLUESCREEN PROCESS; MATTE; OPTICAL PRINTER; PUPPETS; ROTOSCOPING; STOP-MOTION MODEL ANIMATION; TRAVELLING MATTE.

Further Reading
Smith, Thomas G. *Industrial Light & Magic: The Art of Special Effects.* New York: Ballantine Books, 1986.

Gordon, Bert I. (1922–)

Born on September 24, 1922, in Kenosha, Wisconsin, Bert I. Gordon produced, directed, and sometimes wrote science fiction and fantasy films that relied heavily on special effects, many of them featuring giant creatures. Gordon strongly believed that such creatures should not be created with models or miniatures. His monsters were actors in costume, or they were created with photographic tricks. For example, in *Beginning of the End* (1957), Gordon used rearscreen projection and enlarged film of real bugs to make it appear as though actors were standing in front of giant grasshoppers. He also relied on a matte process to make two scenes filmed separately appear to be one. Gordon's films include *Serpent Island* (1954), *King Dinosaur* (1955), *The Amazing Colossal Man* (1957), *Attack of the Puppet People* (1958), *War of the Colossal Beast* (1958), *Village of the Giants* (1965), and *Empire of the Ants* (1977).

The Great Train Robbery

Made in 1903 by filmmaking pioneer Edwin Porter, the eight-minute-long *The Great Train Robbery* was the most successful of the early story films, which had a true beginning, middle, and end. It was also one of the first movies to use a special effect not as a trick meant to dazzle the audience but for strictly practical purposes. Wanting to show a train passing outside the window of a telegraph office, Porter filmed the office using a matte that blocked the area of the window from exposure. He then rewound the film negative, replaced the matte with one that blocked everything but the window, and filmed the train.

In addition to the matte shot, *The Great Train Robbery* also includes the first color tinting of a film frame. In order to simulate a gunshot, Porter handcolored three frames of film with a red "flash." The shot of the gunman shooting was the first closeup ever used in a movie, and it inspired other directors to experiment with different camera placements. *See also* MATTE; PORTER, EDWIN.

Further Reading

Brosnan, John. *Movie Magic*. New York: St. Martin's Press, 1974.
Fry, Ron, and Pamela Fourzon. *The Saga of Special Effects*. Englewood Cliffs, NJ: Prentice-Hall, 1977.
Stensvold, Mike. *In-Camera Special Effects*. Englewood Cliffs, NJ: Prentice-Hall, 1983.

Green Dolphin Street

Released by MGM in 1947, *Green Dolphin Street* won an Academy Award for its special effects, which were supervised by A. Arnold Gillespie. The movie featured an earthquake and resultant tidal wave, which were created primarily with miniature photography and mechanical effects during live-action filming. *See also* GILLESPIE, A. ARNOLD.

Greenscreen *See* BLUESCREEN PROCESS.

Griffith, D.W. (1875–1948)

Director David Wark (D.W.) Griffith was one of the pioneers of the film industry. Not only did he make thousands of movies but he encouraged the use of creative camera techniques, such as varying the angles of shots and intercutting wide shots with closeups. Griffith's cameraman on many of his projects was Billy Bitzer, who contributed many advances to the field of cinematography.

Born in 1875, Griffith began his film career as an actor and screenwriter. After selling several stories to the Biograph Studios, he started directing his work and others, beginning with *The Adventures of Dollie* (1908). Within five years he was directing almost all of Biograph's films, and he launched the ca-

A scene from Edwin Porter's *The Great Train Robbery* (1903). *Photofest.*

Director D.W. Griffith (right) and his cameraman Billy Bitzer (left). *Corbis/Bettmann.*

reers of many new stars. He also lengthened the average viewing time of a movie, using two reels of film instead of one.

During his Biograph period, Griffith refined such techniques as the closeup, the scenic long shot, the fade-in, and the fade-out, as well as the technique of cross-cutting, whereby scenes shot at different locations are intermingled during the editing process. The purpose of the cross-cut is to encourage the audience to perceive that the events at each location happened simultaneously. Griffith and Bitzer also developed mattes that could change the borders of the camera's filming area, so that the film frame was no longer the standard size and/or shape.

In 1913 Griffith left Biograph to become production chief at another studio, Reliance-Majestic, and Bitzer continued to work for him. Together the two made *The Birth of a Nation* (1915), which is considered significant in the history of film specifically because of their artistic approach to filming it. A three-hour epic about the Civil War, the movie was a financial success, even though some people criticized it as racist.

After the release of *The Birth of a Nation*, Griffith joined the Triangle Corporation, a filmmaking company attempting to dominate the industry by demanding that theaters showing its pictures present no other company's work.

Griffith and Bitzer's first film for Triangle was *Intolerance* (1916), which cost more than $2 million to make. The movie received artistic acclaim and offered new approaches to cinematography. Nonetheless, it was a box-office failure and ultimately led to Triangle's dissolution.

Before this bankruptcy occurred, however, Griffith left Triangle for another film company, Artcraft. In 1919 he joined actors Douglas Fairbanks, Mary Pickford, and Charlie Chaplin in forming a studio called United Artists, although he continued to make films for other studios as well. But no matter what studio he worked with, his movies continued to lose money despite some critical success.

Griffith made his last film, *The Struggle,* in 1931, and in 1935 he won an honorary Academy Award for his contributions to the film industry. He died in 1948. *See also* BITZER, G.W.; FADES; *INTOLERANCE.*

The Guns of Navarone

Filmed in CinemaScope and released in 1961 by Columbia Pictures, *The Guns of Navarone* won an Academy Award for its special effects. The movie used extremely detailed miniatures to depict the destruction of a German fortress during World War II. However, the backgrounds for these miniatures, which were matte paintings, have been criticized by some experts as being unrealistic, and the film contains a major error: two cannons blown off a cliff are subsequently shown intact. *See also* MATTE PAINTINGS.

Further Reading
Hayes, R.M. *Trick Cinematography.* Jefferson, NC: McFarland & Company, 1986.

H

Hammer Films

From the late 1950s to the 1970s, Hammer Films was England's most lucrative production company. Most of its films were in the horror genre and featured realistic violence. These movies were made on low budgets and tight shooting schedules, but were also in color, which was atypical for horror movies of the period. Moreover, they used real castles rather than Hollywood sets.

Hammer Films was established as a film distribution company in 1948 by Wil Hammer and Sir John Carreras, who moved into production in 1956. The studio's movies featured such monsters as Frankenstein's monster, Dracula, and the Werewolf, and they were responsible for many new cost-effective makeup and special effects techniques. *See also* MAKEUP.

The character of the Mummy, played here by Christopher Lee, from one of the many low-budget movies of Hammer films. *Photofest.*

Further Reading

Brosnan, John. *Movie Magic*. New York: St. Martin's Press, 1974.

Cohen, Daniel. *Masters of Horror*. New York: Clarion, 1984.

Harryhausen, Ray (1920–)

Ray Harryhausen is considered one of the foremost stop-motion model animation experts in film history. Born in 1920, his first work in model animation was as an assistant to special effects expert George Pal during the early 1940s. In 1946, after a stint in World War II, Harryhausen began working for stop-motion animation expert Willis O'Brien. His first film under O'Brien was *Mighty Joe Young* (1949), which won an Academy Award for its special effects. Harryhausen was placed in charge of the special effects on his next film, *The Beast from 20,000 Fathoms* (1953). He then worked on *It Came from Beneath the Sea* (1955), *Earth Versus the Flying Saucers* (1956), and *Twenty Million Miles to Earth* (1957) before making *The Seventh Voyage of Sinbad* (1959), which was the first Technicolor film to feature stop-motion model animation. *Sinbad* was extremely successful, grossing more than $6 million, as were Harryhausen's subsequent films, which include *Mysterious Island* (1961), *Jason and the Argonauts* (1963), *One Million Years B.C.* (1967), *Sinbad and the Eye of the Tiger* (1977), and *Clash of the Titans* (1981). He received an honorary Academy Award for his technical accomplishments in 1992. *See also* THE BEAST FROM 20,000 FATHOMS; DYNAMATION; MIGHTY JOE YOUNG; O'BRIEN, WILLIS; PAL, GEORGE; STOP-MOTION MODEL ANIMATION.

Haskin, Byron (1899–1984)

Byron Haskin was a special effects expert who eventually became a director. He wrote the screenplay for *War of the Worlds* (1953), a special effects–laden movie that he directed as well, and won a special Academy Award in 1938 for developing a new kind of background projector.

Born in 1899, Haskin worked at various jobs and served in the United States military before becoming a cameraman in 1918. By 1922 he was a director of photography, working on major Hollywood films. During the late 1920s he began to direct, then returned to cinematography and became interested in trick photography. Haskin joined Warner Brothers and was placed in charge of the special effects department there in 1937. He remained in this position until 1945, when he resumed his career as a director, making such films as *The Naked Jungle* (1954), *From Earth to the Moon* (1958), and *Robinson Crusoe on Mars* (1964). Haskin died in 1984. *See also* WAR OF THE WORLDS.

Further Reading

Brosnan, John. *Movie Magic*. New York: St. Martin's Press, 1974.

Henson, Jim (1936–1990)

Jim Henson was a puppeteer who produced and directed many films featuring his own puppets, which he called Muppets. He also provided puppets for such other films as *Teenage Mutant Ninja Turtles* (1990) and *The Witches* (1990).

Born in 1936, Henson got his first job as a puppeteer when he was 18, working on a local television show in Maryland. He held this position while attending the University of Maryland, where he studied theater arts. At the same time, he made his first Muppets and used them to make short films. One of these films, *Time Piece,* was nominated for an Academy Award in 1965.

Four years later Henson was hired to create Muppets for a new Public Television children's program, *Sesame Street*. Henson's work on the show earned him many awards and led to two Muppet television programs, *The Muppet Show* and *Fraggle Rock*. In 1979 Henson made his first Muppet movie, appropriately titled *The Muppet Movie*. His subsequent films include *The Great Muppet Caper* (1981), *The Dark Crystal* (1982), *The Muppets Take Manhattan* (1984), and *The Labrynth* (1986).

In 1990 Henson contracted strep throat and died from complications of the disease. His company, Jim Henson Studios, is now run by Henson's son Brian, in association with Walt Disney Studios. Also under Brian Henson's control is Jim Henson's Creature Shop, a special effects facility that has been responsible for many advances in animatronics.

In 1992 the Creature Shop's technicians received a technical achievement award from the Academy of Motion Picture Arts and Sciences for inventing the Henson Performance Control System. This computerized system allows one puppeteer to operate a variety of mechanisms on a puppet all at once, using a special glove on one hand and operating a joystick with another. Opening and closing the glove in combination with certain joystick movements can create a full range of expressions on the figure's face.

In 1995, the Creature Shop added a computer graphics department, dedicated to creating computer-generated characters similar to their animatronic ones. Its first major assignment was the computer-generated monkey creature in *Lost in Space* (1998). *See also* ANIMATRONICS; *LOST IN SPACE;* PUPPETS.

Further Reading
Bacon, Matt, Brian Henson, and Anthony Minghella. *No Strings Attached: The Inside Story of Jim Henson's Creature Shop.* New York: Macmillan, 1997.
Duncan, Jody. "The Making of a Rockbuster." *Cinefex* 58, June 1994.

Hero Model

A hero model is a model used for closeup shots during miniature photography. Highly detailed and realistic, it is called a hero because it is the "star" of a miniature shoot. More than one version of a model is usually made for a scene, with non-hero models featuring far less detail. Some background models are mere shapes. Others are known as stunt models, because they are specifically designed to be destroyed in crash or pyrotechnics scenes. *See also* MINIATURES AND MODELS.

The Hindenburg

Released by Universal Studios in 1976, *The Hindenburg* won a Special Achievement Academy Award for its elaborate visual effects, which were previsualized using more than 2,700 storyboards. The film relied on a combination of live action on full-sized sets, miniature photography, mechanical effects, and matte paintings.

Three full-sized sets represented different parts of the airship, an 8x36-foot gondola, a fin, and a nose cone. These sets were built on mechanized rockers so they could move and tilt. The nose cone, which was made of more than 8 tons of aluminum, 2 million rivets, 11,000 yards of muslin, and 24,000 feet of sash cord, was set on fire in the climactic scene. First, however, an asbestos chimney was created to vent the fumes out of a hole in the soundstage roof. The heat of this effect was so intense that the asbestos caught on fire and one of the 12 cameras filming the scene was destroyed.

Other scenes were created using a miniature airship built by special effects expert Glen Robinson. Hung on thin wires from an overhead track, it could perform extremely realistic movements and was filmed in front of one of three painted backgrounds: a normal sky, a stormy sky, and a sunset. On the floor beneath the miniature, a machine used dry ice to create clouds. A total of 78 matte paintings were used in the film, created under the supervision of Albert Whitlock. *See also* ROBINSON, GLEN; WHITLOCK, ALBERT.

Further Reading
Brosnan, John. *Movie Magic.* New York: St. Martin's Press, 1974.
O'Conner, Jane. *Magic in the Movies.* Garden City, NY: Doubleday, 1980.

Hitchcock, Alfred (1899–1980)

Director Alfred Hitchcock made movies that were known for their sophisticated special effects. His first use of advanced special effects was in the 1929 film *Blackmail,* which included a scene created with the relatively new "Shuftan process." This technique used mirrors to reflect images of various elements, such as miniatures and matte paintings, into a single scene so they could be filmed together in one camera shot.

Director Alfred Hitchcock on the set of *The Birds* (1963). *Universal Pictures/Photofest.*

Many of Hitchcock's movies, including *Rebecca* (1940), *Saboteur* (1940), *Vertigo* (1958), and *The Birds* (1963), featured elaborate miniatures and matte paintings. For example, for *The Birds*, artist Albert Whitlock created a painting of hundreds of birds sitting on telephone wires and trees; this painting had tiny holes punched in it to allow glittering light to pass through from behind, thereby giving the illusion of movement among the birds. *The Birds* also relied heavily on rearscreen projection. Hitchcock had his cameramen film seagulls swooping to catch tossed food; this film was then projected from behind onto a screen made of special clear plastic, and schoolchildren were placed in front of this screen, where they were filmed reacting to the bird images.

Hitchcock was born in England in 1899. In 1920 he got his first job in the film industry, designing titles for a production company. Eventually he began directing scenes in the company's films, working his way up to assistant director and then director. His first film as director was *The Pleasure Garden* (1925). He made several other silent films before directing England's first sound film, *Blackmail,* in 1929. His first internationally successful film was *The Man Who Knew Too Much* (1934), which Hitchcock remade in 1956 in color.

In the late 1930s Hitchcock moved to the United States, where he made such films as *Rear Window* (1954), *North by Northwest* (1959), and *Psycho* (1960). From 1955 to 1965 he also produced and hosted a television show. He died in 1980. *See also* PROJECTION PROCESSES; WHITLOCK, ALBERT.

Holland, Cecil (1887–1973)

Born in England in 1887, Cecil Holland was a makeup artist who worked on hundreds of films. His first job was as a sailor, but seasickness drove him to become a farmworker. In 1904 he moved to the United States, where he worked for a small theater company, first as an extra and later as an actor. During this time he learned how to do his own makeup so he could play a wide variety of characters.

In 1913 Holland began acting in silent films, once again doing his own makeup. Soon he began doing makeup for other actors as well, and in 1927 he abandoned acting entirely to become the first head of the makeup department at MGM Studios. There he worked on such films as *Son of India* (1931), *Rasputin and the Empress* (1932), *The Mask of Fu Manchu* (1932), and *The Good Earth* (1937).

Howell was particularly skilled at giving a non-Asian actor the appearance of an Asian. He also invented many new makeup techniques. For example, he discovered that a piece of eggshell placed over a person's eyeball, in much the same way as a modern contact lens, could make that person appear blind. In addition, Howard could create extremely realistic colors and textures with facial paint. Eventually he began using his artistic skills to paint commissioned portraits of celebrities. In 1964 he suffered a stroke, and in July, 1973, he died at the age of 86. *See also* MAKEUP.

Honda, Inoshiro (1911–)

Japanese director Inoshiro Honda was responsible for a series of Japanese monster movies that featured such creatures as Godzilla, Rodan, and Mothra. The first of these were *Gojira,* called *Godzilla, King of the Monsters* in the United States, and *Gigantis the Fire Monster;* both were released in 1956. *Rodin* also appeared in 1956 and *Mothra* in 1961. Honda's other films include *Attack of the Mushroom People* (1964), *King Kong Versus Godzilla* (1963), *Godzilla's Revenge* (1969), and *The War of the Gargantuas* (1966). Born in 1911, Honda began making films at the Toho Studios in Japan in 1955 and continued to direct movies there until the 1970s. He also co-wrote several of his screenplays. The special effects expert working on his movies was typically Eiji Tsuburaya. *See also* GODZILLA.

Honey, I Blew Up The Kid

A sequel to *Honey, I Shrunk the Kids* (1989), the 1992 movie *Honey, I Blew Up the Kid* was the first movie to use electronic compositing during postproduction, adding animation to live action via video equipment rather than with an optical printer. The movie

used a total of 210 special effects shots, 185 of them composite or miniature shots, as well as 39 shots of hand-drawn animation, particularly for images of electricity.

The movie also benefited from a new computer software program that enables a programmer to map an image onto a grid. Once this grid map is complete, the software can use it to stretch the image in any direction. This technique enabled the special effects team to make it seem as though a baby were expanding in size. In contrast, in *Honey I Shrunk the Kids* the shrinking and growing illusions were created with camera lenses and optical zooms.

However, the second movie did rely on traditional photographic tricks rather than computer graphics to create some of its scenes. For example, in some cases an old technique called the Shuftan process combined live-action footage with reflected images of miniatures. In others, an effect called the split-scale technique placed a giant baby in a room with tiny parents.

The split-scale technique involves building two scales of a set on one soundstage: a full-sized part in the background and a miniature part in the foreground. In the case of an interior set, the floors, ceilings, moldings, and other linear elements must be carefully aligned to trick the eye into believing that the two halves are actually part of the same, full-sized set. For *Honey, I Blew Up the Kid*, there were eight split-scale sets, each representing a different room in a house. The live actors representing the parents were placed in the full-sized part of a set while the baby was placed in the miniature part, which was 43 percent smaller than life-sized. However, because only one camera position can be used to film a split-scale scene, the filmmakers had to use the bluescreen process for scenes requiring multiple angles, or for scenes in which the parents had to move into the baby's area.

In addition, because the baby actor could be uncooperative, the director sometimes substituted a man in a baby suit for the child. The head of this suit was operated via radio control by four puppeteers. There were also several puppet versions of the baby's family members. For scenes in which the baby puts people in his pocket, 3-inch-tall radio-controlled puppets were placed in the real baby's overalls. Sometimes, however, the real baby was substituted with a fake torso with similar clothing. In this case, either 21-inch-tall cable-controlled puppets or the live actors were put in the pocket.

The oversized torso came in two sizes, 24x32 and 16x12, because the baby grew twice during the movie. Both torsos were made of plywood and foam. To give them a realistic walking movement, they were hung from bungee cords and tugged at by eight men.

Another large prop, the baby's shoes, also came in two sizes, an 8-foot version to represent him at 56 feet tall and a 17-foot version to represent him at 112 feet tall. Like the torso, the shoes had a plywood structure and were filled with rigid Styrofoam. Their surface was made of vinyl, and they had handwoven shoelaces. Each shoe was 20 feet tall, weighed 1,500 pounds, and was attached to a plywood calf that rose approximately 20 feet. The shoes could be raised with a crane and had hinges, cables, and levers to provide some movement in the heel and toe.

In addition to such large-scale mechanical props, the movie also featured several miniatures, including a 1/16-scale, 40x60-foot desert landscape made out of Styrofoam, plaster, sand, and other materials. There were also several miniature helicopters, one in 1/32 scale and two in 1/7 scale. Each of these had puppets inside that could make slight hand and head movements. A miniature car was also built in several scales for scenes in which the baby picks up a car and plays with it. These scenes are set in Las Vegas, which was filmed as background footage and added to bluescreen baby shots during post-production. *See also* BLUESCREEN PROCESS; COMPUTER GRAPHICS; THE WALT DISNEY COMPANY; PUPPETS.

Further Reading

Duncan, Jody. "Blowing Up Baby." *Cinefex 52,* November 1992.
Smith, Dave. *Disney A-Z.* New York: Hyperion, 1996.

Hook

Released in 1991 by Amblin Entertainment and TriStar Pictures, *Hook* inspired the invention of new computer software called the digital pinblock program, which is a tool for aligning various elements of a composited shot, such as foreground images, background images, and bluescreen faces. The movie also featured some of the largest and most detailed soundstage sets ever created for a

Shoe props from *Honey, I Blew Up The Kid* (1992). *Photofest.*

movie, including a pirate town and harbor, a ship's cabin interior, and a treehouse with skateboard ramps.

Building such enormous sets required 1 million board feet of lumber, 25,000 gallons of paint, 260 tons of plaster, 10 miles of rope, and 600,000 gallons of water to fill the harbor. The pirate harbor was constructed on a soundstage 250 feet long and 150 feet wide, with an adjustable roof that could be heightened from 50 feet to 80 feet. For *Hook* the roof was fully extended, because the set included a full-sized pirate ship 35 feet wide and 175 feet long with a mast height of 70 feet. This vessel sat in a water tank with a depth of 3 feet. Towards the back of the tank was a 30-foot-tall tower with a camera crane arm, on a track that lay beneath the surface of the water. This crane made it easier for director Steven Spielberg to film scenes at various locations on the crowded set.

All live action in the movie was filmed on this soundstage or others. No scenes were shot outdoors. Therefore sky elements had to be added later. Clouds were sculptures of polyester fiberfill, filmed on a motion-control stage. During postproduction, digital artists smoothed the edges of the cloud images to make them more realistic and then composited them onto various live-action shots. This and other optical work was performed by Industrial Light & Magic (ILM), under the supervision of visual effects expert Eric Brevig, who had previously won an Academy Award for the effects in *Total Recall* (1990). For *Hook* he was required to oversee more than 243 special effects shots, some involving the most detailed 2-D matte paintings employed in a movie until that time. There were 20 of these paintings, and most included live-action elements such as waterfalls, breaking waves, and sunsets. The moving images were rear-projected onto clear areas of the mattes, which had been painted on glass.

Another difficult visual effect was the character of Tinkerbell, whose image was added to various live-action scenes during postproduction. In many cases she was supposed to be moving very quickly, so the ac-

tress portraying her was filmed at 12–18 frames per second, or approximately half normal speed; the resulting footage was later projected at normal speed. However, this caused a problem with the actress's dialogue, because she could not talk at half normal speed. To solve this problem the filmmakers used a digital device called a voice harmonizer, which can change a voice's pitch instantly, thereby converting half-speed sounds back to normal. The device also lets the actor hear, understand, and mouth dialogue that is being played back at any speed, making it easier for him or her to match lip movements to prerecorded voices.

Hook also involved sophisticated wirework, supervised by mechanical effects expert Michael Lantieri, along with a bluescreen unit of 38 cameramen and other technicians. Tinkerbell's flying scenes were filmed in a bluescreen studio, but those involving the character of Peter Pan were shot not only in a bluescreen studio but also on the live-action set. This allowed the movie's director, Steven Spielberg, to supervise many of Pan's flying scenes himself. In most cases, the actor playing Pan, Robin Williams, hung "heads up," with the wires attached to a harness beneath a costume. In a few instances, however, he had to hang horizontally, which required him to wear a steel-reinforced body cast under his costume. Three wires were then mounted to the cast, one beneath each arm and another between his legs. However, they did not move the horizontal Williams along a track; instead the illusion of flight was created by moving a track-mounted camera towards the actor at high speed.

All wires that appeared in flying scenes were digitally removed during postproduction. There were a total of 60 wire removal shots in the film, representing 10,000 frames of manipulated imagery. Of these, shots involving the pirate set were the most difficult, because with such an elaborate background the digital artists had to struggle to find all parts of the wires for removal. In fact, it took six artists two weeks to complete the wire removal for each shot in the movie. *See also* BLUESCREEN PROCESS; GO-MOTION; LANTIERI,

MICHAEL; *TOTAL RECALL;* WIRE REMOVAL, DIGITAL; WIREWORK.

Further Reading
Vaz, Mark Cotta. "Return to Neverland." *Cinefex 49,* February 1992.

Howard, Tom

British special effects expert Tom Howard received an Academy Award for his work on *Blithe Spirit* (1946), which required him to create the illusion that objects were being moved by an invisible ghost, and again for *tom thumb* (1959), which was directed by special effects expert George Pal. Howard also contributed to the special effects on *The Thief of Bagdad* (1940) and *2001: A Space Odyssey* (1968). For the latter, he designed a new frontscreen projector to create several special effects. He had previously designed and built optical printers for director Alexander Korda.

Howard went to work for Korda in 1934 as a darkroom assistant. His first major special effects assignment was to create the travelling matte shots for Korda's version of *The Thief of Bagdad,* under the supervision of special effects expert Lawrence Butler; this process had never before been used with color film. Howard later developed a new type of split-screen matte for *tom thumb.* He was continually experimenting with special effects, and he made many other contributions to the field. *See also* INVISIBILITY; KORDA, ALEXANDER; PAL, GEORGE; *THE THIEF OF BAGDAD*; TRAVELLING MATTE; *2001: A SPACE ODYSSEY*.

Hydraulics

The term "hydraulics" refers to machines run by hydraulic power. This power is created when a pressurized fluid, usually a water-soluble oil or a mixture of water and glycol, is circulated into a motor. Hydraulic systems provide more power in relation to their size than mechanical or electrical systems, and are used in airplanes, automobiles, and many other kinds of machines.

A wide variety of hydraulic equipment has been used to create mechanical effects, which include moving creatures and sets. One example of a hydraulic set appeared in the movie *Superman* (1978). Representing the planet Krypton, the set was destroyed during a simulated earthquake via hydraulic machinery that pulled various heavy stage pieces apart. In other scenes, hidden hydraulically powered devices raised heavy objects to make it seem as though the title character was lifting them.

New hydraulics are continually being designed for use in animatronics. Major advances in this regard occurred during the making of *Jurassic Park* (1993), when animatronics expert Stan Winston employed hydraulics engineers from the industrial sector to create a large hydraulics system to power his mechanized Tyrannosaurus rex dinosaur. The system proved so successful that it was put to a similar use for *The Lost World* (1997). *See also* JURASSIC PARK; THE LOST WORLD; WINSTON, STAN.

Further Reading
Duncan, Jody. "The Beauty in the Beasts. " *Cinefex* 55, August 1993.

I

I Wanted Wings

Released by Paramount in 1941, *I Wanted Wings* won an Academy Award for its special effects, which were provided by two of the foremost experts in the field: Farciot Edouart and Gordon Jennings. The following year, the two would team up again to provide special effects for another Academy Award-winning effects film, *Reap the Wild Wind*.

Most of their work on *I Wanted Wings* was related to flying scenes, as the movie was about men training to be Air Force pilots. The actors were actually filmed in a studio, in front of rearscreen projections featuring the aerial photography of Elmer Dyer. Edouart was an expert in rearscreen effects; his other works include *Dr. Cyclops* (1940), *A Connecticut Yankee in King Arthur's Court* (1949), *Vertigo* (1958), and *It's a Mad, Mad, Mad, Mad World* (1963). *See also* DR. CYCLOPS; EDOUART, FARCIOT.

Icebox Camera System

Also called simply "the Icebox," the Icebox camera system was invented by Douglas Trumbull to create special effects for *Close Encounters of the Third Kind* (1977). It featured one of the earliest computer-controlled cameras and was the first motion-control device ever used on location.

The Icebox could repeat the same camera pass as many times as necessary, using information recorded on tape. It would also automatically rewind the camera's film between each pass. This enabled Trumbull to build up many layers of special effects on the same piece of negative. He used the system again while making *Blade Runner* (1982) when, for example, he had to add lights and fireballs onto a shot of a miniature city, and again during miniature photography for *Star Trek: The Motion Picture* (1979). *See also* BLADE RUNNER; CLOSE ENCOUNTERS OF THE THIRD KIND; MOTION-CONTROL CAMERA SYSTEMS; STAR TREK MOVIES; TRUMBULL, DOUGLAS.

Independence Day

Released in 1996 by 20th Century Fox, *Independence Day* won an Academy Award for its visual effects. The movie had a budget of $70 million and used more than 250 special effects artists and 512 visual effects shots, including 340 digital composites, to create a total of 50 on-screen minutes of special effects depicting an attack on Earth by alien spacecraft. Its director, Roland Emmerich, and writer/producer, Dean Devlin, were also responsible for the movie *Stargate* (1994), another science-fiction movie that relied heavily on special effects.

To depict widespread destruction during an attack on Earth by aliens, *Independence Day* used 44 modelmakers to create hundreds of miniatures, including aircraft, spacecraft, vehicles, cityscapes, and landmarks such as the Statue of Liberty and the White House.

The White House was built in 1/12 scale and was 14 feet wide and 5 feet tall, and it included miniature furniture. To simulate its destruction by an alien spaceship, experts in pyrotechnics used primacord combined with other explosives, as well as 24 mortars to blast debris through the building, and the scene was filmed in one take with seven cameras set at different angles.

The alien mothership was built in several versions, either whole or in part, and in three different scales. The largest was a 35-foot fiberglass section that weighed approximately 3 tons. The alien fighter ships, called attackers, were also built in three scales; the largest was 63 feet in diameter. A miniature city, constructed to depict a firestorm sweeping through its streets, was turned on its side and filmed with the camera overhead, to make the flames appear to be moving laterally rather than vertically.

All miniature filming was done in front of bluescreens, and the resulting footage was then turned over to one of five special effects companies working on the movie. These companies were responsible for combining the more than 45,000 photographic and computer-generated elements needed to create

the finished product. *See also* BLUESCREEN PROCESS; COMPUTER GRAPHICS; MINIATURES AND MODELS; PYROTECHNICS; *STARGATE*.

Further Reading

Prokop, Tim. "Fireworks." *Cinefex 67,* September 1996.

Indiana Jones Movies

During the 1980s, filmmaker Steven Spielberg created a series of movies featuring a character named Indiana Jones. The first two movies, *Raiders of the Lost Ark* (1981) and *Indiana Jones and the Temple of Doom* (1984), won Academy Awards for their special effects. Together with the third movie, *Indiana Jones and the Last Crusade* (1989), they featured the work of Industrial Light & Magic (ILM), which developed many new special effects techniques for the films.

Raiders of the Lost Ark was ILM's third film after *Star Wars* (1977) and *The Empire Strikes Back* (1980). The special effects supervisor on *Raiders* was Richard Edlund, who later established his own special effects facility, the now-defunct Boss Film Studios; Dennis Muren took over for Edlund on *Indiana Jones and the Temple of Doom.*

Miniature spaceship in composite shot from *Independence Day* (1996). *20th Century Fox/Photofest.*

The effects for *Raiders of the Lost Ark* included elaborate stunts and full-sized sets, miniature photography, pyrotechnics both full-sized and miniature, matte paintings, and cel animation. The latter was originally chosen as the means for portraying all of the ghosts in the film's climactic scene. Test footage, however, proved cel animation to be unsatisfactory. Therefore Edlund decided to try something new, using a 7x7x4-foot cloud tank designed for the 1977 Spielberg movie *Close Encounters of the Third Kind*. Into the tank, which was filled with water, he put miniature armatures, which he then swirled about during filming to create ghost-like motions. For ghosts that were less formed, he filmed swirls of paint that had been injected into the tank. Additional ghosts were created using puppets or live actors in costume. But no matter what its origin, each ghost was photographed separately and then composited into the scene, which meant that many passes of a shot were required.

Another element of this scene involved live actors undergoing a horrific transformation. After the ghosts appear, some Nazi soldiers are hit with rays of light that set them on fire and make them melt. To create the ray hit, each actor wore a concealed harness that held a projector bulb to his chest. When the bulb was turned on, the light illuminated the actor's shirt. To create the illusion that a screaming actor's head was melting, special effects makeup artist Chris Walas made a life mold of the actor's face in that position. He then used the mold to make a sculpture, which subsequently acted as a guide for building a screaming face and head out of gelatin. After the gelatin head was set on fire, it was filmed with time-lapse photography, making it appear to melt. For a head that exploded rather than melted, the head was made of plaster and filled with primer cord, compressed air, and bags of movie blood; it was blown up with a shotgun blast. The fire that appeared in front of this head was filmed separately and matted into the shot later. A long shot of the fire sweeping up the dead Nazis were filmed with a miniature set approximately 4 feet wide and 5 feet deep, with soldiers only 4½ inches long. Matte paintings were used to enhance the scene.

Matte paintings were also used for a scene involving a Pan American "China Clipper" seaplane. A real seaplane was discovered in drydock in San Francisco but it could not be moved. Photographers therefore took pictures of the plane and combined them with matte paintings to make it look as though the craft was really on water at a pier. Another matte painting was used to depict a cliff for a scene of a Nazi car plunging to its doom. The car and flailing Nazis were miniatures filmed with stop-motion photography against a bluescreen.

Bluescreen work, miniatures, and matte paintings were important special effects tools for *Indiana Jones and the Temple of Doom* as well. For example, miniature mining cars were used to film an elaborate chase scene through tunnels. The motion-control cars sat on wide-gauge model railroad tracks in a detailed miniature set. The figures in the cars were animated by stop-motion, or by radio-control in cases where they could not be reached easily. Miniature stop-motion puppets were also used to film a scene of people falling from a damaged bridge into a river; in this case the puppets were photographed not on a miniature set but in front of a bluescreen and composited with the live-action background plates during postproduction. Another puppet, this one radio-controlled, was used for a scene in which someone is put in a cage and lowered into lava, which was actually a mixture of colored glycerin and water composited into the shot later.

Indiana Jones and the Last Crusade features the first digital composite of live-action footage used in a movie. The composite was made using shots of three motion-control puppets, each representing a different stage of aging for a character that turns into a corpse and decays into dust. The movie also relied on special effects techniques developed for the first two movies in the series: matte paintings, bluescreen shots, and miniatures that were accompanied by spectacular full-scale sets and stunts. *See also* BLUESCREEN PROCESS; *CLOSE ENCOUNTERS OF THE THIRD KIND;* COMPOSITING; EDLUND, RICHARD; INDUSTRIAL

LIGHT & MAGIC; MATTE PAINTINGS; SPIELBERG, STEVEN; TRUMBULL, DOUGLAS.

Further Reading
"Creating the Special Visual Effects for *Raiders*." http://www.smartlink.net/~deej7/sfx.htm, 1999.
Duncan, Jody. "20 Years of Industrial Light & Magic." *Cinefex 65,* 1996.
"Spirits of the Lost Ark: Photographic Effects in Raiders of the Lost Ark." http://www.smartlink.net/~deej3/sfx.htm, 1999.

Industrial Light & Magic

Industrial Light & Magic (ILM) is responsible for dozens of advances in the field of special effects, particularly related to computer graphics. The company has provided special effects for more than 140 movies and television programs, more than any other company currently in the business, and it has won 14 Academy Awards for Best Visual Effects and 12 Academy Awards for technical, scientific, and/or engineering achievement. A list of ILM's projects and awards given to the company and/or its employees by the Academy of Motion Picture Arts and Sciences follows.

ILM Projects by Year

(films that have won an Academy Award for special effects are preceded by an asterisk)

1977

Star Wars

1980

The Empire Strikes Back

1981

Dragonslayer

Raiders of the Lost Ark

Scientific and Engineering Award for the engineering of the *Empire* motion picture camera system; recipients: Richard Edlund and Industrial Light & Magic.

Scientific and Engineering Award for the concept and engineering of a beam-splitter optical composite motion picture printer; recipients: Richard Edlund and Industrial Light & Magic.

Technical Achievement Award for the development of a motion picture figure mover for animation photography; recipients: Dennis Muren and Stuart Ziff.

1982

The Dark Crystal

ET: The Extraterrestrial

Poltergeist

Star Trek II: The Wrath of Khan

1983

Return of the Jedi

Twice Upon a Time (animated feature)

1984

The Ewok Adventure(TV movie)

Indiana Jones and the Temple of Doom

The Neverending Story

Star Trek III: The Search for Spock

Starman

1985

Amazing Stories (TV program)

Back to the Future

---

*Cocoon
Enemy Mine
Explorers
The Goonies
Mishima
Out of Africa
Young Sherlock Holmes

1986
"Captain Eo" (a 3D adventure at Disneyland)
The Golden Child
Howard the Duck
Labyrinth
The Money Pit
Star Trek IV: The Voyage Home

1987
Batteries Not Included
Empire of the Sun
Harry and the Hendersons
Innerspace
"Star Tours" (an adventure ride at Disneyland)
Star Trek: The Next Generation (TV series)
The Witches of Eastwick
Technical Achievement Award for the development of a wire rig model support mechanism used to control the movements of miniatures; recipient: Tadeusz Krzanowski.

1988
Caddyshack II
Cocoon, The Return
The Last Temptation of Christ
Space Rangers (TV program)
"Star Trek Attraction" (at Universal Studios)
Who Framed Roger Rabbit
Willow

1989
The Abyss
The Accidental Tourist
Always
Back to the Future, Part 2
"Body Wars Simulator Ride" (at Epcot Center, Walt Disney World)
The Burbs
Field of Dreams
Ghostbusters II
Indiana Jones and the Last Crusade
Skin Deep
Star Trek 5: The Final Frontier

1990
Akira Kurosawa's Dreams

Back to the Future, Part 3
Die Hard 2: Die Harder
Flight of the Intruder
Ghost
The Godfather, Part III
The Hunt for Red October
Joe vs. the Volcano
Kindergarten Cop
Tummy Trouble (animated short)

1991
Backdraft
The Doors
Hook
Hudson Hawk
The Rocketeer
Space Race (Showscan movie)
Star Trek VI: The Undiscovered Country
Switch
*Terminator 2: Judgement Day

1992
Alien Encounter (Showscan)
*Death Becomes Her
Memoirs of an Invisible Man
Phoenix (TV movie)
The Public Eye
Young Indiana Jones (TV program)

Technical Achievement Award for the development and first implementation in feature motion pictures of the 'Morph' system for digital metamorphosis of high-resolution images; recipients: Douglas Smythe and the ILM Computer Graphics Department.

1993
Alive
Fire in the Sky
*Jurassic Park
Last Action Hero
Manhattan Murder Mystery
Meteorman
The Nutcracker
Rising Sun
Schindler's List

Scientific and Engineering Award for the concept and development of the digital motion picture retouching system for removing visible rigging and dirt/damage artifacts from original motion picture imagery; recipients: Douglas Smythe and George Joblove.

1994
Baby's Day Out
Disclosure
The Flintstones
*Forrest Gump

The Hudsucker Proxy
The Mask
Maverick
Radioland Murders
Star Trek: Generations

Scientific and Engineering Award for pioneering work in the field of film input scanning; recipient: Scott Squires.

Scientific and Engineering Award for development and work on a linear array CCD (Charge Coupled Device) film input scanning system; recipients: Lincoln Hu and Michael MacKenzie.

1995

The American President
Casper
Congo
The Indian in the Cupboard
In the Mouth of Madness
Jumanji
Sabrina
Village of the Damned

Technical Achievement Award for pioneering efforts in the creation of the ILM digital film compositing system; recipients: Douglas Smythe, Lincoln Hu, Douglas S. Kay, and Industrial Light & Magic

1996

Daylight
Dragonheart
Eraser
Mars Attacks!
Mission Impossible
101 Dalmations
Sleepers
Special Effects: Anything Can Happen
Star Trek: First Contact
The Trigger Effect
Twister

Scientific and Engineering Award for the development of the ViewPaint 3-D paint system that allows artists to apply color and texture details to computer-generated effects; recipients: John Schlag, Brian Knep, Zoran Kacic-Alesic, Thomas Williams.

Technical Achievement Award for the development of a system to create and control computer-generated fur and hair.

Technical Achievement Award for the creation and development of the Digital Input Device (DID), an encoded armature that allows stop-motion animators to contribute to computer animation; recipients: Phil Tippet, Brian Knep, Craig Hayes, Rick Sayre, and Thomas Williams.

1997

Amistad
Contact
Deconstructing Harry
Empire Strikes Back (Special Edition)
Flubber
The Lost World

Men in Black
Midnight in the Garden of Good and Evil
Return of the Jedi (Special Edition)
Spawn
Speed 2
Starship Troopers
Star Wars (Special Edition)
Titanic
1998
Bunkie and Booboo (Short Film)
Celebrity
Deep Impact
Deep Rising
Jack Frost
The Last Days
Meet Joe Black
Mercury Rising
Mighty Joe Young
Saving Private Ryan
Small Soldiers
Snake Eyes
1999
The Mummy
October Sky
The Phantom Menace
Wild Wild West
Other movies in production for 1999: *Bringing Out the Dead, Sleepy Hollow, Galaxy Quest,* and *Frankenstein.*

ILM currently employs more than 550 people, approximately 300 of which are in the computer graphics department, and the company has given many of the most prominent special effects experts their start in the business, including Ken Ralston and Dennis Muren. Currently located in San Rafael, California, ILM was established in a Van Nuys, California, warehouse in 1975 by George Lucas, who needed a facility that could create the special effects he wanted for his 1977 movie *Star Wars*. This production inspired major advances in the field of special effects, particularly in regard to miniature photography.

Many other ILM movies have also been responsible for new special effects techniques and computer software. For example, *Star Trek II: The Wrath of Khan* (1982) featured the first sequence of realistic images created entirely from computer graphics; *Young Sherlock Holmes* (1985) employed the first fully computer-generated character to appear in a feature film; *Indiana Jones and the Last Crusade* (1989) had the first all-digital composite in a live-action feature film; *The Abyss* (1989) featured the first digital water; *Die Hard 2: Die Harder* (1990) had the first digitally manipulated matte painting; *Terminator 2: Judgement Day* (1991) was the first production to use motion capture to create realistic human movements for a computer-generated character; *Death Becomes Her* (1992) employed the first software to make realistic computer-generated human skin; *The Flintstones* (1994) had the first realistic digital hair; *Dragonheart* (1996) inspired new facial animation software; *Waterworld* (1995) had the first realistic digital water; and *Jurassic Park* (1993) and *The Lost World* (1997) were responsible for several advances in 3-D computer animation and animatronics.

Today ILM continues to stress innovation in its work. One of ILM's most recent inventions was the Sabre system, so named in reference to the lightsaber swords used in *Star Wars* and its sequels. Sabre is a computer system that uses both proprietary and off-the-shelf software to deal with motion picture compositing and editing, allowing artists to manipulate both 2-D and 3-D images in a variety of ways. This system was used in *The Lost World* (1997) to make computer-generated dinosaurs appear to run through live-action grass.

ILM experts experimented with a way to digitally record handheld camera moves for the *Star Wars* movie, *The Phantom Menace* (1999). Some parts of *The Phantom Menace* were shot with high-definition digital tape instead of film, and the result was so satisfactory that George Lucas decided to shoot the movie's sequel entirely with digital tape. *The Phantom Menace* features many other technological advances as well. For example, the production used a new type of lamp to illuminate bluescreens, and suppressed "bluespill," whereby blue lighting reflects in shiny or marble floors, via a new software program. *See also* CASPER; *DEATH BECOMES HER*; DIGITAL EFFECTS; *DRAGONHEART; THE FLINTSTONES; HOOK; INDIANA JONES* MOVIES; *JUMANJI; JURASSIC PARK; THE LOST WORLD;* LUCAS, GEORGE; *MARS ATTACKS!; MEN IN BLACK;* SPECIAL EFFECTS HOUSES; *STARSHIP TROOPERS; STAR TREK* MOVIES; *STAR WARS* MOVIES; *TERMINATOR 2: JUDGEMENT DAY; TITANIC; TWISTER; WATERWORLD; YOUNG SHERLOCK HOLMES.*

Further Reading

Bouzereau, Laurent, and Jody Duncan. Star Wars: *The Making of Episode I,* The Phantom Menace. New York: Del Rey, 1999.

Smith, Thomas G. *Industrial Light & Magic: The Art of Special Effects.* New York: Ballantine Books, 1986.

Vaz, Mark Cotta, and Patricia Rose Duignan. *Industrial Light & Magic: Into the Digital Realm.* New York: Del Rey, 1996.

Innerspace

The 1987 movie *Innerspace* won an Academy Award for its visual effects, which were under the supervision of Dennis Muren at Industrial Light & Magic (ILM). The movie has an important plot point in common with a previous Academy Award–winning special effects movie, *Fantastic Voyage* (1966): a manned submarine is reduced in size and injected into the body of a man. But whereas *Fantastic Voyage* used huge sets to re-create the inside of the human body and place a full-sized submarine within it, *Innerspace* accomplished this with miniature sets and a miniature submarine. The submarine was controlled by puppeteers using rods that were later removed using the bluescreen process. This and other miniatures were typically filmed while in a water tank.

Innerspace also features the transformation of one man's face into another, which was accomplished through makeup and a computer program that could distort an image's shape. This program was a forerunner to digital morphing, a technique developed by ILM for the 1988 movie *Willow. See also* FANTASTIC VOYAGE; MINIATURES AND MODELS; MUREN, DENNIS; *WILLOW.*

Further Reading

Duncan, Jody. "20 Years of Industrial Light & Magic." *Cinefex* 65, March 1996.

Intolerance

The 1916 movie *Intolerance* featured unique cinematography as well as advances in the field of special effects. Filmed on several large sets, it told four separate stories: the fall of ancient Babylon, the St. Bartholomew's Day Massacre in 16th-century France, the crucifixion of Jesus Christ, and the condemnation of a modern man for a crime he did not commit. The movie's director, D.W. Griffith, used complicated editing techniques to weave these stories together, and he mixed shots with different perspectives—long shots, full shots, medium shots, and closeups—in individual scenes.

Griffith also developed a new type of dummy for the movie for a scene in which people were tossed off a high wall. Dummies had been used in place of stuntmen before, but in this case, Griffith determined that they looked fake because they were inanimate. He therefore decided to make them move as they fell, by creating a dummy with joints that bent in a realistic fashion. There were strings inside of the dummy to hold the joints in place; these strings were designed to break as the dummy fell, thereby releasing the joints so that the arms and legs suddenly began to flail.

Griffith also developed several new camera techniques during the filming of *Intolerance,* including the pan and the trucking shot. A pan is a sweeping view of a scene, while a trucking shot is an extreme long shot that moves into a closeup. To accomplish the latter, Griffith built the world's longest camera track. It moved the camera hundreds of feet, beginning far away from a set of the city of Babylon and concluding very close to it, and enabled the director to film the movement in a single shot without a break. *See also* ANGLE, CAMERA; COMPOSITING; GRIFFITH, D.W.; PROPS; STUNTS.

Further Reading

Brosnan, John. *Movie Magic*. New York: St. Martin's Press, 1974.

Fry, Ron, and Pamela Fourzon. *The Saga of Special Effects*. Englewood Cliffs, NJ: Prentice-Hall, 1977.

O'Conner, Jane. *Magic in the Movies*. Garden City, NY: Doubleday, 1980.

Invisibility

Making a man appear to be invisible while wearing visible clothes involves photographic tricks that were first developed by special effects expert John Fulton for the 1933 movie *The Invisible Man,* which won an Academy Award for its special effects. Fulton became such an expert in these techniques that he revived them for several subsequent movies, including *Topper* (1937), *The Invisible Man Returns* (1940), *Topper Returns* (1941), *The Invisible Woman* (1941), *The Invisible Agent* (1942), *The Invisible Man's Revenge* (1944), and *Wonder Man* (1945), which also won an Academy Award for its special effects.

For *The Invisible Man,* Fulton dressed a stuntman entirely in black velvet that did not reflect light, so that every portion of the man's

head and body were completely covered. Over this covering the stuntman wore another set of clothes in light colors, which were the garments meant to show on screen. The man was then placed on a set covered entirely in black velvet and filmed while moving about, being careful not to cover the light clothing with a black-covered hand.

The character of the Invisible Man, who inspired a variety of special effects related to the illusion of invisibility. *Photofest.*

During the filming of any scene, the negative records images in reverse, so that light elements become dark and dark elements become light; these densities are reversed during projection. Therefore after filming the "invisible" man, Fulton had a negative showing a black silhouette of clothing moving against a completely clear background. This black silhouette is called a travelling matte. Fulton then combined it with background scenes in a projection process that created a new negative. The travelling matte was now a moving "hole," which Fulton then filled with images of the moving clothing, again using a projection process. This yielded the final scene in which clothing appeared to move without a person inside.

However, some of the scenes where the invisible man is unwrapping bandages from his face required additional work. The stuntman again wore a black headpiece to film such scenes, with a breathing tube running up his pantleg and under his black suit, and on most occasions his eyes were covered. But sometimes he needed to see, and in these cases his eyes had to be removed from the film frame by frame with a brush and opaque dye. There were more than 64,000 frames of film in the 1933 version of *The Invisible Man* that required some form of brushwork, whether related to the stuntman's eyes or other reasons.

Moreover, because the stuntman often had to act without seeing, props that were supposedly being handled by the invisible man were typically manipulated on the set with wires rather than as part of the black filming process. For footprints that were to appear in the snow, Fulton used foot-shaped boards that were kept at ground level by pegs. When the pegs were removed suddenly via the pull of some wires, the board dropped, making it seem as though the invisible man had stepped there. A layer of plastic snow over the board enhanced the effect.

Fulton used optical rather than mechanical effects to make the invisible man reappear upon his death at the end of the movie. He accomplished this effect in-camera, rather with other equipment during postproduction. He started with a pillow and sheets that seemed indented with the weight of the invisible man's body; they were actually sculpted of plaster and paper mache. He filmed the bedding, then faded out and stopped the camera. Next he placed a real skeleton on the pillow and sheets. He wound the film back slightly, restarted the camera, faded in, filmed the skeleton, and faded out again. While the camera was stopped, he replaced the skeleton with a roughly sculpted dummy, then wound the film back slightly, restarted the camera, and faded in again. He did this several times, using a more refined dummy for each filming and ending with the real actor on the bed. The overlapping fade-ins and fade-outs created a double exposure known as a dissolve, which blends one filmed image into another.

For the movie *Topper,* Fulton advanced his pseudo-invisibility techniques still further, particularly in regard to the manipulation of props. For example, in one scene an invisible ghost writes with a pen. This pen was actually designed so it could stand on its tip, and it was animated using stop-motion photography, which meant that Fulton moved it in tiny increments while filming it in a start-and-stop fashion. Similarly, stop-motion photography and a mechanical device made it seem as though another ghost were drinking a beverage. The glass was manipulated with wires in order to move it to the ghost's invisible mouth, and the camera was stopped again and again to allow someone to siphon 'sips' of liquid from the glass.

When the ghost takes a shower, water appears to cascade around the place where her body would be; this was accomplished with air jets that forced the water to define her shape. Many other illusions in *Topper* were created with wires, which were concealed from viewers' eyes with the help of sets decorated with vertically striped wallpaper.

A 1992 version of *The Invisible Man* relied on the bluescreen process to create its invisibility effects. Actor Chevy Chase wore a bright blue hood and clothing under his costume. His image was then put into a computer that had software capable of erasing anything blue from the scene. This erasure created the modern version of a travelling matte, and its moving "holes" could be filled with digital images of the background scene. Computers can also erase the wires necessary to make objects appear to be moving by the hand of an invisible man, so that more elaborate movements could be performed on the set than in Fulton's time. *See also* BLUESCREEN PROCESS; DISSOLVE; FADES; FULTON, JOHN; MULTIPLE EXPOSURE; TRAVELLING MATTES.

Further Reading

Brosnan, John. *Movie Magic.* New York: St. Martin's Press, 1974.

Duncan, Jody. "20 Years of Industrial Light & Magic." *Cinefex 65,* March 1996.

McKenzie, Alan, and Ware, Derek. *Hollywood Tricks of the Trade.* New York: Gallery Books, 1986.

O'Conner, Jane. *Magic in the Movies.* Garden City, NY: Doubleday, 1980.

The Invisible Man See INVISIBILITY.

Iwerks, Ub (1901–1971)

Ub Iwerks began his film career as an animator but eventually became one of the pioneers of the special effects industry. He invented the multiplane camera, which allows animation cels to be separated from one another during filming to give the illusion of depth, and developed many techniques to improve animation. He also encouraged Disney Studios to use the newly developed sodium-vapor travelling matte system to combine live action with animation. This system used sodium-vapor lamps that cast a monochromatic yellow light against a yellow screen. When an object was filmed in front of the screen using a special camera, its image could later be separated from the yellow background and placed on an animated background instead.

Born in 1901, Iwerks worked as an artist before forming a partnership with coworker Walt Disney in 1919. Their business failed, but in 1923 Iwerks found himself working for Disney, who had formed a new animation business with his brother Roy, and drew the first version of Mickey Mouse. In 1930 Iwerks left the Walt Disney Studios to start his own animation company, making a series of *Flip, the Frog* cartoons. His business never did well, however, and he was soon back at Disney, where he worked on special effects as well as animation. His Disney special effects work includes *20,000 Leagues Under the Sea* (1954), *Davy Crockett, King of the Wild Frontier* (1955), *The Parent Trap* (1961), and *The Three Lives of Thomasina* (1964). He also occasionally supervised special effects on non-Disney films such as *The Birds* (1963).

Iwerks's multiplane camera was first used in a short cartoon, *The Old Mill* (1937), and then in the full-length animated feature *Snow White* (1937). He received Academy Awards in 1959 and 1965 for his technical contributions to the film industry and died in 1971 while still working for Disney. *See also* DISNEY, WALT; THE WALT DISNEY COMPANY.

J

Jennings, Gordon (c. 1900–1953)

Special effects expert Gordon Jennings was one of the pioneers of the film industry. He invented and improved camera, projection, and sound equipment, and he was the first person to make film titles move up the screen. He accomplished this by painting the words on glass sheets that he then slid upwards over painted backgrounds.

Jennings worked as an engineer before taking a job as an assistant cameraman in 1919. After creating title credits, he was hired as a special effects expert by director Cecil B. DeMille, who used Jenning's talents on such films as *Cleopatra* (1934), *Unconquered* (1947), and *Samson and Delilah* (1950). Jennings won an Academy Award for his special effects work on *Spawn of the North* (1938), *Reap the Wild Wind* (1942), *I Wanted Wings* (1941), *When Worlds Collide* (1951), and *War of the Worlds* (1953). He was head of the special effects department at Paramount Pictures from the 1930s until 1953, when he died unexpectedly. *See also* CLEOPATRA; DEMILLE, CECIL B.; PARAMOUNT PICTURES; *WAR OF THE WORLDS.*

Johnston, Joe

Joe Johnston did many of the storyboard sketches for the 1977 movie *Star Wars* and its sequels. His drawings were used to design the character of Yoda, the snow walkers, the Ewoks, and the speeder bikes.

Johnston also worked on *Raiders of the Lost Ark* (1981), for which he won a visual effects Academy Award, as well as *Poltergeist* (1982) and *Indiana Jones and the Temple of Doom* (1984). His first job after graduating from college was his artwork on *Star Wars,* and after making *Indiana Jones and the Temple of Doom* Johnston enrolled in the University of Southern California (USC) Film School to study filmmaking. He then became a director, making such special effects–laden movies as *Honey I Shrunk the Kids* (1989), *The Rocketeer* (1991), *Jumanji* (1995), and *October Sky* (1999). *See also* HONEY I BLEW UP THE KID; INDIANA JONES MOVIES; JUMANJI; STAR WARS MOVIES.

Further Reading

Smith, Thomas G. *Industrial Light & Magic: The Art of Special Effects.* New York: Ballantine Books, 1986.

Vaz, Mark Cotta, and Shinji Hata. *From* Star Wars *to* Indiana Jones: *The Best of the Lucasfilm Archives.* San Francisco: Chronicle Books, 1994.

Judge Dredd

The 1995 movie *Judge Dredd* advanced the field of miniature photography through the development of new equipment and techniques, particularly the smallest VistaVision motion-control camera ever before used in miniature photography. This camera made it possible to film in tiny spaces between miniature buildings.

The movie featured a highly detailed miniature representing a 22nd-century two-tiered city called Mega-City One. The model was built in different scales for different scenes. Most buildings had acrylic windows and fine features created with a new computer-controlled laser cutting system. Some surface details were glued-on pieces made of urethane resin cast from silicone molds.

Motion-control photography on the miniature set was carefully coordinated with motion-control photography of live actors performing in front of a greenscreen, so that these two elements could eventually be composited into one shot. Camera moves were planned in advance via computer so that matching camera angles would be used for the two types of filming. Similarly, for an aerial shot of the miniature city that incorporated a live-action shot of a full-sized swimming pool, a helicopter was equipped with an advanced laser tracking device to record the flight path over the pool. This allowed photographers to exactly match the helicopter's camera moves and angles while filming above the miniature city.

Filmmakers used another relatively new technique to create stand-ins for actors during a difficult chase scene with flying motorcycles: scanning the faces of actors and using them to create digital stuntmen. At the time, it was not possible to scan a full body as well, so they scanned 18-inch body sculptures instead and combined them with the digital heads. They also made computer-generated vehicles to go along with the figures.

Judge Dredd also featured new techniques for its robot, which was a mechanical effect rather than a digital or miniature one. The figure was first created as an 8-inch maquette, sculpted not of clay as was the usual practice but of metal and plasticene with carved details. This made it easier for designers to visualize a realistic robotic surface. The full-sized, 7-foot-tall machine was then built out of a metal armature covered with foam in certain areas to add thickness. The outer "skin" of the robot was fiberglass with electronic surface details. The robot's neck and waist turned on a hydraulically powered motion base developed specifically for *Judge*

Dredd. Its arms were also hydraulically powered. The robot stood on flat metal skis, but was not actually able to walk anywhere. Nonetheless, it took five people 20 weeks to build the robot.

Meanwhile set designers were constructing a full-sized version of Mega-City One at the Shepperton Studios in London. Mega-City One was conceived by Nigel Phelps, who also created Gotham City for *Batman* (1989), with the help of what was then a fairly new design tool, digital previsualization. Digital previsualization allowed Phelps to use computer software to plan his sets before a single building was built, whereas previously the only visualization tools were sketches, foam building mockups, and similar aides. By taking advantage of this and other new techniques, the makers of *Judge Dredd* were able to create a true state-of-the-art film. *See also* BATMAN MOVIES; BLUESCREEN PROCESS; MINIATURES AND MODELS; MOTION-CONTROL CAMERA SYSTEMS; PREVISUALIZATION; ROBOTICS; SCANNING.

Further Reading

Killick, Jane, with David Chute and Charles M. Lippincott. *The Making of* Judge Dredd. New York: Hyperion, 1995.

Vaz, Mark Cotta. "Dredd World." *Cinefex 62*, June 1995.

Jumanji

Released in 1995 by TriStar Pictures, *Jumanji* featured major advances in digital and mechanical effects. The movie was directed by special effects expert Joe Johnston, who won an Academy Award for his visual effects work on *Raiders of the Lost Ark* (1981).

The plot of *Jumanji* features a magic boardgame that presents its players with real dangers, including a large-animal stampede and some marauding monkeys. To create these creatures, special effects experts at Industrial Light & Magic (ILM) divided the duties among several teams. Some people worked on making animatronic figures or puppets of the animals, while others made computer-generated versions of them. Those working on digital images were also divided into teams. There were four groups: one to create an animal stampede and a climactic animal swirl into a vortex, one to work on a lion and a pelican, one to make monkeys, and one to do bats, mosquitoes, some quicksand, and all other computer-generated images.

Another team of modelmakers studied real-life animals and made clay models of them. These models were then laser-scanned into a computer as three-dimensional line drawings, which were subsequently over-drawn with skin and fur and animated to create various actions and facial expressions. In some cases, the digital artists drew the animals freehand, using live animals and non-digital sketches as a reference.

In either case, it took about seven weeks to finish each digital model, which included animation "chains" that told the computer how to move each body part, as well as detailed surface structures with realistic texture and color. The hair on the animals was particularly difficult to create. For this the artists relied on software developed for the movie *The Flintstones* (1994), which was the first to feature computer-graphics hair. For *Jumanji,* the artists customized the software to meet their needs, using it to adjust not only the color, length, thickness, density, and bend of hair strands but also their movements and tangling.

In addition to customizing hair software, the ILM staff also used their work on *Jumanji* to develop better 3-D paint tools and facial animation software. They also improved "flocking" software, which tells digital animals in a flock or herd how to behave in relation to one another. For example, they identified the starting and ending frames within the film where the animal stampede would take place and created a frame-by-frame path of movement for the group of animals, based on how long they calculated it would take real animals to move that distance. Variations of this path were then generated to give each of the more than 60 individual animals within the herd its own course. Once the animal images were placed on the paths, their "run cycles" were checked in relation to one another, and they were given a few unique, hand-animated movements to make them seem more realistic.

Hand animation was also used to make an individual elephant step on a live-action car. The real car was crushed using cable rigs and pneumatics, and the movements of the computer-generated elephant were timed accordingly. Similarly, for a scene in which monkeys destroy a kitchen, the animals were computer-generated, whereas most of the dishes and other objects were real. It would have been too time-consuming and in some cases more difficult to make these props as computer images.

Computer-generated animals also proved inadequate for closeups involving a lion, a pelican, a crocodile, and some bats and spiders. Therefore director Joe Johnson decided to use animatronic animals for these shots. Here again, studies of real-life animals helped the puppetmakers create realistic movements and appearances. The puppets' facial expressions were manipulated by radio control, and other mechanisms were operated using rods, cables, and/or hydraulics. However, in the case of the lion, puppetmaker Tom Woodruff Jr. decided to operate its front legs from inside the body. He looked at a small video monitor and wore headphones to see and hear what was going on in a scene.

Models were used to represent a house that was destroyed during an earthquake. Mechanical devices split the house in half as special effects experts triggered containers to spill debris over the scene. Mechanical devices were also used to animate full-sized objects, such as the car mentioned above, in the animal stampede.

Jumanji's extensive combination of live-action and computer-generated effects made the movie unique at the time it was produced. The film involved dozens of experts and includes 140 special-effects shots. *See also* ANIMATION, COMPUTER; COMPUTER GRAPHICS; *THE FLINTSTONES; INDIANA JONES* MOVIES*;* INDUSTRIAL LIGHT & MAGIC; PUPPETS; TRISTAR PICTURES.

Further Reading

Pourroy, Janine. "The Game Board Jungle." *Cinefex 64,* December 1995.

Robertson, Barbara. "*Jumanji's* Amazing Animals." *Computer Graphics World,* January 1996.

Jurassic Park

Winner of an Academy Award for Best Visual Effects, the 1993 movie *Jurassic Park* is responsible for several important advances in animatronics and computer graphics. Moreover, director Steven Spielberg's decision to use computer-generated images instead of stop-motion and Go-Motion model animation had a tremendous impact on the special effects industry, and today the latter two techniques have largely been abandoned.

Spielberg originally planned to use Go-Motion, and to this end he hired Go-Motion inventor Phil Tippett for his special effects team. Other team members included Dennis Muren, an expert in visual effects; Michael Lantieri, an expert in mechanical effects; and Stan Winston, an expert in puppets, creatures, and animatronics. Spielberg also had computer experts at Industrial Light & Magic working on the film, but initially they were told to create only one scene, a stampede of gallimimus dinosaurs. Computer animation was chosen for this scene because there were so many dinosaurs involved, and a computer would make it possible to duplicate a large number of animals easily. Moreover, these animals would primarily be seen in the distance, and only for a brief time. Spielberg, at this time, believed that computer graphics were not significantly realistic for any other type of shot.

But the animation supervisor, Steve Williams, disagreed with this assessment. To prove that computer graphics were capable of providing more shots for the film, he developed a computer-generated T-rex wireframe skeleton, animated it, and showed it to producer Kathleen Kennedy, who liked it enough to order a more detailed test version. Williams and others then began working to develop the software necessary to perfect the T-rex image.

Eventually, the animators came up with several innovations. First, they developed software that would enable them to rotate the 3-D wireframe during the painting process, whereas previously they had to paint each side of a figure as a 2-D image. This new technique yielded the first realistic computer-generated skin ever seen in a movie. The animators then developed new animation software that allowed them to connect one set of movements to another. For example, they could instruct the computer to make parts of a leg work together, so that the thigh would bulge every time the knee bent at a certain angle. Similarly, part of the belly could be jiggled with each footstep, and the animators could link the movements of an animated sphere inside the animal's chest to its outer skin, thereby making the dinosaur appear to breathe.

Ultimately the computer animators' efforts convinced Spielberg to use approximately 50 computer-generated shots in the film, and he reassigned Phil Tippett to work with computers rather than puppets. By this time, Tippett was an expert on dinosaur shapes and movements, and Spielberg knew that the Go-Motion expert would offer valuable expertise to the project. Tippett soon discovered, however, that it was not easy to go from puppetry to computer animation. His team of animators had great difficulty using a keyboard, and the movements they produced were not as realistic as their puppetry had been.

Tippett and associate Craig Hayes therefore invented a tool that allowed Tippett's team to animate a figure without using a keyboard or computer mouse. Called the Digital Input Device, this tool linked a stop-motion armature, which functioned like a puppet, to a computer. As the animator manipulated the armature, in frame-by-frame fashion just as with stop-motion animation, the computer recorded the movements and used them to drive a corresponding computer-generated wireframe figure. A "quick shade" feature allowed the animator to see how the wireframe would look as a solid shape.

With practice, Tippett's team became quite skilled with this system, and they were assigned 15 computer-generated shots to animate; these shots were related to a T-rex attack on two tourist cars and their occupants and two raptors hunting children in a kitchen. Meanwhile, digital effects experts at ILM were directed to work on 37 other computer-generated shots involving the gallimimus stampede, a battle between the T-rex and the raptors, and a group of browsing brachiosaurs, seen both during the day and at night. The latter included the only traditional matte painting in the film, used to represent the sky and vegetation. The daylight brachiosaur scene employed still photographs for its background, moving footage of a lake to provide water ripples, and images of live actors shot in front of a greenscreen.

Other dinosaur shots in the movie were created with Stan Winston's full-sized animatronic dinosaurs. As with the computer graphics, the animatronics too employed many new techniques. For example, while manufacturing the dinosaurs Winston decided not to make his molds with the customary silicone, because it would have involved too much material. Just one raptor, for example, would have required 50 gallons of silicone. Winston also could not use fiberglass, because that medium would not hold up under the dinosaur's large size. Therefore he relied on new aerospace molding compounds and reinforced his molds with aerospace tubing for strength.

However, Winston still used traditional foam latex for the animals' skins, because the material is easy to patch and repair, and he expected his dinosaurs to experience hard use. The only problem with the foam latex was that it readily soaked up water. This became a problem when the T-rex had to be filmed in a rainstorm, because the weight of the water threw off the creature's hydraulics mechanisms.

The hydraulic mechanisms were another major advance in animatronics technology. Winston hired a team of hydraulics engineers to design them, and the result was impressive. The T-rex had 57 different functions, with hydraulics driving every movement except the radio-controlled eyes. For scenes involving gross body movements, the figure was placed on a hydraulics motion base similar to ones used for flight simulators and amusement park rides such as Disneyland's "Star Tours" and Universal Studios "Back to

the Future" attractions. Such equipment had never before been used on a motion picture shoot.

Another unique feature of Winston's T-rex was the way its hydraulics were controlled. Instead of traditional hand devices, such as joysticks, it was manipulated via a telemetry device, which was a 1/4-scale aluminum duplicate of its armature. Movements on the armature were transmitted to a computer, which in turn immediately sent an electronic signal to produce corresponding movements on the full-sized T-rex. The computer could also record these movements for later playback, although it was rarely used for this purpose. Instead the puppeteers discovered that more realistic movements could be achieved by working the telemetry device spontaneously during filming. This was not done in cases in which the dinosaurs would be extremely close to actors, where it might be too dangerous to vary the preprogrammed routine.

The full-sized velociraptors had a unique feature as well. Although they were controlled with traditional cables and handheld controls, these cables had extensions attached, so that instead of the usual 20-foot length, the cables were 55 feet in length. The additional 25 feet were provided by aircraft cables attached to the animatronics cables. The raptors were also portrayed by men in mechanized suits, which had cables to provide arm and head movements. Only a few people were required to control the suit features, whereas 14 people were necessary to control the fully mechanized raptor. Therefore in scenes in which two raptors were together and neither was computer generated, one or both of the animals were always a man in a suit.

Jurassic Park effectively blended animatronics with computer graphics, so that it is often difficult to tell which type of effect was used for each shot. Generally, however, when the entire body of an animal was seen all at once, particularly if it was making any kind of rapid movement, the dinosaur was computer generated. If the animal was seen in part, especially if the bottom half was missing, or if it was lying still, it was an animatronic figure. The movie also included one of the first computer-generated humans, a lawyer eaten by a T-rex, but the software was not yet available to make him realistic enough for anything but a quick shot. *See also* ANIMATION, COMPUTER; ANIMATRONICS; ARMATURE; DIGITAL INPUT DEVICE; GO-MOTION; HYDRAULICS; *THE LOST WORLD*; MUREN, DENNIS; SPIELBERG, STEVEN; TELEMETRY DEVICE; TIPPETT, PHIL; WINSTON, STAN.

Further Reading

Duncan, Jody. "The Beauty in the Beasts." *Cinefex* 55, August 1993.

———. *The Making of* The Lost World. New York: Ballantine Books, 1997.

K

Keaton, Buster (1895–1966)

Joseph Francis Keaton, nicknamed Buster for his ability to survive falls, was an actor, director, producer, and screenwriter who choreographed and performed spectacular stunts in his films. For example, for a scene in *Sherlock, Jr.* (1924), Keaton runs along the top of a series of moving train cars and, upon reaching the last one, grabs the spout of a water tower, whereupon the spout is pulled down and a rush of water hits Keaton on the head, knocking him to the ground. While performing this stunt, Keaton accidentally fractured his neck, but continued working, although he would suffer from painful headaches for months

Born in 1895, Keaton started doing stuntwork at age three in his parents' comedy act. He performed with them across the country until he turned 21, whereupon he began acting without them in films. His first movie was a short entitled *The Butcher Boy* (1917), which starred Fatty Arbuckle. Keaton went on to make several more shorts with Arbuckle before landing his first starring role in 1921, in the short *The High Sign*. He made his first full-length feature, *The Saphead,* in 1921 as well. He also received financing to set up his own production studio, which eventually became known as Buster Keaton Productions, and consequently released several successful shorts and full-length films during the 1920s, including *One Week* (1920), *The Boat* (1921), *Cops* (1922), *The Navigator* (1924), *Go West* (1925), *The General* (1927), *College* (1927), and *Steamboat Bill* (1928).

Some of Keaton's movies also featured unusual camera tricks, for example, in his short film *The Playhouse* (1921), Keaton walks into a theater filled with people who look exactly like him. He accomplished this using blank-faced dummies, stop-motion photography, and multiple exposures; in some instances he placed himself physically in front of each dummy as the camera panned down a row with filming stops in between each figure, while in others he used multiple exposures to place his image on each blank face.

In 1928 Keaton began working for MGM, where he continued to make movies but lost a great deal of control over his work. His career declined until the late 1940s, when he started doing live performances in Paris, France. These performances were extremely popular and revived interest in his film work. As a result, Keaton was offered small parts in movies, television programs, and commercials. He was enjoying renewed public acclaim when he died in 1966. *See also* STUNTS.

Further Reading

Dardis, Tom. *Keaton: The Man Who Wouldn't Lie Down.* New York: Scribner, 1979.

Moews, Daniel. *Keaton: The Silent Features Close Up.* Berkeley: University of California Press, 1977.

Keystone Kops

The Keystone Kops was a group of silent-film actors who performed stunts and car chases while portraying policemen. Named for their production company, Keystone, they were created by director Mack Sennett, who made hundreds of comedies for Keystone during the early 1900s. Sennett was known as the "king of slapstick," and his Kops represented the height of incompetent silliness. They often crashed through walls, fell off moving vehicles, and got hit with flying custard pies. To enhance this hilarity, Sennett invented fast-motion photography, whereby he filmed an event at half-speed and then played it back at normal speed, which created the illusion that the event was taking place at a much faster pace. *See also* FILMING SPEED; STUNTS.

Kinetoscope

Thomas A. Edison and W.K.L. Dickson invented the Kinetoscope in 1889. At first it was simply a device that played recorded sound, but in 1891 it became a viewing device as well, cranking filmstrips past a peephole that allowed viewers to watch movies 20 seconds to one minute long. The Kinetoscope was extremely popular and typically appeared at such public places as fairs, amusement parks, and dedicated Kinetoscope parlors.

Kinetoscope movies were filmed with one of the first movie cameras, the Kinetograph. Patented in 1891, the Kinetograph was operated with a hand crank that moved film past its lens at a speed of approximately 40 frames per second. Its early movies were of simple scenes, such as a man tipping his hat, but later Edison and Dickson created more elaborate films.

For example, in 1893 the most popular Kinetograph was *The Execution of Mary Queen of Scots,* which used the earliest type of special effect. To simulate the queen's beheading, a real actress was filmed putting her head in the chopping block. Then the filming was stopped, and a dummy was put in the actress's place for the rest of the scene.

Edison and Dickson created this and many other films in the world's first movie studio, a tiny darkened room that Edison named the

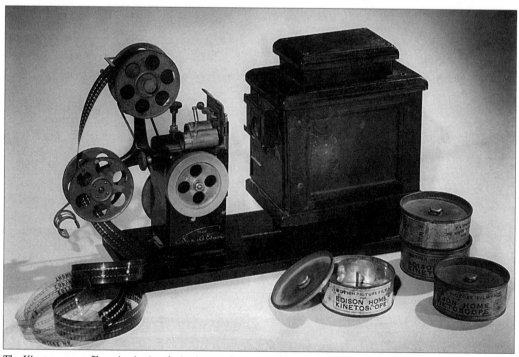

The Kinetoscope, a filmstrip viewing device invented in 1889. *Corbis/Bettmann.*

Black Maria after the common term for police wagons. However, the popularity of the Kinetoscope faded in the late 1890s after projecting devices were invented and audiences could view movies in theaters. *See also* EDISON, THOMAS A.

Further Reading

Kawin, Bruce F. *How Movies Work.* Berkeley: University of California Press, 1992.

Robertson, Joseph F. *The Magic of Film Editing.* Blue Ridge Summit, PA: Tab Books, 1983.

King Kong

There are two versions of *King Kong,* one made in 1933 and the other in 1976; both movies have significance in the field of special effects. The first version is considered a classic example of stop-motion animation, which was created by pioneer animator Willis O'Brien. The second version won a Special Achievement Academy Award for its special effects, which were provided by mechanical effects expert Glen Robinson and creature effects expert Rick Baker.

For the 1933 *King Kong,* O'Brien used the models of Marcel Delgado to depict a gorilla 50 feet tall. The six gorilla miniatures made for the film were each 18 inches tall, and there was an 18-foot-tall model of Kong's head, shoulders, and chest that moved via compressed air and levers operated by three men stationed inside. In addition, there was a Kong hand for a scene in which he tries to grab a man from a cave.

The 1933 *King Kong* used a combination of miniature and full-sized sets. The cave, for example, was full-sized, as was the walled jungle community, whereas the jungle itself was a miniature. In many cases, O'Brien placed his stop-motion models in front of paintings done on glass. The cityscape background in the scene of Kong on the Empire State Building was a 12-foot-wide painting, placed directly on the miniature set. Backgrounds for live action were typically rear-screen projection, using a new kind of screen that was larger and sturdier than previous versions. Various elements of each scene were put together using travelling mattes and an optical printer. For scenes in which Kong is

destroying an elevated train, fleeing people were superimposed onto a miniature set with buildings in 3/4 scale.

The 1976 version of *King Kong* used no miniature sets or stop-motion model animation, preferring to depict Kong using a full-scale, 40-foot-tall mechanical ape constructed out of aluminum framing, electrical wiring, hydraulic tubing, and Argentinean horsehair. The final product required 20 operators and often malfunctioned; therefore a costumed actor was substituted for the mechanical ape about 90 percent of the time.

The costume was actually worn by its creator, Rick Baker, who disagreed with the filmmakers over its design. Baker objected to the fact that the suit was made out of black bearskins: first, he hadn't wanted the animals killed, and, second, the bearskins added too much weight to the costume. The suit weighed approximately 40 pounds and was extremely hot and inflexible, so much so that Baker sometimes sweated off 5 pounds in a day of filming. Baker usually wore the suit for only four hours at a time, after taking 30 minutes to put it on, apply makeup around his eyes, and put in contact lenses.

Beneath the bearskins, the body of the suit was padded with urethane foam sheet rubber covered with polyfoam. The face, chest, and hands were made out of foam latex. The suit had arm and hand extensions, because a gorilla's arms and hands are longer than a man's, and, consequently, Baker could not pick up anything with the fingers. A scene of Kong holding a miniature of an actress had to be accomplished by attaching the figure to the hand. Baker also could not breathe through the suit's mask, and had to depend on a breathing tube beneath the costume.

The animal's facial expressions were controlled by 11 external cables that emerged from the back of the maks, ran down the inside of the suit, and exited at Baker's feet. Sometimes these cables would become caught on something during a scene, tripping Baker. He had a great deal of difficulty working with the miniature helicopters that were attacking Kong. Even more demanding was a scene in which he had to perform in water. The foam latex of the suit absorbed the water, making it extremely heavy. Despite these problems the resulting scenes with King Kong worked well enough that it garnered the special effects award. *See also* BAKER, RICK; DELGADO, MARCEL; O'BRIEN, WILLIS; ROBINSON, GLEN; STOP-MOTION MODEL ANIMATION.

Further Reading

Fry, Ron, and Pamela Fourzon. *The Saga of Special Effects.* Englewood Cliffs, NJ: Prentice-Hall, 1997.

McKenzie, Alan, and Derek Ware. *Hollywood Tricks of the Trade.* New York: Gallery Books, 1986.

O'Conner, Jane. *Magic in the Movies.* Garden City, NY: Doubleday, 1980.

Knoll, John

John Knoll has been the visual effects supervisor for several important special effects movies, including *Star Trek: Generations* (1994), *Star Trek: First Contact* (1996), *Star Wars* (Special Edition) (1997), and the 1999 *Star Wars* prequel *The Phantom Menace*, and an associate visual effects supervisor on such films as *The Hunt for Red October* (1990) and *Hook* (1991). Previously Knoll was a motion-control camera operator for movies like *Star Trek IV: The Voyage Home* (1986), *Innerspace* (1987), and *Willow* (1988), as well as for the television show *Star Trek: The Next Generation* (1987). He was also the computer graphics project designer for *The Abyss* (1989), which featured advances in the field of digital effects. An expert in computer programming, Knoll was one of the inventors of a software program called Photoshop, a high-end image processing program for Macintosh computers that enables the user to enhance and edit images.

Koenekamp, Hans (1891–1992)

Hans Koenekamp was a cameraman who specialized in trick photography in the early 20th century. He developed and patented a system for filming live action in front of moving images, enabling a camera's shutter to be carefully synchronized with the rearscreen projection. This system was later refined by special effects expert Farciot Eduoart.

Born in 1891, Koenekamp began his film career as a projectionist in the early 1920s. At that time, projectors were powered by hand cranks, as were movie cameras. When director Mack Sennett learned that Koenekamp was one of the best hand-crankers in the business, he offered the projectionist a job as a cameraman. Koenekamp's films include *Noah's Ark* (1929), *A Midsummer's Night's Dream* (1935), and *Air Force* (1943). Of these, *Noah's Ark* involved the largest number of special effects and contained some of the most complicated in-camera matte shots in early film history.

Koenekamp died in 1992. By this time his son Fred, who was born in 1922, had become a respected cinematographer himself, having shared an Academy Award for his photography on *Towering Inferno* (1974). *See also* EDUOART, FARCIOT; *NOAH'S ARK*; SENNETT, MACK; *THE TOWERING INFERNO*.

Korda, Sir Alexander (1893–1956)

During the 1930s, producer-director Sir Alexander Korda encouraged the use of elaborate special effects in British films. Many of his movies, such as *The Ghost Goes West* (1935), *The Thief of Bagdad* (1940), *The Man Who Could Work Miracles* (1935), and *Things to Come* (1936), featured trick photography.

Born in Hungary in 1893, Korda worked as a journalist before becoming a publicist and translator in the film industry. He co-directed two films, *The Duped Journalist* and *Tutyu and Totyo*, in 1914. Three years later he was running his own production company. Korda also worked on a government film commission. When the Hungarian government changed hands, Korda moved to Austria, then Germany, the United States, France, and finally England. Korda made films in each of these countries, but his most successful works were those made in London. His 1933 movie *The Private Life of Henry VIII* was one of the most popular international films of the time. The British government knighted Korda in 1942 for his contributions to the movie industry, and he died in 1956. *See also THE THIEF OF BAGDAD*.

Kubrick, Stanley (1928–1999)

Director Stanley Kubrick made major contributions to the special effects industry while filming his 1968 movie *2001: A Space Odyssey*. His work won an Academy Award and became the industry standard for science fiction-related special effects.

Born in 1928, Kubrick became a professional still photographer for *Look* magazine when he was only 17 years old. While photographing a boxer he decided that the man would make a good subject for a documentary, and subsequently he made his first film, *Day of the Fight* (1951). The film was bought by RKO Pictures and showed as part of an RKO series, "This is America," in a New York theater.

Because of this success, Kubrick quit his job at *Look* to concentrate on making films. He made several more documentaries before switching to feature films, beginning with *Fear and Desire* (1953). His first major Hollywood film was *Spartacus* (1960). Additional major projects soon followed, including *Lolita* (1962), *Dr. Strangelove* (1964), *A Clockwork Orange* (1971), and *The Shining* (1980). In 1990, Kubrick joined several other directors, including Francis Ford Coppola, Steven Spielberg, and George Lucas, in forming the Film Foundation, an organization dedicated to promoting film preservation and restoration. Kubrick was awarded the highest honor of the Director's Guild of America, the D.W. Griffith Award, in 1997 for his contributions to his field. He died unexpectedly in 1999 while filming *Eyes Wide Shut*. *See also* COPPOLA, FRANCIS FORD; GRIFFITH, D.W.; LUCAS, GEORGE; SPIELBERG, STEVEN; *2001: A SPACE ODYSSEY*.

Further Reading

Agel, Jerome, ed. *The Making of Kubrick's* 2001. New York: Signet, 1968.

L

Landscapes *See* BACKGROUND PLATE; MATTE PAINTINGS; PROPS.

Lang, Fritz (1890–1976)

Austrian director Fritz Lang made dozens of movies in his career, many of which relied heavily on both mechanical and optical special effects. For example, *Siegfried,* which was the first film in his two-part work *Die Nibelungen* (1924), featured a 60-foot mechanical dragon operated by four men. In *Metropolis* (1927), Lang employed such photographic techniques as dissolves and multiple exposures, both of which were considered advanced at that time. Both *Siegfried* and *Metropolis* also used realistic miniatures filmed and then combined with live-action scenes through two then-revolutionary techniques, travelling mattes and the Shuftan process.

Lang was born in Vienna, Austria, in 1890. He studied architecture and art before serving in the Austrian army in World War I. Wounded in action, he was sent to a Vienna hospital, where he started writing and selling screenplays. After his release from the hospital he was offered a job as a story editor and writer for a German production company. Lang directed his first film there in 1919, and he remained in Germany until 1933, when the government banned one of his films for being anti-Nazi. Fearing for his safety, Lang went to France, directed a film there, and then moved to Hollywood, where he made more than 20 films, including another anti-Nazi movie, *Hangmen Also Die* (1943). In 1957 Lang returned to Germany to direct several more films, the last in 1960, then retired to Southern California. He died in 1976. *See also* METROPOLIS; SHUFTAN, EUGENE; TRAVELLING MATTE.

Lantieri, Michael

Michael Lantieri is one of the leading special effects artists in the film industry. He won an Academy Award for his work on *Jurassic Park* (1993), for which he supervised on-set mechanical effects, and was in charge of special dinosaur effects for its sequel, *The Lost World* (1997). As the supervisor of physical effects for *Hook* (1991), he oversaw construction of an elaborate hydraulic rig to rock and tilt a pirate ship set. For *Mousehunt* (1997) he devised a series of mechanical effects, including a bathtub that appeared to slide across ice and fall into a pond. The tub was actually propelled with a cable and winch system and "fell" via a sinking platform. Several other *Mousehunt* sets were rigged to break apart on cue. Lantieri's other movies include *Indiana Jones and the Temple of Doom* (1984), *Back to the Future II* (1989), *Back to the Future III* (1990), *Who Framed Roger Rabbit?* (1988), *Hook* (1991), *The Flintstones* (1994), *Casper* (1995), *Star Trek IV* (1986), *Death Becomes Her* (1992), *Bram Stoker's Dracula* (1992), *Mars Attacks!* (1996), and

Congo (1995). *See also* BACK TO THE FUTURE MOVIES; *CASPER; CONGO; DEATH BECOMES HER; THE FLINTSTONES; HOOK; INDIANA JONES* MOVIES; *MARS ATTACKS!; MOUSE HUNT; STAR TREK* MOVIES; *WHO FRAMED ROGER RABBIT?*

Latex, Foam

Foam latex is a material used to make models, creatures, makeup appliances, and many other effects-related objects. A type of rubber, foam latex is poured into molds and then baked, whereupon it becomes a solid that is lightweight and flexible yet still retains its shape.

One example of latex work appeared in the movie *The Creature From The Black Lagoon* (1954). To create the body suit for the title character, makeup artist Jack Kevan first made a plaster of paris body cast of the actor playing the monster. The cast was then painted inside with liquid latex, over which was poured a liquid foam latex solution. The cast was then baked for 10 hours in an oven created specifically for the movie's makeup work. Once this basic foam latex suit was finished, it was enhanced with latex fish scales stuck on with special glue.

A more recent example of latex work was for the 1997 movie *The Relic*. To create the movie's monster, the actor had to don a bodysuit and climb onto a special rig. He was then wrapped in plaster bandages, which required several hours to dry. The resulting body cast was slit, carefully removed and repaired, and used to create a fiberglass form. Wire was placed over the fiberglass, and clay was sculpted over the wire. Once the clay hardened, it was used to make another mold for foam latex skin pieces. These pieces were then detailed and applied back over the mold that formed the core of the creature, which also incorporated complex mechanisms.

Another example of foam latex being used with mechanisms was a gorilla head made for the 1998 version of *Mighty Joe Young*. This head had a mechanical device which enabled it to roar. However, because foam latex has a tendency to tear if it is moved too far from its original molded position, the roaring mechanism had to be carefully designed to distribute the stretching evenly over the foam latex, otherwise the mouth would have torn at its corners.

In addition to its fragility, foam latex can also absorb a tremendous amount of water, whereupon it becomes heavy. This was the case with the animatronics Tyrannosaurus rex of *Jurassic Park* (1993), whose skin soaked up so much liquid during a rain shoot that its mechanisms would not work properly. Consequently animatronics designer Stan Winston learned to waterproof his latex skins with a waterproofing silicone coating before painting them.

Such problems working with latex have led special effects experts to experiment with other materials. For the movie *Congo* (1995), for example, the bodies of ape costumes were made out of a new kind of silicone that was extremely soft and yet still able to retain its shape. *See also* JURASSIC PARK; THE LOST WORLD; MAKEUP; MINIATURES AND MODELS.

LaVigne, Emile (1899–1991)

Emile LaVigne was the head of the makeup department at United Artists from 1958 to 1966, during which he supervised makeup on dozens of films. His most famous work was for *Some Like It Hot* (1959), which required him to make actors Tony Curtis and Jack Lemmon look like women, and *The Invasion of the Body Snatchers* (1956), which required him to make life-sized casts of several actors. LaVigne's makeup career began at MGM in the late 1930s, when he became an assistant to Jack Dawn, then head of the makeup department. Under Dawn, LaVigne helped develop the makeup for *The Wizard of Oz*. In later years he worked as a freelance makeup artist on such films as *The Towering Inferno* (1974). *See also* DAWN, JACK, AND ROB DAWN; *THE TOWERING INFERNO; THE WIZARD OF OZ*.

Lee, Bruce (1940–1973)

Bruce Lee was an actor known for performing his own stunts featuring advanced martial arts. Lee's films typically include elaborate hand-to-hand fight scenes with flying kicks, flips, and similar moves. Born in 1940, Lee grew up in Hong Kong, where he appeared in films as a youngster under the name Li Siu Lung. Upon reaching adulthood, Lee went to the United States to attend the University of Washington as a philosophy student, and after graduation he began acting in the Hollywood films and television shows such as *The Green Hornet.* During the early 1970s, Lee returned to Hong Kong to star in action films. In 1973 Lee died unexpectedly at age 32 of brain edema. Ironically, his son Brandon (1965–1993) also died unexpectedly; he was accidentally shot while filming *The Crow* (1994).

Lee, Danny

Danny Lee received an Academy Award for his special effects work on the 1971 Disney movie *Bedknobs and Broomsticks.* He was in charge of mechanical effects at Disney throughout the 1970s, providing effects for such films as *The Love Bug* (1969), *Snowball Express* (1972), *Escape to Witch Mountain* (1975), *The Shaggy D.A.* (1976), and *The Black Hole* (1979). His first film was *Swiss Family Robinson* (1960); his last film was *Last Flight of Noah's Ark* (1980). He also served as a consultant on the 1981 movie *Dragonslayer.*

In addition to his work for Disney, Lee contributed to *It's a Mad, Mad, Mad, Mad World* (1963), which also featured the effects of rearscreen projection expert Farciot Edouart. The movie required Lee to stage several complicated special effects. For example, a real airplane rather than a model crashed through a billboard made of a thin Styrofoam-backed board. The same plane later crashed into a restaurant window, which was made of breakaway glass, with a cable attached to the plane's tail to keep it from going too far into the restaurant. In another scene, a gas station destroyed by an irate truck driver was built in sections and attached to wires, so that Lee could trigger its demolition bit by bit.

Lee also contributed special effects to one serious film, *Bonnie and Clyde* (1968). At the end of the movie, the title characters are killed in a hail of bullets. Lee rigged the tiny explosions that represented each bullet hit and detonated them by remote control at key moments. Some of these chemical explosives were sewn into the actors' clothes with a metal backing to protect the actors' skin, while others were placed into holes made in a car body and then concealed with paint. *See also* THE WALT DISNEY COMPANY; EDOUART, FARCIOT; MECHANICAL EFFECTS.

Actor Bruce Lee (right), an expert in martial arts who performed his own stunts. *Photofest.*

Lloyd, Harold (1893–1971)

During the 1910s and 1920s, silent-film actor Harold Lloyd performed his own stunts in dozens of comedies, including *Haunted Spooks* (1920) and *Safety Last* (1923). While filming the former, an explosion blew off one of his fingers and the thumb of his right hand. Nonetheless, he continually refused to use stunt doubles in his movies, and kept performing even after he experienced more serious injuries. He was particularly noted for his spectacular falls, although the most famous image of Lloyd is of him dangling from the hands of a tower clock in *Safety Last*.

Silent-film actor Harold Lloyd performing a stunt in *Safety Last* (1923). *Photofest.*

Born in 1893, Lloyd's first acting jobs were in the theater. In 1912 he began working as a movie extra, first for the Edison Company and then for Universal Studios, where he met actor Hal Roach. Roach later formed his own production company and hired Lloyd as an actor. Lloyd worked for Roach until 1923, when he formed his own production company. As a producer, Lloyd was the first American filmmaker to regularly release mov-

ies longer than two reels of film. This practice began after he filmed four reels of material for *Sailor Made Man* (1921) and decided that he didn't want to leave anything out.

Lloyd's popularity as an actor waned with the advent of sound, but he continued to make movies until 1947. In 1962 he edited scenes of his old films together to make *Harold Lloyd's World of Comedy,* and this film renewed interest in his work. He made another compilation in 1963, *The Funny Side of Life.* Lloyd died in 1971. *See also* STUNTS.

Logan's Run

Released in 1976 by MGM, *Logan's Run* won an Academy Award for its special effects. The movie featured the work of three prominent special effects experts: Glen Robinson for mechanical effects, L.B. Abbott for miniatures, and Linwood Dunn for optical effects.

Set in the future, the story required many large sets, including an amphitheater housing a carousel-like device. While on this device, characters appeared to rise into the air, where they were incinerated with a force field. The force field was added with an optical printer during postproduction, but the rest of the scene was created mechanically. The carousel was a 40-foot turntable; the actors were raised by wires attached to a corresponding turntable 50 feet above the first on the three-story set. For safety's sake, however, only a few actors were on the wires at a time. Their images were composited together later to make it appear as though the carousel was crowded.

Another full-sized set was a 225-foot tunnel, which required a connection between two soundstages. Full-sized vehicles were made to travel through this tunnel, but 60 miniature vehicles and some plastic tubing were also used to create tunnel scenes. Other miniatures included an exterior view of a futuristic domed city, which was built in 1/400 scale, and a view of the city from within its dome, which was built in 1/48. Landmarks such as the Washington Monument, Lincoln Memorial, and Capitol Building in Washington, D.C., were not miniatures but traditional matte paintings, created from photographs and composited with live action via an optical printer. Filmmakers also used real commercial buildings as settings, most of which were in the Dallas/Fort Worth, Texas, area.

Props were another integral part of the movie's special effects. Of these, the most important was a "disintegrator" ray gun. Its ray was actually an acetylene gas with a greenish flame. After someone had been "shot" by one of these guns, the camera was stopped and the actor replaced with a Styrofoam dummy. The camera was then restarted, and the dummy sprayed from off camera with a mixture of chemicals that made it dissolve. *See also* ABBOTT, L.B.; DUNN, LINWOOD; ROBINSON, GLEN.

The Longest Day

The 1962 movie *The Longest Day* won an Academy Award for its special effects, as well as for its cinematography. The movie re-created D-Day, an event during World War II, and included demanding stuntwork and pyrotechnics. *The Longest Day* also incorporated historic newsreel and documentary footage, expertly blending it with footage filmed for the movie.

Lost in Space

The 1998 movie *Lost in Space* featured the first major digital effects created by Jim Henson's Creature Shop. Because this facility is one of the leading providers of puppets and animatronic figures, its decision in 1995 to develop computer-generated characters is particularly significant to the field of special effects.

Moreover, the character the Creature Shop created for *Lost in Space,* a monkey-like alien, was noted for its complexity. The animal had more than 300 basic facial movements, which could be combined to create even more expressions. In addition, its wireframe shape was made of 209,000 polygons, and its skin was layered with nine different texture maps, ranging from nearly transparent to extremely dense and bumpy.

The Creature Shop also provided two robots for the film, but these were mechanical rather than computer-generated effects. However, their development marks the first time that the Creature Shop had designed a character entirely on a computer rather than with sketches or experimental prototypes. The first robot was 9 feet tall and weighed 1½ tons, while the second was only 6 feet tall and weighed 3/4 tons. Both had an aluminum alloy structure with a fiberglass exterior, and both could move independently on a base capable of reaching 12 mph, although sometimes the robots were placed on tracks. The robot's laser blasts were computer-generated, but all other working parts on the robot functioned as seen in the film.

To make the robot move, animatronics experts employed a hydraulics system and some highly advanced computer technology. A person wearing a bodysuit covered with sensors performed the desired movements, which were recorded and input into a computer. The movements were then sped up, slowed down, or adjusted in other ways to perfect the performance, at which point they were used to drive the robot's actions. This system created a highly realistic performance, particularly for the first robot, which needed to fight some alien spiders. These spiders were animated through conventional 3-D computer animation techniques, but the splatters that they produced when blown up were a mechanical effect, created using paint.

Another computer-generated spider in the movie was more complicated to create. Nine feet tall, its face had to look like the face of the human from which it developed as part of the plot. Therefore the filmmakers decided to use the actor's own face as a model for the computer-generated figure. In addition, after attaching 30–40 motion-capture sensors to the actor's face, they had him perform the scene himself and tracked his movements with six motion-capture cameras. The information they gathered regarding his movements was then digitized and used to animate the computer-generated face.

Lost in Space involved an incredibly large amount of digital work. There were more than 750 digital composites, with a total of 770 shots involving some form of special effects work. Approximately 300 of these shots involved miniatures provided by more than 76 modelmakers. These miniatures included several spacecraft, most notably the *Proteus* and the *Jupiter 2*.

The *Proteus* was 29 feet long and detailed with etched brass sheets. The *Jupiter 2* was made in several versions, including a "hero" version 6 feet across and a 12-foot version for a crash landing. Because it was so large, the *Jupiter 2* was made primarily of two lightweight substances, carbon fiber and kevlar. Wires and a cable attached to the ship for a crash scene were removed digitally. The crash also required a miniature planet landscape that was 150 feet wide and 100 feet deep, constructed with a larger scale in the foreground than in the background to give it the illusion of greater depth. Most of the snow on the landscape was salt, just as was used to create an arctic miniature for *The X-Files* (1998), and the remainder was powdered paper.

All miniature photography in the movie was done in front of a greenscreen and digitally composited with live-action elements during postproduction. Some live action was also shot in front of a greenscreen. For example, an actor in a fighter craft was filmed in a pilot's seat in front of a greenscreen, and his image was later composited into a miniature of the craft. The bubble over the craft was created with computer graphics. In fact, most of the miniatures in the movie were enhanced by computer graphics. For example, for a shot of the fighter craft flying over a city, the city miniature's boundaries were extended digitally with computer-generated buildings. Rain, fog, flying cars, road traffic, and several other elements were also computer graphics.

Interestingly, the city shot was designed to pay homage to a similar shot in the 1982 movie *Blade Runner*, which was made before computer graphics were prevalent. *Blade Runner* had to extend its miniature city with 2-D matte paintings, and rain and other elements were added via an optical printer.

In addition to Jim Henson's Creature Shop, more than 10 London special effects companies worked on *Lost in Space*, including The Film Factory, The Computer Film Company, Men in White Coats, and The Magic Camera Company, whose sister company The Magic Model Company provided the miniatures. All live action was shot in London as well. The movie had a budget of $70 million and was released by New Line Cinema. *See also* ANIMATION, COMPUTER; ANIMATRONICS; *BLADE RUNNER;* HENSON, JIM; MINIATURES AND MODELS; MOTION-CONTROL CAMERA SYSTEMS; *THE X-FILES*.

Further Reading

Cadigan, Pat. *The Making of* Lost in Space. New York: HarperPrism, 1998.
Simak, Steven A. "*Lost in Space:* The Movie Camp Revamped." *Digital World,* April 1998.
Vaz, Mark Cotta. "*Lost in Space:* Lost in London." *Cinefex 74,* July 1998.

The Lost World

Three dinosaur movies have been made with the title *The Lost World,* one in 1925, one in 1960, and another in 1997. The 1925 and 1997 versions both employed special effects techniques that were advanced for their time. The former inspired the development of stop-motion model animation, while the latter furthered animatronics and computer-generated animation.

Stop-motion model dinosaur from the 1925 version of *The Lost World. Photofest.*

Filmmaker Willis O'Brien created stop-motion animation specifically for the 1925 *The Lost World*. This special effects technique is a simple but painstaking process. The animator positions a model, photographs it, stops the camera, and moves the model a slight increment before photographing it again, whereupon the cycle repeats, frame by frame. But of course, only a pliable model can be used for stop-motion model animation.

O'Brien worked with modelmaker Marcel Delgado for two years to develop the models for *The Lost World*. There were 50 in all, averaging 18 inches long and representing 12 different types of dinosaurs. Each had an armature with ball-and-socket joints, muscles of sponge rubber, and skin of latex and rubber. Some had manually operated air bladders to simulate breathing. The creatures were filmed outdoors on a miniature jungle set measuring 6,000 square feet, and during photography O'Brien used seven cameras at once to capture different angles. Live action was added to these scenes during postproduction, using a crude travelling matte process and an optical printer.

In contrast, the 1997 *The Lost World* used sophisticated computers to combine live action with computer-generated instead of stop-motion dinosaurs. The movie was a sequel to *Jurassic Park* (1993), which was the first film to feature realistic digital animals. *The Lost World* not only built on this work but advanced the field of computer special effects still further. Whereas there were approximately 50 3-D computer-generated shots in *Jurassic Park, The Lost World* had 91, of which 80 involved dinosaurs and 11 involved vehicles and trailers. *The Lost World* also had 100 2-D digital effects such as wire and rod removals. Consequently while *Jurassic Park* required eight animators, eight technical directors, and seven months to create the film, *The Lost World* required 25 animators, 23 3-D technical directors, six 2-D technical directors, three painters, eight specialists in match-moving, and 10 months of effort. In both cases, the work was under the supervision of Dennis Muren of Industrial Light &

Magic, who has won eight Academy Awards for his visual effects.

In addition to having more dinosaurs than *Jurassic Park,* the 1997 *The Lost World* showed more interaction between digital dinosaurs and real humans and vehicles. For example, to make it appear as though a Tyrannosaurus rex had hit a bus, mechanical effects experts rigged the bus with pneumatics and cables that worked together to dent it on cue, after which a hydraulic system make it tilt and slide. Meanwhile, special rigs catapulted stuntpeople through the bus windows, which were made of breakaway glass. The various rigs, wires, and machinery used to create this effect were digitally removed from the scene during postproduction. Similarly, during a dinosaur round-up involving real vehicles, live horses were used as stand-ins for the dinosaurs in order to provide the dust they would kick up. The horses were subsequently painted out of the scene digitally, with digital effects artists being careful not to erase dust elements as well.

The 1997 *The Lost World* also used miniatures to create some effects. For example, a San Diego stadium was a 1/48 model 30 feet long, and the car seen with it was a miniature on a slotted track. A dock rammed by a boat was a 1/8-scale, 20x30-foot model made of balsa wood. The boat was also a model; measuring 26 feet in length, it was made primarily of plywood and moved along a track.

Miniatures were a relatively small part of the film, however, compared to its animatronics. As with *Jurassic Park,* most of the dinosaur shots were created with full-sized mechanical animals, provided by Stan Winston and his Stan Winston Studios. Winston advanced the field of animatronics extensively while working on *Jurassic Park,* and he did so again with *The Lost World*. In fact, none of the dinosaurs in *The Lost World* were built and animated in exactly the same way as in *Jurassic Park*.

The main difference from one movie to the next involved the way the animatronics were powered. In *Jurassic Park*, all of the figures except the T-rex were activated by internal mechanisms manipulated via cable or radio waves using hand-held controls. For the T-rex, however, Winston tried a new technique. The figure's internal hydraulics system was electronically linked to a telemetry device, which was a 1/4-scale replica of the figure's armature. Movements on the armature were transmitted to a computer, which in turn immediately sent an electronic signal to produce a corresponding movement on the full-sized T-rex.

This arrangement proved so effective that it was used for most of the figures in *The Lost World,* with important modifications. Winston combined the telemetry device with the cable system and placed the hydraulic mechanisms outside of the figures' bodies. This meant that when the puppeteer manipulated the telemetry device, those movements were transmitted via cables to the hydraulics unit, which in turn transmitted them via cables to the full-sized figure. Moreover, the telemetry device was linked to a computer that could record the movements for later playback. This system required fewer puppeteers and provided much smoother movements.

Another difference between the figures in *Jurassic Park* and those in the 1997 *The Lost World* was in how their skin was made. For the second movie, Winston developed thinner skin that enabled him to make realistic folds. He also added simulated muscles beneath the skin. These muscles were made of foams, elastics, spandex, and other fabrics, while the skin was made of foam latex. In all, Winston used 300 gallons of foam latex for his *Lost World* skins.

The computer-generated dinosaurs were also improved to make them more realistic. Between the time that *Jurassic Park* and *The Lost World* were made, a new type of software called Cari was invented to provide more expressive facial movements for a dragon in *Dragonheart* (1996). Digital effects artists working on *The Lost World* were able to modify Cari to give their dinosaurs such characteristics as muscle flexes and breathing motions. Artists also adapted software used in *Jumanji* (1995) to animate a group of running animals, so that it could vary the speed of each animal. This software enabled the computer to provide the animation once the artist gave each animal a path and a walk/run cycle.

But although a computer was providing the bulk of the movements, the animators still made every effort to ensure naturalism, which is the illusion that a real, imperfect animal is on screen instead of a computer-generated, perfect one. They did this by programming the computer to incorporate irregularites into the animals' movements and by making adjustments to 3-D figures by hand. In the process, the animators made sure that their computer-generated dinosaurs matched Stan Winston's mechanical ones, because many scenes required a combination of both types of animals. For example, in one scene a T-rex eats a man. At the beginning of the shot, the person is a stuntman lifted into the air by a full-sized mechanical T-rex. By the time the dinosaur flips him into the air, however, both the man and the T-rex are computer-generated.

That same scene offers an excellent example of how various kinds of special effects techniques commonly worked together on the 1997 *The Lost World*. To make it seem as though the computer-generated T-rex was damaging a 20,000-pound trailer, the trailer was moved on winches and cables, rocked and jackknifed with hydraulics, and ultimately hung off the side of a five-story parking structure, which was later replaced digitally with a cliff edge. Rain and a cracking trailer window were computer-generated, while shots of the ocean beneath the cliff were live footage. Here and elsewhere, all elements were seamlessly merged to create the final film. *See also* ANIMATRONICS; DELGADO, MARCEL; *DRAGONHEART;* HYDRAULICS; *JUMANJI; JURASSIC PARK;* LATEX, FOAM; O'BRIEN, WILLIS; SPIELBERG, STEVEN; STOP-MOTION MODEL ANIMATION; WINSTON, STAN.

Further Reading

Duncan, Jody. "The Beauty in the Beasts." *Cinefex* 55, August 1993.
———.*The Making of* The Lost World. New York: Ballantine Books, 1997.
——— "On the Shoulders of Giants." *Cinefex 70,* June 1997.

Kaufman, Debra. "Exploring *The Lost World.*" *Digital Magic,* June 1997.

Lucas, George (1944–)

Producer/director George Lucas revolutionized the field of special effects when he made the 1977 movie *Star Wars,* which featured miniature photography techniques that were far advanced for their time. To create this photography and the many other advanced effects in *Star Wars,* Lucas established the Industrial Light & Magic (ILM) special effects house, which continues to be the leading company in the field.

Born in 1944, George Lucas took up amateur racecar driving while in high school, but abandoned the pursuit after he was in a serious off-track automobile accident. This event caused him to reevaluate his life, and he decided to enroll in junior college in his hometown of Modesto, California; two years later, he enrolled in the University of Southern California (USC) film school. There he made several films, including a short called *THX-1138,* and won many prizes for his work.

In 1968 Lucas was awarded a Warner Brothers scholarship to observe the production of *Finian's Rainbow,* which was directed by Francis Ford Coppola. The following year Lucas was hired to work as Coppola's production associate for *The Rain People.* Lucas then made a documentary about the making of *The Rain People* and acted as a cameraman on *Gimme Shelter,* a documentary about the Rolling Stones musical group, before becoming vice president of American Zoetrope, an independent studio newly created by Coppola and bankrolled by Warner Brothers. Lucas directed the studio's first film, *THX-1138,* which was an expanded version of his earlier work. When it was shown the finished product, Warner Brothers so hated *THX-1138* that it withdrew all financial support from the company. Nonetheless, the studio still claimed the movie as its own, cut it severely, and released it without sufficient marketing, which assured its failure at the box office.

Lucas's next film, *American Graffitti* (1973), met a very different fate. Made for only $700,000, it earned approximately $55 million on its initial North American release and remains one of the most profitable movies in history. This success enabled Lucas to establish ILM and a production company, Lucasfilm, Ltd., to assist him in making *Star Wars,* which grossed more than $194 million on initial release. While making the film, Lucas signed over his projected profits to 20th Century Fox in exchange for financing. However, he retained sequel rights as well as the

Producer/director George Lucas on the set of *Willow.* Keith Hamshere, Lucasfilm/Photofest.

profits from *Star Wars* merchandise, which quickly made him a multimillionaire.

Lucas subsequently invested his money in ILM, Lucasfilm Ltd., and a filming and sound recording studio he named Skywalker Ranch, which now also houses his archives and personal headquarters. These companies worked on two *Star Wars* sequels, *The Empire Strikes Back* (1980) and *The Return of the Jedi* (1980)—rereleased in expanded editions in 1997—and on a *Star Wars* prequel, *The Phantom Menace* (1999). Lucas also acted as executive producer for Steven Spielberg's *Indian Jones* trilogy, which comprises the films *Raiders of the Lost Ark* (1981), *Indiana Jones and the Temple of Doom* (1984), and *Indiana Jones and the Last Crusade* (1989).

Lucas has supported several other film projects as well. In addition, he developed a new sound system for motion pictures, THX, and established LucasArts to develop CD games. In 1992 Lucas won the Irving G. Thalberg Award from the Academy of Motion Picture Arts and Sciences for his contributions to the film industry. *See also* COPPOLA, FRANCIS FORD; *INDIANA JONES* MOVIES; INDUSTRIAL LIGHT & MAGIC; *STAR WARS* MOVIES.

Further Reading

Champlin, Charles. *George Lucas: The Creative Impulse—Lucasfilm's First 20 Years.* New York: H.N. Abrams, 1992.

Lumiere, August (1862–1954), and Louis Lumiere (1864–1948)

August and Louis Lumiere were brothers who developed the projected motion picture. Previously, films had been watched not in theaters but with one-person viewers. The Lumieres showed their first projected movie at a private gathering in March 1895 and in December of that year they made their first offering to a paying public. They made the films they projected, and their initial works depicted brief images, such as a moving train and a group of workers leaving a factory at the end of the day. During the late 1880s, the Lumieres hired photographers to film current events throughout the world, and also hired traveling salesmen to sell Lumiere equipment and films. In the early 1900s, Louis Lumiere turned his attention to inventing new film processes.

The Lumieres were born in France, August in 1862 and Louis in 1864. Their father was a photographer who manufactured photographic materials. In 1881 Louis invented a new photographic process that drastically increased the company's profits and helped fund the brothers' experiments with projection equipment. The two also inspired other early filmmakers such as George Melies. August Lumiere died in 1954, Louis in 1948. *See also* MELIES, GEORGE.

M

Makeup

There are three basic types of makeup used in film work. The first, called street makeup, is applied simply to make an actor look better on camera. It employs materials that can be found at any cosmetics counter, including powders, blush, and lipstick and lotions to provide pigment. The second type of makeup, called character makeup, is designed to change the appearance of an actor so that he or she can play a completely different character. The third type of makeup, called special makeup effects, employs a combination of makeup and mechanical devices to create an inhuman appearance, such as an animal, monster, or space alien.

One of the first people to develop cosmetic makeup for use in the movies was Max Factor. In 1914 he invented the first cream-based makeup for silent film stars, and two years later he developed a version for everyday wear. By 1925 Factor's makeup had become an industry standard.

By this time, character makeup for movies had begun to develop as well. This type of makeup can transform an actor in remarkable ways, and is considered one of the earliest forms of special effects. Character makeup requires additional tools besides street makeup, such as bald caps, fake scars, unusual contact lenses, wigs, and various prosthetics or appliances. The latter, usually made of foam latex, are attached directly to an actor's skin with some kind of glue.

Some early actors, such as Lon Chaney Sr., Bela Lugosi, and Boris Karloff, became known for their makeup effects, just as actors like Buster Keaton and Harold Lloyd were known for their stunts. Lon Chaney Sr., who was nicknamed "the man of a thousand faces," not only did his own makeup but developed secret techniques that he guarded jealously.

During the 1930s, actors stopped doing their own makeup and relied instead on skilled makeup professionals such as George and Gordon Bau, Jack Dawn, Charles Schram, William Tuttle, Emile LaVigne, Josef and Gustav Norin, and Jack Pierce, who created makeup for the character of Frankenstein played by Boris Karloff. Pierce's vision of Frankenstein's monster remains its standard appearance today. He created the monster's facial structure with cotton and collodion, which is a mixture of nitrocellulose, alcohol, and ether typically used in the manufacturer of photographic film or as a coating for wounds.

Professional makeup artists experimented with a variety of techniques, but unlike actors who did their own makeup, they generally traded information to advance the field of makeup effects. For example, John Chambers, who created the makeup for *The Planet of the Apes* (1968), established the John Chambers Studio to train young makeup artists. Dick Smith, who invented new types of adhesives, paints, and foam latex facial appliances, not only wrote about his work but became a mentor to Rick Baker, now one of the foremost makeup and creature effects experts in the world.

Creature effects usually fall into the category of special makeup effects, because they incorporate mechanical devices. For example, the foam latex suit worn by the actor playing *The Creature from the Black Lagoon* (1954) featured fake gills operated in one of two ways. While swimming, the actor himself could move the gills, using his jaw movements to squeeze an interior air bulb inside his mask; on land the gills were activated by a crew member, using an off-camera pump to force air in and out of balloons within the suit beneath the gills. Similarly, the actor portraying the monster in *The Thing* (1951) wore foam-rubber appliances to build up his facial features, while a pumping mechanism sent colored water from a special attachment on his chest up to some false veins on his head.

A more recent example of creature effects was Rick Baker's makeup for *Men in Black* (1997). The character of "Edgar" required a device whereby the actor could tighten his

Title character in *The Creature from the Black Lagoon* (1954), an example of special makeup effects. *Photofest.*

own skin on camera. Consequently Baker attached silk threads to the actor's face and tied them to a hidden handle, which the actor pulled when it appeared he was tugging on his scalp. Since the threads were not effective on their own, Baker enhanced the effect with silicone and gelatin makeup, as well as with devices put in the actor's mouth to distort its shape.

Other aliens that Baker created for the film involved animatronics, which are mechanized versions of a creature. Animatronics and special makeup effects often work together to create the final appearance of a character. For example, the character of "Mikey" in *Men in Black* required an ordinary mask of a human as well as a mechanized version that was radio-controlled by two puppeteers, along with a cable-operated alien head and a head that had no cables or moving parts, all manufactured by Baker.

Similarly, Stan Winston had to develop both makeup and robotic devices to create a beast called the Kothoga for the 1997 movie *The Relic*. As in *The Creature from the Black Lagoon*, the Kothoga was actually a man in a suit. However, this suit was extremely sophisticated and employed advanced animatronics. The suit held the actor inside with a harness; his head was located approximately a foot below the creature's shoulder. The actor's job was to act out the Kothoga's gross body movements. However, the head and neck were radio-controlled by puppeteers. The Kothoga had a relatively large range of movement, accomplished through complex mechanisms powered by a cable that ran along the actor's back to the underside of the creature's tail and then out.

Because of such equipment, it was difficult just to get an actor into the suit. There were two men who played the part, each approximately 7 feet tall, and there were actually two mechanized Kothoga suits made, in addition to a "stunt suit" for underwater and fire scenes. When it was time to enter the mechanized suit, the actor had to climb into the stomach while the creature was hung, spine side up, from the ceiling. Arms and legs were not attached until after the actor was in place. Once inside, the actor received fresh air through a tube-and-pump system.

The actor also endured discomfort while the creature was being manufactured. First he had to don a bodysuit and climb onto a special rig. He was then wrapped in plaster bandages, which required several hours to dry. The resulting body cast was slit, carefully removed and repaired, and used to create a fiberglass form. Wire was placed over the fiberglass, and clay was sculpted over the wire. Once the clay hardened, it was used to make another mold for foam latex skin pieces. These pieces were then detailed and applied back over the mold, which formed the core of the creature. Mechanisms were also added to the creature; this machinery was made out of aluminum to keep the weight of the suit down to 35 pounds. It worked extremely well, but a few shots were still not possible to accomplish with the Kothoga suit and had to be created with computer graphics.

Today's special makeup effects artist often have to work with digital effects experts in the design of characters. Makeup artists also have to be experts on a wide variety of makeup techniques and mechanized equipment, and remain open to trying new materials and technologies as they appear. *See also* BAKER, RICK; *BATMAN* MOVIES; BAU, GEORGE, AND GORDON BAU; CHANEY, LON SR.; DAWN, JACK, AND BOB DAWN; FACTOR, MAX; LAVIGNE, EMILE; *MEN IN BLACK;* NORIN, JOSEF, AND GUSTAV NORIN; PIERCE, JACK; *PLANET OF THE APES;* SCHRAM, CHARLES; TUTTLE, WILLIAM; WINSTON, STAN.

Further Reading

Cosner, Sharon. *Special Effects in Movies and Television*. New York: J. Messner, 1985.

Culhane, John. *Special Effects in the Movies: How They Do It*. New York: Ballantine, 1981.

McKenzie, Alan, and Derek Ware. *Hollywood Tricks of the Trade*. New York: Gallery Books, 1986.

Murdock, Andrew, and Rachel Aberly. *The Making of Alien Resurrection*. New York: HarperPrism, 1987.

Pourroy, Janine. "Basic Black." *Cinefex 70*, June 1997.

Street, Rita. "The Calisto Effect." *Cinefex 69*, March 1997.

Swinfield, Rosemarie. *Stage Makeup Step-By-Step*. White Hall, VA: Betterway Publications, 1995.

Taylor, Al. *Making a Monster*. New York: Crown, 1980.

Mann, Ned (1893–1967)

American special effects artist Ned Mann influenced the British special effects industry while working in England. He made several films with British director Alexander Korda, including *The Ghost Goes West* (1935), *The Man Who Could Work Miracles* (1935), and *Things to Come* (1936). The latter employed realistic miniatures and complicated trick photography to depict a future civilization with technological marvels like flying vehicles. Prior to moving to England, Mann worked on the effects for such American films as *The Thief of Bagdad* (1924), which Korda later remade, and *Son of Zorro* (1925).

Born in 1893, Mann acted and directed in the theater before becoming a Hollywood actor in 1920. Shortly thereafter he became involved with special effects, first in the United States and then in England. He returned to the United States in the 1930s, but again worked with Korda in the late 1940s. Finally he settled in Hollywood permanently, creating special effects for such films as *Around the World in 80 Days* (1956). Mann died in 1967. *See also* KORDA, SIR ALEXANDER; *THE THIEF OF BAGDAD*.

Maquette

A maquette is a small clay sculpture of a movie character, typically an animal or other creature. It is a tool that helps all people involved with the film visualize the three-dimensional shape of that character. Puppetry experts use maquettes in the design of animatronics, and digital effects artists can scan their image into a computer to re-create them as computer graphics. Maquettes can also be painted to establish color schemes for an animal, as was the case for *Jurassic Park* (1993) and *The Lost World* (1997), where nearly every dinosaur was first made as a maquette before being built as an animatronic or computer-generated figure. *See also* ANIMATION, COMPUTER; ANIMATRONICS; *JURASSIC PARK; THE LOST WORLD;* PUPPETS; SCANNING.

Marooned

The 1969 movie *Marooned* won an Academy Award for its special effects, which were created by Robbie Robertson. He used standard optical effects and miniature photography to make it seem as though two astronauts had become stranded in space due to a rocket malfunction. *See also* MINIATURES AND MODELS; OPTICAL EFFECTS.

Mars Attacks!

The 1996 Warner Brothers movie *Mars Attacks!* inspired a major advance in computer animation software, which enabled digital artists to create and animate several computer-generated characters at once. The movie features approximately 140 computer-generated spaceship and robot shots provided by Warner Digital Studios, as well as more than 300 shots of computer-generated Martians created by Industrial Light & Magic (ILM). Supervising the work at Warner was Michael Fink; the visual effects producer at ILM was Mark Miller, who was also in charge of visual effects for the 1995 movie *Jumanji*.

Interestingly, the Martians were originally intended to be made as stop-motion animation models. *Mars Attacks!* director Tim Burton, an aficionado of stop-motion, used the technique to film *Nightmare before Christmas* (1993) and *James and the Giant Peach* (1996). Therefore he designed 15-inch-tall Martian puppets for *Mars Attacks!* intending to have ILM shoot them in front of a bluescreen backdrop, extract them from the shot, and add their images to live-action shots during postproduction.

Burton's Martians had to look like those created for a series of Topps trading cards first issued in 1996, on which the *Mars Attacks!* movie was based. These Martians had glass helmets that would be hard to keep clean during stop-motion animation; therefore Burton decided to have a computer create the helmets instead. As a result, ILM made test footage of the alien that included not only the glass helmet but the rest of the Martian. The result was so impressive that Burton decided to abandon his idea to use stop-motion for *Mars Attacks!*

Burton also realized that a computer would be able to generate the Martian footage much faster than stop-motion animators could. Since he was on a tight shooting schedule, he gave Warner and ILM only eight months to create their 440 computer-generated shots. Consequently animators worked on many shots at once, using specialists for each step in the computer graphics process.

The first step was to create a digital Martian using the puppets and other models as a guide. This process involved establishing a skeletal structure, also called an armature or

Computer-generated Martians with actor Jack Nicholson in *Mars Attacks!* (1996). *Warner Bros./Photofest.*

wireframe, and then instructing the computer on how its joints would move. In addition, the final shape and appearance of the Martian was determined and the computer given instructions regarding how to paint and texture the figure. The computer process that adds paint, texture, shade and shadow to an image is called rendering.

In the early years of computer graphics, rendering was the last step in computer animation, and had to take place after the wireframe figure had already been animated. By the time *Mars Attacks!* was made, however, ILM visual effects expert Cary Phillips had created a new software tool called Caricature, also known as Cari, that makes it possible to animate a figure in its rendered rather than wireframe form. Cari is vitally important to computer animators because it allows them to manipulate a realistic, seemingly three-dimensional figure rather than a skeleton, which makes it easier to determine how a scene will look in final form.

Not only did Phillips use Cari to animate the Martians for *Mars Attacks!* but he advanced the software still further. In its original version, which was created for the 1996 movie *Dragonheart,* Cari could animate only one rendered figure at a time, but for *Mars Attacks!* it could animate up to 20 at once. This was a major development in the field of computer graphics. However, the software was not capable of recognizing the solidity of a surface, which meant that it was possible for the Martian to move his elbow through his cape. Digital artists therefore had to correct this problem in individual frames.

Similarly, artists had to change some images generated by the computer during the animation process. To animate a character, the artists often told the computer the figure's position at various points, or key frames, in a scene, and then directed it to fill in the movement necessary to get the figure from one key frame to another. These intermediary images, or "in-betweens," were so perfect that they did not appear realistic. Digital artists therefore altered each one slightly to make it imperfect.

Digital artists also created new software that could generate a crowd of Martians from a master image. The software made "placeholders" for the Martians, but these were rough versions that had to be replaced individually with more detailed Martians. Spaceships for the movie's opening scene were also created from a master image. Since these ships flew in a triangular eight-ship formation, animators began by drawing and animating triangles rather than individual spaceships. They then replaced each animated triangle with eight copies of the master image, which had been animated to perform a long cycle of movements. Each copy began its movements at a different point in the animation cycle, so that the spaceships would not move in unison.

In addition to computer-generated images, *Mars Attacks!* included many detailed miniatures. For example, the surface of Mars was a miniature set of 35x50 feet, made of foam painted red and textured with red wax. The top half of London's Big Ben was recreated as a 16-foot-tall model. It had only two sides, made of a steel frame covered in plaster and breakaway glass. However, it took five weeks to build, because it had to be rigged with pyrotechnics for its explosive destruction by the Martians. First the clock's face was hit with an explosive device, then its base. An explosive tripwire ensured that the model would collapse in the way the director wanted it.

Another important miniature was a Martian saucer that crashed at the end of the film. It was an extremely large model, with a diameter of 25 feet and a weight of 3,500 pounds, and was made of a steel framework with wooden bulkheads. The ship had to be built in three sections to enable it to fit through the doorway of the shop where it was constructed. Once outside, it was reassembled and its fiberglass shell was painted. The model was then attached to a 100-ton crane, swung over a lake at Universal Studios, and dropped to complete the shot. The model ordinarily would have been made in a smaller scale, but it was originally designed to be used with the stop-motion puppets. The same was true for a miniature of the ship's interior. It was 18 feet wide and 11 feet tall because it was initially built for the puppets.

Consequently the director decided to use the puppets to help block out camera moves on the set and determine where images of live actors and computer-generated Martians would be placed.

The actors that would appear to be in the spaceship were filmed in front of a bluescreen, and their images digitally composited onto the miniature set. This scene and others in the movie benefited from new ILM software that automatically linked motion-control camera moves with the moves of the computer's "camera." In other words, the computer's viewpoint and the camera's viewpoint could be matched exactly. In addition, a move created in the computer could be used to guide the motion-control camera on the set, so that the animation in essence drove the shooting session. Similarly, the Martian puppets could be linked to their computer-generated counterparts, so that their movements could drive the animation. This interface between live action and computer-generated animation was an important tool in creating many of the *Mars Attacks!* Martian and spaceship scenes.

The movie also contained several live action scenes that involved traditional special effects such as pyrotechnics, makeup tricks, and mechanical effects. Of these, one of the most complicated involved the only Martian in the movie not created via computer graphics. Played by actress Lisa Marie, this Martian was disguised as a woman, with an extremely tall hairdo to cover up her large Martian brain and glass helmet. She had an elaborate costume that included an eyeball ring that functioned as a camera and could move in all directions. This prop was controlled via a hidden wire that went inside the actress's sleeve, along her arm, and down to her feet, where two operators were sitting. The Martian woman also had an unusual walk. Some of it was created from the actress's own movements, but in most cases she was simply pulled along the floor on a dolly. Interestingly, this technique was used years earlier to propel the Martian in the 1953 film *The War of the Worlds*. *See also* ANIMATION, COMPUTER; BURTON, TIM; COMPOSITING;

COMPUTER GRAPHICS, COMPUTER HARDWARE AND SOFTWARE; *DRAGONHEART*; FINK, MICHAEL; *JUMANJI*; HARRYHAUSEN, RAY; PUPPETS; *WAR OF THE WORLDS*.

Further Reading
Jones, Karen R. *Mars Attacks! The Art of the Movie.* New York: Ballantine Books, 1996.
Mitchell, Jim, and Ellen Poon. "Our Favorite Martians." *Digital Magic*, February 1997.

Mary Poppins

Released in 1964 by Walt Disney Studios, *Mary Poppins* won an Academy Award for its special effects. It also earned a special scientific Academy Award for Ub Iwerks and other people on the special effects team for their creation of color traveling matte composite cinematography.

Mary Poppins employed travelling mattes in order to add, or composite, live action onto animated backgrounds. The actors were filmed in front of an illuminated screen, and their images were removed from the background using special photographic techniques. This not only isolated the live-action footage but resulted in a series of silhouettes that enabled artists preparing the animated background to leave "holes" for the live-action images. Once this background was complete, the live-action footage and the background were rephotographed together, making it appear as though the actors had been dancing with animated penguins and other cartoon characters. *See also* COMPOSITING; THE WALT DISNEY COMPANY; IWERKS, UB; TRAVELLING MATTE.

Further Reading
Fry, Ron, and Pamela Fourzon. *The Saga of Special Effects.* Englewood Cliffs, NJ: Prentice-Hall, 1977.
Matlin, Leonard. *The Disney Films.* New York: Bonanza Books, 1973.
Smith, Dave. *Disney A-Z.* New York: Hyperion, 1996.

The Mask of Zorro

The 1998 movie *The Mask of Zorro* provides excellent examples of modern stuntwork. It employed seemingly dangerous swordfights, whip tricks, and horse leaps, yet no one was seriously hurt during production.

Elaborate planning and safety precautions went into every stunt. For example, extensive stunt rigging was used during a mine scene in which stuntmen had to catapult off high platforms, and deaccelerators were attached to their safety equipment to slow their descent. The filmmakers also relied on the expertise of stuntwork professionals. Horse stunts were performed by Tad Griffith, a trick rider who is also the son of a trick rider and rodeo star. Fencing scenes with live actors were choreographed by Bob Anderson, a fencing master who has trained many other Hollywood stars. Whip training was handled by Alex Green, a whip master and stuntman who has performed in more than 100 movies. All of these people had a great deal of experience, which enabled them to create spectacular stunts without the need for computer-generated effects. *See also* STUNTS.

Further Reading
Curtis, Sandra. *Zorro Unmasked*. New York: Hyperion, 1998.

Masks *See* MAKEUP.

Match-Modeling

Used in computer animation, match-modeling involves creating a shape that matches a live-action figure, then animating that shape to correspond to that figure's real-life movements. Match-moving can be used to create placeholders for the live action that will appear within a computer-generated scene, or to make shadows that will later be pasted onto the live-action figure. A match-modeled shape can also be colored and layered over the live-action image to increase the image's intensity. *See also* ANIMATION, COMPUTER.

Match-Mover

A match-mover is a digital effects artist who makes sure that computer-generated characters and/or miniatures interact properly with the live actors in a scene. One part of the job is to match the movements of the virtual camera to those of the live-action camera. Another is to place a computer-generated or miniature figure in its correct position in a live-action frame.

To facilitate these tasks, the match-mover makes wireframe versions of all objects in the live-action environment and lays them over the background plate as a reference. The crew on the live-action shoot make the match-mover's job easier by taking detailed measurements on the set, by placing match-move markers at various locations, and/or by taking laser surveys of the terrain to provide information about how computer-generated figures would move across the landscape.

The match-move department is usually the first stop of any scene that includes a computer-generated character, and while some projects require only one or two match-movers, others require several. *The Lost World* (1997), for example, employed eight match-moving experts to add its computer-generated dinosaurs to live-action scenes. *See also* ANIMATION, COMPUTER; *THE LOST WORLD*.

Further Reading
Duncan, Jody. *The Making of* The Lost World. New York: Ballantine Books, 1997.

The Matrix

The 1999 movie *The Matrix* employed a new technique called Bullet-Time Photography Super Slow Motion, also known as "Flow-Mo." This process allows the filmmaker to control the speed of moving objects in a scene. For example, with Flow-Mo, a man can leap into the air and appear to freeze several feet off the ground. He can then kick rapidly and appear to descend slowly.

To create the illusion that a man is capable of changing speed in mid-air, he is first filmed on a set at normal speed using regular movie cameras. (The actor is raised off the ground with a wire that will be digitally removed from shots during postproduction.) This film is then scanned into a computer, which converts the man into a wireframe figure that is used to establish camera movements for the scene. Once such movements have been decided upon, the path of the camera is "mapped" by the computer, and a series of sophisticated still cameras are placed along this path on the live-action set. For example, at one point in the movie the camera sweeps completely around two figures hovering in mid-air; this required 120 still cameras set in a circle on a greenscreen set.

The still cameras photograph the actors as they perform the scene, and these photographs are scanned into computer, which creates a strip of still images. Much as a series of animation cels can be flipped from one image to the next at varying speeds to slow down or speed up a cartoon figure's movements, so too can the digital still photographs be presented at varying speeds to slow down or speed up the actors' movements. The computer also smoothes out the transitions from one image to the next. The lead actors in *The Matrix* performed their own martial arts stunts, after training for four months prior to filming.

The Flow-Mo technique was developed by visual effects supervisor John Gaeta and his special effects house, Manix. Meanwhile, another special effects company, Animal Logic Film, developed new shading software that allowed digital artists to create two unique visual images for the movie, gun blasts that looked like lightning, and a cascading matrix code made by blending a live-action water flow with a series of randomly generated numbers. There are many other digital images in the film, and one complicated sequence in which a field of babies is harvested was created entirely with computer graphics. *See also* BLUESCREEN PROCESS, COMPUTER GRAPHICS.

Matte

A matte is any covering, or mask, that blocks out part of a camera shot. The simplest mattes are stationary, or fixed, mattes made of substances like black tape, wood, masonite, opaque cardboard, metal, or painted glass. More sophisticated mattes are travelling mattes, whose silhouettes alter their shape and/or position from frame to frame.

The purpose of a matte is to make it possible to combine two or more shots into one. One of the earliest examples of a matte shot occurred in the 1903 movie *The Great Train Robbery*. Filmmaker Edwin Porter had to shoot his actors on an indoor set, but he wanted the audience to see a real train passing outside the window of a telegraph office. Therefore he made a window-shaped matte and carefully positioned it to block the window from his camera negative during filming. He then shot the live-action scene, rewound the negative, replaced the matte with one that blocked everything but the window, and photographed a moving train. The result was two shots that looked as though they were filmed at the same time.

Another early type of matte was the glass shot, whereby a matte painting was used to change certain aspects of a scene. An artist would paint a background on a piece of glass, leaving the area where the live action would take place transparent. The scene was then filmed through this piece of glass, so that the live action appeared to be taking place amidst the painted scenery. The glass shot was developed by matte painter Norman O. Dawn, who first used it in the 1907 film *Missions of California* to restore missing parts to damaged historic buildings so that they would appear new again.

Camera equipped with matte box for in-camera matte work. *Courtesy of Arriflex Corporation.*

Both of these examples are called in-camera mattes, because they take place entirely within the camera during filming. However, mattes are also used during postproduction, when shots are combined via either an optical printer or a computer. Invented in 1931, the optical printer projects different images together so they can be rephotographed as one shot, and travelling mattes are employed to cover various areas during this process just as with an in-camera matte.

A travelling matte is simply a matte that changes shape from one frame of film to the next. In some cases its shapes are hand drawn. For example, hand-drawn travelling mattes blocked out the area where lightsaber "blades" would appear in the movie *Star Wars* (1977). However, in most cases modern filmmakers create a travelling matte using an illuminated screen or other flat surface, typically in the color blue but also in green, red, or orange.

Filming actors or a miniature spaceship in front of a bluescreen, for example, distinguishes the filmed subjects from their background, which can then be replaced using either an optical printer or a computer. Similarly, inserting a screen within a window can allow an image to be matted into the scene during postproduction. In *Alien Resurrection* (1997), for example, a miniature observation room built in 1/6 scale had 14 chambers meant to hold aliens. During filming, orange cards were placed in the chamber windows, and in postproduction, the orange areas were removed so the computer-generated creatures could be matted into the scene digitally. *See also* BLUESCREEN PROCESS; DAWN, NORMAN O.; GLASS SHOT; *THE GREAT TRAIN ROBBERY;* OPTICAL PRINTER; *STAR WARS* MOVIES; TRAVELLING MATTE.

Further Reading

Hutchison, David. *Film Magic: The Art and Science of Special Effects.* New York: Prentice-Hall, 1987.

Imes, Jack. *Special Visual Effects: A Guide to Special Effects Cinematography.* New York: Van Nostrand Reinhold, 1984.

Kawin, Bruce F. *How Movies Work.* Berkeley: University of California Press, 1992.

McAlister, Michael J. *Language of Visual Effects.* Los Angeles: Lone Eagle Publishing, 1993.

Matte Paintings

A matte painting is a large painting used to enhance a live-action scene, either during filming or through postproduction processes. The painting can provide a background of scenery, buildings, and/or stationary objects, or it can be used to alter some of the foreground live-action elements within a shot.

One of the first uses of a matte painting was as part of a glass shot, invented by Norman O. Dawn to "restore" missing pieces of a rooftop to make it appear new in his 1907 film *Missions of California.* In this instance, a piece of glass was placed between the camera lens and a building with a damaged rooftop. An artist then painted an undamaged roof on the glass, which had been positioned so that it would obscure the real one during filming.

Matte paintings were also commonly created on cardboard and combined with live action via a double-exposure process. This was how MGM Studios added the images of the Emerald City and the Yellow Brick Road to the live action in their 1939 film *The Wizard of Oz.* During postproduction, foreground images of live-action characters were combined with background images of paintings. The *Oz* paintings were 4 feet wide, but most matte paintings of the period were 16 to 48 inches wide. MGM's paintings also varied from the norm in that they were made with crayon pastels on black cardboard, whereas it was more typical to use oil paints on white cardboard.

Currently, matte paintings are combined with live action via either an optical printer or computer software. Matte paintings are typically painted on glass, with the areas that will be filled with live action blacked out. Some modern filmmakers have replaced traditional matte paintings with digital matte paintings, which are created with a computer. One of the most extensive uses of digital matte paintings in recent years has been for the movie *The Fifth Element* (1997), which also features advanced miniatures. *See also* COMPUTER GRAPHICS; DAWN, NORMAN O.; *THE FIFTH ELEMENT;* GLASS SHOT; *INDIANA JONES* MOVIES; MATTE; OPTICAL PRINTER; *THE WIZARD OF OZ.*

Further Reading

Elrick, Ted. "Elemental Images". *Cinefex 70*, June 1970.

Harmetz, Aljean. *The Making of* The Wizard of Oz. New York: Knopf, 1977.

Kawin, Bruce F. *How Movies Work*. Berkeley, Los Angeles, and London: University of California Press, 1992.

Stensvold, Mike. *In-Camera Special Effects*. Englewood Cliffs, New Jersey: Prentice-Hall, (1983).

Matte World Digital

Located in Novato, California, Matte World Digital is a special effects house dedicated to creating digital mattes, 3-D digital environments, and digital composites. The house has provided shots for more than 50 films, including *Batman Returns* (1992), *Independence Day* (1996), *Star Trek: First Contact* (1996), *Con Air* (1997), *Titanic* (1997), *The Truman Show* (1998), and *Armageddon* (1998). *See also* ARMAGEDDON; BATMAN MOVIES; INDEPENDENCE DAY; STAR TREK MOVIES; TITANIC.

McCreery, Mark (1960–)

An art director for the Stan Winston Studios, Mark McCreery has worked with such directors as James Cameron, Tim Burton, and Steven Spielberg. He helped design makeup for the Penguin character in *Batman Returns* (1992), created dinosaur sketches and illustrations for *Jurassic Park* (1993), and worked with Stan Winston to develop the monster in *The Relic* (1997). For *Jurassic Park* he also learned puppeteering so he could help Winston with the movie's animatronic scenes. McCreery didn't commit himself to a career in art until the age of 24, when he became a student at the Art Center in Pasadena. He graduated in 1988 and began working for Stan Winston shortly thereafter. *See also* JURASSIC PARK; WINSTON, STAN.

Further Reading

Shannon, John. "Crash McCreery: Doing Dinosaurs and Such." *Cinefext 69*, March 1997.

McQuarrie, Ralph (c. 1930–)

Artist Ralph McQuarrie made many of the matte paintings for the movie *Star Wars* (1977) and its sequel *The Empire Strikes Back* (1980). He was also production designer for the movie *Cocoon* (1985).

After graduating from high school in 1948, McQuarrie studied art for two years before getting a job as an artist at the Boeing Company, where he worked until he was drafted into the Korean War. After his service was over, he returned to Boeing for a brief time before becoming a freelance illustrator. His specialty was doing technical paintings of spacecraft and space equipment; he frequently worked for the National Aeronautics and Space Administration (NASA).

In 1974, *Star Wars* creator George Lucas hired McQuarrie to create sketches and paintings of several *Star Wars* characters. These illustrations enabled Lucas to get backing for the movie from 20th Century Fox Studios, and McQuarrie was consequently hired to work on the film. *See also* COCOON; INDUSTRIAL LIGHT & MAGIC; LUCAS, GEORGE; STAR WARS MOVIES; 20TH CENTURY FOX.

Further Reading

Smith, Thomas G. *Industrial Light & Magic: The Art of Special Effects*. New York: Ballantine Books, 1986.

Mechanical Effects

A mechanical effect, also called a practical effect, is a physical effect that takes place on the set during live-action filming. Mechanical effects can be as spectacular as large explosions or as subtle as the shaking of a tree branch that will later be "nibbled" by a computer-generated dinosaur. Wirework that enables an actor or a model spaceship to "fly" is also a mechanical effect, as are creatures such as the whale in *Moby Dick* (1956) and the shark in *Jaws* (1974).

Moby Dick actually used three steel-frame, 85-foot-long whale models to create its whale-hunt scenes. Beneath their plastic skin was a layer of sponge rubber soaked in a red liquid, so that each whale would "bleed" when poked with a harpoon. These models, each weighing 14 tons, had complex mechanisms to enable them to dive, spout water, and perform other movements, which were directed by remote-control. One of the whales was designed to fit on rails in an 80,000-gallon tank.

The mechanical shark in *Jaws* also moved along rails set in an underwater tank, operated by remote control and propelled with a combination of hydraulic, pneumatic, and electronic machinery. There were actually three versions of the animal, one for left-sided filming, one for right-sided filming, and another for full-face filming. Areas that would not be photographed were left uncovered so that operators could get to the inner workings, which frequently malfunctioned. All three sharks were designed by Bob Mattey, who had previously created a giant squid for the 1954 movie *20,000 Leagues Under the Sea*.

Similarly, *Congo* (1995) employed the expertise of mechanical effects expert Michael Lantieri to move a hippopotamus along a track and a split a set into pieces during an earthquake. The set was built on air bearings that floated it above the stage, and it was shaken with jackhammers powered by pneu-

matics. At a key moment, the bolts holding it together were released all at once, and the structure came apart.

Mechanical effects are often used to change the physical appearance of a set. Some of this work is quite extensive. To make a cruise ship appear to turn over in *The Poseidon Adventure* (1972), for example, set designers re-created the dining room of a real ship with a set 118 feet long, 60 feet wide, and 28 feet high, rigged to tilt up to 30 degrees. The set had an interchangeable ceiling and floor, so that filmmakers could switch the carpeted floor with the ornately decorate ceiling to make the ship appear upside-down.

More recently, *Armageddon* (1998) used a large asteroid set that was designed to break apart, *Dante's Peak* (1997) had a full-sized freeway ramp set rigged to collapse, and *Mouse Hunt* (1997) featured a house that was destroyed during the course of the movie. *Poltergeist* (1982) employed a variety of mechanical effects to make a house appear to be haunted. Of these, one of the most impressive made it appear as though a mother and child were falling through a ceiling; the ceiling was actually thin material placed over a hole, and the mother and child were foam

Mechanical shark with actor Robert Shaw in *Jaws* (1975). *Photofest.*

dummies on a rope-and-pulley system. As this example illustrates, sometimes very simple techniques can create an impressive mechanical effect. *See also* ARMAGEDDON; CONGO; DANTE'S PEAK; LANTIERI, MICHAEL; MOUSE HUNT; PYROTECHNICS; STUNTS; *20,000 LEAGUES UNDER THE SEA;* WIREWORK.

Further Reading

McCarthy, Robert E. *Secrets of Hollywood Special Effects.* Boston: Focal Press, 1992.

McKenzie, Alan, and Derek Ware. *Hollywood Tricks of the Trade.* New York: Gallery Books, 1986.

Vaz, Mark Cotta. *Visions of* Armageddon. New York: Hyperion, 1998.

Melies, George (1861–1938)

One of the pioneers of filmmaking, French filmmaker George Melies invented such photographic tricks as stop motion, fast motion, slow motion, double exposure, and multiple exposure. Melies was born in 1861 in Paris but moved to London in 1884 to attend an art school. There he became interested in magic, and in 1888 his family bought him a theater in Paris where he could perform magic shows. Melies was very successful in this pursuit. Then he saw the Lumiere brothers demonstrate the first theater projection device, and he decided to show movies in his theater as well. He purchased a version of the device made by instrument maker Robert William Paul, improved it, and developed a camera that would enable him to create his own films rather than rely on those being produced by the Edison Company, which was supplying the rest of the industry.

Melies made his first movie in 1896, and within a year he had made a total of 78 extremely short films. In 1897 he made 53 more. His first works were brief images of common events, such as people walking down the street or playing cards. Then he made an important discovery. While filming the Place de l'Opera in Paris, his camera jammed. It took him a few moments to fix it, whereupon he resumed filming the same site. When he developed the film, he discovered that by stopping the film and restarting it, he had made an omnibus appear to be transformed into a hearse. This was the first use of stop-motion photography.

Melies was fascinated with his trick and featured it in many of his films. For example, in *Cinderella* (1899), he used it to turn a pumpkin into a carriage and a plain dress into a beautiful gown. He also hand-colored individual frames for one scene and used slow motion in another. For *Battleship Maine* (1897), he filmed through a fish tank to create the illusion that some scenes were taking place under water, and for *The One Man Band* (1900), he used multiple exposures to allow himself to play seven different roles. Because of such work, he quickly became famous for his staged special effects. He also made what he called "reconstructed actualities," an early form of newsreel.

To make his movies, Melies built the first film studio in Europe, and from 1897 to 1902 his production company, Star Film, was very successful. His best known work from this period is *Le Voyage dans la Lune,* or *A Trip to the Moon* (1902), which features a scene of a rocket plunging into the eye of the Man in the Moon. By 1913, however, Melies was experiencing financial difficulty. The novelty of his photographic tricks had worn off, and competitors like Edwin S. Porter had begun to offer audiences more sophisticated films with real plots.

In 1915 Melies went back to performing magic in his theater, but even that failed to improve his financial situation. He filed for bankruptcy in 1923, and three years later he started running a toy concession at a railway station. He lived in relative poverty until 1928, when his works were rediscovered by a more appreciative public. In 1931 the French government awarded him a Legion of Honor medal, and in 1932 he was given a rent-free apartment, where he remained until his death in 1938. *See also* CINDERELLA; FILMING SPEED; MULTIPLE EXPOSURE; LUMIERE, AUGUST, AND LOUIS LUMIERE; STOP-MOTION MODEL ANIMATION.

Further Reading

Brosnan, John. *Movie Magic.* New York: St. Martin's Press, 1974.

Fry, Ron, and Pamela Fourzon. *The Saga of Special Effects.* Englewood Cliffs, NJ: Prentice-Hall, 1977.

McKenzie, Alan, and Derek Ware. *Hollywood Tricks of the Trade.* New York: Gallery Books, 1986.

Men in Black

Released in 1997 by Amblin Entertainment and Columbia Pictures, *Men in Black* features more than 200 special effects shots by Industrial Light & Magic (ILM), as well as the makeup and creatures of Rick Baker's Cinovation Studios. Baker won an Academy Award for his work on the film.

One of the most elaborate creatures that Baker made for *Men in Black* was "Mikey," an alien who pretends to be a human. Mikey's human "mask" was made in two versions, one without movement and the other with self-contained mechanisms operated via radio-control by two puppeteers. The Mikey figure had a cable-operated head capable of several movements, as well as radio-controlled flippers. However, for a few shots the head was replaced with one that had no cables or moving parts. In addition, while the animatronic alien was roaring, he was replaced with a computer-generated one, in preparation for a sprint across the desert. This was because it was difficult for the actor to run in the Mikey suit, not only because he could barely see while wearing the head but also because he wore 2½-foot-long leg extensions that made Mikey 7 feet tall.

Both the Mikey costume and the computer-generated Mikey were built using a maquette sculpted by Rick Baker. Once the computer-generated figure was finished, it was animated in part using a software program called Cari. Cari was originally created to give the dragon in *Dragonheart* (1996) more expressive facial features, and it did the same for Mikey in *Men in Black*. It also provided Mikey with realistic skin and muscle movements.

Another Baker creation was an alien who takes over a farmer's lifeless body. The actor playing "Edgar" the farmer had relatively loose skin, and Baker used this to his advantage in order to make the alien appear to tighten Edgar's skin. Baker attached silk threads to the actor's face and tied them to a hidden handle, which the actor was actually pulling when it appeared he was tugging on his scalp. However, the threads were not enough to create the desired effect, so Baker applied silicone and gelatin makeup to the actor's face and put devices in the actor's mouth to distort its shape.

Baker also made a small alien that appears inside the head of a human-like robot. The alien was made in two scales, one life-sized and the other 4 feet tall inside a head 8 feet tall. The larger version was necessary because the alien had to move, and its mechanism would not fit in the smaller figure. This mechanism was fairly sophisticated, and had a motion-control system that made it possible to program lip movements to match the alien's dialogue.

Two other complex Cinovation figures were an alien baby born in a car and a group of "worm guys" that appear in a coffee room. The animatronic baby was able to move, blink, and throw up a mixture of oatmeal and methylcellulose. The "worm guys" were 3-foot-tall animatronic figures, each operated by two puppeteers using cables, radio-control devices, and rods that came through a cabinet behind the creatures. When the worm guys were seen outside of the coffee room, they were not animatronics but computer graphics. Some of the other aliens seen in the MIB headquarters were also computer-generated images, while a few were animatronics provided by companies other than Cinovation, which could not meet the demand for additional background alien figures.

The giant bug seen emerging from Edgar in the movie's climax was the responsibility of Rick Baker, but it was a makeup and computer graphics effect rather than an animatronic figure. The decision not to use animatronics came at the last minute, after Baker had spent several months working on a complicated 15-foot-tall mechanized bug. Once the decision was made, Baker developed a mask for Edgar that was designed to break apart in the back from head to waist. The actor was placed in the costume wearing a bluescreen hood, so that when Edgar split apart, the bluescreen could be replaced with a computer-generated bug.

Bluescreen was also used to make the giant bug appear to eat someone. A computer-generated stuntman was used to plan the shot with the computer-generated bug. The digital figure's movements were then duplicated by a live stuntman performing in front of a bluescreen, and the footage of the live figure was substituted for the computer-generated man during postproduction.

A similar blend of live action and computer graphics was used for a scene in which an actor, Will Smith, is grabbed by an alien's tentacles. Smith was suspended on wires in front of a bluescreen and filmed flailing about. This live action was then composited into a background plate, and the computer-generated tentacles added. Great care had to be taken to make the tentacles appear to be moving the actor, and it was particularly demanding work because there were more than 700 frames in the shot. Far easier was a scene in which a pug dog appears to talk. Digital experts simply replaced the live animal's mouth with a computer-generated muzzle, mouth, and lips, and animated them using Cari software. The entire head of another character, a pawnbroker, was replaced with computer graphics for another scene and animated to disappear and grow back.

Computer graphics were also used in concert with mechanical effects for some shots. For example, a sequence showing a computer-generated spaceship crashing into a real truck required careful rigging. First the truck was placed in a 25-foot-diameter, 9-foot-deep hole, on top of a stack of wooden boxes. Then a 4,000-pound wrecking ball was dropped onto the truck from a height of 90 feet. At the same time, to make it appear as though a large spaceship were making the crater, a series of buried air rams pushed dirt up around the crater's perimeter. Another scene in which mechanical effects were required to enhance computer graphics involved a ball bouncing wildly about a room, destroying various objects in its path. The objects were rigged with trip wires, while the ball was computer-generated.

In some cases, computer graphics were used in concert with miniature photography. For example, a car that transforms itself while in a tunnel was computer-generated, while the tunnel itself was a 1/8-scale model 3 feet wide, 96 feet long, and 20 inches high. The 50 other cars in the scene were also 1/8-scale models, made of epoxy resin. Motion-control cameras slowly filmed a passage through the miniature tunnel, and this footage was later composited with the computer-generated car. Also added was live-action footage of the actors, filmed in a full-sized car mockup in front of a bluescreen.

But perhaps the most spectacular miniature work in the movie concerned a spaceship that crashes into a park. Built of fiberglass in 1/6-scale, the spaceship model was 9 feet in diameter and had working lights. It was propelled into the crash by an hydraulic rig that enabled the ship to travel at 30 mph for a distance of 35 feet. As it crashed, the ship struck a 1/6 scale "Unisphere" structure made of sheet metal, brass, and tubing before hitting soil made of colored peatmoss, and along the route, timers and trip wires triggered pyrotechnics. These explosions were made with smokeless powder, black powder bombs, and barium nitrate, the latter of which provided a greenish glow. Shots of the miniature crash were later composited with live action, making it appear as though the ship had come close to striking the movie's heroes. *See also* ACADEMY AWARDS; ANIMATRONICS; BAKER, RICK; MINIATURES AND MODELS; PYROTECHNICS.

Further Reading
Pourroy, Janine. "Basic Black." *Cinefex 70*, June 1997.

Metro-Goldwyn-Mayer

Metro-Goldwyn-Mayer, commonly known as MGM, is one of the oldest film production companies in the United States. The studio has created hundreds of major films, including *The Good Earth* (1937), which featured advanced makup effects, and *The Wizard of Oz* (1939) and *Ben-Hur* (1959), both of which employed advanced miniature and stuntwork.

Established in 1924 when the Metro Picture Corporation joined with the Goldwyn Picture Corporation, MGM was extremely powerful during the 1930s and 1940s, when it controlled some of the biggest stars in the film industry. During the 1950s, however, this power waned. The company began to have financial trouble, and a series of take-overs and reorganizations soon followed.

In an attempt to strengthen its position, MGM acquired another film company, United Artists (UA), in 1981. Nonetheless, MGM/UA Entertainment continued its downward slide. In 1986 the corporation was bought by the Turner Broadcasting System, which sold off most of MGM's assets but kept its library of more than 3,300 films. Having gutted the company, Turner then passed MGM to the Rome-based Pathe Communications Corporation. After more restructuring, MGM-Pathe was acquired by one of its creditors. Finally in 1996 MGM was purchased by Kirk Kerkorian, a Las Vegas businessman who also owned MGM in the 1970s. *See also* BEN-HUR; THE WIZARD OF OZ.

Further Reading
Harmetz, Aljean. *The Making of* The Wizard of Oz. New York: Knopf, 1977.

Metropolis

Made in 1927, *Metropolis* was one of the first films to use the Shuftan process, a technique whereby mirrors reflect images of models, miniatures, or paintings onto a set so that they can be filmed as part of the live action. The movie was made by noted German filmmaker Fritz Lang, who was noted for employing elaborate special effects.

Lang took two years to complete *Metropolis,* at a cost of more than 1 million marks. Half of this money was spent on re-creating a futuristic city of towers connected with ramps, both with miniature and full-sized sets. The miniature set had 5,000 feet of roadways, and the full-sized set had a hidden dump tank capable of flooding the city on cue.

All of the sets in *Metropolis* were built in forced perspective, which means that they were angled to make it appear as though they were larger than they actually were. This was a fairly new concept in filmmaking. Another new element was Lang's use of photographic techniques such as dissolves and multiple exposures to express the emotions of his characters. For example, a series of multiple exposures to show different background images was used to reflect a character's attempts to decide between two choices in her life.

But perhaps the most memorable scene in *Metropolis* was its depiction of a robot being created in a laboratory. It featured a great deal of electricity and drama and was later re-created almost in its entirety in the 1931 movie *Frankenstein,* in which a scientist creates a monster from cadaver body parts. *See also* LANG, FRITZ; SHUFTAN, EUGENE.

Further Reading
Brosnan, John. *Movie Magic*. New York: St. Martin's Press, 1974.
Fry, Ron, and Fourzon, Pamela. *The Saga of Special Effects*. Englewood Cliffs, NJ: Prentice-Hall, 1977.
Kawin, Bruce F. *How Movies Work*. Berkeley: University of California Press, 1992.

Mighty Joe Young

The 1949 version of *Mighty Joe Young* won an Academy Award for its special effects, which were provided by two of the pioneers of stop-motion model animation: Willis O'Brien and Ray Harryhausen. The movie's title character, a giant ape, was actually a model that could be manipulated into various poses. It was created in basically the same fashion as the ape for *King Kong* (1933), which also featured O'Brien animation; artist Marcel Delgado made the stop-motion figures for both movies. *Mighty Joe Young* also employed the same basic photographic techniques as *King Kong*.

A 1998 version of *Mighty Joe Young,* however, provided new advances to the field of special effects. Rather than use stop-motion animation and a model to create the giant ape, the film featured a live actor wearing a sophisticated animatronic costume. Designed by Rick Baker, whose company, Cinovation, is a leading supplier of creature effects, this costume employed a new hot-melt adhesive in its chest area and had a new eye-blink mechanism that made its expressions more realistic. The costume's arms were stronger than those in previous ape costumes, allowing the actor to put significant weight on them, the way a real gorilla would.

The 1998 *Mighty Joe Young* also inspired the creation of new photographic technology, which was provided by Dream Quest Images. In order to film background footage for a scene in which the gorilla would run through a jungle, Dream Quest devised a new compact, high-speed, real-time motion control system. Called the Zebra dolly, this system could propel a camera at 15 mph along a precision track on a location shoot. Dream Quest also commissioned Eastman Kodak to make a new film stock for the movie, because the ones already available left a magenta line around the gorilla image when it was separated from a bluescreen background; the reason for this had to do with the color of the gorilla, which was a dark brown-red. Previous filmmakers had dealt with this problem by eliminating the border of the image, but for the gorilla this would mean that it would have a smooth edge instead of ruffled fur.

The company also caused advances in the field of digital effects. For example, Dream Quest computer experts developed a new software program to create digital hair, so that for some scenes they could employ a computer-generated gorilla that matched the costumed one. Digital hair had already been developed for *The Flintstones* (1994) and *Jumanji* (1995), but the artists at Dream Quest felt that it did not accurately reproduce the varied directional growth of fur. Dream Quest also created new proprietary software tools to animate the creature's face, to shade any skin that was not covered by hair, and to create realistic muscle jiggle when the animal moved. *See also* DELGADO, MARCEL; DIGITAL EFFECTS; DREAM QUEST IMAGES; HARRYHAUSEN, RAY; MINIATURES AND MODELS; O'BRIEN, WILLIS; STOP-MOTION MODEL ANIMATION.

Miniatures and Models

A model is a replica of an object. It can be full-sized (typically called a mock-up), or it can be a miniature. Both types of special effects have been used since the beginning of filmmaking. Some of the first miniatures seen in a motion picture were model ships that appeared in the 1899 short film *The Battle of Manilla Bay.*

Miniatures are typically discussed in terms of scale, which is a means of comparing the model's size to that of the full-sized object it represents. For example, a miniature built in a scale of 1/200 has 1 foot for every 200 feet of the full-sized object. The same miniature built in a scale of 1/24 is far larger, with 1 foot for every 24 feet of the full-sized object.

Miniatures built in fairly large scales that represent huge objects can therefore be quite big. For example, the 1/6-scale model of a cliff used in *Cliffhanger* (1993) was 60 feet wide, 50 feet high, and 30 feet deep, and a Martian spaceship in *Mars Attacks!* (1996) had a diameter of 25 feet and a weight of 3,500 pounds. The volcano miniature featured in *Dante's Peak* (1997) was 30 feet tall and 110 feet at its base.

Most miniatures used in special effects work are built to be extremely durable, because they must be able to withstand repeated filming over several months, usually under hot lights. Miniature sets are often made of carved polystyrene sprayed with foam, onto which various details, such as miniature trees, are attached. Spaceships and other vehicles are constructed of a metal framework covered by foam, urethane, styrene, and/or plastic. Many miniature sets have complex electronics, working lights, and some form of internal air conditioning to keep these electronics from overheating with constant use under hot stage lights.

Surface details on spaceships, vehicles, and buildings are often done in etched brass. For buildings, windows might be backed with light boxes displaying miniature interiors to provide the model with depth and realism. This technique has also been used for spaceships in the most recent *Star Trek* movies (1994–1998).

The earliest model spaceships were sleek in appearance. However, in 1972 special effects expert Douglas Trumbull changed movie audiences' expectations with his spaceships for *Silent Running.* These miniatures had a hodgepodge of surface details, created with parts cannibalized from plastic model kits sold in hobby shops. This model-building practice would later be used for the spaceships in *Star Wars* (1977), *Close Encounters of the Third Kind* (1977), *Star Trek: The Motion Picture* (1979), and *Blade Runner* (1982).

Models with the most detail, used for closeup work, are called hero models, because they are the miniature "stars" of the movie. Background models are much less detailed. Stunt models, which are used for crashes, pyrotechnics, and other destructive work offer some details but are also made of different materials from a corresponding hero model. For example, there were two space station models used to film miniature work on *Armageddon* (1998). The hero version was a 1/20-scale, highly detailed Plexiglas and styrene model, while the pyrotechnics version was a 1/12-scale model made of cardboard and epoxy resins. While filming the explosion of the pyrotechnics model, special effects experts used a device that timed blasts to the millisecond. This device was linked to the same computer that was driving the motion-control camera.

Aside from the miniatures themselves, the motion-control camera is the most important component of model photography. Although crude motion-control devices were used earlier, the first motion-control system used for extensive miniature work was developed for the 1977 movie *Star Wars*. This system completely changed the field of miniature photography. A motion-control system makes it possible for a miniature to be photographed repeatedly using the same camera moves and settings each time. Not only can the camera be programmed to move, but the model itself can move on a stand called a support pylon that has motors driven by the same computer that controls the camera.

The ability to repeat a filming session, or pass, using the exact same movements, angles, and camera settings, is important because miniature effects require many layers of a particular image. The reason for this involves the different film speeds required to shoot the model's different working devices, which include lights, moving parts, and pyrotechnics. Some of these elements must be shot with a faster film than others, and motion control allows a person to shoot the same move but with different levels of exposure for each pass. For example, in *Armageddon,* the tiny lightbulbs on the shuttle model had to be shot at a speed of 2 to 8 seconds/frame, but the beauty pass, which is a sustained closeup of a model with none of its devices working, had to be shot at a speed of 1 second/frame.

In other situations, a separate pass is used to add live action within a model. For example, if a filmmaker wants the image of a live actor added to the window of a model, a pass is done with a bluescreen insert in that window and the live action is composited there later. By using the motion-control camera to exactly duplicate the model's position and the camera angles, each pass can be precisely lined up with all the others during the compositing process. This not only makes it easier to insert live-action elements but enables the filmmaker to manipulate the various layers of the spaceship image to adjust their relative color and brightness.

Whether they include interior bluescreen elements or not, all miniatures are typically filmed in front of a bluescreen, greenscreen, or similar background, so that the miniature can be pulled from that background and composited into a live-action background plate or a computer-generated background. In the case of miniature buildings, often only a few floors of the model are built, with the rest supplied with computer graphics. This was the case with *The Fifth Element* (1997) and the most recent *Batman* movies (1995–1997).

Creating an entirely computer-generated city, however, would require too much computer storage space and processing speed. Similarly, although movies such as *Star Trek: First Contact* (1996) have employed some computer-generated spaceships instead of miniature ones, they were not used for all spaceship shots because they proved a less impressive substitute for long closeups of the real miniatures. However, the technology for such work is changing, and consequently the *Star Trek* movie, *Star Trek: Insurrection*

(1998), relies entirely on computer-generated spaceships. Still, in some cases it is possible for an audience to discern a computer-generated image from a real object, whether miniature or full-sized, if the camera lingers on the image long enough. Therefore although a few special effects experts believe that computer graphics will eliminate the need for miniatures, others argue that it will take major advances in technology for this to occur. Moreover, several recent movies, including *Dante's Peak* (1997), *Volcano* (1997), and *Armageddon* (1998), have relied on miniatures to create the bulk of their special effects shots. *See also* ARMAGEDDON; CLIFFHANGER; DANTE'S PEAK; MARS ATTACKS!; STAR TREK MOVIES; VOLCANO.

Further Reading

Cadigan, Pat. *The Making of* Lost in Space. New York: HarperPrism, 1998.

Sammon, Paul M. *Future Noir: The Making of* Blade Runner. New York: Harper Collins, 1996.

Vaz, Mark Cotta. *Visions of* Armageddon. New York: Hyperion, 1998.

Vaziri, Todd. "Boldly Trekking into the Digital World." *VFX/HQ Spotlight*. http://vfxhq.com/spotlight98/9805b.html, May 1998.

Mix, Tom (1880–1940)

A skilled rider, actor Tom Mix is representative of the cowboy actors/stuntmen of the silent-film era. He performed his own horse stunts during the 1910s and 1920s in more than 100 Western movies, leaping onto horses and galloping over rough terrain in such movies as *The Daredevil* (1920), *The Trouble Shooter* (1924), and *Son of the Golden West* (1928). He was also skilled at the horse transfer, whereby he leapt from a galloping horse onto another moving object such as a wagon or train. He could also transfer from a moving train to a ladder dangling from an airplane.

In the 1930s and 1940s Mix had an extremely popular radio show. Born in 1880, Mix joined a Wild West Show in 1906 and won a national rodeo championship in 1909. His first movie role was in *Ranch Life of the Great Southwest* (1910), in which he had a bit part. In addition to his movie career, he had a three-year tour with the Ringling Broth-

ers Circus performing horse tricks. Mix died in 1940 in an automobile accident when his car plunged into a desert gully.

Model Mover

A model mover is a mechanized cradle that holds a model during miniature photography. The device can be programmed to pitch, roll, tilt, or otherwise move the model while the camera is filming. *See also* MINIATURES AND MODELS.

Morphing

Morphing is the gradual transformation of one image into another. The segue from one image to the next has always been accomplished with computer software. However, the images themselves were originally of live actors and/or puppets. For example, the first use of morphing, which appeared in *Willow* (1988), was done with an actress and a series of animal puppets photographed in front of a bluescreen. Computer software automatically merged one image into the next.

The first morph to employ a computer-generated figure appeared in *Terminator 2* (1991), when a digital robot, or cyborg, took on a human form. First, digital experts created the computer-generated image from films of the live actor, and then they used morphing software to transform one image into the other.

Example of morphing in *Terminator 2: Judgement Day* (1991), in which an alien transforms itself from a section of floor into a human figure. *Industrial Light & Magic. Terminator 2: Judgement Day. (Tri-Star, 1991)/Photofest.*

A subsequent morph, in *The Abyss* (1989), involved a more complicated computer-generated creature, which appeared to be made of water. This creature transformed its face to match various humans. To make these matches more exact, the actors' faces were scanned with a laser, digitized, and used to shape the face of the computer-generated creature.

Today morphing is a common effect in movie and television work. In addition, inexpensive morphing software is available commercially that will run on a home computer. Easy to operate, it allows the user to morph a photograph of one person into another. *See also* THE ABYSS; COMPUTER GRAPHICS; *TERMINATOR 2: JUDGEMENT DAY; WILLOW.*

Further Reading

Vaz, Mark Cotta, and Patricia Rose Duignan. *Industrial Light & Magic: Into the Digital Realm.* New York: Del Rey, 1996.

Motion Capture

Motion capture is the means by which the movements of a live actor are recorded, turned into digital information, and used to create computer-generated actors.

There are many ways to accomplish motion capture. One of the most common is to put the live actor in a bodysuit onto which approximately 30 reflective plastic balls, each less than 1 inch in diameter, have been attached. The actor is then placed in a motion-capture studio to perform various movements, sometimes in conjunction with props and set pieces. Several high-speed cameras record the actor from various angles; these cameras emit an infrared light that illuminates a special coating on the plastic balls. The result is an image of white dots moving against a black background. A computer then translates this information into animated digital wireframe skeletons onto which costumes can be placed.

A modification of this approach was tried for the movie *Titanic* (1997). Experts at a motion-capture facility called House of Moves decided to record actors in full costume rather than in a body suit. They pinned or velcroed as many as 68 plastic balls onto the clothing, which included long, swaying skirts, thereby sparing digital artists the work of determining the clothing movements themselves. However, a great deal of digital work was still required to clean up the images, because sometimes the computer would mix up one dot with another as their paths crossed, and other times the clothing would obscure a marker entirely. Digital animators also had to work with the images frame by frame to make them more lifelike or more unique, to create smoother motions, and to duplicate them as necessary. In all, approximately 30 actors were used to create as many as 500 digital passengers in some scenes.

Early motion-capture systems could only capture a small part of the body at one time, so the head, body, face, and hands were recorded separately and pieced together later. In addition, animators did not use reflective balls; instead they linked a bodysuit or headgear directly to the computer via cables, which greatly restricted the actors' movements.

Today's motion-capture systems are far more sophisticated, and they allow a moving figure to be viewed from any angle. This makes them superior to the alternative, which is to film a live actor, digitally reduce his or her image, and then insert that image into a computer-generated scene, because the filmed, live-action image is two-dimensional and cannot be rotated during postproduction. *See also* TITANIC.

Further Reading

Shay, Don. "Back to *Titanic*." *Cinefex 72*, December 1997.

Motion-Control Camera Systems

Motion-control camera systems allow the camera to perform the exact same movements and functions in the exact same way over and over again. Camera movements, shutter action, lens adjustments (such as zooms and closeups), lighting elements, and other components of a shot are all controlled automatically rather than manually. This is important for visual effects work, much of which requires repeated filmings, or passes, of the same shot.

The earliest motion-control camera system was the Repeater, invented by Gordon Jennings for his work on *Samson and Delilah* (1950). Operated by remote control, the device used prerecorded tape to instruct the camera to repeat movements such as tilts and pans. However, the camera body stayed in the same location.

The first sophisticated motion-control camera system was Dykstraflex, which was created to allow repeated photography of miniatures. In this case, both internal and external camera movements were electronically controlled, enabling John Dykstra, who invented the system, to make sweeping shots of spaceship models for the 1977 movie *Star Wars*. That same year, Douglas Trumbull developed the Icebox camera system for *Close Encounters of the Third Kind* (1977). His device recorded camera movements during live-action filming for replay during miniature photography.

Motion control is invaluable not only for miniature photography but also for scenes in which one actor is required to play more than one part in a movie. Because the camera can repeat the exact same movements for each pass, an actor can perform a scene as one character, move to a new position, and perform the same scene as a different character, making it appear as though the actor is talking to his twin. The path of a motion-control pass can be worked out on computer or manually with the motion-control camera; the camera is capable of recording these manual movements for later duplication.

Today's motion-control cameras are computerized devices that can either remain stationary or move along tracks or other predetermined courses. However, special effects experts working on the *Star Wars* movie, *The Phantom Menace,* experimented with a way to digitally record hand-held camera moves. *See also* CAMERAS, MOTION PICTURE; COMPUTER GRAPHICS; DYKSTRA, JOHN; ICEBOX CAMERA SYSTEM; *STAR WARS* MOVIES; TRUMBULL, DOUGLAS.

Further Reading
Kawin, Bruce F. *How Movies Work*. Berkeley: University of California Press, 1992.
Ohanian, Thomas A., and Michael E. Phillips. *Digital Filmmaking*. Boston: Focal Press, 1996.
Smith, Thomas G. *Industrial Light & Magic: The Art of Special Effects*. New York: Ballantine Books, 1986.
Vaz, Mark Cotta, and Patricia Rose Duignan. *Industrial Light & Magic: Into the Digital Realm*. New York: Del Rey, 1996.

Mouse Hunt

Released in 1997 by DreamWorks SKG Studios, *Mouse Hunt* is significant because it inspired new techniques in animatronics and mechanical effects, as well as improvements in existing computer animation software.

Most of the movie's special effects center around the plot of a mouse's attempts to keep two men from restoring and selling an old house. Animal trainer Boone Narr, owner of Boone's Animals for Hollywood, provided 60 mice for the film. He spent six months training them to perform various acts, and was so successful that the filmmakers ended up using real animals in more scenes than intended. However, the mice had difficulty keeping still, so for closeups director Gore Verbinski relied on animatronic mice made by the Stan Winston Studio. In order to hold the complicated animatronic mechanisms, each animatronic mouse was built $4\frac{1}{2}$ times larger than life-sized, which meant that it had to be operated on correspondingly scaled-up sets.

Each mouse had remote-controlled facial features and a cable-controlled head and neck, and its arms were controlled via a telemetry device. One of the six puppeteers operating the soft-foam figure could also place a hand inside to create additional torso movements when necessary. In addition, the animatronic mouse had an air-controlled bladder that simulated breathing.

Stan Winston Studio also built an animatronic cat with six different detachable heads, each one featuring a different facial expression. Its front and hind legs could move in a variety of ways, and its shoulders and body were mechanized as well. The cat was operated via an external, computer-controlled telemetry device that sent a radio signal to the figure, a system that Stan Winston had developed for his dinosaur animatronics in

The Lost World (1977). Like the mouse, the cat was built larger than life, at 150-percent scale.

About 150 of the mouse shots were not done with real animals or animatronics but with computer-generated animals provided by Rhythm & Hues, the company responsible for the "talking" animals in the movie *Babe*. To create its digital mice, artists first sculpted a maquette (model) and used it as a guide to create their own wireframe images. They then used custom software to create the illusion of real bone and muscle, to provide lifelike skin and fur, and to animate the animal in a realistic fashion.

Digital techniques were also used to change footage of the real mice, particularly in regard to subtle facial features, or even the real actors, when they were caught looking in the wrong place for a computer-generated image. In one instance, a computer-generated olive was combined with footage of a real mouse, to make it appear as though the mouse were rolling the olive into a hole.

In filming the real mice, the director had to experiment with various lighting conditions and camera lenses in order to make the animals look more appealing and humanistic. Similarly, sometimes it was necessary to vary filming speed to make the mice appear to move more purposefully. In addition, the motion-control camera often shot from a "mouse perspective," which created various problems relating to focusing, depth of field, and the dirt found on the floor of the set.

One of the most difficult mouse-perspective scenes depicts the mouse running inside the walls and flooring of the house. This required a number of sets, each one representing a different part of the house. The camera would film the mouse's path on one set, stop, and then film the mouse's path on another set. A bluescreen was placed at the end of each set, so that the image of the next set's leading edge could be placed over the bluescreen to make the shot appear seamless.

Another impressive digital effect was a group of moths that explodes from an opened box of mothballs. The insects were created using new particle animation software that generated 2-D images in a chaotic fashion and then rendered them to appear 3-D.

In addition to digital and animatronic effects, *Mouse Hunt* featured a number of elaborate mechanical effects, which were under the supervision of Michael Lantieri. For example, in one scene a bathtub had to slide out over a frozen pond and then fall through the ice. The tub was actually propelled with a cable and winch system along an 8-foot-wide, 90-foot-long pier painted to look like ice. The fall through the ice was enacted separately, by placing the tub on a mechanism that could sink it. In both cases, the pond had been sprayed with paraffin to make its surface seem like thick ice.

Another mechanical effect involved an exterminator being pulled out from underneath the house by a cable. The exterminator was actually a stuntman acting on specially designed breakaway sets. Similarly, for a scene in which water build-up within the walls is supposed to explode into a room, the set was placed in a tank, and one of its breakaway walls was hit with 45,000 gallons of water.

To make a room full of mousetraps go off en masse, the floor of the set was riddled with tiny holes, through which wires were attached to the trap mechanisms. Three crew members sat underneath the floor to cut wires at key moments, thereby causing the mousetraps to snap and fly up to 18 feet in the air. A few more vigorous mousetraps were added to the scene via computer graphics.

Other mechanical effects involved pyrotechnics. For example, in one scene a character shoots at the floor of the house and accidentally hits a bug bomb canister, which then explodes. This required the special effects crew to replace the hard floor of the set with one made of tempered glass. The glass was painted black, dusted with black powder, and then covered with fabric. Beneath the floor were wooden beams wrapped with primacord, which were exploded to create the effect. Stuntmen standing on top of the floor wore special fireproof clothing to protect them during the explosion, and hung from wires that controlled their descent. The collapse of the house near the end of the film was also accomplished with pyrotechnics, although the shot involved only a 56-foot-tall façade and its support system, rigged to fall. *See also* ANIMALS; ANIMATRONICS; *BABE;* DREAMWORKS SKG; LANTIERI, MICHAEL; *THE LOST WORLD*; MECHANICAL EFFECTS; SPIELBERG, STEVEN; WINSTON, STAN.

Further Reading
Shay, Estelle. "Of Mice and Men." *Cinefex* 73, March 1998.

Multiple Exposure

A multiple exposure occurs when several images, each photographed at a different time, are placed on the same frame(s) of film. A double exposure is when only two such images are joined together.

In the early years of filmmaking, the multiple exposure effect was created in-camera by exposing the film's negative to light to record an image, then rewinding it and exposing it again, this time to a different image. Today a multiple exposure is made during postproduction using an optical printer; this device uses a projection system to place filmed elements from various sources into one frame and photograph them together. Elements can also be put together digitally, via computer software that composites, or layers, them onto a background plate. *See also* COMPOSITING; OPTICAL PRINTER.

Further Reading
Kawin, Bruce F. *How Movies Work*. Berkeley: University of California Press, 1992.

Multiplicity

Released in 1996 by Columbia Pictures, *Multiplicity* was responsible for the development of a new digital compositing system and a new motion-control tracking system, both of which were necessary to meet the demands of its storyline. The movie featured one actor, Michael Keaton, playing five parts, himself and four clones; this required more than 100 special effects shots, many of them involving elaborate clone interactions.

To help create these shots, Boss Film Studios invented a digital compositing system that could provide a rough videotape of a scene within minutes of filming it. The special effects facility had been founded by Richard Edlund, an expert in such work. Boss also developed the idea of using a handheld video playback system to guide an actor playing a multiple role, a technique that is common today. In the case of *Multiplicity*, Michael Keaton acted the role of Character A as the video system recorded him from the position of Character B. When Keaton acted the scene a second time as Character B, the Character A position was held by a stand-in with a video monitor on his shoulder. This video monitor provided Keaton with an image of himself as Character A, thereby enabling the actor to see his counterpart in the scene and respond accordingly.

Another Boss Film Studio invention for *Multiplicity* was a motion-control tracking system that recorded an actor's actions on the set during the first pass. As the scene was acted the second time, this system projected laser graphics onto the set to show the actor where he had walked the first time. The laser's light was timed to be projected only when the camera shutter was closed; it blinked off when the shutter was open. This blink was so fast that the human eye could not detect it, yet it ensured that the camera would not photograph the light.

Filmmakers also used small, portable greenscreens to isolate the actor within scenes. These portable screens were made either with a special digital green cloth or with foam core pieces painted with digital green paint. When placed on one half of the set, they created a split screen. In addition, sometimes a stand-in was dressed in a digital green suit and hood to act as a "place-holder" for Keaton. This occurred, for example, in the scene where Keaton has to bump chests with his clone. *See also* BLUESCREEN PROCESS; EDLUND, RICHARD; SPLIT-SCREEN PHOTOGRAPHY; MOTION-CONTROL CAMERA SYSTEMS.

Further Reading
Pourroy, Janine. "Split Personalities." *Cinefex* 67, September 1996.

The Mummy

Featuring the visual effects work of Industrial Light & Magic (ILM), the 1999 movie *The Mummy* employed several new computer animation tools to create a realistic computer-generated decayed, but living, human. Of these tools, the most important was innovative software that automatically made the skin of a digital character move realistically as the character walked. For previous movies such as *The Lost World* (1997), computer animators had to manually identify which areas of skin on a creature should move. The new software also created realistic bone, muscle, flesh, and organ movements; these body parts could often be glimpsed through the title character's decayed skin.

The mummy's gross body movements were established via motion capture, in order to match its walk and other characteristic gestures with those of the actor who would portray the mummy once it was restored to normal human form. This actor was photographed with eight video cameras as he performed in a motion-capture suit on a motion-capture set. The resulting data was then refined and altered using sophisticated motion-capture tools to suit the needs of a particular scene. For example, new motion-capture software allowed animators to retime

Computer-generated mummy with actors Brendan Frasier (left) and Rachel Weisz in *The Mummy* (1999). *Industrial Light & Magic/Photofest.*

movements, so that the computer-generated mummy would reach a particular spot sooner than the actor had while performing the scene.

The character's more subtle movements were not supplied by motion capture but by frame-by-frame animation. For facial animation, the digital artists used Caricature (or Cari) software, a computer program originally developed for the 1996 movie *Dragonheart*. Some shots, however, combined a digital effect with images of the live actor. In such shots, only part of the mummy's face was decayed; this part was the digital effect. To make it easier for animators to place the digital decay, the actor wore a prosthetic makeup device that incorporated tracking markers. These markers were diodes that gave off a red light whenever they reached a certain position in respect to the camera. But while this visual reference made placement easier, it did not eliminate the need for animators to blend digital features with the actor's features by hand.

Another unique digital effect involved a large sandstorm. This image was created with particle animation software, which generates and moves a swarm of dots. Although this technique had been used previously for such movies as *Twister* (1996) and *Starship Troopers* (1997), its use in *The Mummy* required the development of new shading software that could create swirling streams of sand within the storm. A face that appears in the sand was created using a scanned image of an actor's face.

There were more than 120 shots depicting sweeping desert sands, but none of these were as complicated as a shot depicting a fiery hailstorm that destroys Cairo, Egypt. This single shot featured more than 100 elements, including miniatures, matte paintings, footage of both a moving cloud and real palm trees, 3-D computer-generated buildings, 3-D hail, and 3-D fires.

There are many other digital effects in the film, including a swarm of flies, deadly beetles, and several mummified soldiers and priests, the latter of which are cut into pieces during a climactic battle. The whole mummies in this scene were stunt performers in suits and makeup. Their costumes were scanned into a computer and, as with the main mummy character, their movements motion-captured so that digital artists could match them to their computer-generated counterparts. *See also* ANIMATION, COMPUTER; *DRAGONHEART;* INDUSTRIAL LIGHT & MAGIC; *THE LOST WORLD;* MOTION CAPTURE.

Further Reading
Shay, Estelle. "Thoroughly Modern Mummy." *Cinefex 77,* April 1999.

Muren, Dennis (1950–)

As a visual effects supervisor at Industrial Light & Magic (ILM), Dennis Muren has been involved with some of the greatest visual special effects work in filmmaking. He shared Academy Awards in visual effects for *The Empire Strikes Back* (1980), *ET: The Extraterrestrial* (1982), *Return of the Jedi* (1983), *Indiana Jones and the Temple of Doom* (1984), *Innerspace* (1987), *The Abyss* (1989), and *Terminator 2: Judgement Day* (1991). He also worked on *Dragonslayer* (1981), *Jurassic Park* (1993), *Dragonworld* (1994), *Casper* (1995), and *Jumanji* (1995).

Born in 1950, Muren became interested in movies as a boy. During his freshman year in college, he borrowed $8,000 from his friends to finance a science fiction film called *The Equinox* (1970). Muren not only produced and directed the movie but acted in it himself. Assisted by his friend Jim Danforth, an expert in stop-motion photography, he shot *The Equinox* on 16 mm film and then sold it at a profit to a film distributor who blew it up to 35 mm.

After the film distributor replaced all but Muren's special effects with new footage, Muren decided that he was better suited for special effects work than directing. He continued to experiment with effects, making extra money in college by working on television commercials part-time. After graduation, however, he had trouble finding a special effects job. Just as he was beginning to despair of breaking into the field, he was hired to work at ILM, which was then preparing to make *Star Wars*, as a specialist in stop-motion animation and miniatures. Eventually he became senior effects supervisor at ILM. In the 1999

The Phantom Menace, Muran was in charge of all visual effects related to underwater scenes featuring an alien city, a submarine, and three sea monsters. He was also responsible for a climactic battle scene involving the Gungan army and the Trade Federation. For this scene Muran placed computer-generated characters within an environment created by scanning his own still photographs of hills and valleys into a computer and altering the landscape to make it look alien. He also scanned in images of explosions that had been filmed on a soundstage. *See also* *DRAGONSLAYER;* *ET: THE EXTRATERRESTRIAL;* *INDIANA JONES* MOVIES; INDUSTRIAL LIGHT & MAGIC; *JUMANJI; JURASSIC PARK; STAR WARS* MOVIES.

Further Reading
Bouzereau, Laurent, and Jody Duncan. Star Wars: *The Making of* Episode I: The Phantom Menace. New York: Ballantine, 1999.
Shay, Don. "Dennis Muren: Playing It Unsafe." *Cinefex* 65, March 1996.
Smith, Thomas G. *Industrial Light & Magic: The Art of Special Effects.* New York: Ballantine Books, 1986.

Murnau, Friedrich Wilhelm (F.W.) (1888–1931)

German filmmaker F.W. Murnau is best known for his 1921 silent film *Nosferatu,* which featured many cinematographic and special effects techniques unique for their time. For example, in one scene Murnau chose to show the film's negative image rather than its positive one, so that areas normally dark would appear light and vice versa. In another scene, he used a dissolve to make the main character, a vampire, seem to fade away when exposed to sunlight. Murnau also shot much of the film on location, a rare practice in German cinema of the period.

Another of Murnau's films, *The Last Laugh* (1924), featured only one intertitle, or caption; the silent film expressed its story through visuals rather than words. The plot concerns a hotel doorman who loses his job, then steals a uniform and pretends he is still employed so he won't have to reveal the truth to his family. In telling this tale, Murnau's cameraman, Karl Freund, used freeform

Vampire in F.W. Murnau's 1921 silent film *Nosferatu*. *Photofest.*

camera movements, unusual in an era when cameras were traditionally stationary.

Murnau made more than 20 films between 1919 and 1931. Born in 1888, he studied art and literary history at the University of Heidelberg before becoming a protégé of Max Reinhardt (1873–1943), a director and theater owner in Berlin who trained many of Germany's most famous filmmakers and actors. Murnau served as a pilot in World War I, and during one flight he landed in Switzerland, where he remained until the end of the war. At that point he returned to Germany and began directing films.

In 1927, Fox Studios asked Murnau to come to the United States to make movies. His first American work was *Sunrise* (1927). After two more movies he made *Tabu* (1931), which was filmed on location in the South Pacific. A week before the movie was released, Murnau was killed in a car accident. *See also* FREUND, KARL.

My Favorite Martian

The 1999 movie *My Favorite Martian* featured one of the most complex puppets ever constructed. Representing a Martian in his natural form (as opposed to the human shape he later takes), the life-sized figure was oper-

ated by 12 puppeteers. A large hydraulic mechanism allowed the body to stretch and contract, and the creature could rise on its legs via rod-puppeteering or by being lifted on a boom. The arms were moved by cables, while the head contained 47 servo-mechanisms to control facial movements. A head of the Martian in human form was created for another scene in which the alien falls apart. This head did not move; its eye blinked and other facial twitches were a digital effect.

Many other scenes combined digital and physical effects. For example, in one scene, the Martian levitates ice cream scoops, cones, and buckets. Some of these items were real props on the set, hanging from strings attached to a mechanism that revolved them, while others were computer-generated. In another scene, a dress-clad monster hurls a man across a room. The monster was computer-generated; the man was a real stuntman who performed on a greenscreen set and was flung by a mechanical arm. Still other shots employed models and miniatures. For example, an automobile featured in a chase scene and the Martian's spaceship appeared as full-scale mockups, miniatures, and 3-D computer-generated images. The movie also featured a great deal of morphing, whereby computer software converts a live-action image into a digital one, or vice versa.

One of the most complicated computer-generated images in the film was the Martian's suit, Zoot, which had a personality of its own. Made to look like a real suit that would be worn on the set, it was typically animated via motion capture, which acquires data related to a performer's movements and digitally applies them to a computer-generated image. However, animators had to adjust these movements manually. In some cases, shots were created entirely through manual computer animation, such as when the suit twisted into a ball or wrung itself out after being in the wash. *See also* ANIMATION, COMPUTER; MORPHING; MOTION CAPTURE; PUPPETS.

Further Reading

Martin, Kevin H. "Martian Chronicles." *Cinefex* 77, April 1999.

N

Needham, Hal (1931–)

Director Hal Needham began his career as a stuntman, and his movies often feature automobile stunts. Born in 1931, he first began performing car and motorcycle stunts as a teenager, when he worked for various circuses. During the Korean War he became a paratrooper whose job was to test parachute designs for the United States military. He subsequently worked as a tree trimmer before meeting a stuntman and deciding to join the profession himself.

Needham's first assignment was to parachute from the wing of a flying airplane. He subsequently climbed trees, executed falls, and did car and motorcycle stunts, performing as a stuntman and movie extra for several years before working his way up to being a stunt coordinator and second-unit director. In this capacity he was responsible for the stunts on such films as *McLintock!* (1968), *Beau Geste* (1966), *Little Big Man* (1970), and *Semi-Tough* (1977). He then became a director specializing in action movies that featured car stunts. These include *Smokey and the Bandit* (1977), *The Cannonball Run* (1981), and *Stroker Ace* (1983). *See also* STUNTS.

Further Reading
Miklowitz, Gloria D. *Movie Stunts and the People Who Do Them.* New York: Harcourt Brace Jovanivich, 1980.

Negative, Film

A film negative is the undeveloped celluloid strip that runs through a still or movie camera. Motion picture film comes in different widths, including 35mm and 70mm. However, a 70mm negative is actually only 65mm wide, with the extra 5mm allotted for the six soundtracks that are added to the final print.

The film is held in the camera by sprockets that go through perforations, or perfs, along the sides of the film. With standard 70mm film, each frame has five perfs. Standard 35mm film has four perfs per frame, but 35mm VistaVision widescreen film has eight perfs, because it runs the film through the camera horizontally rather than vertically to give each frame more width. *See also* ANAMORPHIC PROCESS; CAMERAS, MOTION PICTURE; PERFS; VISTAVISION.

Further Reading
Woods, Mark. "Formats, Fields, and Standards." *International Photographer*, March 1998.

Noah's Ark

Made in 1929, *Noah's Ark* included some of the most complicated in-camera matte shots of its time. A few pieces of film were exposed, rewound in the camera, and reexposed 18 different times to create the illusion that a wide variety of zoo animals were together in one shot. This work was supervised by optical effects expert Hans Koenekamp, who was one of the pioneers of trick photography.

The most elaborate special effect in the movie, however, was not an optical but a mechanical effect that occurred on the set during live-action filming, for a scene that depicts the destruction of the world by a massive flood. In one shot, thousands of people gathered at a temple are swept away by a rush of water. The director of photography, Hal Mohr, wanted to photograph this rush of water separately and then matte it into the live-action scene, believing that re-creating a real flood on the set would be too dangerous. When the producer refused Mohr's request, Mohr quit the picture, and the scene was staged as planned. A device was built to spill tons of water onto the soundstage, and at a key moment the flood was released to slam into thousands of extras, only 40 or 50 of which were qualified stuntmen. The result was chaos. Several people died and many were injured, including one man who lost his leg.

Scenes of the flood destroying the rest of the city were done with a miniature set spread out over an area 300 feet wide and 250 feet deep. This set took four months to build, at a cost of $40,000, partly because the models had to be rigged to break apart when 600,000 gallons of water released from a huge water tank slammed into them. Fifteen cameras recorded the scene, four at normal speed and 11 at high speed.

After its release, *Noah's Ark* was acclaimed for its realism but condemned for the injuries incurred by extras during filming. Consequently new safety procedures were established for the film industry to avoid a repeat of the incident. *See also* ACCIDENTS; KOENEKAMP, HANS; STUNTS.

Further Reading

Brosnan, John. *Movie Magic*. New York: St. Martin's Press, 1974.

Norin, Joseph (b. 1883), and Gustaf Norin (b. 1905)

Born in 1883 and 1905 respectively, Joseph and Gustaf Norin were father and son makeup artists who were responsible for many advances in the field. For example, they improved bald caps and created new appli-

ance materials for such movies as *The Good Earth* (1937) and *The Wizard of Oz* (1939). Both were artists before joining the MGM makeup department in 1935, which was then under the supervision of Jack Dawn. Now that the Norins are deceased, their work has been continued by Gustaf's sons Bob and John. Bob has provided makeup effects to such films as *Planet of the Apes* (1968), *Paint Your Wagon* (1969), and *The Towering Inferno* (1974), while John has concentrated on television shows. *See also* PLANET OF THE APES; THE TOWERING INFERNO; THE WIZARD OF OZ.

Further Reading

Taylor, Al. *Making a Monster*. New York: Crown, 1980.

The Nutty Professor

The 1997 film *The Nutty Professor* advanced the field of special effects makeup through the work of Rick Baker, one of the foremost experts in the field. The movie also furthered greenscreen and digital techniques developed during the making of *Multiplicity* (1996).

To make the professor, played by Eddie Murphy, appear to undergo an instantaneous transformation from fat to thin, Baker first made a lifecast of Murphy, then created a "fat suit" for him out of foam latex. Foam latex was also used for appliances to make Murphy's face and chin appear fat. The neck appliance contained a liquid-filled bladder to add to the illusion of fat. In addition, bladders were used to bulge Murphy's clothes at the beginning of a transformation. The rest of the transformation was done with a computer morphing program that, when provided with a beginning and ending shot of an image, simply filled in the steps between. A combination of makeup and computer software was used for a scene in which Murphy's lip appears to enlarge.

Digital effects and makeup also made it possible for Murphy to play all six characters in one scene. The actor played the scene once for each character he was portraying, talking to tennis balls hung at eye level so he would know where to look. He wore a concealed earpiece so he could hear tape recordings of his dialogue for the other parts. For each pass, he worked directly in front of a portable greenscreen so that his image could be composited later with others. The most complicated of these multiple-character scenes was one in which he walks through a screen door followed by himself. The second character through the doorway, Sherman, must catch the screen door as the first character, Sherman's mother, lets it go. To accomplish this, the door frame without its screen was filmed in front of a greenscreen with a motion-control camera. During this filming, Murphy as Mama walked through the door, and the doorframe was caught by an off-camera rod. For the second pass, with Murphy as Sherman, the action of the camera and the door were motion-controlled, thereby exactly duplicating the first sequence. The door screen was photographed later and digitally composited into the screen. In all, *The Nutty Professor* required approximately 150 special effects shots, many of them involving greenscreen work such as this. *See also* BAKER, RICK; BLUESCREEN PROCESS; MOTION-CONTROL CAMERA SYSTEMS; SPLIT-SCREEN PHOTOGRAPHY.

Further Reading

Duncan, Jody. *"The Nutty Professor:* Pleasingly Klump." *Cinefex* 67, September 1996.

Nye, Ben Sr. (b. ca. 1920)

Makeup artist Ben Nye Sr. developed many new makeup colors as well as a liquid plastic substance that, when applied and dried on skin, makes the skin appear wrinkled and old. He began his career in makeup in 1935 at Fox Studios. In 1939 he worked at MGM on the movie *Gone With the Wind,* and later he contributed to films at Warner Studios and Paramount. Eventually he became head of the makeup department at 20th Century Fox. He later worked on some of Fox's most important musicals, including *Oklahoma!* (1958) and *The King and I* (1956), and designed the fly mask worn by the lead actor in *The Fly* (1958). Nye left Fox in 1967 to develop his own line of movie makeup. *See also* MAKEUP; PARAMOUNT PICTURES; 20TH CENTURY FOX; WARNER BROTHERS.

O

O'Brien, Willis (1886–1962)

Special effects artist Willis O'Brien was the inventor of stop-motion model animation, which he called "animation in depth." Stop-motion animation was already in use when he entered the film industry, but he created many new techniques related to its use. He also employed clay and cloth figures, or models, as opposed to puppets, as previous stop-motion filmmakers had done.

Born in 1886, O'Brien was a cartoonist and sculptor before making his first stop-motion animation film, a short of a boxing match, in 1915. He was unable to sell the film, but his second short, *The Dinosaur and the Missing Link* (1915), was bought by the Edison Company for $525. O'Brien subsequently made several more shorts, experimenting with different animation techniques and figuring out how to combine animation with live action, before making his first full-length feature film, *The Lost World* (1925). This immensely successful movie depicted dinosaurs fighting with each other and stampeding through London.

O'Brien followed *The Lost World* with *King Kong* (1933), which is considered a film classic, and made several more movies before winning an Academy Award for his special effects for *Mighty Joe Young* (1949). Working with O'Brien on this film were modelmaker Marcel Delgado, who also worked on *King Kong*, and stop-motion model animator Ray Harryhausen, who went on to create his own classic special effects movies, which include *The Seventh Voyage of Sinbad* (1959), *Mysterious Island* (1961), and *Jason and the Argonauts* (1963). O'Brien's last animation work was for the 1963 movie *It's a Mad, Mad, Mad, Mad World*. He died in 1962. *See also* DELGADO, MARCEL; HARRYHAUSEN, RAY; *KING KONG; THE LOST WORLD; MIGHTY JOE YOUNG*.

Further Reading

Archer, Steve. *Willis O'Brien: Special Effects Genius*. Jefferson, NC: McFarland & Company, 1998.

Fry, Ron, and Pamela Fourzon. *The Saga of Special Effects*. Englewood Cliffs, NJ: Prentice-Hall, 1977.

Jenson, Paul M. *The Men Who Made the Monsters*. New York: Twayne, 1996.

Optical Effects

Optical effects, also known as opticals, are effects that have been created using an optical printer during postproduction. They were first used in the early 1930s, when the optical printer was invented, for such work as multiple exposures, dissolves, and the compositing of live-action footage with miniature photography. Prior to the 1930s, such effects were accomplished in-camera during filming and were known as photographic effects or trick photography. *See also* OPTICAL PRINTER.

Optical Printer

Invented in 1931, an optical printer is a device used to take a picture of a picture. It is composed of a process camera and a projector, called a printer head, that face each other, so that a projected image can be focused onto the film in the camera. The camera and printer head are on rails, enabling the distance between them to be adjusted in order to reduce, enlarge, or exactly duplicate the size of the projected image.

Modern optical printers, which are controlled by computer, have more than one projector. These projectors are placed at different angles; mirrors or prisms send their images to the camera lens, and multiple strips of film are run through the printer at a speed of approximately 2 to 3 frames per second.

Optical printers have many uses during postproduction. For example, they can create fades and dissolves by changing the size of the lens opening on the process camera. They can also put several images, filmed at different times, into one shot. Special effects elements such as matte paintings and miniatures can therefore be combined with live action to create a final shot called an optical composite, or simply a composite. An optical is any special effect made using an optical printer.

Optical printers are still used in modern special effects work, but many of their functions are gradually being replaced by computers, which can combine scanned-in images from various sources digitally rather than through projection. Digital compositing is highly effective and efficient, but it is also more expensive. Traditional optical techniques for compositing shots typically cost around 50 cents per frame, whereas digital scanning costs about $3 a frame. *See also* CAMERAS, MOTION PICTURE; COMPUTER GRAPHICS; DISSOLVE; DUNN, LINWOOD; FADES; MATTE PAINTINGS; MINIATURES AND MODELS; MULTIPLE EXPOSURE.

Further Reading

Imes, Jack. *Special Visual Effects: A Guide to Special Effects Cinematography.* New York: Van Nostrand Reinhold, 1984.

Kawin, Bruce F. *How Movies Work.* Berkeley: University of California Press, 1992.

Langford, Michael. *The Darkroom Handbook.* New York: Alfred A. Knopf, 1986.

McAlister, Michael J. *Language of Visual Effects.* Los Angeles: Lone Eagle Publishing, 1993.

Pincus, Edward, and Steven Ascher. *The Filmmaker's Handbook.* New York: Plume, 1984.

Robertson, Joseph F. *The Magic of Film Editing.* Blue Ridge Summit, PA: Tab Books, 1983.

P

Pal, George (1908–1980)

George Pal was an Academy Award-winning special effects expert who eventually became a producer-director. One of the pioneers of stop-motion model animation, he helped launch the career of Ray Harryhausen, who was responsible for many advances in the field.

Born in Hungary in 1908, Pal studied art, illustration, and cartooning at the Budapest Academy of Art. He then became an animator at the Hunnia Film Studio in Budapest. In 1931 he went to Berlin, Germany, to work for the UFA Studio before moving to Paris, where a cigarette manufacturer paid him to make an animated short film advertising cigarettes. It was extremely popular and led to other advertising work. Pal soon accepted a job with an advertising agency in Holland, which allowed him to make stop-motion model animation films for entertainment as well as advertisement purposes. He called his entertaining films "Puppetoons."

In 1939, Pal moved to Los Angeles, California, where he agreed to make Puppetoons for Paramount Pictures. Paramount also financed the establishment of Pal's own studio, George Pal Productions. In 1943 he received an Academy Award for the techniques he developed in making his Puppetoons. He also received an Academy Award for his special effects work on *Destination Moon* (1950), *When Worlds Collide* (1951), *War of the Worlds* (1953), *tom thumb* (1958), and *The Time Machine* (1960). Pal died in 1980. *See also* HARRYHAUSEN, RAY; *DESTINATION MOON; WAR OF THE WORLDS.*

Further Reading

Brosnan, John. *Movie Magic*. New York: St. Martin's Press, 1974.
Fry, Ron, and Pamela Fourzon. *The Saga of Special Effects*. Englewood Cliffs, NJ: Prentice-Hall, 1977.
Johnson, John. *Cheap Tricks and Class Acts*. Jefferson, NC: McFarland & Company, 1996.

Paramount Pictures

Paramount Pictures originated in 1914 as a film distribution company. That same year, it was given the right to distribute movies from several important production companies, including Adolph Zukor's Famous Players Film Company and Jesse L. Lasky's Feature Play Company. These two companies soon merged with each other and then with 12 other major studios before joining with Paramount Pictures Corporation.

The name of this large entity was the Paramount Famous Lasky Corporation, and later Paramount Publix Corporation. During the 1920s it was one of the biggest and most lucrative silent-film studios in the United States, creating such blockbusters as Cecil B. DeMille's *The Ten Commandments* (1923). Nonetheless, the company went bankrupt in 1933. Two years later it was reestablished as Paramount Pictures Inc. and quickly became profitable again. The studio's success continued throughout the 1940s and 1950s, helped by regular offerings by prominent directors like Alfred Hitchcock. In 1954 Paramount introduced a major widescreen filming process, VistaVision, which was later used to create *Star Wars* (1977).

In 1966, Paramount became part of the Gulf & Western Industries Corporation, which eventually changed its name to Paramount Communications, and continued to produce major motion pictures. Some of these films were of crucial importance to the history of special effects, including *Star Trek: The Motion Picture* (1979) and its sequels and *Raiders of the Lost Ark* (1981) and its sequels. In 1994 the company was acquired by Viacom International but retained its Paramount label.

Park, Ray (1975–)

British stuntman Ray Park is best known for his portrayal of Darth Maul in the 1999 *Star Wars* movie *The Phantom Menace*. He was originally hired to choreograph the film's lightsaber fight sequences, a job that was subsequently filled by stunt coordinator Nick Gillard. During this sequence, Park performed an aerial backwards somersault during which he traveled 40 feet across a soundstage. He was launched into the air by a pneumatic ram; when jumped on, this device uses air pressure to propel a stuntperson upwards with great force.

Park began studying martial arts at age 7, and is an expert in those arts (particularly kendo), as well as in kickboxing, fencing, Oriental weaponry, and gymnastics. He previously performed stuntwork for *Mortal Kombat 2: Annihilation* (1997). *See also* STAR WARS MOVIES; STUNTS.

Paul, Robert W. (1869–1943)

Robert W. Paul designed one of the first theater projectors. Born in 1869, he manufactured scientific instruments until 1894, when two Greek showmen asked him to make six duplicates of an Edison and Dickson Kinetoscope they owned. This device enabled individuals to view its motion pictures through a peephole. Since Edison's patent on the Kinetoscope did not apply in England, Paul agreed to manufacture the duplicates, then made 60 more over the next year.

When the Edison Company refused to supply films for the copied machines, Paul manufactured a camera and began making his own movies for them, including *The Last Days of Pompeii* (1897), *The Haunted Curiosity Shop* (1901), and *The Butterfly* (1910). Some of his work featured innovative photographic effects such as animation, slow motion, and closeups; however, his movies did not bring him the fame of contemporary trick photographer George Melies.

Similarly, although Paul devised a way to project movies onto a screen, his fame was eclipsed by rival inventors August and Louis Lumiere, who demonstrated their own theater projection device in London on the same day as Paul (February 20, 1896). Nonetheless, Paul continued to perfect his moviemaking equipment until 1910, when he retired from the industry to manufacture scientific instruments again. He died in 1943. *See also* KINETOSCOPE; LUMIERE, AUGUST, AND LOUIS LUMIERE; MELIES, GEORGE.

Further Reading
Brosnan, John. *Movie Magic*. New York: St. Martin's Press, 1974.

Perfs

The term "perfs" is short for perforations, which are the slots along the side of a film negative used to hold the film in the camera. Different types of film have different numbers of perfs along a frame of film, and filmmakers often speak in terms of perfs when discussing their work. For example, they might say they are shooting in eight-perf, rather than state that they are using VistaVision, a 35mm widescreen film that has eight perforations per frame. *See also* VISTAVISION.

Pierce, Jack (1889–1968)

Makeup expert Jack Pierce created some of the most famous movie monsters of the 1930s and 1940s, including Frankenstein's monster,

Dracula, the Mummy, and the Wolf Man. Born in 1889, Pierce worked as a projectionist and theater manager before becoming a stuntman, character actor, cameraman, and finally a makeup artist. He was named the head of the makeup department at Universal Studios in 1936.

At Universal, Pierce developed unusual shades of greasepaint for the character of Dracula, which was played by actor Bela Lugosi, and for Frankenstein's monster, which was played by Boris Karloff. In fact, Pierce's vision of Frankenstein's monster remains its standard appearance today. He created the monster's facial structure with cotton and collodion, which is a mixture of nitrocellulose, alcohol, and ether typically used in the manufacturer of photographic film or as a coating for wounds. Pierce also made Karloff into the character of the Mummy, using cloth that had been cooked until it looked rotted, and he created the character of the Wolf Man, played by Lon Chaney Jr., with a rubber nose and some yak hair.

Eventually, however, Pierce's makeup techniques were replaced with more modern ones. He made his last film, *The House of Dracula,* for Universal in 1942. He was then let go from the company and began doing freelance work for television programs. Pierce died in 1968. His film credits include *Frankenstein* (1931), *The Mummy* (1932), *The Invisible Man* (1933), *Son of Frankenstein* (1939), *Frankenstein Meets the Wolf Man* (1943), *Abbott and Costello Meet Frankenstein* (1948), and *The Devil's Hand* (1961). *See also* INVISIBILITY; MAKEUP; UNIVERSAL STUDIOS.

Pixar

Pixar is a computer animation studio that created the first full-length movie made entirely with computer-generated images. Entitled *Toy Story,* the movie was released in 1995 and won several prestigious awards. It was also the first animated film nominated for a Best Picture Academy Award. In 1988, Pixar's *Tin Toy* won an Academy Award for Best Short Film, the first computer-animated film

to receive the honor. Another Pixar offering in 1988, *Geri's Game*, received the Academy Award for Best Animated Short.

In addition to awards for film content, Pixar has received numerous awards for its technical innovations. The company's vice president of creative development, John Lasseter, received an Academy Award for advancing 3-D computer animation; the executive vice president and chief technical officer, Dr. Ed Catmull, and the director of effects animation, Thomas Porter, won Academy Awards for achievements in the field of digital image compositing. Catmull is one of the pioneers of the field of computer graphics and created the first computer-generated image for a major motion picture.

Under the direction of such computer experts, Pixar developed two important software systems: Marionette, an animation software that models, lights, and animates figures, and RenderMan, a rendering software that creates photorealistic images. RenderMan is one of the most widely used software programs in the field of computer graphics; Pixar has proprietary rights to the program but also licenses it to other companies. Marionette is a proprietary software used in-house, as is Pixar's database of thousands of digital models, sets, textures, and surfaces.

Pixar was originally part of the Lucasfilm Computer Graphics Division, but it was spun off into a separate company in 1986. Located in Point Richmond, California, Pixar currently employs approximately 350 people. Its chairman and chief executive officer is Steve Jobs, the creator of Apple Computer. In addition to film work, Pixar develops CD-ROM software for personal computers. *See also* ANIMATION, COMPUTER; COMPUTER GRAPHICS; COMPUTER HARDWARE AND SOFTWARE; LUCAS, GEORGE.

Further Reading
Shay, Estelle. "Company File: Pixar." *Cinefex* 55, August 1993.
Street, Rita. *Computer Animation: A Whole New World.* Gloucester, MA: Rockport, 1998.

Planet of the Apes

The 1968 movie *Planet of the Apes* had a major impact on the field of makeup effects. The story required makeup artist John Chambers to design facial appliances that would make actors look like realistic talking apes. While working on this project, Chambers discovered that the conventional material for such appliances, rubber, was so thick and stiff that it muffled the actors' voices and did not allow the ape lips to move as they spoke. He therefore worked with chemists to develop a new type of rubber compound for the appliances, along with new adhesives, glues, and paints.

These substances were porous, so that the actors' skin could breathe and sweat through the appliances. Moreover, some of these appliances could be reused, which reduced makeup costs to approximately $700 to $800 per day. Chambers also streamlined the makeup application and removal process, using a large staff and teamwork to cut the time from approximately 10 hours to four and a half. All of these advances were quickly put into use by other makeup professionals. *See also* CHAMBERS, JOHN; MAKEUP.

Further Reading

Essman, Scott. "John Chambers: Maestro of Makeup." *Cinefex 71*, September 1997.

Taylor, Al. *Making a Monster*. New York: Crown, 1980.

Pleasantville

The 1998 movie *Pleasantville* employed revolutionary color-correction technology in order to selectively turn images filmed in color into black-and-white ones. This is different from colorization, which turns black-and-white images into color ones.

Color film was scanned into a computer, digitally manipulated, and then scanned back out onto film, which resulted in nearly 1,700 visual effects shots appearing in approximately 100 minutes of screen time. Because of this high volume of work, the filmmakers had to find a faster way to scan the film. They consequently acquired a new type of telecine device under development in Europe. Called the Spirit Datacine, the device transfers film

Actors Kim Hunter (left) and Roddy McDowall both before and after their ape makeup was applied for *Planet of the Apes* (1968). *Photofest.*

to digital files and puts them on videotape for editing at a speed of 4 frames per second. In contrast, the average scanner completes this process at a rate of 1 frame per 10–30 seconds. *See also* SCANNING.

Further Reading
MacDonald, Matthew J. "Color My World." *Cinefex* 76, January 1999.
Wallace, Amy. "Showing His True Colors." *Los Angeles Times Calendar*, September 20, 1998.

Plymouth Adventure

Released by MGM in 1952, *Plymouth Adventure* won an Academy Award for its special effects. The movie concerns the journey of the Mayflower from England to New England in the 17th century, and its effects primarily relate to a storm at sea. To re-create this storm, filmmakers primarily used optical effects that combined miniature photography and dramatic live-action footage.

Polo, Eddie (1875–1961)

Eddie Polo was a silent film actor who performed his own stunts. Born in 1875, he worked as a circus acrobat before making his first movie in 1913 as a stuntman. His first acting role occurred in 1915. That same year, he gained notoriety by being the first man to parachute off the Eiffel Tower. He subsequently starred in many movie serials, including *The Vanishing Dagger* (1920), *King of the Circus* (1920), *Captain Kidd* (1922), and *With Stanley in Africa* (1922). With the advent of sound, Polo discovered that he was unsuited for leading roles, and his career as a star ended. He died in 1961. *See also* STUNTS.

Further Reading
Miklowitz, Gloria D. *Movie Stunts and the People Who Do Them.* New York: Harcourt Brace Jovanivich, 1980.

Porter, Edwin S. (1869–1941)

Edwin S. Porter was one of the pioneers of the film industry. Many of his movies featured trick photography, and most employed those tricks not simply to dazzle audiences, as was the case with other filmmakers of the time, but to enhance the storytelling process. Also two of Porter's earliest films, *The Life of an American Fireman* (1903) and *The Great Train Robbery* (1903), were among the first movies to have a true beginning, middle, and end.

Born in 1869, Porter held a variety of jobs before becoming a projectionist in the late 1880s. He also developed his own projector and marketed it as an improvement over existing ones. In 1899 he started filming newsreels and selling them to the Edison Company. Two years later, Edison hired him to work as a cameraman, producer, and director. Porter's films were extremely popular, particularly *The Teddy Bears* (1907). Only a few minutes long, it featured seven small, moving teddy bears and is one of the earliest examples of stop-motion model animation. Another of his films, *Dreams of a Rarebit Fiend* (1906), employed an in-camera matte to create the illusion that a bed was flying over New York City.

Porter made films for Edison until 1909, when he started his own production company. In 1912 he became involved with the creation of a new studio that later evolved into Paramount Pictures. Porter oversaw the production of all of this studio's films, while continuing to direct his own pictures. He also experimented with new photographic techniques, including the widescreen and 3-D formats, and developed new projection equipment. Eventually Porter stopped making movies to concentrate on his inventions. He died in 1941. *See also* DISSOLVE; FADES; THE GREAT TRAIN ROBBERY; MATTE; MULTIPLE EXPOSURE; STOP-MOTION MODEL ANIMATION; 3-D.

Further Reading
Brosnan, John. *Movie Magic.* New York: St. Martin's Press, 1974.
Fry, Ron, and Pamela Fourzon. *The Saga of Special Effects.* Englewood Cliffs, NJ: Prentice-Hall, 1977.

Portrait of Jennie

The 1948 movie *Portrait of Jennie* won an Academy Award for its special effects. The movie concerns a woman who ages rapidly during the course of the story, and eventually the audience discovers that she is a ghost.

Makeup effects were therefore an important part of the film. However, *Portrait of Jennie* also included a climactic hurricane and tidal wave, created using full-sized and miniature sets as well as optical effects. *See also* OPTICAL EFFECTS.

The Poseidon Adventure

One of a series of disaster films created by producer Irwin Allen, the 1972 movie *The Poseidon Adventure* earned L.B. Abbott and A.D. Flowers Academy Awards for their special effects. The most significant effects were related to the overturning of a cruise ship.

To create the illusion that the ship was flipping over, set designers first re-created the dining room, or Grande Salon, of a real ship, the Queen Mary. This set was 118 feet long, 60 feet wide, and 28 feet high, and had an interchangeable ceiling and floor. Simply by switching the carpeted floor with the ornately decorated ceiling, the Grand Salon would appear upside-down.

For the moment when the ship begins to flip, the set was rigged to tilt up to 30 degrees. It was also reinforced to hold 4 feet of water, because, according to the plot, after the ship is upside-down a window bursts and floods the room. The window, which was made of breakaway glass, was blown out using explosives, and then shot with water by water cannons fueled by compressed air.

Three high-pressure water pumps were used to the create the subsequent flood, which created mayhem in a crowd of passengers a scene that included 125 stuntpeople. Many other stunts, including falls, jumps, and swimming, were featured in the film, most performed by stuntpeople but some by the actors themselves. *See also* ABBOTT, L.B.; ALLEN, IRWIN; BREAKAWAYS; FLOWERS, A.D.; PYROTECHNICS; STUNTS.

Further Reading

Fry, Ron, and Pamela Fourzon. *The Saga of Special Effects*. Englewood Cliffs, NJ: Prentice-Hall, 1977.
Kawin, Bruce F. *How Movies Work*. Berkeley: University of California Press, 1992.
McCarthy, Robert E. *Secrets of Hollywood Special Effects*. Boston: Focal Press, 1992.
Miklowitz, Gloria D. *Movie Stunts and the People Who Do Them*. New York: Harcourt Brace Jovanivich, 1980.
O'Conner, Jane. *Magic in the Movies*. Garden City, NY: Doubleday, 1980.
Stuntmen and Special Effects. New York: Ripley Books, 1982.

Postproduction

Postproduction is the stage of creating a movie that comes after the principle photography is complete. During postproduction the film is edited and many special effects are added to it via optical printing and/or computer software programs. Not only are shots visually composited during postproduction, but sound effects and soundtracks are added as well. At the end of postproduction, the film is in final form, ready to be copied and released for public viewing. *See also* COMPUTER GRAPHICS; OPTICAL PRINTER.

Further Reading

Kawin, Bruce F. *How Movies Work*. Berkeley: University of California Press, 1992.

Previsualization

Previsualization is any method that helps a filmmaker conceive how scenes will look before they are shot. This is especially important for movies that feature elaborate special effects. One example of previsualization is the storyboard, a series of sketches that illustrate the progression of scenes within a film. Storyboards were originally drawn by hand, but now storyboarding software has been developed to allow their creation on a computer.

The earliest digital previsualization occurred in the early 1990s, when directors began using an architectural design program called Virtus WalkThrough to plan sets. Today there are more sophisticated software programs available, such as LightWave, which was used to design a 3-D house exterior and other sets for the 1994 movie *Forrest Gump*.

In some cases, digital previsualization is used to envision how the actor will interact with a set. First a tentative set is established with computer software. Then a stand-in for an actor, vehicle, or other moving scene element is filmed in front of a bluescreen, and the filmed images are scanned into the computer background. This allows the filmmaker to see exactly how the actor or other moving elements will relate to a set's stationary elements, so that the set designer can make decisions regarding the building and arranging of furniture and other props.

Computers are also used to previsualize miniature sets. The alien transport machine in *Contact* (1997) was created using digital previsualization, as were the miniature buildings and vehicles in *Batman and Robin* (1997). For *Batman and Robin,* digital previsualization was also used to explore how the miniature vehicles would move around miniature buildings. This enabled the filmmakers to experiment with camera angles for important chase scenes and alter building designs, prior to construction, to suit their needs.

In addition, digital previsualization can be used to plot out entire special effects sequences, just as in traditional storyboarding. One recent example of this occurred during the making of *The Fifth Element* (1997). All but four or five of its 225 special effects shots were previsualized on computer. This kind of previsualization helps directors see exactly what a final shot will look like after compositing, and also help special effects houses estimate the complexity, and therefore the cost, of a particular effect. The 1999 *Star Wars* movie, *The Phantom Menace,* was the first film to use digital previsualization for every shot in the movie, rather than for just select special effects sequences. Digital storyboards, called animatics, were shown on a monitor on the set to guide the director during filming.

Many makeup designers, such as Rick Baker, also use computers to previsualize an actor's makeup. The shape of the actor's face is established via a scanned drawing or photograph, and then makeup appliances and prosthetics are designed digitally. Again, this helps both with design and with complexity/cost estimates. It also helps the special effects artist communicate with the director, so that both know exactly what the final product will look like. *See also* ANIMATICS; BAKER,

RICK; *BATMAN* MOVIES; COMPUTER GRAPHICS; MAKEUP; SCANNING; *STAR WARS* MOVIES; STORYBOARD.

Further Reading

Ohanian, Thomas A., and Michael E. Phillips. *Digital Filmmaking.* Boston: Focal Press, 1996.

Vincenzi, Lisa. "Digital Previsualization." *Digital Magic,* July 1997.

Production Designer

Also called an art director, the production designer works with a film's producer and director to establish the visual appearance of live-action shoots. This means that the production designer oversees the design and construction of sets and costumes, as well as the selection of props and filming locations.

Projection Processes

Projection processes involve the use of projectors to create special effects either during filming or in postproduction. There are two types of projection processes used during filming: rearscreen projection and front-screen projection.

Rearscreen projection originated in the 1930s, when filmmakers developed it as a way to make live actors in a studio appear to be elsewhere, usually outdoors in an exotic and/or dangerous environment. To create this illusion, the actor was placed in front of a screen onto which images were being projected from behind, either directly or via the reflection of a mirror. The actor was then filmed in concert with the projected, moving background.

Rearscreen projection has also been used to combine live action with stop-motion model animation. For example, in the 1959 movie *The Seventh Voyage of Sinbad,* stop-motion animator Ray Harryhausen employed this technique to create a scene in which a man engages in a swordfight with a skeleton. The actor rehearsed the scene with an Olympic fencer, then performed the same moves alone during filming. This film was then projected onto a miniature screen placed behind the 8-inch-tall skeleton stop-motion figure, and the figure was carefully animated, frame by frame, to make its actions appear to be taking place in concert with the live footage.

However, the rearscreen projection process often fails to create the illusion that foreground figures, whether puppets or live actors, are actually within the projected background. This is because the foreground figures are closer to the camera than the background images. In contrast, the front-projection process, which was developed in the 1950s, uses mirrors to merge the foreground and background images at the same distance from the camera, thereby creating a more realistic effect.

To accomplish this, the actor is first placed in front of a background screen. Then a two-way mirror is placed in front of the actor, so that the reflective side of the mirror is towards the actor and the see-through side of the mirror is facing the camera. A projector off to the side, working with a system of mirrors, then sends background images onto the reflective side of the mirror, which in turn bounces them past the actor, back onto the screen behind him. Meanwhile, the camera films the combined live action and projected background through the see-through side of the mirror, recording the actor as a part of the projected images rather than separate from them. Bright foreground lighting keeps projected images from showing on the actor's face and ensures that the shadow he casts back onto the screen is blocked by his own body.

Mirrors are also used in a projection process that adds special effects during postproduction. This process is called optical printing, which takes place via a device called an optical printer. The optical printer reflects projected images from different sources onto one piece of film for rephotographing. In this way, several images are put together, or composited, to create one shot. *See also* COMPOSITING; OPTICAL PRINTER.

Further Reading

Hines, Bill. "Techniques for In-Camera Effects." *International Photography*, December 1997.

Kawin, Bruce F. *How Movies Work*. Berkeley: University of California Press, 1992.

McKenzie, Alan, and Derek Ware. *Hollywood Tricks of the Trade*. New York: Gallery Books, 1986.

Stecker-Orel, Elinor. *Special Effects Photography Handbook*. Buffalo, NY: Amherst Media, 1998.

Stensvold, Mike. *In-Camera Special Effects*. Englewood Cliffs, NJ: Prentice-Hall, 1983.

Props

A prop is any accessory used in a scene, such as a food item, weapon, or writing implement. The prop might be life-sized but it might also be smaller or larger than life, depending on whether the filmmakers want an actor to appear to be a giant or a tiny creature dwarfed by ordinary objects.

Some scenes require numerous props. For example, filming the Exodus scene in *The Ten Commandments* (1956) required 172,000 props that included dishes, baskets, bundles, and carts. *Judge Dredd* (1995) employed 30 truckloads of props, as well as 200 neon signs and 150 lights, to create a futuristic city. *Small Soldiers* (1998) used more than 100 props, most of which were tiny weapons. However, whereas the props in *The Ten Commandments* and *Judge Dredd* were real, those in *Small Soldiers* were made with computer graphics.

Once a prop has been created as a digital image, it can be stored in a digital image database for repeated use. Real props are sometimes stored for reuse as well, but with storage space at a premium it is more typical to destroy them and recycle their materials for use in other props. In addition, some types of props are meant to be destroyed during filming. Called breakaways, they look real but have been manufactured to break easily during stuntwork. *See also* BREAKAWAYS; DIGITAL IMAGE DATABASE; *JUDGE DREDD*; *SMALL SOLDIERS*; STUNTS; *THE TEN COMMANDMENTS*.

Further Reading

Killick, Jane, with David Chute and Charles M. Lippincott. *The Making of* Judge Dredd. New York: Hyperion, 1995.

Prosthetics *See* MAKEUP.

Puppets

When a character in a movie cannot be portrayed by live animals or actors, it might be represented by a puppet. Modern puppets are extremely sophisticated. Designed using sketches and a series of models, they have realistic skin or fur, expressive faces, and fully posable armatures, and they often contain complex mechanisms.

Some puppets are powered simply by placing a hand inside of them. For example, in the 1958 movie *The Fly,* a spider seen attacking a fly at the end of the movie is a hand puppet, with the scene enhanced by stock footage of a real spider. Other puppets are marionettes, which are manipulated by hand using strings connected to the puppet's movable parts. However, the most common tool for moving a puppet today is a lightweight, flexible rod. In most cases the rod is colored blue and shot in front of a bluescreen, so that it blends in with the background, which is digitally removed from the shot during postproduction. The rod can be manipulated either by a puppeteer or by a computer via a process called Go-Motion, which was invented by Phil Tippet for *Dragonslayer* (1981). In either the case, the end result is that the puppet appears to be moving under its own power, with no strings or puppeteer evident in the camera shot.

Prior to bluescreen and Go-Motion, a technique called stop-motion model animation was used to make a puppet appear to move on its own. With this method, the puppet is photographed, the motion-picture camera stopped, the puppet moved slightly, and the camera started again. The pioneers of this technique were Willis O'Brien and Ray Harryhausen, who typically animated highly detailed clay figures.

Modern puppeteers use lifelike puppets rather than clay ones, and they often combine rod puppetry with other means of moving a figure in order to create a realistic effect. *Alien Resurrection* (1997) used these techniques to create alien puppets. Covered with artificial slime made of methocel, the puppets had silicone skin with gel patches beneath to simulate fat pockets, and their arms were made with foam latex skin to support the weight of hydraulic rams. These puppets were placed on booms and operated with a

combination of hydraulics, cables, and puppetry rods, which were later removed from their scenes digitally. It took five body puppeteers, five facial puppeteers, and several support technicians to move the alien queen figure.

A rod puppet of a compsognathus, or compy, dinosaur built for *The Lost World* (1997) was equally complex. Its head, neck, and body were manipulated from above using traditional rod techniques. However, its eye blinks were created with a unique device that fitted inside in the creature's walnut-sized head. Directed by remote-control, this device was a pneumatic cylinder and valve that sent a pulse of air through a tube to make the eye blink. The puppet had another pneumatic system to simulate breathing, as well as a servo-controlled jaw. Other versions of the compy were made for a scene in which compies attacked someone; they had no machinery, except for a spring that made the head bob, and were mounted on the actor's body with magnets.

The *Lost World* puppets were designed by Stan Winston, one of the foremost experts in the field. Another expert in puppetry was Jim Henson, who not only advanced rod techniques but was among the first to combine simple puppets with sophisticated machinery. Although Henson is now deceased, his Creature Shop continues to provide puppets for filmmakers, as does Stan Winston Studios.

One of the most recent films to involve Stan Winston puppetry was *Small Soldiers* (1998), which used extremely sophisticated techniques. The movie used more than 200 rod, cable-operated, and radio-control puppets, representing a total of 14 different characters.

The first character to be built was "Chip the Commando." Initially a 2-foot-tall prototype, in final form he was 1 foot tall and had metal joints, a polyurethane body, and a soft, flexible silicone head. He was made in three versions, one powered by handheld rods, another by electric cables, and a third by self-contained batteries. The filmmakers originally intended to use the rod puppets for most shots, but eventually they decided to rely primarily on the battery-operated ones. Thanks to tiny, watch-sized mechanisms within their skulls, these puppets had heads and facial features that moved on their own, but their arms and legs had to be manipulated using stop-motion model animation techniques.

Constructing all of these puppets proved a major undertaking. In sculpting the maquettes from which the figures were designed, artists used more than 375 pounds of clay. During the manufacturing process they used 400 molds, 3,500 feet of electrical wire, and 103 microprocessors, as well as other equipment. Thirty-four transmitters and 72 radio receivers were needed to control the puppets during a large battle scene, and puppeteers had to use 52 different radio frequencies to handle all of the transmissions. Fourteen to 23 puppeteers worked on the film at any given time, along with the 50 artists and technicians needed to construct the puppets. *See also* ALIEN MOVIES; ANIMATRONICS; BLUESCREEN PROCESS; *DRAGONSLAYER;* GO-MOTION; HARRYHAUSEN, RAY; HENSON, JIM; *THE LOST WORLD;* O'BRIEN, WILLIS; *SMALL SOLDIERS;* STOP-MOTION MODEL ANIMATION; TIPPETT, PHIL.

Further Reading

Duncan, Jody. "A *Small Soldiers* Story." *Cinefex* 75, October 1998.

Pyrotechnics

Pyrotechnics are special effects that deal with incendiary devices such as fire or explosives. Great care must be taken in setting up this type of special effect, which can be quite elaborate. For example, pyrotechnics expert Robert McCarthy reports that his work for the 1989 movie *Kill Me Again* required more than 200 separate steps to prepare, check, and execute a shot of a car crashing into a gas storage tank.

To create explosions, pyrotechnics experts mix various types of combustible substances. The most common is black powder, which is a mixture of potassium nitrate, sulfur, and charcoal that can be handmade or purchased commercially in granular or finely powdered form. Another pyrotechnics substance is nitrocellulose, which is smokeless, but there are many others. Gasoline is also frequently used to fuel an explosion, but again, many other ingredients can be used. Napthalene, for example, can create a huge blast when ignited; it is the primary ingredient in mothballs. To

Characters in *Small Soldiers* (1998) were created with both puppets and digital effects. *Photofest.*

create debris for an explosion, nonpyrotechnic substances such as fuller's earth, cork, peat moss, Styrofoam, sand, and/or balsa wood are often added to the black powder.

Another common material used in pyrotechnic effects is Det core, which is a flexible cord with an explosive core. It is typically ignited with a blasting cap to create an explosion that then triggers other explosions along the path of the cord. There are many other kinds of detonating devices, such as electricity and wires, flares, and black-powder fuses. Flash powders and sparking devices create sparks, as do fireworks.

Some explosions are created simply with air. Air mortars filled with debris use 300 pounds of air to blow out doors, windows, and walls. Air mortars can also create underwater explosions. A similar device called a trunion gun blows out car windows by firing a glass or steel ball through them.

Pyrotechnical experts are skilled at creating whatever type of explosion is needed for a scene, but digital artists have also become experts in pyrotechnics, as they try to re-create explosions using computer graphics. For example, to keep costs down, *Star Trek: Generations* (1994) employed digital pyrotechnics instead of real ones for its space battles, although it did use real pyrotechnics in a climactic fight scene. Another recent development is to combine real pyrotechnics with other scene elements digitally during postproduction, so that a valuable miniature will not be touched by flames. In such cases, a metal form called a buck, which is generally cut in the shape of the miniature, is used as a stand-in, so the flames will curve around the object appropriately.

But despite advances in computer pyrotechnics, large-scale on-set pyrotechnics are still being used. Some of the most extensive work in this regard was for the 1997 movie *Starship Troopers*, in which giant alien bugs battle with human beings. At one point in the movie, an airstrike appears to create a wall of flames nearly 1/2 mile long, moving at a speed of 300 miles per hour. To create this effect, pyrotechnics experts filled 28 50-gallon drums with a plastic-lined bag of gasoline and an igniter charge. These drums were then placed on their sides at regular intervals along the set, with one end of each drum left open to allow the burning fuel to exit. The fuel was ignited with buried dynamite ground charges mixed with fuller's earth and cement dust. *See also* BUCK; FIRE.

Further Reading

McCarthy, Robert E. *Secrets of Hollywood Special Effects*. Boston: Focal Press, 1992.

R

The Rains Came

Released in 1939 by 20th Century Fox, *The Rains Came* featured a spectacular flood and won an Academy Award for its special effects, beating both *Gone With the Wind* and *The Wizard of Oz*. The movie's effects supervisor was E.H. Hansen, who employed full-sized sets, miniature sets, and optical effects in his work. In 1955 *The Rains Came* was remade as *The Rains of Ranchipur;* this movie was nominated for an Academy Award in special effects but lost to *The Bridges of Toko-Ri*.

Ralston, Ken (1955–)

Ken Ralston won Academy Awards for his visual effects work on *Return of the Jedi* (1983), *Cocoon* (1985), and *Who Framed Roger Rabbit?* (1988). He also contributed special effects to such prominent films as *Star Wars* (1977), *Back to the Future II* (1989) and *III* (1990), *Forrest Gump* (1994), and *Jumanji* (1995).

Born in 1955, Ralston became interested in stop-motion animation as a boy. With the help of friend Jon Berg, who already worked in the field, Ralston learned puppetry and animation and made his own 8 mm film, *The Bounds of Imagination,* which won an honorary mention in a Kodak Film contest. At age 17, Ralston was hired by Berg's employer, Cascade Pictures, to make commercials. He also attended the California Institute of the Arts for a short time.

In 1975 Jon Berg and another special effects expert, Dennis Muren, approached Ralston with the script for *Star Wars* (1977). Ralston joined the project as Muren's assistant, working for the Industrial Light & Magic (ILM) special effects studio. Ralston continued to work for ILM after *Star Wars* was released, designing creatures for *Return of the Jedi* (1983) and creating the movie's initial space battle. He also worked as the co-supervisor of visual effects for *Star Trek II: The Wrath of Khan* (1982) and supervised special effects for *Contact* (1997) as the president of Sony Pictures Imageworks, a major special effects house. *See also* INDUSTRIAL LIGHT & MAGIC; *JUMANJI;* MUREN, DENNIS; SONY PICTURES IMAGEWORKS; SPECIAL EFFECTS HOUSES; *STAR TREK* MOVIES; *STAR WARS* MOVIES; *WHO FRAMED ROGER RABBIT?*

Rank, Joseph (1888–1972)

Lord Joseph Arthur Rank was a wealthy businessman who controlled much of the film production, processing, and distribution industries in England during the 1930s and 1940s. He owned several British film studios and more than 1,000 movie theaters. His significance in terms of special effects lies not just in his dominance of British filmmaking but in his decision to establish a major special effects department in England that would rival those in the United States. He consequently gave many important British special effects experts their start and contributed financial support to many advances in the industry. Rank was made a baron in 1957 and died in 1972.

Reap the Wild Wind

Directed by Cecil B. DeMille and released by Paramount in 1942, *Reap the Wild Wind* won an Academy Award for its special effects. The movie's plot concerns a marine salvage operation, and its effects include underwater photography, which was an advanced technique at the time. *Reap the Wild Wind* also featured a climactic battle between a man and a giant squid during a hurricane, which was accomplished through both mechanical and optical effects supervised by Gordon Jennings and Farciot Edouart. The two men won an Academy Award a year earlier for their work on *I Wanted Wings. See also I WANTED WINGS;* EDOUART, FARCIOT; JENNINGS, GORDON.

Rendering

Rendering is the process by which computer graphics are converted from wireframe skeletons to realistic-looking images with shading, color, texture, and other features. To render a scene, the digital artist must tell the computer how to enhance each wireframe. The computer must also be given instructions regarding the lighting of the scene, so that shadows will be accurately cast.

Once instructions regarding this and other details have been given, the computer is left alone to render the scene. This process can be extremely long, depending on how many different elements are being combined in a shot. For example, scenes of two bug swarms in the 1997 movie *Starship Troopers* had so many layers of elements and so much digital data that each time a version of the scenes was rendered, it took the computer an average of 60 hours per frame to complete the task; however, through research and development during the course of the production, digital experts decreased the rendering time to 25–30 hours per frame.

Various programs help a digital effects artist render a scene. Currently, one of the most popular is called RenderMan. Created by Pixar, it automatically calculates the three-dimensional physical properties within a computer-generated shot, such as the placement of computer-generated characters and the components of their set, the position of the virtual camera, and the lighting. The software then uses this 3-D data to determine such details as how shadows should be cast in order to make the scene look as realistic as possible. *See also* ANIMATION, COMPUTER; COMPUTER HARDWARE AND SOFTWARE; PIXAR.

Further Reading
Duncan, Jody. "The Making of a Rockbuster." *Cinefex 58*, June 1994.

Sammon, Paul M. "Bug Bytes." *Cinefex 73*, March 1998.

Street, Rita. *Computer Animation: A Whole New World*. Gloucester, MA: Rockport, 1998.

Vaz, Mark Cotta, and Patricia Rose Duignan. *Industrial Light & Magic: Into the Digital Realm*. New York: Del Rey, 1996.

Rhythm & Hues Studios

Rhythm & Hues Studios is a visual effects and animation studio that has contributed special effects to several major films, including *Babe* (1995), which won an Academy Award for visual effects; *Waterworld* (1995); *Batman Forever* (1995); *The Nutty Professor* (1996); *Mouse Hunt* (1997); and *Babe: Pig in the City* (1998). The company is particularly noted for being able to make live animals appear to talk via 2-D and 3-D mouth animation techniques.

Rhythm & Hues was founded in 1987 by computer software expert Keith Goldfarb and four of his co-workers at Robert Abel & Associates, one of the oldest computer graphics studios in the industry. In March 1999, Rhythm & Hues purchased the VIFX portion of Blue Sky/VIFX, a visual effects and digital animation company that contributed to *Star Trek: Insurrection* (1998), *Armageddon* (1998), and *The X-Files* (1998). This acquisition made Rhythm & Hues the largest privately owned visual effects and animation studio in Los Angeles, California. *See also* ANIMATION, COMPUTER; *BABE; BATMAN* MOVIES; COMPUTER GRAPHICS; *MOUSE HUNT; THE NUTTY PROFESSOR; WATERWORLD.*

Robinson, Dar

Dar Robinson was a stuntman noted for his falls from great heights. One of his most spectacular falls was for the 1984 movie *Highpoint;* he tumbled from the roof of a 117-story building and seemed to hit the ground, but he actually opened a hidden parachute after dropping approximately 800 feet. For other movies, Robinson relied solely on an airbag to cushion his fall, and eventually he developed his own cable system to decelerate his body before it hit the ground.

Robinson also performed stunts with moving vehicles, jumping from one plane to another while both were in flight, flinging himself from a car that was plunging off a cliff, and hanging on to a helicopter as it took off. In addition, he was an expert motorcyclist, skilled at leaping from an airborne bike onto an airbag.

In 1983, while working on the 1987 movie *Million Dollar Mystery,* Robinson was injured during a motorcycle stunt at a remote site in Arizona. The area had no trained medical personnel, and after waiting two hours for an ambulance, Robinson's co-workers drove him to the hospital themselves. He died along the way. *See also* ACCIDENTS; STUNTS.

Further Reading

Michael McCann. "Medical Services on Set and Location." http://www.tmn.com/Artswire/csa/arthazards/performing/filmmed, May 1999.

Miklowitz, Gloria D. *Movie Stunts and the People Who Do Them.* New York: Harcourt Brace Jovanivich, 1980.

Robotics *See* ANIMATRONICS.

Rosher, Charles (1885–1974)

Cinematographer Charles Rosher was one of the pioneers of the film industry and contributed many technical and practical improvements to the business. For example, he was the first to suggest the use of stand-ins to replace actors for dangerous stunts. He also made a special stand to hold a camera in place. This device was particularly important for matte work and multiple exposures, because it could ensure that a camera filming a scene more than once didn't change position between each take.

Born in England in 1885, Rosher moved to the United States in 1908. Three years later he was working in the film industry. In 1918 he helped establish the American Society of Cinematographers. He remained in the field for more than 40 years, first as a cinematographer and later as a director of photography. His movies include *Little Lord Fauntleroy* (1921), *Pollyanna* (1920), *My Best Girl* (1927), *The Call of the Wild* (1935), *Annie Get Your Gun* (1950), *Show Boat* (1951), and *Kiss Me Kate* (1953). Rosher won an Academy Award in cinematography for *Sunrise* (1927) and *The Yearling* (1946). He died in 1974.

Rotoscoping

First developed by animator Max Fleischer in 1915, rotoscoping is the process of isolating a filmed object by tracing around its edges in order to create a silhouette. This silhouette, which changes shape and/or position as the film advances from one frame to the next, can then be replaced during postproduction by another image.

Prior to computers, the rotoscope artist sat at an easel, over which was mounted a rotoscope camera capable of either photographing or projecting an image. Footage from the movie would be loaded into the camera, and each frame would be projected onto the easel. Working in a dark room, the artist could then trace each projected image, one at a time, onto individual animation cels or thin sheets of paper to create a series of silhouettes, also called a travelling matte. Later this matte could be used to eliminate the traced image from the scene.

For the 1980 movie *The Empire Strikes Back,* for example, actors used a weapon called a lightsaber, which was actually a stick sword. During postproduction, rotoscope artists at Industrial Light & Magic (ILM) projected live-action footage of these fights onto their easels and laboriously traced the weapons' blades frame by frame onto animation cels. Next they painted the traced blades either red or blue and photographed them against a black background, using a camera lens that would blur the blades to create a glowing effect. They then turned their work over to the optical department, which used a device called an optical printer to replace the stick blades with the seemingly illuminated ones.

Today's rotoscope artists typically add or remove objects digitally, using a computer rather than an optical printer. Their primary job is to eliminate wires, cables, flying rigs, and other equipment used to perform a stunt or special effect. In order to remove wires, the artist examines each shot to locate the starting and ending points of the wires, so that the course of each line can be plotted. Once this has been accomplished, the artist directs the computer to sample the colors on either side of each line, erasing the wire or cable by blending in the colors that appear on its left and right.

Similarly, during live-action filming, *The Lost World* (1997) employed equipment to make computer-generated dinosaurs seem to be interacting with their environment. For example, they made bushes shake when a dinosaur was supposedly rustling them. Later ILM's rotoscope department removed this equipment and replaced it with images that roughly matched the live-action background.

Rotoscope artists also digitally remove any markers placed at live-action sites; these markers are used during postproduction to help line up different takes of the same shot. Sometimes a computer-generated image, such as foliage, is used to conceal the marker instead of remove it. For *Jerry Maguire* (1996), rotoscope artists covered up an actor rather than a marker, using a computer-generated potted plant to conceal a child who had been replaced during the production. For *The Lost World,* the rotoscope department added extra computer-generated dinosaurs in the foliage of a shot that was deemed to have too few animals.

Rotoscoping is also used to help integrate a digital character into a scene. For example, the 1998 movie *Star Trek: Insurrection* featured a computer-generated creature called a palmpet, which was added to scenes during postproduction. When the creature was required to sit on actor's hand, digital artists rotoscoped, or outlined, the live-action footage of that hand in order to determine the palmpet's placement and its movements in relation the surface on which it sat.

Further Reading

Erdman, Terry J. *The Secrets of Star Trek: Insurrection.* New York: Pocket Books, 1998.

McNary, Dave. "Cause of Effects." *Los Angeles Daily News,* September 28, 1997.

Smith, Thomas G. *Industrial Light & Magic: The Art of Special Effects.* New York: Ballantine Books, 1986.

S

Samson and Delilah

Directed by Cecil B. DeMille, *Samson and Delilah* (1950) is significant because it employed an early motion-control device, the Repeater. The Repeater was co-invented by special effects expert Gordon Jennings, who needed a way to repeat camera moves for matte work. Operated by remote control, the device used prerecorded tape to instruct the camera to repeat such movements as tilts and pans. *See also* JENNINGS, GORDON; MATTE; MOTION-CONTROL CAMERA SYSTEMS.

Further Reading
Fry, Ron, and Pamela Fourzon. *The Saga of Special Effects*. Englewood Cliffs, NJ: Prentice-Hall, 1977.

Scale

Used in modelmaking, the term "scale" refers to the relationship between the size of the miniature and the size of the real-life item it represents. For example, a model built at a scale of 1/24 measures 1 foot for every 24 feet of the full-sized object. A model in 1/6 scale is far larger, measuring 1 foot for every 6 feet of the object. *See also* MINIATURES AND MODELS.

Scanning

Scanning is a process by which a laser device transfers visual information into a computer and then back out again onto film. The visual information scanned into the computer can be a two-dimensional (2-D) object such as a photograph or sketch or a three-dimensional (3-D) one such as a clay maquette.

Scanning a 2-D object is fairly simple. A sketch, for example, can be placed face-down on a device called a flatbed scanner, and the computer instructed to execute the transfer process.

Scanning a 3-D object requires much more work. First the physical object is covered with a grid made of thin tape, and then each section, such as a leg or an arm, is digitized by pressing a scanning stylus or digital wand against various points of line intersection on the grid. This process orients each point within the computer. Once all of the points have been scanned, the computer can connect them to create a wireframe image, which is then used to develop a realistic computer-generated 3-D image.

3-D scanning was used by digital effects experts at Blue Skies Studios to scan casts of a live-action alien costume into a computer. Working with the digitized images, they were able to create a corresponding computer-generated alien for the movie *Alien Resurrection* (1997).

Once a computer-generated image is in final form and has been composited with various other film elements, it can be scanned back out onto film. New scanning hardware and software is continually being developed to improve this process, as well as the way that information is scanned into the computer. During the making of *Jurassic Park* (1993), for example, Industrial Light & Magic created color-correction software that would work in concert with scanning software to ensure that each shot would be consistent with others in a sequence. For *Pleasantville* (1998), filmmakers used a new type of telecine device, which is a device that converts film into video. Called the Spirit Datacine, the device scans film to digital files and puts them on videotape for editing at a speed of 4 frames/second. In contrast, the average scanner completes this process at a rate of 1 frame/10-30 seconds. *See also* COMPUTER GRAPHICS.

Further Reading
Duncan, Jody. "The Beauty in the Beasts." *Cinefex* 55, August 1993.
———. "The Making of a Rockbuster." *Cinefex* 58, June 1994.
Murdock, Andrew, and Rachel Aberly. *The Making of* Alien Resurrection. New York: HarperPrism, 1997.

Schiffer, Robert (b. 1900)

Makeup artist Robert Schiffer is perhaps best known for being the person who trained Stan Winston, one of the most famous special effects artists of all time. But Schiffer also accomplished a great deal in his own career, which began at RKO Pictures in 1934 and included stints at MGM, Columbia, and Walt Disney Studios, where he was head of the makeup department. Perhaps his most challenging work at Disney was creating the transformation of an actor into a dog for the 1977 movie *The Shaggy D.A.* His other films include *Annie Oakley* (1935), *The Picture of Dorian Gray* (1945), *Bedknobs and Broomsticks* (1971), and *Island at the Top of the World* (1975). *See also* BEDKNOBS AND BROOMSTICKS; MAKEUP.

Schoedsack, Ernest B. (1893–1979)

Director Ernest Beaumont Shoedsack made several films during his career, but his most important in terms of special effects were *King Kong* (1933), *Dr. Cyclops* (1940), and *Mighty Joe Young* (1949). Born in 1893, he began working in the film industry in 1914 as a cameraman. He co-directed his first movie, a documentary called *Grass,* in 1926. Shoedsack died in 1979. *See also* DR. CYCLOPS; KING KONG.

Schram, Charles (1911–)

Makeup artist Charles Schram worked on several important films during his career, including *The Good Earth* (1937), *The Wizard of Oz* (1939), *Dr. Jekyll and Mr. Hyde* (1941), *The Seven Faces of Dr. Lao* (1964), and *Papillon* (1974). Born in 1911, he attended the University of Southern California (USC) as an art student, and in 1935 he was discovered there by Jack Dawn, then head of MGM's makeup department. Schram worked at MGM until 1965. He then became a freelance makeup artist and eventually established his own makeup laboratory in Los Angeles, the Windsor Hills Makeup Lab. *See also* MAKEUP; THE SEVEN FACES OF DR. LAO; THE WIZARD OF OZ.

Scott, Ridley (1937–)

Ridley Scott has directed several movies known for their special effects, including *Alien* (1979) and *Blade Runner* (1982). Born in 1937 in South Shields, England, he attended the Royal College of Art in London before getting a job as a set designer for BBC-TV. He eventually worked his way up to director, creating episodes for popular television series, and decided to establish his own production company, Ridley Scott Associates. At first he devoted himself to producing television commercials, but in 1977 he directed a movie entitled *The Duellists,* which won the Best First Film award at the Cannes Film Festival. This led to his job directing *Alien,* followed by *Blade Runner.* His subsequent films include *Black Rain* (1989), *Thelma and Louise* (1991), *White Squall* (1996), and *GI Jane* (1997). *See also* ALIEN MOVIES; BLADE RUNNER.

Further Reading
Sammon, Paul M. *Future Noir: The Making of* Blade Runner. New York: Harper Collins, 1996.

Second Unit

A unit is a portion of the film's personnel, or crew. The first unit works with the director and the actors who star in the film. The second unit deals with the stuntpeople, action scenes, location shots, and other shots that do not revolve around the main actors. The second-unit director is in complete charge of the filming of such scenes, just as the first-unit director is in charge during first-unit filming sessions.

Sennett, Mack (1880–1960)

Mack Sennett was an actor, producer, and director who established his own production company, Keystone. This company is significant in terms of special effects because its comedies often featured stunts and photographic tricks such as fast motion, stop motion, and double exposures.

Born in 1880, Sennett worked in a factory before becoming an actor, first on the Broadway stage and later at the Biograph Studios in New York. Eventually he began directing Biograph pictures as well. In 1912 he left the studio to create Keystone, and three years later the company became part of the Triangle Film Corporation.

In 1917 Sennett severed his association with Keystone to form a new production company, Mack Sennett Comedies. He continued to make movies and to experiment with film techniques until his retirement in 1935, then consulted on a few productions during the late 1930s. In 1937 he received an Academy Award for his contributions to the film industry. Sennett died in 1960.

Further Reading

Fry, Ron, and Pamela Fourzon. *The Saga of Special Effects.* Englewood Cliffs, NJ: Prentice-Hall, 1977.

Sensurround

Sensurround is a special effects projection system that was developed by Universal Studios for the 1974 movie *Earthquake.* The system adds a code to the soundtrack of a film that triggers a response from special theater speakers, which then produce sounds and air vibrations that make audience members feel as though they are experiencing extreme shaking. After *Earthquake,* the system was used for *Midway* (1976) and *Rollercoaster* (1977). *See also* EARTHQUAKE; UNIVERSAL STUDIOS.

Further Reading

Fry, Ron, and Pamela Fourzon. *The Saga of Special Effects.* Englewood Cliffs, NJ: Prentice-Hall, 1977.
McKenzie, Alan, and Derek Ware. *Hollywood Tricks of the Trade.* New York: Gallery Books, 1986.

Destruction seen in *Earthquake* (1974), which employed Sensurround to simulate shaking in movie theaters. *Universal Pictures/Photofest.*

The Seven Faces of Dr. Lao

Released in 1964, *The Seven Faces of Dr. Lao* was the first film to receive Academy Award recognition for its makeup. The star of the film, actor Tony Randall, was made up to play seven different characters. Many of them were created with masks, which were first designed in watercolor by makeup expert Bill Tuttle. To make the masks, Tuttle took a plaster cast of Randall's head, from which he created two molds. He used one mold to sculpt mortician's wax into facial features that would fit on Randall's face. He used the other cast to duplicate these wax features in sponge rubber.

The rubber appliances were then glued onto the actor's face using spirit gum and enhanced with various makeups. For the character of Merlin, who had to appear quite old, Tuttle created wrinkles out of a liquid adhesive and painted on liver spots. Despite their complexity, each of Tuttle's creations only took two hours to apply to Randall's face, but the actor sometimes had to change into a different character as many as three times in one day.

Tuttle won an honorary Academy Award for his makeup work for the film. In addition to his expertise, *The Seven Faces of Dr. Lao* featured the stop-motion model animation of Jim Danforth, who had to create a Loch Ness Monster in various stages of growth from infant to adult. The movie's special effects were overseen by director George Pal, who was an experienced stop-motion animator himself. *See also* DANFORTH, JIM; MAKEUP; PAL, GEORGE; STOP-MOTION MODEL ANIMATION; TUTTLE, WILLIAM.

Further Reading

Jenson, Paul M. *The Men Who Made the Monsters.* New York: Twayne, 1996.

O'Conner, Jane. *Magic in the Movies.* Garden City, NY: Doubleday, 1980.

Taylor, Al. *Making a Monster.* New York: Crown, 1980.

Shot

A shot is a continuously filmed segment of a scene. In regard to a composited scene, the word also refers to a continuously moving image created by computer graphics, as though the computer were the camera.

The number of special effects shots in modern movies is often high. For example, *Men In Black* (1997) required 200 special effects shots, *The Fifth Element* (1997) 223, *What Dreams May Come* (1998) 240, *Batman and Robin* (1997) more than 400, *Starship Troopers* (1997) 600, and *Return of the Jedi* (1983) more than 900. *See also* BATMAN MOVIES; THE FIFTH ELEMENT; MEN IN BLACK; STAR WARS MOVIES; STARSHIP TROOPERS; TITANIC; WHAT DREAMS MAY COME.

Showscan

Showscan is a filming process that gives depth to two-dimensional screen images, making them appear three-dimensional. Movies created with Showscan have been filmed at more than twice the normal speed and must be projected at that rate too. In addition, Showscan movies must be shown on a special type of screen. Special effects expert Douglas Trumbull invented the process and used it to create the movie for Universal Studios' "Back to the Future" amusement park ride. *See also* FILMING SPEED; 3-D; TRUMBULL, DOUGLAS.

Shuftan, Eugene (1893–1977)

Eugene Shuftan invented the Shuftan process, which used projectors and mirrors to reflect images of models, miniatures, and/or paintings onto a set so that they could be filmed together with live action. The first major film to employ the technique was *Metropolis* (1927), in order to combine live-action foregrounds and miniature backgrounds; Shuftan created the process in 1923.

Born in 1893 in Germany as Eugen Shüfftan, Shuftan worked as an artist, sculptor, cartoonist and architect before becoming a cameraman and experimenting with photographic effects. In 1933 he moved from Germany to France to escape the Nazi regime, and in 1940 he settled in the United States. Shuftan made films not only in Germany, France, and the United States but in Great Britain as well. His works include *Queen Louise* (1927), *Ulysses* (1955), and

The Hustler (1962), for which he won an Academy Award for cinematography. Shuftan died in 1977.

Further Reading
Brosnan, John. *Movie Magic*. New York: St. Martin's Press, 1974.

Silicon Graphics

Silicon Graphics Inc. (SGI) manufactures computers used by most major special effects houses. The company provided the systems used to make such movies as *Toy Story* (1995), *Terminator 2: Judgement Day* (1991), *Starship Troopers* (1997), *Flubber* (1997), and the *Star Wars* prequel *The Phantom Menace* (1999) as well as software related to 2-D image processing and 3-D animation. SGI computers are large machines that employ a UNIX operating system.

Founded in 1982 by Kurt Akeley and Jim Clark, the company's first customers were manufacturers, engineers, scientists, and government agencies. Within a few years, Akeley and Clark decided to start marketing computers to Hollywood filmmakers. Consequently SGI developed a prototype of a computer designed for digital effects work and gave it to George Lucas free of charge. The company then sold a similar system to Robert Abel, a computer graphics pioneer who set up his own digital effects house.

Today SGI, along with Sun Microsystems and Hewlett Packard, sells 83 percent of all computers used in major special effects work. In addition, SGI's subsidiary, Alias/Wavefront, provides some of the most important digital effects software on the market, including Animator, Dynamation, and Composer, the latter of which is a digital compositing tool. Many software packages made by other companies, such as Pixar's RenderMan, are also designed to run on SGI computer systems. *See also* DYNAMATION; COMPUTER HARDWARE AND SOFTWARE; PIXAR; SPECIAL EFFECTS HOUSES.

For Further Reading
DiOrio, Carl. "The After-Effect: Slowing Follows the FX Explosion." *Hollywood Reporter*, 10 December 1997.
Wolff, Ellen. "SGI at 15." *Variety*, 20–26 October 1997.

Slit-Scan

Slit-scan is a photographic process invented by special effects artist Douglas Trumbull to create streaks of light on film. Trumbull first used the process in *2001: A Space Odyssey* (1968) in a scene in which a lone astronaut is being propelled through a time-traveling corridor in space.

Slit-scan takes place in a completely dark room. The process requires the camera's shutter to remain open a long time, while a light is brought towards it. This light is not constant but modulated, so that it changes in intensity in a complicated pattern, and as it moves towards the lens the camera must keep it in focus. Trumbull invented a slit-scan device to make this process automatic. The movement of the light, which is on a track, and its modulation pattern are controlled by a computer, as is the camera's shutter. *See also 2001: A SPACE ODYSSEY.*

Further Reading
Agel, Jerome (ed). *The Making of Kubrick's* 2001. New York: Signet, 1968.

Slow Motion *See* FILMING SPEED.

Small Soldiers

The 1998 movie *Small Soldiers* was responsible for the creation of new scanning tools and computer software that enabled digital artists at Industrial Light & Magic (ILM) to input more perfect information into a computer about some puppets used in the film. This allowed them to match computer-generated versions of the puppets nearly exactly with their manufactured counterparts.

The scanned digital information took up so much computer space that each part of a computer-generated character had to be stored in a separate file, to be reassembled during the final compositing process. Each computer-generated character took nine modelers three to six weeks to create, with the most complex character, Freakenstein, taking three months. In addition, digital artists had to make more than 100 props, primarily weapons, for the characters. These props were not scanned from hard objects but were drawn using computer software tools. There were more than 200 computer-generated shots in the final movie, all blended seamlessly with live-action puppet shots.

Actress Kirsten Dunst with one of the title characters in *Small Soldiers* (1998). *Photofest.*

The movie also used more than 200 rod, cable-operated, and radio-controlled puppets during live-action filming. Designed by Stan Winston Studios, the puppets represented a total of 14 different characters. The first to be built was "Chip the Commando." Initially a 2-foot-tall prototype, in final form he was 1 foot tall and had metal joints, a polyurethane body, and a soft, flexible silicone head. He was made in three versions, one powered by handheld rods, another by electric cables, and a third by self-contained batteries. The filmmakers originally intended to use the rod puppets for most shots, but eventually they decided to rely primarily on the battery-operated ones. Thanks to tiny, watch-sized mechanisms within their skulls, these puppets had heads and facial features that moved on their own, but their arms and legs had to be manipulated using stop-motion model animation techniques.

Constructing all of these puppets proved a major undertaking. In sculpting the maquettes from which the figures were designed, artists used more than 375 pounds of clay. During the manufacturing process they used 400 molds, 3,500 feet of electrical wire, and 103 microprocessors, as well as other equipment. It took 34 radio transmitters and 72 radio receivers to control the puppets during a large battle scene, and puppeteers had to use 52 different radio frequencies to handle all of the transmissions. Fourteen to 23 puppeteers worked on the film at any given time, along with the 50 artists and technicians needed to construct the puppets. *See also* ANIMATION, COMPUTER; INDUSTRIAL LIGHT & MAGIC; PROPS; PUPPETS; STOP-MOTION MODEL ANIMATION; WINSTON, STAN.

Further Reading
Duncan, Jody. "A *Small Soldiers* Story." *Cinefex* 75, October 1998.

Smell-O-Vision

Smell-O-Vision was a theater gimmick promoted by producer Mike Todd Jr. in the late 1950s. It incorporated a system of tubes that went directly from scent vials to each audience member's seat. At certain points in a film, a "smell track" would trigger the release of a particular odor. Only one movie was ever made to take advantage of this system: *Scent of Mystery* (1960). A competing system called Aroma-Rama was also developed during this period. It used theater air-conditioning ducts to deliver smells to the audience during the documentary *Behind the Great Wall* (1959). In 1981, a different type of smell enhancement was tried for the movie *Polyester*. Called Odorama, it required audience members to scratch and sniff special cards at particular moments during the film, as indicated by numbers on the movie screen.

Further Reading
Fry, Ron, and Pamela Fourzon. *The Saga of Special Effects.* Englewood Cliffs, NJ: Prentice-Hall, 1977.

Smith, Dick (1922–)

Dick Smith is one of the foremost makeup artists in the special effects industry. His specialty is making actors appear older than they really are, and he has developed many new makeup techniques and devices in this regard. He improved foam latex facial appliances, came up with innovative ways to use adhesives and paints, and invented his own adhering facial makeup, PA-X or Pax, which combined the medical adhesive Pros-Aide with Liquitex artist's acrylic paint. He first used Pax to attach fake hair over facial appliances for the 1983 movie *The Hunger,* which featured aging vampires.

Born on June 26, 1922, in Larchmont, New York, Smith began his career as a makeup artist in 1945, working in television before turning his attention to movies. His first major film was *Little Big Man* (1970), which required him to make 32-year-old actor Dustin Hoffman appear to be 120 years old. Smith subsequently made 44-year-old Max von Sydow appear to be a 70-year-old priest for *The Exorcist* (1973), and made actor F. Murray Abraham age from 42 to 75 as the character Salieri in *Amadeus* (1984). The latter earned him an Academy Award.

Smith also received acclaim for his work on *The Exorcist* (1973). The movie required elaborate makeup effects to make it appear as though actress Linda Blair were possessed by the devil. At one point, for example, Blair had to spew bile. To accomplish this she wore tubes concealed beneath her cheek makeup, through which a combination of pea soup and oatmeal was pumped. Her horrific face was made with latex appliances and makeup that took two hours to apply.

While working on *The Exorcist,* Smith hired a young makeup artist named Rick Baker to work as his assistant. Baker is now one of the leading makeup and creature experts in the movie industry, contributing to such films as *The Nutty Professor* (1996), *Men in Black* (1997), and *Mighty Joe Young* (1998).

Smith's other works include makeup for *The Godfather* (1972), *The Sunshine Boys* (1975), *Ghost Story* (1981), and *Altered States* (1981). Retired from full-time work, Smith continues to act as a consultant working on such films as *Death Becomes Her* (1992), as well as teaching and giving seminars on makeup techniques. *See also* DEATH BECOMES HER; MAKEUP.

Further Reading
Timpone, Anthony. *Men, Makeup, and Monsters.* New York: St. Martin's Press, 1996.
Shay, Don. "Dick Smith: 50 Years in Makeup." *Cinefex 62,* June 1995.

Smith, Doug

Doug Smith won an Academy Award for his visual effects work for *Independence Day* (1996), which included shots of a mothership in space and several alien craft hovering over major cities. He was also visual effects supervisor for *Flubber* (1997), creating several flying car sequences and a number of digital effects related to a robot named Weebo.

Smith began his career as a camera assistant on *Star Wars* (1977) and subsequently worked as a camera operator for *Star Trek: The Motion Picture* (1979) and as the person in charge of visual effects photography for the 1994 movie *True Lies.* He also spent several years as a partner in Apogee Inc., a special effects company that went out of business in 1993, before he moved to Rhythm & Hues, another full-service special effects company. *See also* APOGEE INC.; INDEPENDENCE DAY; RHYTHM & HUES STUDIOS; STAR TREK MOVIES; STAR WARS MOVIES.

Smith, George Albert (G.A.) 1864–1959)

G.A. Smith was an inventor and film director who patented a number of early special effects techniques. In 1897 he patented the double exposure after using it in the 1897 movie *The Corsican Brothers.* He also created some of the first glass shots, whereby live action is filmed through a piece of glass onto which some background images have been painted.

Born in 1864 in Brighton, England, Smith began his career as a portrait photographer. In 1896 he built his own movie camera and subsequently became a filmmaker. In 1900 he and filmmaker Charles Urban became partners to establish one of the first motion picture studios. Together they not only made movies but worked to develop a color film technique, which they patented as Kinemacolor in 1906. Smith died in 1959. *See also* GLASS SHOT; URBAN, CHARLES.

Sony Pictures Imageworks

Founded in Culver City, California, in 1992, Sony Pictures Imageworks has provided visual effects for more than 30 films, including *Starship Troopers* (1997), *Contact* (1997), *Godzilla* (1998), and *Star Trek: Insurrection* (1998). A division of Sony Pictures Entertainment, the company also works on multimedia projects. Sony's president is Ken Ralston, one of the most respected special effects experts in the business. *See also* CONTACT; *GODZILLA;* RALSTON, KEN; *STAR TREK* MOVIES; *STARSHIP TROOPERS.*

Spawn of the North

Released in 1938 by Paramount, *Spawn of the North* was the first movie to receive an Academy Award for its special effects work. At the time, there was no Best Special Effects category among the awards, so the movie was given a citation for outstanding achievement in creating special photographic and sound effects. The following year, Best Special Effects did become an official, regular category.

Spawn of the North, which is about a fight between Alaskan salmon fishermen and Russian poachers at the end of the 19th century, features the rearscreen projection work of Farciot Edouart. The movie's special effects supervisor was Gordon Jennings. Jennings and Edouart teamed up to make many subsequent films, including *I Wanted Wings* (1941) and *Reap the Wild Wind* (1942), both of which also won Academy Awards for their special effects. *See also* ACADEMY AWARDS; EDOUART, FARCIOT; *I WANTED WINGS;* JENNINGS, GORDON; *REAP THE WILD WIND.*

Special Effects Houses

According to the Bureau of Labor Statistics, there are currently 276,000 visual effects artists working today, employed by dozens of special effects companies (also called houses). A few of the largest special effects houses are "full-service" facilities, which means that they can provide a filmmaker with any kind of special effect needed for a movie. This can include digital, mechanical, and optical effects, as well as makeup, puppetry, pyrotechnics, models, and miniature photography. Most companies, however, specialize in one particular category of effect or even in one particular job within a category. For example, the House of Moves motion-capture studio is dedicated to digitizing images of live action using their own motion-capture system; the Stan Winston Studio specializes in animatronics, puppetry, and other creature effects; Matte World Digital has created digital mattes, 3-D environments, and digital composites for more than 50 films; and the Computer Film Company has provided digital compositing, wire removal, and other computer effects for approximately 120 movies.

Because so many effects houses are specialized, filmmakers often rely on more than one effects company for their shots, even when one of those houses is a full-service facility. In part this is because filmmakers have realized that not all shots need to be done by the most experienced, and therefore more expensive, full-service houses such as Industrial Light & Magic (ILM). Therefore a particularly difficult shot might be given to ILM, while another might be assigned to a newer, less experienced company.

Sometimes, however, such cost-cutting measures can backfire. For example, the creators of *Star Trek V: The Final Frontier* (1989) decided to save money by using a less experienced company than ILM, which had worked on previous *Star Trek* films, and were then disappointed when the effects on the movie were not of as high a quality as they had hoped.

A director's budget is a major factor in special effects work, and many filmmaking decisions are made on the basis of cost. Moreover, special effects houses usually work on a fixed-cost basis, which means that they have to study a particular job and determine a flat fee for their work before signing an agreement to provide certain effects for a particular price. If they underestimate the amount of money their work will cost them, they will make little or no money on the job. Therefore the special effects business entails some financial risk.

In addition, the field is highly competitive. This is partly because computers have become more affordable lately, which not only makes it easier for special effects houses to buy or lease equipment but also makes it easier for new competitors to spring up. Consequently several important special effects houses have gone out of business in recent years, including Boss Film Studios, Warner Brothers Digital, Stetson Visual, and Apogee Inc., and some major studios have closed down their own special effects divisions and bought existing independent ones. For example, the Walt Disney Company shut down their in-house Buena Vista Imaging and acquired Dream Quest Images.

As a result of such closings and acquisitions, many other special effects companies in the industry have undertaken cost-cutting measures, eliminating personnel and/or becoming even more specialized. Because of such uncertainty within the industry, any listing of special effects facilities is subject to sudden change. However, the *Hollywood Reporter* magazine does endeavor to keep a current list of the addresses and phone numbers of most special effects companies, as well as other businesses and people involved in the movie industry. Its directory, updated annually, is called the *Blu-Book Film and TV Production Directory. See also* APPENDIX C: SPECIAL EFFECTS HOUSES; APOGEE, INC.; BLUE SKY/ VIFX; BOSS FILM STUDIOS; DIGITAL DOMAIN; COSTS, SPECIAL EFFECTS; HENSON, JIM; INDUSTRIAL LIGHT & MAGIC; MATTE WORLD DIGITAL; RHYTHM & HUES STUDIOS; *STAR TREK* MOVIES; WARNER DIGITAL.

Further Reading

Dowling, Robert J. *The 1998 Hollywood Reporter Blu-Book*. Hollywood: Hollywood Reporter, 1998.

Huffstutter, P.J. "Visual Effects Pioneer Tells How Digital Showed His Studio Who Was Boss." *Los Angeles Times,* 20 October 1997.

Karon, Paul. "Left Brain vs. Right: F/X Wizards Try to Conjure Equity in Pic Biz." *Variety,* 24–30 August 1998.

Spielberg, Steven (1946–)

Steven Spielberg is, to date, one of the most successful American filmmakers in history and is well known for making movies that inspire advances in the special effects field. These include *Close Encounters of the Third Kind* (1977), *Raiders of the Lost Ark* (1981) and its sequels *Indiana Jones and the Temple of Doom* (1984) and *Indiana Jones and the Last Crusade* (1989), *ET: The Extraterrestrial* (1982), *Hook* (1991), and *Jurassic Park* (1993) and its sequel *The Lost World* (1997).

Born in 1946, Spielberg spent his childhood making amateur movies as a hobby. One of them won a prize in a filmmaking contest, and another was shown in a theater near his home in Phoenix, Arizona. After graduating from high school in Phoenix, Spielberg attended the California State University at Long Beach and continued to make films. In 1969 he entered a 24-minute short, *Amblin'*, in the Atlanta Film Festival, and it was so well received that he received a seven-year contract with Universal Studios to direct television shows, which made him the youngest director ever to receive a long-term contract with a major motion picture studio.

Spielberg's first task at Universal was to direct the pilot episode of *Night Gallery*. The program was critically acclaimed and led to many other assignments, including work on *Columbo* and *Marcus Welby*. Spielberg then began directing television movies. The most successful of these was *Duel,* which was first aired in 1972.

In 1974, Spielberg directed his first motion picture, *The Sugarland Express,* followed by *Jaws* in 1975. While both movies received critical acclaim, the latter was also extremely lucrative, grossing $260 million after a cost of only $8.5 million. Spielberg's next movie, *Close Encounters of the Third Kind,* earned him an Academy Award nomination for Best Director. He was nominated again for *Raiders of the Lost Ark,* but he did not win an Academy Award until 1993, for directing *Schindler's List.*

Spielberg had created his own production company, Amblin Entertainment, which he created in 1984, that was responsible for such films as *The Color Purple* (1985), *Always* (1985), and *Empire of the Sun* (1987). None of these films, however, were as successful as *Jurassic Park,* which grossed $100 million during just the first nine days of its 1993 release but cost only $70 million to produce.

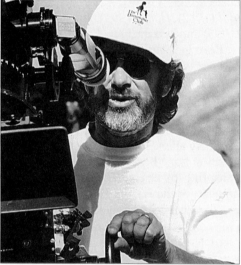

Director Steven Spielberg. *Murray Close/Universal Pictures/Photofest.*

The following year, Spielberg decided to create his own entertainment studio, DreamWorks SKG, in conjunction with entertainment executives Jeffrey Katzenberg and David Geffin. The company's first major film was *The Peacemaker* (1997), followed by *Amistad* (1997) and *Saving Private Ryan* (1998), which earned him another Academy Award for Best Director. Other offerings include *Mouse Hunt* (1997), *Deep Impact* (1998), *Small Soldiers* (1998), and *Antz* (1998), which is an animated movie whose characters were all computer-generated. Spielberg has produced other animated work as well, including the television shows *Tiny Toon Adventures* (1990–1995), *Steven Spielberg Presents Animaniacs* (1993–present), and *Steven Spielberg Presents Pinky and the Brain* (1995–present). *See also* ANI-MATION, COMPUTER; *CLOSE ENCOUNTERS OF THE THIRD KIND; ET: THE EXTRATERRESTRIAL; HOOK;* *INDIANA JONES* MOVIES; *JURASSIC PARK; THE LOST WORLD; MOUSE HUNT.*

Further Reading

Sanello, Frank. *Spielberg: The Man, the Movies, the Mythology.* Dallas, TX: Taylor Publishing, 1996.

Split-Screen Photography

Split-screen photography involves filming images for two halves of a frame separately and then combining them. Early split screens were created to show the audience two completely different shots side by side, such as one of a murderer sharpening a knife and the other of his unsuspecting victim getting ready for bed. Currently split screens are primarily used to make it appear as though two images filmed separately were actually filmed together, with the split line unnoticeable. For example, a shot of the same man on both sides of the split can make it appear as though one actor is playing two parts. Alternatively, a split screen is often used to combine a shot of a man at normal size with one of a man at smaller-than-normal size, so that the latter appears to have shrunk.

Split screens have been created in various ways. The earliest method was to use an in-camera matte to block first one half of the film and then the other from exposure. In other words, the cameraman would cover the right side of the film, shoot a scene in which the actor was on the left, rewind the film, cover the left side of the film, and shoot the actor on the right.

After 1931, when the optical printer was invented, this technique no longer had to be accomplished in-camera but could be done during postproduction. The scene would be filmed twice using the mattes, but with no rewinding, and the two images would be put together later in the optical printer, which combines projection and rephotography.

For the 1956 movie *tom thumb,* special effects expert Tom Howard invented a new matte process that enabled the cameraman to split the image automatically within his camera, blackening one half of the shot while leaving the other intact, and to change the location of this split as the scene progressed. This meant that with careful timing, an actor could appear as though he were walking around himself.

In current films, special effects experts often use bluescreens or greenscreens to create split-screen effects. For example, a small, portable greenscreen made of either a special digital green cloth or foam core pieces painted with digital green paint might be placed on one half of the set and the actor filmed on the other. The position of the greenscreen and the actor would then be reversed and the scene filmed again, this time with the actor playing his twin. This method was used to make *Multiplicity* (1996), which featured one actor playing five parts.

Multiplicity also employed a handheld video playback system that guided the actor in his split-screen work. The actor performed the role of Character A as the video system recorded him from the position of Character B. When he acted the scene a second time as Character B, the Character A position was held by a stand-in with a video monitor on his shoulder. This video monitor provided the actor with an image of himself as Character A, thereby enabling him to see his counterpart in the scene and respond accordingly. Moreover, within minutes of completing the scene, a digital compositing system provided filmmakers with a rough videotape of the final version, showing both halves of the split together.

A similar system was used to film the 1998 version of *The Parent Trap,* which featured one young actress playing two parts. A 1961 version of the movie, however, primarily used double exposure create the same illusion, as did the 1921 film *Little Lord Fauntleroy* (1921). *See also* BLUESCREEN PROCESS; MULTIPLICITY; TOM THUMB; WONDER MAN.

Further Reading

Brosnan, J. *Movie Magic.* New York: St. Martin's Press, 1974.

Hines, Bill. "Techniques for In-Camera Effects." *International Photography*, December 1997.

Pourroy, Janine. "Split Personalities." *Cinefex 67*, September 1996.

Stensvold, Mike. *In-Camera Special Effects.* Englewood Cliffs, NJ: Prentice-Hall, 1983.

Squires, Scott

Scott Squires was one of several video effects supervisors for the 1999 *Star Wars* movie *The Phantom Menace.* He also supervised visual effects for *The Mask* (1994) and *Dragonheart* (1996), both of which earned him Academy Award nominations, and for *Starship Troopers* (1997), which featured several advanced digital effects techniques. Squires is an expert in the field of computer

Actor Michael Keaton playing two parts in *Multiplicity* (1996) via split-screen photography. *Stephen Vaughn, Columbia Pictures/Photofest.*

and digital technology as it relates to film, and in 1994 he received an Academy Award for his pioneering work in film input scanning, whereby filmed images are converted into digital images. Squires also developed the "Cloud Tank Effect" for the 1977 movie *Close Encounters of the Third Kind,* under the supervision of Douglas Trumbull, and served as technical director for such films as *Willow* (1987) and *Who Framed Roger Rabbit?* (1988). One of the founders of Dream Quest Images, Squires served as president of the special effects company from 1979 to 1995. *See also* CLOSE ENCOUNTERS OF THE THIRD KIND; CLOUD TANK; *DRAGONHEART*; DREAM QUEST IMAGES; *STARSHIP TROOPERS*; *STAR WARS* MOVIES; TRUMBULL, DOUGLAS; *WHO FRAMED ROGER RABBIT?*; *WILLOW.*

Star Trek Movies

A series of movies based on the *Star Trek* television show provides an excellent example of how budget constraints can affect the quality of a movie's special effects, as well as how special effects can enhance or detract from a film.

The first movie, *Star Trek: The Motion Picture* (1979), was given a relatively generous budget by Paramount Pictures and earned an Academy Award nomination for its visual effects, which were supervised by Douglas Trumbull. However, the movie was widely criticized upon its release for having too many special effects shots in relation to dialogue and dramatic scenes. Saddled with a weak plot, the characters spent most of their time staring at a viewing screen, which was actually a bluescreen, watching images that were created later using miniature photography.

In contrast, the second *Star Trek* film, *Star Trek II: The Wrath of Khan* (1982), accompanied its special effects with a powerful story. Consequently the movie is generally considered one of the best in the series. Moreover, like the previous film, the special effects were of extremely high quality for the time. Provided by Industrial Light & Magic (ILM) under the supervision of Jim Veilleux and Ken Ralston, effects included the first digital matte painting ever created by ILM. This painting depicted a planet that had been transformed from a barren world into an Eden through a scientific process called Genesis. In addition to the final matte painting, several computer-generated images were created for the Genesis transformation, including a rocket blast, a firestorm, and a background of computer-generated stars. However, the gaseous nebula seen elsewhere in the movie is not a computer-generated shot, but was instead created by filming the injection of latex rubber into a water tank.

As did the first *Star Trek* movie, *The Wrath of Khan* used extensive motion-control photography of miniatures against a bluescreen.

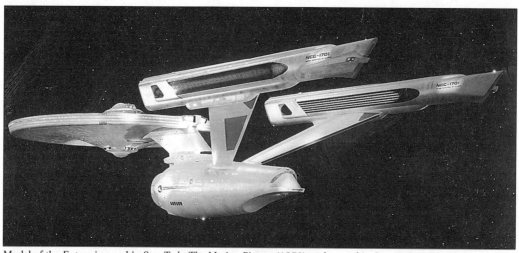

Model of the *Enterprise* used in *Star Trek: The Motion Picture* (1979) and reused in *Star Trek II: The Wrath of Kahn* (1982). *Photofest.*

It also featured a new ship, the *Reliant,* which was made of vacuformed plastic. However, the *Enterprise* spaceship model seen in the first movie was the same as in the second. Built by Entertainment Effects Group (EEG), this metal model was extremely heavy and difficult to lift into position for photography, and ILM's modelmakers badly wanted to design a new *Enterprise* for their film. Unfortunately, *Wrath of Khan* was on an extremely tight budget and they were forced to reuse the original model.

In fact, budget constraints affected many of ILM's decisions regarding special effects on *Star Trek II.* This situation grew worse during the filming of the third movie in the series, *Star Trek III: The Search for Spock* (1984). Once again ILM's Ken Ralston wanted to make a new *Enterprise* model, and once again he was refused, even though the old model required refurbishing. He also had to refurbish and reuse the unwieldy 20-foot-diameter spacedock model featured in the first movie. However, *Star Trek III* did offer ILM some opportunities for new work. Digital artists used computer animation to create a holographic game, and computer-programmed lighting effects altered the appearance of the *Enterprise*'s transporter beams. In addition, *Star Trek III*'s special effects shots were far longer than in the previous movies; some took up more than 500 frames of film.

But despite the success of *Star Trek III,* Ken Ralston's budget was even tighter on the fourth film, *Star Trek IV: The Voyage Home* (1986). Consequently Ralston tried to accomplish most of his effects in-camera through traditional optical methods. In order to save additional money, models from the previous films were refurbished and used yet again. A model of a whaling ship not featured in the earlier films was actually an old 140-foot model of a World War II minesweeper, which had been altered to look like a whaling vessel. The only computer-generated images in the film appear in a dream sequence in which one person transforms into another. However, the film did employ fairly sophisticated techniques to create fake whales. There were only two shots of live whales in the film; otherwise the creatures were either models of full-sized whale parts, such as a tail or head, or a mechanized miniature. This miniature could actually swim, using only the motions of its own flippers and tail.

Star Trek IV made more money than any of the previous *Star Trek* films, grossing approximately $110 million. Nonetheless, Paramount saddled *Star Trek V: The Final Frontier*

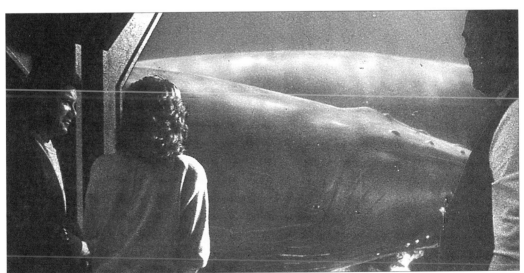

Actors William Shatner (left), Catherine Hicks (center), and James Doohan (right), observe humpback whales (which are sophisticated puppets) in *Star Trek IV: The Voyage Home* (1986). *Photofest.*

with another highly restricted budget. Consequently the filmmakers decided to cut costs by not hiring ILM for their special effects work. Instead they relied on Associates and Ferren (AF), which was vastly less experienced than ILM. Moreover, the head of AF, Bran Ferren, did not believe in using the bluescreen process or computer-generated mattes. He preferred the more traditional process projection technique, in which images are composited together via projection and rephotography. This method proved extremely unsatisfactory, not only to the film's many critics, but also to its director, William Shatner, who later complained that the process kept him from using broad, sweeping shots and made his scenes choppy. Ferren also saved money by copying footage from *Star Trek IV* so he wouldn't have to reshoot certain images, and like Ralston before him, he used the original *Enterprise* model. Ultimately, the special effects budget on *Star Trek V* proved so tight that a substantial part of the movie, including its ending, was rewritten to keep the required number of special effects shots to a minimum.

After the movie's release, extensive criticism of its effects led the filmmakers to rehire ILM to work on the sixth movie in the series, *Star Trek VI: The Undiscovered Country* (1991). This time it was not Ken Ralston but Scott Farrar who supervised the special effects, and once again budget constraints affected ILM's decisions. The company's original cost estimate was double what Paramount Pictures wanted to pay, so to reduce their cost ILM redesigned some shots, cut others, and figured out a way to reuse footage from earlier *Star Trek* films. They also farmed some of the special effects work out to cheaper facilities.

As before, the studio reused the original *Enterprise* model, as well as models from other movies in the series. By this time, however, many of them needed extensive work, particularly paint and electrical repairs. ILM added new paint and interior lighting to a Klingon battlecruiser used in the first movie, and it rewired the *Enterprise* so that all of the ship's lights could be photographed in a single pass. Prior to this, the running lights, window lights, and sensor dome each had to be photographed in a separate pass. As with earlier films, the models were shot in front of a bluescreen, although sometimes a black cloth was used. Pyrotechnical effects were created separately and added to the miniature photography using a motion-control optical printer. The explosion of the Klingon ship, however, was done as a staged effect, using a dummy vessel made of brittle epoxy, with the detonation filmed against a black background.

A scene in which a shockwave blasts a starship required computer-generated effects. First the shockwave was created in black and white, and then color was added. Digital artists had to do much experimenting to get the look they wanted for the wave. When it was complete, they scanned in images of the model ship and put them in the path of the wave, which required further manipulation of the wave's direction, color, and texture.

Elsewhere in the film, digital work was reserved primarily for cases where it would be more expensive to create an effect any other way. For example, to avoid having to tear any uniforms, rips in fabric were added digitally. Similarly, to avoid difficult wirework, floating props in a zero-gravity scene were actually computer-graphic images. However, the actors in the scene did use wires, because at the time it was impossible to create a realistic computer-generated human. The same scene included computer-generated floating blobs of blood, as well as computer-generated shadows on live-action figures. Another scene featured advanced morphing software developed by Industrial Light & Magic. To generate a sequence in which a shape-shifting alien changes from one creature to another, the software merely required a scanned image of the first creature and a scanned image of the second, and from these then was able to supply the shift in between.

The makeup for the morphing creature and other aliens in the film was supervised by Richard Snell, who had a staff of 38 makeup artists and 25 hairstylists. Snell's laboratory, which had a staff of 25, designed custom makeups for 22 principal characters and supplied over 300 prosthetics for *Star Trek VI*. The Klingon appliances were particularly thin to allow the actors' facial expressions to come out. Nonetheless, each Klingon required three and a half hours to make up. To avoid having to use thousands of Klingons for a scene in which they are assembled for a trial, the filmmakers employed a trick that was used for the 1925 version of *Ben-Hur*: creating a crowd scene with miniature moving puppets. Similarly, *Star Trek VI* used 200 miniature Klingon dolls, which were sold commercially, for the scene, attaching them to a motion-control device that would rock them back and forth in the 10-foot-long model courtroom. Such techniques helped hold makeup costs down; however, makeup was considered the most important aspect of the film's special effects, and so the makeup department was allowed to go somewhat overbudget, whereas the visual effects department was not.

The next movie in the series, *Star Trek: Generations* (1994), was also hampered by a tight budget. To circumvent this problem, director David Carson decided to save money by shooting the film in 50 days instead of the scheduled 70 or more. He was confident that he could do this because he had experience directing two *Star Trek* television shows, *Star Trek: The Next Generation* and *Deep Space Nine*. For his special effects, Carson turned to special effects houses that had worked on these shows. These included ILM, Digital Magic, and Santa Barbara Studios. The visual effects supervisor for *Star Trek: Generations,* Ron Moore, had also worked on the television shows. In addition, Carson was able to use stock footage, computer-generated images, miniatures, props, and makeup techniques from the television show, as well as from the previous *Star Trek* movies.

Fortunately, by the time *Star Trek: Generations* was made, digital effects had become more cost-effective, which enabled Carson to feature many new computer-generated images in his film. Most of these images were created by the computer graphics team at ILM, which was responsible for the miniature bluescreen photography as well. However, Santa Barbara Studios (SBS) created the opening shot of the champagne bottle flying through space and the 3-D map of the stellar cartography room, the latter of which required a great deal of difficult bluescreen work in addition to digital artistry.

ILM's most important digital image for *Star Trek: Generations* was that of an energy ribbon. Five different computer models were created to represent this ribbon for different types of shots. The ribbon used in distance shots was created as a 2-D image, whereas the rest were 3-D. Computer-generated ships seen with the ribbon were not made from digitized models but were created freehand. ILM also made a computer-generated collapsing star and its subsequent shockwave, digital pyrotechnics for a space battle, and digital matte paintings seen throughout the movie.

One of these digital matte paintings depicts the *Enterprise* after it has crashed on a forested planet. To re-create the crash itself, ILM used a 12-foot-diameter fiberglass model of the ship's saucer and an 80-foot-long miniature set representing the planet's surface. During the first part of the scene, the saucer was flown on cables. Subsequently it was placed on a dolly rig pulled by a truck, which required ILM photographers to work outside, an unusual circumstance for them. During postproduction, digital experts removed the saucer's cables and other unwanted elements from these shots, while adding images of trees and similar elements that had been filmed in front of a bluescreen.

The movie's climactic scene, which involved a fight scene on a rickety bridge, was filmed on a full-sized set. However, this scene still required much digital work. The bridge was held by cables that had to be removed digitally after the scene was shot. At the same time, the structure was rotated digitally to make it appear more tilted. A digital matte painting and computer-generated falling metal debris were added to make the bridge appear far higher off the ground than it really was. The digital effects for this scene were done in only three days, which helped keep the movie within its budget, but after the movie was released the effects were severely criticized for being inferior in quality.

Fortunately, Paramount Pictures was not as strict about keeping costs down for the eighth movie in the series, *Star Trek: First Contact* (1996). Moreover, by the time the film was made, computer graphics were even more economical to use than before, and of course there were even more resources available from previous films and television episodes. As with *Star Trek: Generations,* the special effects houses working on the movie, which included Industrial Light & Magic, Matte World Digital, Illusion Arts, and Pacific Ocean Post, had experience working on the *Star Trek: The Next Generation* and *Deep Space Nine* television series, as well as a new entry into the *Star Trek* franchise, the television show *Voyager.*

Makeup for *Star Trek: First Contract* was provided by another *Star Trek* veteran, makeup artist Michael Westmore. He developed all of the Borg makeup for the movie, in conjunction with the designer of the Borg suits, Todd Masters. To create the appearance of these aliens, which were part machine, required a variety of makeup appliances and prosthetics. In addition to robotic arms, both working and nonworking, there were a total of 36 Borg eyepieces, some with regular lights called blinkies and some with lasers. The eyepieces and other Borg makeup pieces could be rearranged or turned in different ways to create many unique characters, making it possible for only eight actors to play the dozens of Borg characters depicted in the movie.

The Borg Queen required unique makeup and costuming, also provided by Westmore and Masters. Her latex skull had tiny holes in it, with light-emitting diodes (LEDs) beneath to suggest electrical activity. The actress wore a battery pack under her costume to power the lights. She was also required to perform some complicated bluescreen work for her first scene in the movie. She initially appears as a head and spine, which is then lowered into a mechanical body. To create this effect, the actress donned a bluescreen suit with only her head showing. She was then attached to the prosthetic spine, so that it

hung from her neck, and to a bluescreen rig with wires that raised her into the air. Her descent into the mechanical body was then filmed. This bluescreen work was composited with a background plate of the set, which was a three-story engine room. Digital effects experts made the head and body appear to connect perfectly, and added images of the suit fastening itself up.

There were many other digital effects in the film. In addition to digital matte paintings, they include a computer-generated vortex, nebula, and Earth, the hairs on a character's arm, the gas that kills the Borg Queen, and a Vulcan spaceship landing on Earth. In fact, all of the starships in the space battle with the Borg were computer-generated, with the exception of the *Enterprise* and the *Farragut,* which were state-of-the-art models.

The *Farragut* had been used on *Star Trek: The Next Generation,* but the *Enterprise* had been rebuilt specifically for this movie. It was a 10-foot motion-control model made strong enough to last through at least three more films. Behind its windows were tiny light boxes holding photographs of *Star Trek: The Next Generation* interior sets, which gave the model realistic depth. The ship also had a heavy-duty model mount to hold it, as well as many other advanced features. A model of the Borg spaceship, which is cube-shaped, was also built especially for the movie, although another model of it had been used for the *Star Trek: The Next Generation* television show. The new Borg ship had sides 30 inches square, each with a surface textured to a depth of 5 inches. Other models for the film include the *Phoenix* rocket and its stages and a starship deflector dish, built in a 16-inch and a 30-inch size. The latter was for a pyrotechnics scene in which the model was blown up.

For the ninth movie in the series, *Star Trek: Insurrection,* the filmmakers decided to rely entirely on computer-generated starships rather than miniatures. In fact, not only all of the ships but also the planets and meteors in the film were created through computer graphics, under the supervision of digital effects experts at Santa Barbara Studios. Santa Barbara Studios also made digital matte paintings for *Star Trek: Insurrection.* However, unlike *Titanic* (1997), crowds were made larger not by adding computer-generated people but by hiring more live actors. More than 200 extras were employed for several scenes involving an alien village.

This village was constructed along a lake in Westlake Village, California, along with a cave entrance built by set designers out of wood, fiberglass, plaster, and paint. The inside of the cave was on a soundstage. The movie employed several other large soundstage sets as well, including a "metaphasic particle collector," which was a 36-foot-tall, 60-foot-diameter structure made of thousands of steel bars. The concrete floor beneath this structure was covered with greenscreen; later this greenscreen was replaced with digital images, so that the structure would appear to extend downwards for hundreds of feet.

Another set, that of a "body shop" in which a character's face is altered, was recycled from an episode of *Voyager,* in which it appeared as a Kyrian museum in an episode called "Living Witness." But despite this type of cost-cutting, *Insurrection* was the most expensive of the *Star Trek* films, with a budget of more than $70 million.

Nonetheless, *Star Trek: Insurrection* did not receive an Academy Award nomination for its effects, nor was it critically acclaimed. As with the first *Star Trek* movie, a large special effects budget does not necessarily guarantee that a movie will be well received. *See also* ANIMATION, COMPUTER; *BEN-HUR;* COST, SPECIAL EFFECTS; COMPUTER GRAPHICS; INDUSTRIAL LIGHT & MAGIC; MATTE PAINTINGS; OPTICAL PRINTER; PARAMOUNT PICTURES; RALSTON, KEN; SPECIAL EFFECTS HOUSES; *TITANIC;* TRUMBULL, DOUGLAS.

Further Reading

Gross, Edward. *The Making of the Trek Films*. New York: Image, 1992.

Martin, Kevin H. "Kirk Out." *Cinefex 61*, March 1995.

——. "Letting Slip the Dogs of War." *Cinefex 49*, 1992.

——. "Phoenix Rising." *Cinefex 69*, March 1997.

Mason, Dave. "A Bold New 'Trek': Santa Barbara Firm Creates Digital Universe." *Ventura County Star Television Guide*, November 15-21, 1998.

Shatner, William. Star Trek *Movie Memories*. New York: Harper Collins, 1994.

Star Wars Movies

Written and directed by George Lucas, the 1977 movie *Star Wars* was responsible for revolutionary new visual effects techniques, and its sequels, *The Empire Strikes Back* (1980) and *Return of the Jedi* (1983), pushed these advances still further. A 1999 prequel to *Star Wars, The Phantom Menace,* employed state-of-the-art digital effects. In addition, *Star Wars* inspired the creation of Industrial Light & Magic (ILM), the foremost special effects house in the industry.

Lucas established ILM specifically to provide special effects for his film. Prior to beginning production on *Star Wars,* Lucas hired a team of special effects experts to help him set up the facility in a Van Nuys, California, warehouse. He first tried to recruit Douglas Trumbull, who had earlier supervised the effects on *2001: A Space Odyssey* (1968) and had his own special effects company. When Trumbull turned him down, Lucas instead hired John Dykstra, one of Trumbull's staff. He then hired bluescreen expert Richard Edlund to work with Dykstra in developing new miniature photography equipment and travelling matte techniques.

While writing the script for *Star Wars,* Lucas had decided that he wanted to include starship battles that were similar to World War II aerial dogfights. To do this, he needed a camera that could perform quick tracking shots, which meant that it would have to move forward, backwards, and sideways on a track or dolly. At the same time, he wanted to be able to layer several separate elements into one shot, and to have a large number of such multilayered shots. However, he did not want to do this compositing in-camera, by shooting a miniature, rewinding the film, and shooting the miniature again with a new element added. This meant that he needed a way to exactly duplicate camera moves as many times as necessary. As a result, Dykstra developed an electronic motion-control camera system, which he named Dykstraflex. This system not only provided Lucas with a way to repeatedly film a miniature so that various lighting, animation, and live-action elements could be added to the shot, but also made it possible for him to film one model spaceship and turn it into a fleet.

Using the Dykstraflex system, the camera hung from a type of boom arm on a track and was capable of tilting and rolling as well as forward, backwards, and sideways movement. The type of camera equipment used for this system was selected by Richard Edlund, who discovered an old VistaVision optical printer last used for Cecil B. DeMille's *The Ten Commandments* (1956). The VistaVision format had been largely abandoned by this time in favor of other widescreen formats, but Edlund decided that it would be perfect for use with Dykstra's system, because it was known for limiting image degradation during the compositing process. The VistaVision format did indeed prove to be the best camera for the system, and other filmmakers subsequently began using it for special effects photography themselves.

Along with the motion-control system, Edlund and other members of the ILM team were responsible for advances in bluescreen procedures. They set a new standard in the industry by switching from alternating-current (AC) to direct-current (DC) power sources to backlight their bluescreens, which eliminated flickering, and they used better fluorescent lighting tubes. In addition, they put their miniature spaceships on supports, called model pylons, that were the same blue color as the bluescreens, which reduced the need for rotoscoping during postproduction.

ILM developed the first dedicated rotoscope department, whose staff had the job not only of eliminating unwanted elements in a shot but of adding animation artwork to provide bursts of light. Interestingly, although the lightsaber rays were added with animation during *The Empire Strikes Back* and *Return of the Jedi*, for *Star Wars* they were created by wrapping front-projection material around stick swords. Light was then reflected onto the sabers during filming.

Originally the ILM team also planned to create miniature pyrotechnics effects during filming. However, after experimenting with a few explosions, they discovered that the blasts were too powerful for their models. A spaceship would go from intact to dust so quickly that the effect did not register well on film. Therefore they had pyrotechnician Joe Viskocil create separate explosions that they then layered over their miniature effects footage during postproduction. One exception involved the Death Star, which was a large model that covered 1,600 square feet of a parking lot. The model was built from 2-foot-square foam panels, which were carved and detailed with cellophane tape for windows. Pyrotechnics were detonated directly on this model, as well as on three versions of the Death Star trench that were set up in a similar fashion.

Other spaceship miniatures were photographed inside the ILM facility. The models sat on pylons mounted on a track and then were moved along the track via the Dykstraflex system to perform tilts and rolls. The models therefore had to be fairly sturdy, so they were built with a metal armature with multiple mounting points for the pylons. The models also had internal lights. Designed by Steve Gawley and Joe Johnston, their surface details were created with parts from commercial model kits such as those sold in a hobby shop. Some of the exterior panels were scribed and airbrushed to provide the illusion of age and weathering. This simulated damage was revolutionary, because previous science fiction films such as *2001: A Space Odyssey* (1968) had always depicted spaceships in pristine condition.

In fact, executives at 20th Century Fox, which was providing financial backing for *Star Wars*, were disappointed with the way the miniatures looked. They were also unhappy with how long it was taking Lucas to make the movie. Establishing ILM and creating the Dykstraflex system and other technological advances were so time-consuming that after one year the special effects team had completed only four shots. By this time, 20th Century Fox had spent approximately $1 million on the movie. Therefore the company briefly shut down the production, and when they allowed filming to continue they did so on a provisional basis, providing very limited funds to the project. This meant that the effects team had very little time or money to waste, and they began shooting miniatures around the clock, using a day team and a night team.

The day team was supervised by Richard Edlund, while nights were handled by Dennis Muren, assisted by Ken Ralston. Muren and Ralston would later become two of the most influential special effects experts in the industry, along with two other ILM team members, makeup expert Rick Baker and stop-motion expert Phil Tippett. Rick Baker created the alien creatures for the cantina scene. Phil Tippett also contributed to these designs, along with Jon Berg, and worked with Dennis Muren to provide stop-motion model animation for a holographic chess game.

This stop-motion work was so effective that ILM created a stop-motion department for *The Empire Strikes Back*. Overseen by Dennis Muren, this department experimented with using motion control to move its stop-motion figures, thereby laying the groundwork for Go-Motion. However, most of the models were moved by hand, including those involving the Empire's walkers. The walker models and other miniatures were shot on miniature sets that had painted backgrounds and foreground glass paintings to provide additional details. Other glass paintings were combined with live action by front-projecting live-action images onto parts of the glass.

The Empire Strikes Back also employed a new type of optical printer for postproduction work, as well as an improved VistaVision camera for miniature photography. The movie contained approximately 400 special effects shots employing over 50 miniatures. This work was not done in ILM's original facility, because after completing *Star Wars* George Lucas decided to move his company to Northern California. Some of his effects experts, such as John Dykstra, refused to relocate, and subsequently founded their own

effects house, Apogee, in the ILM Van Nuys facility. Richard Edlund, Dennis Muren, and Ken Ralston did make the move to Northern California, however, and worked on *Return of the Jedi*.

Return of the Jedi had more than 900 special effects shots, and once again the ILM team had to come up with new techniques to create them. For example, they developed an improved version of their motion-control system that could perform much faster moves, and they devised a form of motion control that could be used on location. They used animatics rather than traditional sketched storyboards to plan an elaborate speeder bike scene, which was created with motion-control bikes, human figures, and live actors filmed in front of a bluescreen. In addition, they employed Go-Motion in place of stop-motion model animation to animate the walkers, and they invented a new multiplane matte camera to make postproduction compositing easier.

In order to create the numerous creatures seen in *Return of the Jedi,* ILM established a department dedicated to this type of effects work. The new creature effects department was under the supervision of Phil Tippett, who formerly had handled stop-motion model animation. In addition, ILM's parent company, Lucasfilm, established a computer graphics division to develop the art of computer animation. However, 3-D computer animation software was still relatively primitive, so there was not much difference between the computer-generated tactical display of the Death Star in *Return of the Jedi* and the one in *Star Wars*.

Advances in computer animation allowed Lucas to rerelease all three *Star Wars* movies in 1997 with new computer-generated images inserted into various shots. Lucas had decided to remake the movies largely because he was dissatisfied with some of his creature and animation effects. For example, in one *Star Wars* shot of two characters walking into a cantina, a creature in the background was a rubber figure with limited movement. In the new version of *Star Wars,* however, the creature is a fully animated, lifelike computer-generated figure.

Lucas continued his reliance on new computer animation techniques in his *Star Wars* prequel, *The Phantom Menace,* which was released in 1999. There were approximately 2,200 visual effects in the film, and almost 70 percent of the movie featured computer-generated elements. More than 60 computer-generated characters appear in roughly 800 character animation shots. One of the main characters, Jar Jar Binks, was created entirely with computer graphics; he appears in approximately 350 shots and is often seen next to live actors.

On the live-action set, Jar Jar was often represented by the actor who provided his voice, Ahmed Best. Best wore a model of his character's head atop his own, which elevated Jar Jar's eyes to the proper height and showed other actors where to look when speaking to him during a scene. Best also wore a suit colored like his character, so digital artists would later know how to light the computer-generated figure that would completely replace Best.

Jar Jar was originally conceived through computer drawings, but other computer-generated figures were first developed as clay sculptures called maquettes and then scanned into a computer. In either case, these stationary digital images were subsequently provided with wireframe skeletons and animation "chains" that perform much like muscles, connecting various points on a figure to make them move in concert.

After this work was complete, artists used a proprietary ILM 3-D paint program called Viewpaint to add color, texture, and surface details to each character. Meanwhile, animators used wireframe or gray-shaded versions of the characters to work out their movements. In the case of a robot, or "droid," army, movements were provided via a motion-capture system that transferred a man's walk into the computer for replication in hundreds of soldiers. For clothed characters, a new software program was developed to make clothing movements more realistic.

Once the digital characters were in final, animated form, digital experts integrated them into live-action background plates, so that they appeared to be real creatures filmed at the same time and with the same lighting as live actors. The same basic step-by-step process was used to create computer-generated spaceships and other objects.

However, not all objects or characters were created wholly through computer graphics. Typically a mixture of effects was used. For example, in closeup shots, the Queen's spaceship was a 10-foot-long miniature; in shots involving complex animation, the ship was a richly detailed 3-D computer-generated image, while in quick cuts it was a low-resolution 2-D computer-generated image.

Computer-generated character of Jabba the Hutt placed into a 1977 scene with actor Harrison Ford for the 1997 *Star Wars* re-release. *Lucasfilm Ltd./Photofest.*

The Mos Espa podracing arena was also created with both computer graphics and miniature sets. In a few shots of a large stadium crowd, the cheering spectators were actually variously colored Q-Tips cotton swabs, moved in their miniature seats by blowing air.

Similarly, in underwater sequences, which were supervised by visual effects expert Dennis Muren, the terrain of the sea floor was a miniature set, filmed through smoke to make it look murky, while the Gungan city was computer-generated, as were a submarine and three sea monsters. A scene within a Gungan room was created using a miniature set as well as a partial full-sized set. Live actors were shot on the full-sized set in front of bluescreens, and their images were later composited into the miniature set alongside several computer-generated characters.

Of the 60–70 full-sized interior sets used for the film, most had some areas of bluescreen, so that digital matte paintings or other types of computer-generated images could be added to them. In fact, 60–75 percent of all shots in *The Phantom Menace* employed some amount of bluescreen work. The bluescreens used in the production were of a new type, with lamps two times more powerful than previous versions, and those used during live-action filming could be as tall as 20 feet. Some were also extremely long; for example, a 300-foot-long bluescreen was used behind the set of the Jedi Council chamber. Smaller, portable bluescreens were used on location, and miniature ones were used during miniature photography.

In all bluescreen work, particularly on sets involving shiny floors, there is the risk that the lights from the bluescreen will be reflected onto other surfaces, a problem known as blue spill. During work on *The Phantom Menace,* the movie's visual effects supervisor, John Knoll, invented software that would suppress blue spill during postproduction.

Other technological innovations were inspired by the movie as well. One of the most significant was a new technique to record camera movements on live-action sets. A data-capture module was attached to the camera to gather detailed information regarding lens operations and camera movements; this information was immediately transmitted to a laptop computer. Digital artists then used the data to help them integrate computer-generated characters into live-action footage. This eliminated the need for matchmovers to calculate angles, distances, and other data themselves using film footage that had been scanned into the computer. However, because digital experts were not certain the new system would work properly, matchmovers still took careful measurements on the set of *The Phantom Menace* in case manual calculations were needed.

Another new technique was the use of high-definition digital videotape for approximately 10–20 shots in the movie. Lucas interspersed these digital shots with filmed shots to determine whether audiences would be able to distinguish the difference between the two types of images. When he discovered that the quality level of both was the same, he announced that he will make future *Star Wars* movies using only digital videotape, which will eliminate the process of transferring filmed images into the computer for special effects work.

The Phantom Menace also marked the first time that computerized animatics were used to previsualize an entire film. Using a 3-D animation program, animatics expert David Dozoretz worked with George Lucas to make a digital representation of every shot prior to filming, establishing the placement of objects such as spaceships, characters, and landscape elements as well as camera movements and angles. These animatics were played on a monitor on the set during filming, so that Lucas could show his cast and crew exactly what he had in mind for each scene.

The Phantom Menace employed advances in puppetry, animatronics, and creature effects as well. For example, the puppet used to portray Yoda in all but one shot in the film (when he was a computer-generated figure) was made of silicone, whereas for previous films he had been made of foam latex. He also had more sophisticated mechanisms, including a brow movement that was operated by remote radio control rather than by the puppeteer holding the figure. Two Neimoidans, aliens who plotted to destroy a queen, were portrayed by actors wearing sophisticated radio-controlled puppet heads.

As in earlier films, R2-D2 was portrayed by actor Kenny Baker in a costume; however, for some shots in *The Phantom Menace* the robot was instead powered by wheelchair motors. Another robot, C-3PO, who had previously been portrayed by costumed actor Anthony Daniels (who continues to provide the character's voice) was a puppet controlled from behind. The puppeteer wore clothing in a color that blended with his background, whether that background was a greenscreen (rather than a bluescreen because of the blue metallic sheen of the puppet), black material, white material, or part of a live-action set. This made the puppeteer easier to eliminate digitally during postproduction.

Postproduction equipment was also very different in comparison to earlier *Star Wars* films. For example, *The Phantom Menace* employed a larger RenderFarm than any previous ILM project. RenderFarm is a visual effects term for the computer equipment used to process and render digital data. Digital artists working on *The Phantom Menace* had access to 250 computer workstations wired to Silicon Graphics hardware, as well as to new software tools developed specifically for the production. Existing software was also upgraded to meet the demands of the movie. For example, the Caricature program used for such films as *Dragonheart* (1996) was improved and linked with the software used to create realistic digital clothing.

Some effects, however, were created more traditionally. For example, the blades of lightsaber weapons were made of aluminum tubing covered with fluorescent-painted plastic shrinkwrap to prevent pieces of aluminum from flying off during fight scenes. After filming, lightsaber footage was scanned digitally into a computer and the blades' glow was painted onto them frame by frame, after which the scene was recorded back out to film. Fight scene stunts were enhanced with

pneumatic rams, which used air pressure to propel actors into the air for leaps and flips. *See also* ANIMATICS; ANIMATION, CEL; ANIMATION, COMPUTER; BLUESCREEN PROCESS; CAMERAS, MOTION PICTURE; COMPOSITING; DEMILLE, CECIL B.; DOZORETZ, DAVID; DYKSTRA, JOHN; EDLUND, RICHARD; GAWLEY, STEVE; GO-MOTION; INDUSTRIAL LIGHT & MAGIC; JOHNSTON, JOE; LUCAS, GEORGE; MINIATURES AND MODELS; MOTION-CONTROL CAMERA SYSTEMS; MUREN, DENNIS; RALSTON, KEN; ROTOSCOPING; *THE TEN COMMANDMENTS;* TIPPETT, PHIL; TRAVELLING MATTE; TRUMBULL, DOUGLAS; *2001: A SPACE ODYSSEY;* VISTAVISION.

Further Reading

Bouzereau, Laurent, and Jody Duncan. Star Wars: *The Making of* Episode I: The Phantom Menace. New York: Ballantine Books, 1999.

Duncan, Jody. "20 Years of Industrial Light & Magic." *Cinefex* 65, March 1996.

Martin, Kevin H. "War Stories." *Cinefex* 65, March 1996.

Shay, Don. "30 Minutes with the Godfather of Digital Cinema." *Cinefex* 65, March 1996.

Smith, Thomas G. *Industrial Light & Magic: The Art of Special Effects*. New York: Ballantine Books, 1986.

Woods, Bob (ed.) Star Wars Episode I: The Phantom Menace: *The Official Souvenir Magazine*. Lucasfilm Ltd, 1999.

Starewicz, Wladyslaw (1882–1965)

Born in Vilna, Poland (subsequently part of Russia), in 1882, Wladyslaw (later Ladislas) Starewicz was a filmmaker in Moscow beginning in 1909 and in France from 1920 until his death in 1965. His first movies were short documentaries about insects, and as part of this work he began to experiment with stop-motion techniques using dead beetles that he had rigged with tiny wires. The result was *The Battle of the Stag Beetles* (approximately 1911), which is considered the first stop-motion "puppet" film to tell a story. Prior to this time, the technique was used by stop-motion animator Emile Cohl, but only as part of a short public-announcement piece.

Starewicz went on to produce several more stop-motion puppet films, including *The Grasshopper and the Ant* (1912), *Insects Aviation Week* (1912), *The Rat of the City and the Rat of the Country* (1927), and *The*

Tale of the Fox (released in German in 1937 and in French in 1941). The latter took more than 10 years to make and is considered one of the greatest stop-motion puppet films ever made. *See also* COHL, EMILE; STOP-MOTION MODEL ANIMATION.

Stargate

The 1994 MGM/UA science-fiction movie *Stargate* is notable because it increased the size of cities and crowds with computer graphics as a way to cut costs. For example, for a scene showing thousands of slaves in an alien city, the movie's director, Roland Emmerich, filmed approximately 800 actors with spaces between them, and then had computer experts replicate these actors to fill in the crowd. The same thing occurred with the alien city itself. Model makers created relatively few miniature buildings, and computer experts filled in the rest with replicated images, some of which were reversed.

This computer graphics work was more economical than hiring thousands of actors and building lavish sets. By conserving money in this way, Emmerich had more to spend on the movie's most important special effect, the stargate. In the movie, the stargate is an alien transportation device activated on Earth by a team of humans who use it to travel to a distant planet. Twenty-two feet tall, it was constructed of metal and fiberglass in a Long Beach, California, building that once housed a famous airplane, the Spruce Goose. The stargate was also wired for electricity, so that its outer ring really turned when it was activated.

The rest of the stargate effect was accomplished with a computer. Thirty-eight digital shots made the surface of the gate's entrance seem to ripple like water, and footage of actor James Spader pulling his face from a tank of water was played in reverse to make it seem as though he is slowly pushing himself through the gate. Then a rush of light and color makes it appear as though he is being sucked through the stars.

Two other important effects in *Stargate* relate to a strange yak-like animal and a group of alien spaceships that attack an unruly crowd. The animal was a Clydesdale horse in a special costume. The horse's rider was concealed under the beast's huge hump, and its facial expressions were created with a radio-controlled mask. Most of the spaceships were models, many of which were made to "fly" on wires outdoors in Arizona. The rest were computer-generated.

Emmerich's extensive reliance on computer graphics kept *Stargate*'s cost at approximately $50 million, despite the fact that it featured more than 280 special effects shots. When the film grossed more than $70 million in the United States alone, the director learned the value of digital effects, and went on to employ similar techniques in his 1996 blockbuster *Independence Day*. *See also* ANIMATION, COMPUTER; EMMERICH, ROLAND; *INDEPENDENCE DAY*.

Further Reading
Vaz, Mark Cotta. "Through the Stargate." *Cinefex 61,* March 1995.

Starship Troopers

The 1997 TriStar Pictures movie *Starship Troopers* was responsible for several new technological advances, particularly in the field of digital effects. Approximately 200 of the film's 600 special effects shots featured hundreds of giant alien bugs, which were created under the supervision of Phil Tippett. Some of his work employed the Digital Input Device (DID), a computer-puppet interface that he developed for *Jurassic Park* (1993) with computer expert Craig Hayes and improved while making *Starship Troopers*.

Tippett hired 100 digital artists, compositors, animators, and technicians to design and create six different types of bugs for the movie, including the warrior, which was 8 to 10 feet tall, the tanker bug, which functioned like a tank and shot a flaming acid, and the brain bug, which controlled all of the other alien insects. Except for the tanker bug, all of the insects began as 2-D digital drawings that were then used to sculpt maquettes, which in turn provided information to a computer so it could turn the figures into 3-D wireframe computer images. The tanker bug was created directly as a 3-D image, without the preceding digitizing process. The computer models were then painted, shaded, and animated. Approximately 70 percent of this animation work was done by digital artists, while 30 percent was animated using a DID, with the help of new software that improved communication between the device and the computer.

Digital work on *Starship Troopers* also benefited from Dynamation software, which animates points or particles. In this case, the software generated dozens of dots that could be applied to the background plate to represent swarming bugs. Each dot was assigned its own radius, speed, and direction capabilities, and given information about the terrain in the scene, so that once it was animated it would not hit rocks or other bugs. In this way, the Dynamation software allowed digital experts to create a background filled with moving insects, without having to animate each one individually.

These images were placed on background plates made from photographs taken at the live-action setting. At the same time, 3-D aerial topography maps of the setting were made so that animators could determine how the bugs would move over the landscape. However, the composited scenes had so many layers of elements and so much digital data that it initially took the computer 60 hours to render a single frame. Even after extensive research and development, this time was only reduced to 25–30 hours per frame. This meant that a 10-second shot could take 300 hours to render in final form. The average number of layers for each shot was between 75 and 100, with some having as many as 200. In one starship battle scene alone, there were 150 different pyrotechnics elements.

The film also included computer-generated humans, created either to fill in crowds of troops or to depict soldiers being attacked and torn apart by bugs. In the case of the former, live extras were filmed in front of a greenscreen, duplicated, and placed in the appropriate locations, whereas the latter required freestyle drawing and manipulation.

However, most shots of bugs interacting with soldiers were filmed using live actors and full-scale bug puppets or props. There were 300 extras working on the large battle scenes, but this meant that there were not enough men to play both living soldiers and wounded men. Therefore, in addition to digital extras, 35 crude dummies were made to represent dead bodies in background scenes, with five more detailed ones for foreground scenes.

Bug attack scenes also featured full-sized warrior bug puppets, which were driven by pneumatic cables and hydraulic mechanisms. One of them had jaws that could lift an actor, and another, which was 10 feet tall and 15 feet long, was capable of performing 30 separate movements. There were also 15 bug puppets incapable of movement, primarily used to represent dead bodies, as well as several bug props representing individual body parts; for example, several claws with handles that could be manipulated by puppeteers.

More complicated machinery was required to move a tank bug used for a scene in which a character jumps on the beetle's back, drills a hole in its shell, and drops in an explosive grenade to explode the bug. Only the bug's back was constructed, which was done by joining two handpainted fiberglass shells 28 feet long and 18 feet wide and attaching them to a 20-foot-long tractor. This tractor was connected to the shells through a series of complex mechanisms that enabled it to buck and rock the back. The actor was tethered to the bug by thin wire attached to a belt under his costume.

This arrangement was only used for closeups, however. For wide shots, a computer-generated bug and human were used. To create the human the animators tried a unique approach. They photographed the actor, wearing only his underwear, in front of a grid, and used these photos as reference material to help them plot out the human figure in the computer. They also used a photograph of a Trooper uniform as a visual reference for color and texture. With careful work, they managed to create an impressive computer-generated copy of the character.

The explosion of the computer-generated bug was also done digitally, but most of the other pyrotechnics in the film were done live on the set because the director did not believe that fires and explosions could be made well using computers, although other filmmakers had begun to take this approach. Consequently *Starship Troopers* featured some of the most spectacular on-set pyrotechnics of recent films.

Some explosions were created on location, while others were created in a studio for later compositing with photographs of miniature spaceships. In the case of the latter, bucks, or metal forms, shaped like spaceships were used as placeholders, so that the flame would form a realistic shape around it. Miniature pyrotechnics also required experimentation with various scales of fire, so that the fire would not appear the wrong size in proportion to the models, and with chemicals, in order to discover how to make the fires smokeless yet colorful.

Miniature photography for the film's 120 space battle shots was provided by Sony Pictures Imageworks (SPI), which had a staff of 270 special effects experts working on *Starship Troopers*. SPI created their shots using computer-generated starfields and planets, but employed models and motion-control photography, with digital enhancements, for the other elements in their scenes. There were several different types of ships featured in the movie, requiring more than 100 models built out of foam, wood, metal, and plastic. To create digital planets, artists first created traditional matte paintings on glass panels, digitized their images, imported them into a computer, and wrapped them around a 3-D globe. They then further enhanced the images by adding clouds and similar effects.

At one point in the film, a battle cruiser called the *Rodger Young* is hit by a plasma burst, which is a computer-generated image, after which the ship cracks in half. To create this event, first an 18-foot-long model of the spaceship was photographed in its entirety in front of a bluescreen. It was then replaced with another model that had been built as two 9-foot-long sections. This model was mounted on a mechanism called a model mover that gradually pulled it apart during filming. While this separation was happening, two stop-motion model animators manipulated various details on the models in between frames, to make it appear as though wires were bending and debris falling. Just before the scene's climactic explosion, the ship was replaced with a pyro-model, a model specifically designed to blow up.

Live-action filming related to the *Rodger Young* took place on a set that had been built on a 40x50-foot steel gimbal. This gimbal weighed 20,000 pounds and could support an additional 60,000 pounds, which enabled it to tilt and shake violently. It was operated by pulleys, wires, and cables, using a computer-controlled electronic joystick.

Live-action filming was also used for the final scene in which the Troopers capture the brain bug. However, as in the battle scenes, there were not enough extras to create a crowd of 800 cheering Troopers. Therefore one extra was hooked up to a motion-capture device and told to perform various actions. This device then digitized his movements so that the computer could insert computer-generated cheering Troopers into the scene. Here and elsewhere, *Starship Troopers* demonstrated that computer graphics could be used practically to enhance a movie and create images that otherwise would not have been possible, either because of physical or budgetary constraints. *See also* ANIMATION, COMPUTER; COMPUTER GRAPHICS; DIGITAL INPUT DEVICE; MOTION CAPTURE; PYROTECHNICS; RENDERING; TIPPETT, PHIL; WIREFRAME.

Further Reading

Mallory, Michael. "Twist & Shout & Scream." *VISFX*, February 1998.

Sammon, Paul M. "Bug Bytes." *Cinefex 73*, March 1998.

Stop-Motion Model Animation

Stop-motion model animation is a process whereby a model or puppet is animated by hand, without any computer intervention. The object is filmed frame by frame, with the animator moving it by tiny increments between frames and when the filmed scene is run at the conventional speed of 24 frames per second, the model appears to be moving. The term "stop-motion" is derived from the fact that the camera must be stopped intermittently during the filming process while the model is moved. This is in contrast to the Go-Motion process, whereby the object is moved continuously by machine so the camera need not be stopped.

Among the earliest stop-motion animation was the work of Willis O'Brien, who animated clay dinosaurs for his 1925 film *The Lost World*. He later went on to make the stop-motion classic *King Kong* (1933). Most of O'Brien's models were made by Marcel Delgado, who developed more sophisticated model construction techniques as time went on. For example, while his earliest figures had simple wire armatures, his later ones had ball-and-socket joints.

Prior to O'Brien's work, animators like Emile Cohl and Wladyslaw Starewicz used stop-motion photography to animate puppets as opposed to clay models. In fact, Starewicz was the first filmmaker to use puppet animation to tell a story in *The Battle of the Stag Beetles* (approximately 1911), although his "puppets" were actually dead beetles manipulated with tiny wires. Starewicz went on to make several other acclaimed stop-motion puppet animation films, including *The Tale of the Fox* (1937), which many consider to be the best work in the genre.

Another pioneer of stop-motion model animation was Ray Harryhausen, who created such famous stop-motion movies as *The Beast from 20,000 Fathoms* (1953) and *Jason and the Argonauts* (1963). Harryhausen used stop-motion in concert with other optical effects, including miniature rearscreen projection, to make highly realistic scenes. For example, *Jason and the Argonauts* features a swordfight between seven skeletons and three of the movie's main characters. This scene was created by projecting the live action, which had been filmed the previous year in Italy, frame-by-frame onto a miniature screen behind miniature skeletons. These skeletons were only 8 inches high and could be ma-

nipulated into many different poses. Nonetheless, the process was extremely time-consuming. It often took an entire day to film only 13 or 14 frames, and the entire five-minute swordfight scene took more than four months to complete.

Skeletons created with stop-motion model animation for a scene in *Jason and the Argonauts* (1963). *Photofest.*

A more recent film to use stop-motion model animation was *The Nightmare Before Christmas* (1993), directed by Tim Burton. However, it did not combine stop-motion with live action at all; the entire movie was made with stop-motion figures. Burton did intend to use both stop-motion and live-action filming for his 1996 movie *Mars Attacks!* but ultimately decided that the computer-animated motions looked more impressive and would save time on his tight shooting schedule.

Computer animation has largely replaced the stop-motion model animation in modern films, although the latter is still used to animate certain aspects of miniatures and models. For example, photographers working with miniatures for *Starship Troopers* (1998) placed one spaceship model on a mechanism called a model mover, which gradually pulled it apart during filming, while two stop-motion model animators manipulated various details on the models between frames, making it appear as though debris were falling and various structural supports were bending and twisting. In this way, stop-motion animation provided a richness of detail that enhanced the final shot. *See also* THE BEAST FROM 20,000 FATHOMS; BURTON, TIM; DELGADO, MARCEL; HARRYHAUSEN, RAY; *KING KONG; THE LOST WORLD; MARS ATTACKS!;* MINIATURES AND MODELS; MODEL MOVER; O'BRIEN, WILLIS; *STARSHIP TROOPERS.*

Further Reading

Archer, Steve. *Willis O'Brien: Special Effects Genius.* Jefferson, NC: McFarland and Company, 1998.

Bernard, Wilkie. *Creating Special Effects for TV and Film.* New York: Hastings House, 1977.

Culhane, John. *Special Effects in the Movies: How They Do It.* New York: Ballantine, 1981.

Johnson, John. *Cheap Tricks and Class Acts.* Jefferson, NC: McFarland and Company, 1996.

Storyboard

A storyboard is a series of sketches, photographs, or other visual representations of the individual images within a movie scene, typically accompanied by technical notes and other written comments. It is a planning tool that can help directors visualize a scene and develop a step-by-step guide to filming a special effects sequence or an entire movie, particularly an animated one. A storyboard also gives cameramen, set designers, lighting experts, and other members of a live-action movie crew an idea of what their final product should look like, thereby aiding them in making critical decisions during the preproduction process.

Over the years, the art of storyboarding has developed from rather crude sketches to fairly sophisticated drawings. In addition, several storyboarding computer software programs have recently been created to generate more sophisticated storyboards, also called digital previsualization tools. These programs allow the user to "build" a three-dimensional setting out of various scene components such as trees, streets, cars, buildings, doorways, and furniture. In doing so, the user can explore different types of set design, lighting sources, and other aspects of a filming location. After this work is completed, the user places generic characters within the setting and develops a motion path to depict the char-

acters' movements in real time. This motion path can be extremely helpful to live actors during filming, particularly when they must act out a complicated special effects scene that involves careful timing. *See also* ANIMATICS; ANIMATION, COMPUTER; COMPUTER GRAPHICS; PREVISUALIZATION.

For Further Reading

Ohanian, Thomas A., and Michael E. Phillips. *Digital Filmmaking.* Boston: Focal Press, 1996.

Smith, Thomas G. *Industrial Light & Magic: The Art of Special Effects.* New York: Ballantine Books, 1986.

Stunts

Stunts are acting feats that typically involve some element of physical risk, such as falls, fights, vehicle chases and/or crashes, aerobatic tricks, and wirework. The earliest stuntpeople were the actors themselves. Buster Keaton, Harold Lloyd, Tom Mix, and Pearl White, for example, all performed their own stunts, as did many other silent-film stars. Most of these stunts involved leaps, flips, tumbles, and falls from heights small and great. Performers used little or no padding to protect their bodies during the execution of such stunts, and as a result they sometimes sustained injuries that delayed the completion of a movie. This led filmmakers to start asking unimportant actors, known as extras, to perform stars' stunts instead, whereupon the extras became known as stunt doubles.

During the 1920s, it was easy to find extras willing to perform dangerous stunts, because at that time an extra made only $2 to $3 a day, while doing a stunt paid an extra $5. But because of the extreme risks involved with aerial work, people who performed stunts with airplanes banded together in 1925 to set higher rates for their performances. They required $150 to jump from an airplane to a train, $500 to blow up a plane in the air and parachute to safety, and $1200 to crash a plane into a tree or a house. The latter was called a controlled crash, but it was still extremely dangerous, and many stuntpilots died attempting the stunt.

Many other types of early stuntwork also involved a great deal of danger. From 1925 to 1930, more than 10,000 people were injured and 55 were killed performing stunts. Many of these injuries were caused during falls, often when untrained extras jumped off a precipice into piles of straw. Other injuries involved large, staged events. For example, several people died and one man lost his leg during the filming of *Noah's Ark,* when tons of water slammed into them as part of a planned stunt. The producer had been warned that the stunt was extremely dangerous, but had disregarded this advice. Similarly, both men and horses were injured and more than 100 horses died while filming the chariot race in the 1926 version of *Ben-Hur,* when stuntpeople were paid to run a real race with no regard to safety.

Today the humane society regulates the use of animals on a movie set. Humans are also subject to strict safety policies and procedures, and special equipment has been developed specifically to keep them safe during stuntwork. In the case of falls, for example, stuntpeople land in airbags or large mattresses, sometimes using parachutes or other equipment to break their fall. When falls are made into water, a safety boat is always on hand to recover the stuntperson as quickly as possible. Various padding devices are available to protect a stuntperson's body during any type of stuntwork, and windows, walls, furniture, and/or other props that will come into contact with the stuntperson during a fall or crash are made from materials that will not inflict injury. Some pieces of equipment, such as flying rigs, have made stuntwork safe enough to allow actors to perform some of their own stunts.

Most stunts, however, are left to trained professionals physically fit to withstand the rigors of their work. These people practice their stunts carefully and repeatedly before filming begins, and they know when a stunt is too dangerous or difficult to perform. In such situations, filmmakers can now substitute a computer-generated figure for the live actor. For example, while filming *Titanic* (1997), special effects experts filmed a real stuntperson falling into a bag using motion-capture equipment, which created a digital duplicate of his movements. They then created a computer-generated stuntperson who performed every fall from a height of more than 50 feet.

But despite such digital accomplishments, real stuntwork is still a requirement in many situations, often in concert with complicated mechanical effects. In *True Lies* (1994), for example, some of the stunts were performed on a full-sized mockup of a Harrier jet, constructed using more than two dozen fiberglass molds of a real Harrier. This mockup was mounted on a computer-controlled hydraulic motion base that could be programmed to tilt and turn the plane in a variety of ways as the stuntmen performed.

Full-sized Harrier jet mockup used for stunts in *True Lies* (1994). *Photofest.*

For some scenes, this system was set up in front of a greenscreen 120 feet wide and 35 feet tall. For others it was mounted on the top of a high-rise office building. The plane was also detached from the motion base and attached to a truck-mounted crane for filming, so that it could be maneuvered on wires and made to "land" on a street or a Florida causeway. For one fight scene, during which the stuntmen were safety-cabled to the plane, the mockup was held 200 feet above the ground and filmed from a helicopter. This stunt and others in the movie had to be carefully choreographed prior to filming, as are all movie stunts.

Several professional associations exist to support stuntpeople, including the

Stuntmen's Association of Motion Pictures, the Stuntwomen's Association of Motion Pictures, and the Professional Drivers Association. Many stuntpeople also belong to the Screen Actors Guild (SAG), which lists their names and skills in a directory of stunt performers.

Further Reading

Miklowitz, Gloria D. *Movie Stunts and the People Who Do Them*. New York: Harcourt Brace Jovanivich, 1980.

Shay, Don. "Mayhem Over Miami." *Cinefex 59*, September 1994.

Stuntmen and Special Effects. New York: Ripley Books, 1982.

Superman

Released in 1978, *Superman* earned a Special Achievement Award for Visual Effects for its special effects team. The movie featured the most advanced flying rigs of its time.

The actor who played Superman, Christopher Reeve, was held in the air by one of three methods. One was a harness that dangled him from a boom 50 feet above the ground. Another was a system of wires, tracks, and pulleys that could move him from one end of a soundstage to another; for scenes in which he needed to be moving rapidly, he was slammed into a net at a speed of 30 miles per hour. The third flying method was a then-new filming system that used zoom lenses to make a subject appear to move close to or away from the camera when it was actually standing still. All Reeve had to do in such cases was shift his weight and lean slightly to create the illusion of flying while he was held aloft by a sophisticated system of vibrating wires.

Reeve often "flew" in front of an 80-foot-wide bluescreen whose blue area was even-

Christopher Reeve "flying" in *Superman* (1978). *Photofest.*

tually replaced with background footage shot from the underside of a helicopter flying over New York. This system was so effective that Superman's normally blue costume had to be made in blue-green, so it would not be eliminated as well. On other occasions Reeve "flew" behind a large front projection screen, which showed moving images of the scenery he was passing.

Mechanical effects enabled the actor to lift seemingly heavy objects without effort. For example, a truck was equipped with hydraulic machinery that made it rise when a young Superman appears to move it. Hydraulic equipment also lifted and shook the set representing the planet Krypton, which breaks apart at the beginning of the movie. *See also* BLUESCREEN PROCESS; HYDRAULICS; MECHANICAL EFFECTS; PROJECTION PROCESSES; WIREWORK.

Further Reading

O'Conner, Jane. *Magic in the Movies*. Garden City, NY: Doubleday, 1980.

Stuntmen and Special Effects. New York: Ripley Books, 1982.

T

Technicolor

Invented in 1917 by scientist Herbert T. Kalmus, Technicolor is a color process that originally used a camera with two apertures, one with a red filter and one with a green filter, and two strips of film. The red and green filmed images were then processed, dyed, and combined during projection.

Several popular movies of the 1920s were filmed with this two-color process, including *The Black Pirate* (1926). Nonetheless, the technique was expensive and was eventually abandoned in favor of a superior three-color Technicolor process, developed in 1932. This used a more complicated camera and special negatives sensitive to the colors red, green, and blue. At first, special proprietary Technicolor cameras were needed to create a Technicolor film; no one but a Technicolor cameraman could operate them. This was the case during the filming of *The Wizard of Oz* (1939), the first major film to employ the new three-color Technicolor process. However, in the 1940s the process was changed so that any type of motion picture camera could film in Technicolor. *See also* APERTURE; CAMERAS, MOTION PICTURE; FAIRBANKS, DOUGLAS SR.

Further Reading

Harmetz, Aljean. *The Making of* The Wizard of Oz. New York: Knopf, 1977.
Kawin, Bruce F. *How Movies Work*. Berkeley: University of California Press, 1992.

Telemetry Device

A telemetry device is a small-scale replica of an animatronic figure connected electronically, through a computer, to that animatronic figure. When the telemetry device is manipulated by a puppeteer, the animatronic figure immediately duplicates that movement. In other words, to move the animatronic figure, a person simply moves the small replica. This is extremely helpful when the animatronic figure is large and cumbersome to move, such as with the large animatronic dinosaurs of *The Lost World* (1997). *See also* THE LOST WORLD; PUPPETS.

Further Reading

Duncan, Jody. *The Making of* The Lost World. New York: Ballantine Books, 1997.
Smith, Thomas G. *Industrial Light & Magic: The Art of Special Effects*. New York: Ballantine Books, 1986.

The Ten Commandments

Directed by Cecil B. DeMille, the 1956 version of *The Ten Commandments* featured the special effects of John P. Fulton, who won an Academy Award for his work. The movie had a budget of $13 million, of which $1 million was spent on one scene alone: the parting of the Red Sea and subsequent flooding and destruction of the Egyptian pharoah's troops, which took six months to film.

The wall of water seen when the Red Sea parts was created with 24 dump tanks that released water down an inclined ramp. The rate of release was controlled manually through a series of 15 valves, and the resulting waterfall was actually in 1/5 scale. For the flooding portion of the scene, a 20,000-cubic-foot tank released 360,000 gallons of water in two minutes using special hydraulic equipment. In contrast, a 1920 version of *The Ten Commandments*, also directed by DeMille, created the flooding on a full-sized set without much concern for controlling the water. Large vats released the water on cue, but it not only flooded the set but rushed out of the filming area to flood Hollywood streets as well.

The 1956 version of the movie also used many full-sized sets. In fact, the movie featured the biggest set of its time: a 60-acre Egyptian city, which had an avenue of 16 sphinxes and an archway more than 100 feet high. There were also massive numbers of extras used for certain scenes. For example, the Exodus, wherein Moses leads his people from Egypt, required 10,000 extras accompanied by 172,000 props such as utensils and carts, and took 20 days to film. *See also* BLUE-SCREEN PROCESS; DEMILLE, CECIL B.; FULTON, JOHN P.; MATTE; MINIATURES AND MODELS; PROPS.

Further Reading

Brosnan, John. *Movie Magic*. New York: St. Martin's Press, 1974.

Fry, Ron, and Pamela Fourzon. *The Saga of Special Effects*. Englewood Cliffs, NJ: Prentice-Hall, 1977.

Terminator 2: Judgement Day

A sequel to *Terminator* (1984), *Terminator 2: Judgement Day* (1991) won an Academy Award for its visual effects, which were supervised by Dennis Muren at Industrial Light & Magic (ILM). The movie features spectacular stunts, pyrotechnics, animatronics, and mechanical effects; however, its most significant contributions were related to digital effects. Every shot in the film was composited digitally rather than with an optical printer. In addition, the movie's T-1000 cyborg character was a major advance in computer-generated imagery.

In the story of *Terminator 2,* the T-1000 was a liquid metal that could take on any form, including a human one. Digital effects artists therefore developed computer software that could create a realistic 3-D human shape. This was the first time a computer-generated image was able to approximate the human form. However, its surface was still metallic, because the technology was not yet available to give it a realistic human appearance.

A real actor played the part of the cyborg in human form. To make it seem as though the metallic shape had transformed itself into the person, the digital effects experts used a

Parting of the Red Sea in *The Ten Commandments* (1956). *Photofest.*

morphing program originally developed for the movie *Willow* (1988). With morphing, a computer automatically fills in the intermediary steps from one image to the next. In the case of *Willow*, these images were puppets; *Terminator 2* was the first film to include a computer-generated image in a morph.

To create this computer-generated image, digital experts drew grid lines on the live actor's body, filmed him in motion, and then scanned his image into the computer. They then made a wireframe skeleton of him and animated it using new software that smoothed out its joints and shaded it in a realistic fashion. Finally the artists merged the computer images with background plates through digital compositing.

In order to have the equipment and personnel for this work, ILM invested in more than $3 million in new hardware and increased its computer graphics department by 35 people. The company also invented a new type of scanner, which could scan in and digitize all types of 35mm film as an original negative, an intermediate positive for compositing, or a final positive print. To bring final work out of the computer and onto film, ILM used a camera system that recorded the visual images.

A total of 44 shots in *Terminator 2* were done with computer graphics. For other shots involving the T-1000, filmmakers used foam rubber and urethane puppets designed by noted effects expert Stan Winston. Several versions of the cyborg's head were hinged and mechanized to come apart when "blasted" by a shotgun. Several more were built with a system of springs and pneumatic rams to make the abdomen blow apart.

Another cyborg in the film, the Terminator, was also created as a mechanical effect, as well as a makeup effect. Winston used a series of prosthetic appliances to make an actor appear to be part human, part machine, and to make him appear to deteriorate during the course of the movie. For some shots, puppets or animatronic cyborgs were used in place of the actor. The animatronic cyborgs were operated by a combination of radio, rod, and cable controls. *See also* ANIMATION, COMPUTER; MORPHING; SCANNING.

Further Reading

Duncan, Jody. "20 Years of Industrial Light & Magic." *Cinefex 65,* March 1996.

Timpone, Anthony. *Men, Makeup, and Monsters.* New York: St. Martin's Press, 1996.

Texture Mapping

Texture mapping is a term related to computer graphics. It refers to the process of painting and shading a patch and then pasting it onto a 3-D computer-generated figure, much as one would stick wallpaper onto a wall. Texture mapping is one step in creating realistic skin or other surface features. *See also* ANIMATION, COMPUTER.

The Thief of Bagdad

The 1940 version of *The Thief of Bagdad* won an Academy Award for its special effects, which were under the supervision of Lawrence Butler. The movie featured the first travelling matte ever used in a color film. There were more than 100 such mattes, many used to make a magic horse appear to fly.

A 1924 version of *The Thief of Bagdad* is also significant in that it had a budget of $1 million, which was huge for its time. The movie featured many elaborate sets; for instance, "underwater" scenes were filmed in a 52-foot-deep waterless tank filled with kelp that had been hung from wires. Wires were also used to "fly" a magic carpet. *See also* BUTLER, LAWRENCE W.; TRAVELLING MATTE.

Further Reading

Brosnan, John. *Movie Magic.* New York: St. Martin's Press, 1974.

Fry, Ron, and Pamela Fourzon. *The Saga of Special Effects.* Englewood Cliffs, NJ: Prentice-Hall, 1977.

Thirty Seconds over Tokyo

Released by MGM in 1944, *Thirty Seconds over Tokyo* won an Academy Award for its special effects, which were under the supervision of A. Arnold Gillespie. The movie recreated World War II bombing raids on Japan using miniatures, rearscreen projection, and other physical and optical effects. *See also* GILLESPIE, A. ARNOLD; MECHANICAL EFFECTS; OPTICAL EFFECTS.

3-D

3-D stands for three-dimensional. A 3-D object has depth as well as height and width, whereas a two-dimensional, or 2-D, object has width and height but no depth. A movie is a 2-D medium, but many methods have been tried to make its images appear 3-D, the first in the 1900s. None of these methods proved popular until the 1950s, when an advanced 3-D technique called the anaglyphic process was developed. It resulted in a rash of 3-D movies, including *House of Wax* (1953), *It Came from Outer Space* (1953), and *Creature from the Black Lagoon* (1954). However, the process required that the audience wear special glasses, and for this and other reasons it was gradually abandoned. There was one attempt to revive it, via the 1983 movie *Jaws 3-D,* before it was discovered by the amusement park industry, which has used the technique to create 3-D effects in rides and attractions such as Disneyland's "Honey I Shrunk the Audience" experience.

In addition to referring to a three-dimensional image on a movie screen, the term "3-D" is also used in discussing computer graphics. It applies to a computer-generated person or object that has been digitally created in three-dimensional form, so that the computer can rotate the image to show all of its sides. Of course, the image on the computer screen is not truly three-dimensional, because the computer screen is two-dimensional. But the computer creates the person or object as a 3-D figure so that it will move within its setting as though it were real. *See also* ANAGLYPHIC PROCESS; COMPUTER GRAPHICS.

Further Reading

Grove, Chris. "Size Matters." *The Hollywood Reporter Large-Format Cinema Special Issue*, September 8-14, 1998.

Hayes, R.M. *3-D Movies: A History and Filmography of Stereoscopic Cinema.* Jefferson, NC: McFarland & Company, 1998.

Thunderball *See* BOND MOVIES.

The Time Machine

The 1960 movie *The Time Machine* won an Academy Award for its special effects, which were under the supervision of cinematographer Paul Vogel. The most advanced of these effects involved a sequence in which time appeared to be passing more rapidly than normal. To create this illusion, Vogel had to change the lighting in the scene to indicate the transitions from dawn to day to dusk to night. He consequently filmed through a rotating disk that had four sections of glass tinted according to the time being depicted; the dawn section was tinted pink, day was clear, dusk was amber, and night was blue. At some point, however, the lighting had to change so rapidly that a two-section disk—representing day and night—had to be substituted for the four-section one. In addition, Vogel employed stop-motion photography to show items changing in a shop window as time progressed. *See also* VOGEL, PAUL C.

Tippett, Phil (1951–)

Academy Award-winning special effects expert Phil Tippett specializes in stop-motion model animation. Much of his work has been done for Industrial Light & Magic (ILM), the foremost special effects company in America.

Tippett's first job for ILM was to do model animation for the 1977 movie *Star Wars,* creating some living chess pieces. For the *Star Wars* sequel *The Empire Strikes Back* (1980), Tippett designed and animated the tauntaun, a creature ridden through the snow by the character Luke Skywalker. For *Return of the Jedi* (1983), Tippett worked on scenes involving a beast called the Rancor, as well as those with All Terrain-Scout Transport (AT-ST) walkers, which were machines used by the film's villains. He was also placed in charge of ILM's Creature Shop, supervising production of the movie's models.

But Tippett's most significant contributions to the special effects industry have involved interfaces between puppetry devices and computers. One such device is the Go-Motion system, whereby a computer drives a figure that would previously have been animated through stop-motion. Tippett first used this system to animate the dragon in the 1981 film *Dragonslayer*. Another interface system is the Digital Input Device (DID), which Tippett developed with Craig Hayes for *Jurassic Park* (1993) and improved during the making of *Starship Troopers* (1997).

Born in 1951, Tippett became fascinated with model animation as a boy. He began working professionally as a model animator when he was only 17 years old, creating scenes for television commercials. However, he made very little money at his work, so he decided to quit his job and go to art school. After graduation he returned to the field of animation, both for commercials and movies. One of his responsibilities was to animate the Pillsbury Dough Boy. Tippett received an Academy Award for his work on *Return of the Jedi* and currently has his own special effects studio, Tippett Studio. In addition to *Dragonslayer, Jurassic Park,* and *Starship Troopers,* his recent works include *Indiana Jones and the Temple of Doom* (1984), *Robocop 2* and *3* (1990, 1993), and *My Favorite Martian* (1999). *See also* DRAGONSLAYER; GO-MOTION; INDIANA JONES MOVIES; INDUSTRIAL LIGHT & MAGIC; JURASSIC PARK; STAR WARS MOVIES.

Further Reading

Painter, Jamie. "An Insider Interview with Phil Tippett." *Star Wars Insider 33*, Spring 1997.

Smith, Thomas G. *Industrial Light & Magic: The Art of Special Effects*. New York: Ballantine Books, 1986.

Titanic

The 1997 movie *Titanic* won an Academy Award for its visual effects and featured some of the most innovative and advanced sets, miniatures, and digital effects ever produced. All special effects were created under the supervision of writer and director, James Cameron, who co-founded his own special effects company, Digital Domain.

Cameron decided to make *Titanic* after meeting Robert Ballard, who discovered the wreckage of the great oceanliner. Real footage of this wreck is incorporated into the movie. Cameron and the crew of his production company, Lightstorm Entertainment, visited the site of the wreck even before the film project was finalized, travelling to its remote location in the Atlantic Ocean on a Russian marine research vessel, *Keldysh*.

Their ship was equipped with two deep-sea submersibles, *Mir 1* and *Mir 2*, and carried two camera systems built specifically by Lightstorm for filming the *Titanic* wreck. The first was a motion picture camera that could be attached to the outside of *Mir 1*. Operated from inside the submersible, the camera had been customized to hold a widescreen film that lasts two times longer than normal; however, even using this film, as well as a slower-than-normal filming speed of 14–16 frames per second, the load would last for only 15 minutes per dive. The second camera was a video camera attached to an ROV, or remotely operated vehicle, that would be tethered to *Mir 2*. Both cameras required cases strong enough to withstand the water pressure at deep depths and filmed through portholes four inches thick and 9½ inches in diameter.

It took the submersibles two hours to travel down to the wreck, with another 2½ hours to reach the surface again after filming. Given film limitations, this meant that Cameron had little time to photograph the wreck. In all, had had to make 12 dives to get the footage he wanted, and he sent the ROV camera deeper into the ship than any device had gone before.

The wreck was also represented in the movie by a 1/20-scale model. Actually, only the front half of the ship appeared in miniature, because that is the only part seen in the videotapes that Cameron made underwater. To simulate the appearance of the real wreck, the model was sprayed with a product called Instant Iron, which creates rust, and crusty formations were added. These formations were made of bran flakes and Cheetos that had been spraypainted brown. The model was then sprayed again, this time with an artificial silt made from paint, glue, and spackling paste.

Another 1/20-scale model represented the undamaged ship. Built by more than 50 modelmakers, it was 40 feet long and had a steel armature, a birch plywood hull coated with fiberglass, and laminated plywood decks with acrylic structures. Its portholes were brass with plastic windows. There were also brass railings and many other fine details made of a variety of materials, as well as more than 1,000 rivets that were actually pins stuck in predrilled holes.

Three large-scale models of the *Titanic* were also used for scenes of it sinking. One was a 60-foot-long, 1/8-scale model of the stern, one a 40-foot long, 1/6-scale model of the bridge-to-bow section, and another a 1/4-scale model of the ship's funnel. As with the 1/20-scale models, they were highly detailed, but reinforced to withstand being attached to hydraulic devices and submerged repeatedly in real water. The models were filmed in a large tank built especially for the shoot; it had been equipped with several air mortars used to create water turbulence during filming, to hide the fact that the models were not of the same scale as the water.

Other models used in the film included a 20x30-foot miniature engine room section, 2-foot-long models of the tugboats that would be seen with the ship as it went out to sea, and two 1/20-scale *Mir* deep-sea submersibles for underwater scenes with the wreck. The tugboats were filmed on a motion-control stage, where machinery had been programmed to pitch them about in a manner consistent with real tugboats on the open sea. The submersibles were mounted upside-down on dolly-like platforms that would move along tracks in the floor. Above the tracks was the *Titanic* wreck, which had been placed upside-down on the ceiling so that the subs would look as though they were passing over, instead of beneath, the ship. This was a much easier system than the one James Cameron had used while making *The Abyss* (1989), which also involved submersibles passing over a submerged vessel; for that film he placed

the vessel on the floor and the subs on a large overhead gantry.

Both *The Abyss* and *Titanic* relied on a motion-control system for their model photography. This enabled cameras to duplicate moves, lens settings, and other operations as many times as necessary. For *Titanic*, motion control was particularly helpful in creating shots of the present-day wreck morphing into the undamaged *Titanic* of the past. The two models were each photographed using the exact same camera moves, and then one image was dissolved into the other. Computer-generated images were subsequently added to complete the scene of the *Titanic* right before its launch. The dock, birds, and smoke were digital, as were most of the passengers on the ship.

In filming the models for this and other daylight scenes, photographers did not use a bluescreen. Instead they either used a black background or a fluorescent orange screen lit with ultraviolet light. The orange screen method was first developed for model photography on the *Star Trek: The Next Generation* television show. The orange screen is known for creating matte lines that are smooth and soft rather than crisp and hard, as is the case with bluescreen photography, which makes images easier to blend during digital compositing. Nonetheless, the process was still difficult and time-consuming.

One of the most complicated scenes involving model photography was for a sweeping shot of the ship from bow to stern, which begins with two of the principal actors on the bow. Since it was a continuous shot, it had to look as though the live actors were part of the same motion-control camera sweep used to film the miniature. However, at that time Digital Domain did not have a motion-control system that was adequate for live-action filming. They were set up to work at speeds as slow as 2 frames per second, because model photography requires slow passes rather than real-time filming. Therefore the technicians at the special effects house designed a new motion-control rig specifically for the shoot. Fast enough for live-action filming, it had a 6-foot arm and operated on 60 feet of track. In addition, the actors were placed on a turntable so that the camera did not have to go around them.

Most of the live-action filming for *Titanic* involved a spectacular full-sized set that represented the oceanliner. After discussing several options for re-creating the gigantic ship and the possible sites where this could take place, Cameron convinced one of the film's financial backers, 20th Century Fox, to purchase 40 acres of oceanfront land in Mexico for a new studio. Several soundstages and a water tank were then built on this site, which was approximately 30 miles south of San Diego, California, near Rosarito, Mexico.

The water tank covered 8½ acres right beside the ocean and had an irregular shape to better house the massive reproduction of the Titanic built within its walls. Made of steel framing, the ship was constructed in two sections placed together between its second and third funnel. When it was finished, its deck rose 45 feet above the floor of the water tank, which had been built with different depth zones. Since the ship would sink at the front, the 100x200-foot zone of water there was 40 feet deep. A 25-foot-wide zone running along the right, or starboard, side of the ship, was 15 feet deep to allow stuntpeople enough water for safe plunges off the deck. The rest of the tank was only 3½ feet deep. An area at the back, or aft, section of the ship was partitioned off and left dry to provide an area for production equipment.

The left, or port, side of the ship had no hull, leaving the steel scaffolding of the set exposed. This was possible because the port side of the set was never shown on film. Whenever a shot of the port side was required, a shot of the starboard side was used instead, and its image simply flipped during postproduction. This meant, however, that all printed signs on the ship had to be made in two versions, one with the words written normally and one with them written in mirrored form.

In addition to its missing port hull, the ship was missing its forecastle, which is a section of the bow. The model was also built to be 10 percent shorter than the real *Titanic*, with its masts, stacks, and lifeboats shortened by the same percentage to allow them to fit properly on the ship. Nonetheless, the ship was approximately 700 feet long, with a starboard hull made of plywood textured with metal panels, and had more than 3,000 lights requiring 140 cables for illumination. Its Plexiglas windows and portholes had appropriate photographs behind them to give the illusion that rooms were inside.

There were, however, no rooms within the ship set; it was used for exterior filming only. Interior ship scenes were filmed on other soundstages at the Mexico site. These not only included cabin interiors but also the first-class dining room and accompanying staircase, which were built on a 200-foot-long platform that could be lowered like an elevator into a 30-foot-deep tank of water. This tank was later reused for scenes of flooded corridors and other waterlogged sections of the ship's interior. Scenes of passengers drowning after the ship sank were shot on yet another soundstage, which held a tank of heated freshwater. To simulate extreme cold, icy breath vapors were added during postproduction.

Scenes on the large, exterior ship set were filmed either on the deck itself or from a tower crane that ran along rails the length of the tank. Once all of the pre-sinking scenes were filmed, the ship was lifted with jacks at one end and its steel framing reduced at the other so that it tilted, first by 3 degrees and later 6. After these scenes were filmed, the tank was drained and the front section of the set was detached from the rest. This section was then put on a computer-controlled hydraulic system that would tilt it and plunge it into the sea. Once this equipment was in place, the tank was refilled and shooting commenced.

The tilting of the rear section of the ship, or poop deck, had been filmed earlier, with no water involved. In fact, the poop deck was built before the rest of the set was finished, and after it was used to film the tilting scenes it was attached to the newly completed ship. Like the forward section, the poop deck was placed on a hydraulic mechanism that could tilt it 90 degrees, and in order to make it safer for stuntmen, its railings and other hard surfaces were covered with painted foam. An airbag was placed at its base to catch stuntmen making intentional falls, although several accidents caused the director to order that no more such stunts be performed. Instead, computer graphics would depict the falling victims.

To create the digital stuntmen required a new technique called roto capture, whereby footage of real stunt falls was scanned into a computer and used as a reference for computer animators, who duplicated the live moves on a computer mannequin using freehand techniques. This method was used to create more than 1,000 falling figures for scenes of the ship sinking.

Other computer-generated characters, such as those seen in crowd scenes or strolling along the deck, were created using a motion-capture system. It recorded and digitized movement information from 30 extras walking, waving, or performing more complex actions such as chasing a ball or roughhousing. This information was then used to animate computer-generated characters, sometimes as many as 500 in one scene. However, this animation still had to be refined freehand.

There were more than 100 shots in the film employing digital characters, with one-fourth of these involving scenes of the ship sinking. In addition to those falling and sliding from the deck, computer-generated characters were added to shots of stunt people floundering in the water. Although in most of these shots the water was real, in others it was a digital effect. For example, the water is computer-generated in one shot of a rocket going off over the ship. The people in the shot are also computer-generated, while the rocket was a full-sized effect and the ship was a miniature.

Digital artists also designed a computer-generated ship, which was used for a variety of purposes. For example, the ship helped with the placement of computer-generated people into a scene, and it provided a way for the filmmakers to previsualize camera moves for both live-action and model photography. The computer-generated ship was also used as the starting point in designing computer-generated propellers for an underwater shot of the seagoing *Titanic*, and it appeared in three aerial shots of the ship under steam. In addition, parts of the digital ship were used to complete missing sections of the live-action ship set, particularly the forecastle.

The forecastle was also created with shots of a model ship. In fact, the model was used to create the digital ship, with the assistance

Scene shot on full-sized oceanliner set for *Titanic* (1997). *Photofest.*

of a digital wand. The wand input information about the dimensions of the model into the computer, so that digital artists would have a basic structure they could paint and texture. The artists had to work very carefully to match details of their computer-generated ship to details on the model.

During postproduction, such digital elements were carefully composited with live-action and miniature elements, to make it look as though all had been filmed together. Compositing work on *Titanic* was extensive, as was rotoscoping, which is a digital process that removes unwanted film elements such as cables, rigs, and, in one case, a broom that accidentally slid into view while a crewmember was making ice spill onto the deck.

A total of 17 effects companies provided more than 450 visual effects for *Titanic,* with Cameron's Digital Domain providing the bulk of the shots. Their work was financed by both 20th Century Fox and Paramount Pictures. These companies spent approximately $200 million to make the film, all of which was recovered in profits. *See also* THE ABYSS; ACCIDENTS; ANIMATION, COMPUTER; BLUESCREEN PROCESS; CAMERON, JAMES; COMPUTER GRAPHICS; MINIATURES AND MODELS; MOTION CAPTURE; MOTION-CONTROL CAMERA SYSTEMS; STUNTS.

Further Reading

Clark, Douglas. "Effects Wizard Lends *Titanic* Touch to Film." *Los Angeles Daily News*, 28 December 1997.

Duncan, Jody. "*Titanic* Aftermath." *Cinefex 72*, December 1997.

Shay, Don. "Back to *Titanic*." *Cinefex 72*, December 1997.

———. "Ship of Dreams." *Cinefex 72*, December 1997.

Toland, Gregg (1904–1948)

Gregg Toland was an independent director of photography who contributed a great deal to the field of cinematography. He experimented with lighting and optical techniques and developed the deep focus, which he used in such films as *Citizen Kane* (1941) and *The Best Years of Our Lives* (1946). He won an Academy Award for his cinematography for *Wuthering Heights* (1939).

Born in 1904, Toland got his first job as an assistant cameraman when he was only 16 and worked his way up to cameraman by 1929. At one point he was a student of noted German cinematographer Karl Freund. During World War II, Toland served as a lieutenant in the U.S. Navy's camera department and worked on a war documentary, *December 7th* (1943). Toland's other films include *Les Misérables* (1935), *The Grapes of Wrath* (1940), *The Bishop's Wife* (1948), and *A Star is Born* (1948). He died of a heart attack in 1948. *See also* DEEP FOCUS; FREUND, KARL; WELLES, ORSON.

tom thumb

Produced and directed by George Pal, the 1958 MGM movie *tom thumb* won an Academy Award for its special effects, which were supervised by Tom Howard. Howard created the illusion that a 6-foot-tall actor had been shrunk to a height of 5½ inches via enlarged props that included a 16-foot-tall top hat, an 80-foot-long cobblers bench, and a 55-foot-long baby's cradle.

More significantly, Howard developed new techniques for the movie's miniature scenes. For example, one scene was filmed with an 18-inch-high cradle and animated puppets. But instead of using regular photographic equipment, Howard employed three small-sized cameras built on miniature booms and dollies.

Howard also invented a new matte process called Automotion, which enabled the cameraman to split the image within his camera, blackening one half of the shot while leaving the other intact, and to change the location of this split as the scene progressed. This meant that with careful timing, an actor could appear as though he were walking around himself. *See also* HOWARD, TOM; MATTE; MINIATURES AND MODELS; PAL, GEORGE; PROPS; SPLIT-SCREEN PHOTOGRAPHY.

Further Reading

Fry, Ron, and Pamela Fourzon. *The Saga of Special Effects*. Englewood Cliffs, NJ: Prentice-Hall, 1977.

Kawin, Bruce F. *How Movies Work*. Berkeley: University of California Press, 1992.

Tora! Tora! Tora!

Released by 20th Century Fox in 1970, *Tora! Tora! Tora!* won an Academy Award for its special effects, which were provided by two of the foremost experts in the field: A.D. Flowers and L.B. Abbott. The movie features re-creations of World War II battles using detailed miniatures. Some of these miniatures were actually quite large; for example, one battleship was 40 feet long. Built at a scale of 1/16, it represented a real battleship of approximately 640 feet. The film's miniature ships also had to be specially weighted in order to make them appear as heavy on the water as a real vessel. *See also* ABBOTT, L.B.; MINIATURES AND MODELS.

Further Reading
O'Conner, Jane. *Magic in the Movies*. Garden City, NY: Doubleday, 1980.

Total Recall

The 1990 movie *Total Recall* earned a Special Achievement Academy Award for its visual effects experts. With the exception of a few location exteriors, the movie was shot entirely on 35 full-sized sets, each of which took up an entire soundstage. Since there were only eight soundstages available to the filmmakers, each set was removed after three to five days of filming so another could be built to take its place; it typically took as long as four to six weeks for construction to be complete, and another 10 days or so to set up the lighting.

The film also used miniature photography to enhance various shots. For example, one exterior location, used to represent a Martian landscape, was a relatively small area among some rocks in Mexico. To make it look like a vast landscape, special effects experts used an optical printer to combine live action filmed on the set with photographs of a miniature and matte paintings.

Just as with the full-sized sets, miniature sets were filmed, then taken apart so their pieces could be used to build additional miniature sets. One of these sets was the most complex miniature set ever constructed to date. Representing an alien reactor beneath the surface of Mars, the set was made in two scales and featured a miniature canyon spanned by a bridge supported by towers. Three scales of miniatures were used to represent the reactor and its rods. These and other models were filmed using motion-control cameras, and live actors were either rear-projected into miniature scenes or composited with them using bluescreen photography and an optical printer.

Total Recall also used extensive special makeup effects, as well as computer graphics. The latter were created by Metrolight in association with Dream Quest Images. One example of Dream Quest's work was for a scene in which the main character walks through a futuristic x-ray machine that shows his skeleton. At one point, this computer-generated skeleton breaks through the x-ray machine glass, thereby shattering the image and becoming a solid human again. The human was a live-action element, filmed with a stuntman, and his movements had to be matched with the skeleton's at the moment his image merged with the computer-generated one. This was a difficult effect to create at the time, because computer experts did not have the advantage of later developed match-modeling tools to help them line up the two images. Therefore they had to match the images freehand, in a painstaking manner. *See also* ANIMATION, COMPUTER; COMPUTER GRAPHICS; MATCH-MODELING; MATCH-MOVER; OPTICAL PRINTER.

Further Reading
Lee, Nora. "*Total Recall*: Interplanetary Thriller." *American Cinematographer*, July 1990.
Magid, Ron. "Many Hands Make Martian Memories." *American Cinematographer*, July 1990.

The Towering Inferno

Produced by Irwin Allen, the 1974 movie *The Towering Inferno* featured the work of noted special effects expert L.B. Abbott, but is perhaps best known for its stuntwork, during which many sets and props were destroyed by fire and water. Of the 57 full-sized interior sets built for the movie, only nine of them would be left undamaged by the end of production.

Great care was taken to ensure the safety of stuntpeople during the mayhem of the shoot. Windows were made of breakaway glass to prevent injury, and stuntpeople who portrayed burning victims were carefully prepared to withstand the flames. They wore triple layers of clothing made from a lightweight, nonflammable material called Nomex, as well as facemasks and wigs to protect their heads.

Stuntpeople who were to be set ablaze also wore hidden breathing equipment that contained three minutes of air. Right before the cameras began filming, their outer layer of clothing was painted with a mixture of gasoline and alcohol and set on fire. After a few moments the fire was extinguished with a blast of carbon dioxide. More than a hundred stuntpeople were involved in these "body burns," and no one got hurt.

At the end of the movie, a water tank atop an office building is exploded in order to extinguish the burning floors below. The resulting rush of water slams down onto the Promenade Deck, where many of the main characters are located. This scene was carefully planned using more than 2,600 storyboards. During filming, more than 8,000 gallons of water were dropped on actors and stuntpeople from a height of 40 feet. In order to make it seem as though the water then continued its downward rush, set designers had built the 11,000-square-foot Promenade Deck set on stilts. The set was surrounded by a 340-foot curved painting, or cyclorama, of the San Francisco skyline.

The movie also used a 70-foot-high miniature of the 138-story glass office building, built in 1/2-inch scale. The model needed to be that big in order to make the size of the flames seem realistic in relation to the size of the building. These flames were created by a mixture of butane and acetylene, fed through gas jets located in various "rooms" of the model. Airjets added oxygen to the fires, which made the heat so intense that cameraman could not shoot from above the model. Consequently the camera was mounted on a steel platform elevated over the site and operated by remote control. *See also* ABBOTT, L.B.;

ALLEN, IRWIN; BREAKAWAYS; FIRE; PYROTECHNICS; STORYBOARD; STUNTS.

Further Reading

Fry, Ron, and Pamela Fourzon. *The Saga of Special Effects*. Englewood Cliffs, NJ: Prentice-Hall, 1977.

Miklowitz, Gloria D. *Movie Stunts and the People Who Do Them*. New York: Harcourt Brace Jovanivich, 1980.

O'Conner, Jane. *Magic in the Movies*. Garden City, NY: Doubleday, 1980.

Stuntmen and Special Effects. New York: Ripley Books, 1982.

Travelling Matte

A matte creates an opaque area on a piece of film, where the image of a like-shaped object will later be placed. A travelling matte is a matte that changes shape and/or position from frame to frame, so that it moves just as the object it represents will move in the final film.

There are several ways to create this moving silhouette. The most basic is to use a series of handmade drawings of the object. In order to make these drawings, special effects artists use a process called rotoscoping, whereby a frame of film is projected so that the object can be traced onto an animation cel or other surface, then filled in to make the silhouette.

Another way to make a travelling matte is with special filming techniques. One of the earliest examples of such a technique was used for the 1933 movie *The Invisible Man,* which required travelling mattes to create the illusion that a man was invisible yet still wearing clothes. To accomplish this, a stuntman was dressed entirely in black velvet that did not reflect light. He wore black tights, gloves, and a headpiece, so that every portion of his skin and face were covered, and over his covered skin he wore a second set of clothes in light colors, which were the garments meant to show on screen. The stuntman was then placed on set covered entirely in black velvet and filmed while moving about.

During the filming of any scene, images are recorded onto the film negative in reverse, so that light elements become dark and dark elements become light; these densities are reversed during projection. Therefore after filming the "invisible" man, the negative showed a black silhouette of clothing moving against a completely clear background. This black silhouette was the travelling matte.

Once a negative of a travelling matte's moving silhouettes is obtained, it can be combined with the background scene in an optical printer, which rephotographs two projected images to create a new negative. The travelling matte leaves a "hole" in the film that is subsequently replaced by a positive print, or nonreversed, film of the item that was matted out, once again using an optical printer.

Another way to create a travelling matte is to use special lighting during filming in order to make it easier to separate live action from its background. An early example of this is a process called beam-splitting. There are many types of beam-splitting techniques. One of the most common has been the sodium-vapor process, which uses sodium-vapor lamps. The lamps cast a monochromatic yellow light onto a screen, in front of which a live-action person or object is photographed using a special camera. The camera holds two rolls of film, one of which cannot pick up monochromatic yellow. The camera has a prism that splits the incoming light so that the exact same image is photographed on both rolls of film. When filming is complete, one roll has recorded the live-action person or object, but not the yellow background, while the other roll has done the opposite.

Beam-splitting processes were used for many movies during the 1950s and 1960s. For example, the sodium-vapor process was used to add a spider monster to the 1955 movie *Tarantula*, and a more sophisticated variant was used to isolate live-action images so they could be added to animation for *Mary Poppins* (1964), which won an Academy Award for its travelling matte compositing technique.

A more modern method of creating a travelling matte is the bluescreen process, which is also a way of isolating live action from its background. In this case, an actor or object is filmed in front of a screen that has been illuminated in blue, green, red, or orange, and a computer digitally removes the background color from the shot. *See also* BLUESCREEN PROCESS; INVISIBILITY; *MARY POPPINS;* MATTE; OPTICAL PRINTER; ROTOSCOPING.

Further Reading

Kawin, Bruce F. *How Movies Work*. Berkeley: University of California Press, 1992.

O'Conner, Jane. *Magic in the Movies*. Garden City, NY: Doubleday, 1980.

A Trip to the Moon

First shown in 1902, *A Trip to the Moon* was one of the earliest films of special effects pioneer George Melies, who relied on basic photographic tricks such as stop-motion, superimposition, and double exposure. For example, he would stop the camera in mid-take to substitute a person with a puff of smoke or a grinning cartoon of the Man in the Moon with a grimacing one, over which he had superimposed footage of a rocket. But although these special effects techniques were basic, they were also time-consuming. *A Trip to the Moon* was only 30 minutes long, yet it took took Melies four months to film it. *See also* MELIES, GEORGE; MULTIPLE EXPOSURE; STOP-MOTION MODEL ANIMATION.

Further Reading

Fry, Ron, and Pamela Fourzon. *The Saga of Special Effects*. Englewood Cliffs, NJ: Prentice-Hall, 1977.

Kawin, Bruce F. *How Movies Work*. Berkeley: University of California Press, 1992.

A cartoon "Man in the Moon" after a rocket landing in George Melies' *A Trip to the Moon* (1902). *Photofest.*

TriStar Pictures

TriStar Pictures is a motion picture production and distribution company that has been responsible for many popular special effects movies, including *Terminator 2* (1991) and *Cliffhanger* (1993). It was founded in 1982 by three entertainment-industry giants: CBS, Home Box Office (HBO), and Columbia Pictures. Eventually Columbia Pictures took control, and in 1987 TriStar became part of Columbia Pictures Entertainment. Two years later this corporation was bought by the Sony Corporation of Japan. Sony then split TriStar and Columbia back into two separate entities, both under the umbrella of Sony Pictures Entertainment. *See also* COLUMBIA PICTURES; SONY PICTURES IMAGEWORKS; TERMINATOR 2: JUDGEMENT DAY.

Tron

Released by Walt Disney Studios in 1982, *Tron* was the first movie to create a three-dimensional world using computer imagery. Its plot centers around a man transported into a computer. This setting was created through computer graphics done by a scientific-based group, Mathematic Applications Group Inc. (MAGI). To speed communications between MAGI and Walt Disney Studios, the two companies used a transcontinental computer hook-up between New York and California. This was the first time such a link was used in the making of a major film. *See also* ANIMATION, COMPUTER; COMPUTER GRAPHICS; THE WALT DISNEY COMPANY.

Further Reading

Matlin, Leonard. *The Disney Films*. New York: Bonanza Books, 1973.

Smith, Dave. *Disney A-Z*. New York: Hyperion, 1996.

Smith, Thomas G. *Industrial Light & Magic: The Art of Special Effects*. New York: Ballantine Books, 1986.

Trumbull, Douglas (1942–)

Special effects expert Douglas Trumbull has worked on many important films featuring special effects, including *2001: A Space Odyssey* (1968), *The Andromeda Strain* (1971), *Close Encounters of the Third Kind* (1977), *Star Trek: The Motion Picture* (1979), and *Blade Runner* (1982). He also directed *Silent Running* (1971) and *Brainstorm* (1983), created the film for Universal Studios' "Back to the Future" amusement park ride, and invented two special effects processes, slit-scan and Showscan.

Born in 1942, Trumbull studied architecture at a junior college in Southern California but dropped out to become an artist. He worked as a technical illustrator for various advertising agencies, and eventually was hired by a company called Graphic Films to make animated promotional films for the National Aeronautics and Space Administration (NASA).

One of these films, *To the Moon and Beyond,* was shown at the 1964 World's Fair. There it attracted the attention of director Stanley Kubrick, who hired Trumbull to supervise special effects on *2001*. Trumbull's work on that movie brought him fame within the special effects industry, and he subsequently established his own special effects company, Future General Corporation, which became the Entertainment Effects Group (EEG). Although Trumbull later sold EEG to Richard Edlund, who turned it into Boss Film Studios, he continues to work in the industry today. Trumbull is also credited with inventing a new kind of artificial limb for amputees, which he originally developed as a mechanical arm for the robots in *Silent Running*. *See also* BLADE RUNNER; CLOSE ENCOUNTERS OF THE THIRD KIND; EDLUND, RICHARD; KUBRICK, STANLEY; SHOWSCAN; SLIT-SCAN; STAR TREK MOVIES; 2001: A SPACE ODYSSEY; UNIVERSAL STUDIOS.

Further Reading

Brosnan, John. *Movie Magic*. New York: St. Martin's Press, 1974.

Fry, Ron, and Pamela Fourzon. *The Saga of Special Effects*. Englewood Cliffs, NJ: Prentice-Hall, 1977.

Sammon, Paul M. *Future Noir: The Making of* Blade Runner. New York: Harper Collins, 1996.

Tsuburaya, Eiji (1901–1970)

Eiji Tsuburaya was in charge of special effects at Japan's Toho Studios when the first Godzilla movie, *Gojira,* was made there in

1954. He subsequently supervised special effects on many other monster movies, including *Rodan* (1956), *Mothra* (1961), and *King Kong Versus Godzilla* (1963).

Born in Japan in 1901, Tsuburaya became interested in photography as a boy, teaching himself how to use a camera and then how to build one. He first worked in a studio photo laboratory, and when he was 21 he became a cinematographer. He joined the special effects department at Toho Studios a few years later. To create his monster scenes for the studio, he put men in monster suits and filmed them rampaging through miniature cities. Tsuburaya died in 1970. *See also* GODZILLA.

Further Reading
Engel, Volker, and Rachel Aberly. *The Making of Godzilla*. New York: HarperPrism, 1998.

Tuttle, William (1911–)

William Tuttle worked in the makeup department of MGM for more than 35 years, first under the supervision of makeup artist Jack Dawn and then as department head, a position he held from 1950 to 1969. He is best known for creating the Morlock makeup for the 1960 movie *The Time Machine* and for his work on the 1964 movie *The Seven Faces of Dr. Lao,* which earned him an honorary Academy Award. He also provided makeup for *Young Frankenstein* (1974).

Born in 1911, Tuttle was a musician before becoming an assistant to Jack Dawn in 1934, initially at 20th Century Pictures and later at MGM. His last film was *Same Time Next Year,* released in 1978. Tuttle taught makeup techniques at the University of California at Los Angeles (UCLA) and created his own line of movie makeup, Custom Color Foundation. *See also* DAWN, JACK, AND ROB DAWN; MAKEUP; *THE SEVEN FACES OF DR. LAO.*

20th Century Fox

20th Century Fox is a major American motion picture company whose successful special effects films include *The Poseidon Adventure* (1972), *Star Wars* (1977) and its sequels, and *Independence Day* (1996). The company was established in 1935 when two other production companies, Fox and 20th Century, merged.

Fox had been founded in 1915 as Fox Film Corporation, and during the 1920s it had many major stars under contract. It also created the first system to put a soundtrack directly on movie film. 20th Century had been established in 1933; one of its founders was the former chief of production at Warner Brothers, Darryl F. Zanuck.

After the merger, 20th Century Fox attracted many high-quality stars and film projects. In addition, in the 1950s it developed the CinemaScope widescreen filming process and projection system. During that same decade, Darryl Zanuck left the company, but he returned in 1962 to rescue 20th Century Fox from declining fortunes. He remained there until 1971, whereupon Dennis C. Stanfill became chairman and CEO of the company. It was under Stanfill's direction that the company produced *The Poseidon Adventure* and *Star Wars.* During the 1980s, 20th Century Fox was sold several times, with Stanfill being replaced by a series of other executives. *See also* CINEMASCOPE; *INDEPENDENCE DAY; THE POSEIDON ADVENTURE; STAR WARS MOVIES;* WARNER BROTHERS.

20,000 Leagues Under the Sea

Released by Walt Disney Studios in 1954, *20,000 Leagues Under the Sea* won an Academy Award for its special effects. The movie was also the first Disney feature shot in CinemaScope, a widescreen filming process.

The movie's most elaborate special effect was a mechanical giant squid, which at a cost of $200,000 was the most expensive movie monster of the 1950s. Made by Bob Mattey, the same mechanical effects expert who made the shark for the movie *Jaws* (1975), the squid's body weighed 2 tons and had steel-spring coils, flexible tubing, tension cables, hydraulic cylinders, ball joints, and steel rods. The creature was covered with a combination of glass, cloth, rubber, plastic, and an acrylic resin called Lucite. A hydraulic lift operated by remote control could move the head 8 feet in any direction, and a pneumatic ram on a piston made the squid's beak snap open and shut.

In addition, the creature had 40 feet of tentacles, each weighing 175 pounds. Inside of the tentacles were steel springs and flexible pneumatic tubing which coiled and uncoiled according to the actions of compressed air forced through an air pump. The tentacles were further manipulated with a system of wires operated by men who stood on a rail either above or alongside the creature, which was filmed in a 90x165-foot water tank constructed especially for this movie on a Disney soundstage. When this tank, which was 3–12 feet deep, was not needed, it could be covered with a wooden floor, so that other scenes could be shot in the same studio.

Besides its realistic squid, *20,000 Leagues Under the Sea* featured more actual underwater footage than had been shot for any movie up to that time. Filmed near the Bahamas, the shoot used natural sunlight filtering down from the ocean's surface. Twenty divers acted underwater, each wearing 225-pound diving suits with two tanks of air. Although the tanks provided two hours of oxygen, the divers typically worked no more than 55 minutes at a time.

The submarine in the movie was represented by several miniatures, which ranged in size from 18 to 22 inches. There was also a full-sized submarine for live-action filming, but it was only built from the waterline up. The backgrounds for the live-action and miniature work were created by Peter Ellenshaw as matte paintings on glass. Artists also created more than 1,300 storyboard drawings for the film in order to plan out the film's intricate special effects. *See also* ANAMORPHIC PROCESS; CINEMASCOPE; THE WALT DISNEY COMPANY; ELLENSHAW, PETER; MATTE PAINTINGS; MECHANICAL EFFECTS; MINIATURES AND MODELS; STORYBOARD.

Further Reading

Fry, Ron, and Pamela Fourzon. *The Saga of Special Effects*. Englewood Cliffs, NJ: Prentice-Hall, 1977

Johnson, John. *Cheap Tricks and Class Acts*. Jefferson, NC: McFarland & Company, 1996.

McKenzie, Alan, and Derek Ware. *Hollywood Tricks of the Trade*. New York: Gallery Books, 1986.

Twister

The 1996 movie *Twister* was responsible for the development of new particle animation software, created by Industrial Light & Magic (ILM). All of the tornadoes, or twisters, seen in the film were digital. In some cases their debris was a mechanical effect, made with two Boeing 707 jet engines mounted on 40-foot tiltable trailers; 20-foot-long containers over the engines released tons of lightweight, biodegradable debris, which was then blown all over the set. The finest dust, however, was added digitally by special effects experts, and it was this effect that inspired the new computer software.

Special effects crew releasing debris during the filming of *Twister* (1996). *David James, Warner Bros., and Universal City Studios Inc./Photofest.*

Animating the dust and other flying debris required a program that could not only isolate and move individual particles within a larger image but allow for random patterns of chaos based on turbulence, gravity, and other factors. This software was used to create the biggest computer-generated tornadoes seen in the movie. The smaller ones were created more simply, by instructing the computer to transform a conical shape to approximate the motions of a tornado.

There were a total of 135 tornado shots in the movie, along with 165 other special effects shots. Digital mattes were frequently used to change the look of the sky, because the film was shot primarily on sunny days rather than gray ones. Digital artists also sometimes had to alter the landscape. The crops in the fields where the movie was filmed grew rapidly, and without digital work their height would have varied dramatically from one scene to the next.

As with the debris, the movie's hailstorms were created with a combination of mechanical and computer-generated effects. An ice machine was adjusted to make hailstones out of ice and milk, which where then blown onto the set, and digital artists later enhanced this footage. In one case, computer work was used to replace something that had already been filmed—a full-sized aluminum and fiberglass model of a tanker trunk that exploded on cue. The pyrotechnic effect, which employed explosives and 400 gallons of gas, was spectacular, but footage of the truck itself was disappointing. Therefore it was eventually replaced with a computer-generated truck, which provided more interesting camera angles.

For a scene in which two people are almost sucked into a tornado, mechanical effects worked so well that no computer replacement was necessary. The two actors were placed in a mechanical room that could spin them upside down. After the actors had tied themselves down with belts, as the scene required, the room was activated; the violent motion caused them to lose their grip, and when the film was turned upside-down, it looked as though a tornado were pulling them skywards. *See also* INDUSTRIAL LIGHT & MAGIC; MATTE; MECHANICAL EFFECTS; PYROTECHNICS; TRAVELLING MATTE.

Further Reading
Luskin, Jonathan. "Riders on the Storm." *Cinefex* 66, June 1996.

2001: A Space Odyssey

The 1968 movie *2001: A Space Odyssey* won an Academy Award for its special effects, which were supervised by Douglas Trumbull.

Trumbull later worked on *Close Encounters of the Third Kind* (1977), *Star Trek: The Motion Picture* (1979), and *Blade Runner* (1982), but he found *2001* particularly challenging because the movie's director, Stanley Kubrick, preferred for all mattes to be created in-camera. This meant that instead of using an optical printer to composite separate elements of a scene, such as live-action and miniature photography, into one shot during postproduction, these elements were photographed together on the set using projection techniques. For example, the windows of a miniature spacecraft were made of reflective material, and live-action shots of actors were projected onto them during filming.

Similarly, actors wearing ape costumes performed on a set where background shots from Africa were being projected. The method used for the Africa projection was developed specifically for *2001* by special effects expert Tom Howard. Called large-screen front projection, it employed mirrors and a highly reflective 40x90-foot screen to make it seem as though the apes were part of the landscape.

The apes' makeup featured a technique that was later used for the character of Chewbacca in *Star Wars* (1977), whereby an actor's mouth manipulated a device that moved the mouth and lips on his mask. The ape mask had a plastic skull with a hinged jaw, rubber skin, animal hair, and eyeholes.

The movie's miniatures were made of wood, fiberglass, Plexiglas, steel, brass, and aluminum. They included a space station set 6 feet long, a space station set 300 feet long, and two versions of the *Discovery* spaceship, one 54 feet long and another 15 feet long. To add detail and depth to the models' surface, modelmakers added pieces of plastic taken from commercial model kits for railroad cars, battleships, aircraft, and Gemini spacecraft.

The interior set of *Discovery* included a centrifuge that was commissioned from an engineering group. Constructed of steel, it was 38 feet in diameter and could rotate at a speed of 3 mph. The camera was attached to the centrifuge so that it rotated along with the machine, making it appear as though an actor was running within a stationary treadmill so that at one point he was upside-down. A similar shot involved a stewardess walking around a treadmill until she is upside-down. In this case the camera was locked to the front of a set that rotated 180 degrees. The actress wore velcro-lined shoes that stuck to a velcro-lined floor.

Another unique effect was a light show viewed by the main character near the end of the movie. To create this light show in-camera, Douglas Trumbull invented a technique called slit-scan filming. It involved a specially designed 65 mm camera with an automatic focus, working in concert with a complicated machine that projected a movie onto rotat-ing screens. Trumbull's slit-scan movie was made from artwork of abstract paintings, architectural drawings, and electronic microscope photographs of molecules and crystals.

Such devices made *2001* a relatively expensive movie for its time. It cost $10.5 million to produce, with $300,000 allotted merely for the centrifuge set. *See also* KUBRICK, STANLEY; MATTE; OPTICAL PRINTER; PROJECTION PROCESSES; SLIT-SCAN; *STAR WARS* MOVIES; TRUMBULL, DOUGLAS.

Further Reading

Agel, Jerome, (ed). *The Making of Kubrick's 2001*. New York: Signet, 1968.

U

Universal Studios

Founded in 1912, Universal Studios is an American motion picture company with a history of employing state-of-the-art special effects. The company first gained prominence in the 1930s, when it produced a string of popular horror movies that included *Dracula* (1931), *Frankenstein* (1931), and *The Invisible Man* (1933). Humorous versions of these titles were created in the 1950s with comedians Bud Abbott and Lou Costello.

Universal has changed hands several times over the years, and is currently owned by the Seagrams Company. But regardless of its ownership, it has continued to make successful films and television programs. Both types of work are supervised from the company's studios in Universal City, a 230-acre community the studio established in 1915.

During the 1970s, director Steven Spielberg established his production company, Amblin Entertainment, on the Universal backlot, where he created such notable films for the studio as *Jaws* (1975), *ET: The Extraterrestrial* (1982), *Back to the Future* (1985), and *Jurassic Park* (1993). In 1994 Spielberg created his own studio, DreamWorks SKG, which is a rival to Universal in some ventures but a partner in others. For example, DreamWorks SKG and Universal jointly produced *Small Soldiers* (1998).

In addition to making such films, Universal operates an amusement park at the site of its studios at Universal City and at a similar facility in Orlando, Florida. *See also* BACK TO THE FUTURE MOVIES; *ET: THE EXTRATERRESTRIAL;* INVISIBILITY; *JURASSIC PARK; SMALL SOLDIERS.*

Urban, Charles (1871–1942)

Charles Urban was a filmmaker who developed one of the first workable color systems, Kinemacolor, in association with a chemist. He also experimented with trick photography. His most famous film in this regard is *The Airship Destroyer* (1909), which was later renamed *Aerial Warfare*, then *Aerial Torpedo,* followed by *Battle in the Clouds*. The film used models to depict a group of airships bombing London and ultimately being destroyed by radio-controlled flying torpedoes.

Born in the United States in 1871, Urban managed the London office of the Edison Company, which made projectors and films. He quarreled with the company after inventing his own projector in 1897 and left to start his own filmmaking business. In 1911 he hired Edgar Charles Rogers to work as his studio's art director, and supported Rogers in the development of many new special effects techniques, including the glass shot.

Urban moved to the United States in 1912 and set up two studios there in an attempt to exploit his Kinemacolor technology. He made several color films and enjoyed moderate success, but his fortunes declined when color systems superior to his own were developed by rival studios. He died in 1942. *See also* EDISON, THOMAS A.

V

VistaVision

VistaVision is a widescreen projection system that was extremely popular in the 1950s, and its filming process continues to be used for some special effects scenes today. Whereas other widescreen systems use special lenses to make a widescreen image fit on a standard-sized piece of film, VistaVision creates more width by running its negative through the camera horizontally rather than vertically. The image that this negative produces on the screen varies from a width-to-height ratio, also called an aspect ratio, of 1.33: 1 to 1.96:1.

The most common VistaVision aspect ratios during the 1950s were 1.66:1 and 1.86:1. Two other popular widescreen projection systems, CinemaScope and Panavision, both have an aspect ratio of 2.35:1. These two systems use the squeezing, or anamorphic, process to film widescreen images; this distortion process makes them difficult to use for special effects shots.

The advantage of the VistaVision process is that it results in sharp pictures. However, there is not much film in a pack, which means that it is generally considered unsuitable for situations in which it is difficult to change film frequently. For example, the makers of *The Truman Show* (1998) determined that to create aerial shots using a motion-control camera mounted beneath a helicopter, VistaVision film would yield only two minutes of shooting time per load; they therefore decided to use a full-aperture 35mm film format known as Super35 for their movie. Super35 is a 35mm full-aperature film, which means that the full width of the film negative is exposed during the photographic process. This provides enough width to create widescreen movies without the squeezing of the anamorphic process. It also provides superior quality when the film is transferred to video. The Super35 format has been used for such effects-laden films as *The Abyss* (1994), *Terminator 2* (1991), *True Lies* (1994), *Apollo 13* (1995), *Dragonheart* (1996), *Independence Day* (1996), *The Fifth Element* (1997), *Titanic* (1997), *Godzilla* (1998), and *The X-Files* (1998). *See also* ANAMORPHIC PROCESS; APERTURE; CINEMASCOPE.

Further Reading

Kawin, Bruce F. *How Movies Work*. Berkeley: University of California Press, 1992.

Martin, Kevin H. "*The Truman Show:* The Unreal World." *Cinefex* 75, October 1998.

Smith, Thomas G. *Industrial Light & Magic: The Art of Special Effects*. New York: Ballantine Books, 1986.

Vogel, Paul C. (1899–1975)

Paul Vogel was a cinematographer who worked at MGM during the 1940s, 1950s, and 1960s as director of photography. He won an Academy Award for his special effects for *The Time Machine* (1960).

This movie included one particular special effect that was advanced for its time, which was used to make it appear as though time was passing more rapidly than normal. To accomplish this effect, Vogel had to change the lighting in the scene to indicate the transitions from dawn to day to dusk to night. He consequently filmed through a rotating disk that had four sections of glass tinted according to the time being depicted; the dawn section was tinted pink, day was clear, dusk was amber, and night was blue. At some point, however, the lighting had to change so rapidly that a two-section disk—representing day and night—had to be substituted for the four-section one. Vogel also had to show items changing in a shop window as time progressed. He accomplished this with stop-motion photography.

Born in 1899, Vogel began his film career in the 1920s as a lighting cameraman. He became a director of photography in the late 1930s. In 1949 he won an Academy Award in cinematography for *Battleground*. His other films include *Angels in the Outfield* (1951), *High Society* (1956), *The Wonderful World of the Brothers Grimm* (1962), and *The Money Trap* (1966). Vogel died in 1975.

Volcano

Released by 20th Century Fox in 1997, *Volcano* featured the most extensive use of fire on a live-action shoot. Each night for 26 nights, pyrotechnics experts used 1,700 gallons of propane, 300 cans of sterno, and 8 gallons of rubber cement to burn a set that was 3/4 of a mile long and approximately 750,000 square feet in area. Representing a section of Los Angeles, California, known as the "Miracle Mile," the set had buildings that were close to full scale in size, with the tallest being 75 feet, and it included a 550,000-gallon lake. Every part of this set was shielded with fireproof materials such as metal sheeting. Even its real palm trees were rigged to withstand fire; they had metal sleeves concealed with real palm fronds.

To simulate ash on the set, mechanical effects experts used undyed gray paper, distributed with insulation blowers lifted on cranes 50 feet above the set. They also rigged manhole covers to explode 75 feet into the air on a jet of steam. The steam was actually material from a device used to create fog, and the covers were propelled with blasts of compressed air. The covers themselves were made not of metal but of plywood and cast foam. Trenches were dug beneath them to allow room for the air compression system.

The Miracle Mile set was also made as a highly detailed miniature, which was subject to additional pyrotechnics. Like the full-sized set, it was relatively large; even at 1/8 scale it was 200 feet long, covered 21,000 square feet, and had to be housed in two Air Force hangars. The entire set was elevated on a 4-foot-tall platform so that wires and other pyrotechnic equipment could be placed underneath. Certain buildings were rigged with primacord for explosions and made of breakaway plaster and concrete so that they would collapse easily. One building had 900 windows, which were triggered to blow out during an explosion. Ash on the set was snow flocking dyed gray.

Another miniature set was used for lava effects. Its buildings were not detailed at all; in fact, they were simply clear acrylic shapes that had been glued to a tabletop with clear acrylic cement. They were not seen on screen, but were used as "placeholders" around which the lava would flow. This lava would later be composited into shots made with the detailed miniature or the live-action set.

The lava was a mixture of methylcellulose, also called methocel, and other biodegradable materials such as cork to add thickness. The lava was colored with a pigment that is sensitive to ultraviolet (UV) light, then placed on a clear surface and lit from underneath with a UV light, which made the substance glow. By tilting the table, the lava could appear to flow, and by placing small air bladders or bags filled with explosive black powder beneath its surface, it could be made to bubble or splatter. Splatters were also made by shooting air blasts or tiny clay balls at the lava flow. The crust of the lava was made by covering it with Christmas tree flocking that had been dyed black or by spraying it with black paint. Geysers were created by shooting the lava skyward with air cannons. Different thicknesses of lava were required for each of these techniques, and at the end of the production, the special effects experts determined that they had used 45,500 gallons of methocel and 650 pounds of pigment.

Computer-generated clouds, smoke, steam, and flames were added to some shots during postproduction, as were flying "bombs" of lava and a few background helicopters. Computer graphics were also used to make the edges of the lava seem more a part of the miniature or live-action footage, and to keep the color and illumination of the lava consistent from one shot to the next. In one scene, computer graphics were also used to replace the face of a stuntman who had to wear a protective mask. In addition, *Volcano* employed digital compositing to put scene elements together, with an average of 30–40 elements layered into each shot.

Further Reading

Simak, Steven A. "Graphics That Sizzle!" *Digital World*, April 1997.

Street, Rita. "Toasting the Coast." *Cinefex 71*, September 1997.

W

War of the Worlds

Directed by George Pal, the 1953 movie *War of the Worlds* featured the visual effects of Gordon Jennings, who won an Academy Award for his work. The film's plot concerns the invasion of Earth by Martians. On only two occasions is any part of a Martian creature seen, initially in a destroyed farmhouse and later while it is dying. During the death scene, only the Martian's arm is visible, in the doorway of a Martian spaceship. This arm was mechanically operated and had air-filled tubes to make it pulse. When the Martian dies the air is deflated. The whole-body Martian was made of wire, wood, paper mache, and sheet rubber, and it too had rubber tubing in it that "pulsed." The actor who wore the costume had to be on his knees; when he had to "run away," he was pulled from the set on a dolly.

The Martian menace was therefore represented not by their physical presence but by the presence of their spaceships. These flying, hovering craft are among the most impressive effects in the movie. The spaceships were copper-hulled miniatures 42 inches in diameter, each one supported by 15 wires suspended from a trolley system. An optical printer was used during postproduction to superimpose a plastic force-field bubble around the ship as well as force-field beams underneath the ship's legless body.

The ships were originally designed to have legs, just as in the novel, *The War of the Worlds* by H.G. Wells, on which the movie was based. Before Pal decided to eliminate the legs, they were intended to be the conduit whereby the Martians shot people with fiery rays. Once the ship was redesigned, these rays came from the tips of its wings as well as from a snake-like device that emerged from the top of the ship. The rays' fire was added in postproduction, using film of a melting welding wire sparked by a blowtorch. The pulsing light on the snake-like device, which appeared when it was not firing, was made with a lightbulb shielded with red plastic. A miniature fan revolved in front of the bulb, intermittently covering it and uncovering it to create the "pulse."

Another realistic miniature was that of the Los Angeles City Hall, which the Martian ships blow up. Made larger than what was then the norm for miniatures in order to allow for more detail, the building was 8 feet tall. The model was destroyed by a layered blast. First its foundation was detonated, then its dome, then its middle section, in quick succession. The background of this scene was a matte painting incorporating the sky, the surrounding city, flames, and some Martian ships; it was combined with the live action in postproduction using an optical printer.

Many other matte paintings were used to make the film, as were other forms of mattes, not only for miniature scenes but for live-action scenes as well. For example, in one scene a soldier is hit by a Martian ray and evaporates gradually to become bone and then dust. To create this image, 144 separate mattes were made of his figure, which was drawn with inks. This series of mattes was then used to add the series of ink drawings to background footage, using an optical printer. In all, there were approximately 4,000 frames of film that featured some form of matte painting. Mattes were combined with live action via custom-built optical printers that provided more finely tuned adjustments than regular optical printers.

It took more than six months of miniature model work and two months of special optical effects to create *War of the Worlds,* and there were 40 days of live-action filming. In addition, sound technicians worked three months to develop new sounds for the Martian creatures and ships. The Martian in the farmhouse lets out a scream made by scraping dry ice across a microphone and mixing that sound with that of a woman's scream replayed backwards. The spaceship and death ray sounds were made with electric guitars, whose chords were recorded, played backwards, and reverberated.

The special effects work for the movie was not only time-consuming but expensive. Whereas live-action filming cost about $600,000, the special effects cost $1.4 million, which was a considerable amount during the 1950s. However, this $2 million dollar budget was recouped shortly after the movie's release. *See also* ACCIDENTS; JENNINGS, GORDON; MATTE; MATTE PAINTINGS; MINIATURES AND MODELS; OPTICAL PRINTER; PAL, GEORGE; PYROTECHNICS.

Further Reading

Brosnan, John. *Movie Magic.* New York: St. Martin's Press. 1974.

Fry, Ron, and Pamela Fourzon. *The Saga of Special Effects.* Englewood Cliffs, NJ: Prentice-Hall, 1977.

Hayes, R.M. *Trick Cinematography.* Jefferson, NC: McFarland & Company, 1986.

Johnson, John. *Cheap Tricks and Class Acts.* Jefferson, NC: McFarland & Company, 1996.

Kawin, Bruce F. *How Movies Work.* Berkeley: University of California Press, 1992.

O'Conner, Jane. *Magic in the Movies.* Garden City, NY: Doubleday, 1980.

Warner Brothers

Warner Brothers was one of the first motion picture companies in Hollywood. Established in 1923 by four brothers—Harry, Albert, Sam, and Jack Warner—it gained international fame in 1927 with its release of *The Jazz Singer,* the first movie with an actor who was actually heard as well as seen. Called a "talkie," *The Jazz Singer* heralded the end of the silent-film era.

Throughout the ensuing years, Warner Brothers produced hundreds of notable films in several genres. In 1956, it sold much of this film library to a company called Associated Artists, which in turn sold it to United Artists; but now most pre-1950s Warner Brothers movies are the property of billionaire Ted Turner. Turner also owns most of the films of another historically significant movie company, Metro-Goldwyn-Mayer.

In 1967, Warner Brothers itself was sold to a Canadian company called Seven Arts Productions, which in turn sold it to a conglomerate called Kinney National Service. Kinney renamed the company Warner Communications in 1971. Prior to this time, Warner Brothers had been undergoing financial difficulties. However, as Warner Communications, it soon flourished, producing many money-making films.

The company's most notable special-effects work of this time appears in such movies as *The Exorcist* (1973), *The Towering Inferno* (1974), *Superman* (1978), *Gremlins* (1984), and *Batman* (1989). Such successes brought the company to the attention of publisher Time Inc., which bought Warner in 1989. The resulting company, Time Warner, is one of the largest communications corporations in the world. *See also* BATMAN MOVIES; SUPERMAN; THE TOWERING INFERNO.

Warner Digital

Warner Digital was a major special effects house that lasted little more than two years. Although it employed more than 150 people and worked on such films as *Mars Attacks!* (1996), *Batman and Robin* (1997), and *Contact* (1997), the company found that it could not generate enough profit, primarily because it was only allowed to work on projects for its parent company, Warner Brothers. This was an unusual situation; most special effects houses backed by major film studios are able to work on other studios' projects.

Warner Digital began in 1995 as Warner Brothers Imaging Technology (WBIT), a division of Warner Brothers. Its first project was a fully computer-generated skyline in *Batman Forever* (1995). The following year the company became Warner Digital. Its senior visual effects supervisor at that time was Michael Fink, who became head of the company in 1997. That same year Warner Digital closed its doors, leaving Warner Brothers to hire outside special effects houses for future visual effects work. *See also* FINK, MICHAEL; SPECIAL EFFECTS HOUSES; WARNER BROTHERS.

Waterworld

Released by Universal Pictures, the 1997 movie *Waterworld* is best known for its economic failure at the box office; its budget of $175 million was never recouped. However, the film is also notable for having the largest rear-lit bluescreen ever used underwater, the first realistic computer-generated water, and the largest movie set ever constructed to date.

The bluescreen measured 24x36 feet and was submerged in a 70-foot-diameter, 33-foot-deep tank in order to film live action. To keep the actors in front of the screen, massive pumps pushed water against them head-on so they could only swim in place. Their images were later composited with shots of miniature buildings representing a ruined underwater city. The city model was built in 1/24-scale, with some small sections done in 1/12-scale as well, and was filmed on a smoky set to simulate the poor visibility at great ocean depths. Computer-generated water was added during postproduction.

To create *Waterworld*'s realistic computer-generated water, digital artists at a company called Cinesite experimented with existing water simulation software that had been developed for government oceanographic stud-

Actor Kevin Costner in *Waterworld* (1997). *Ben Glass, Universal City Studios/Photofest.*

ies. The software was designed primarily to show the dynamics of the sea, but eventually the artists developed a way to make the water's surface sparkle, shimmer, and ripple. Their work made it possible for photographers to film a 1/8-scale, 110-foot-long tanker model in the desert rather than in the ocean, because computer-generated water, waves, and swells could be added during postproduction.

For the climactic scene in the movie, the tanker model was exploded using propane jets, propane mortars, and fire boxes. Pyrotechnics were also used on a full-sized, 600-foot-long set representing part of the tanker, where more than 9,000 gallons of propane were used during each day of live-action filming. There were many other pyrotechnical effects in *Waterworld*, not just related to explosives but to machine-gun fire as well. For example, a machine-gun attack on an atoll required that the pyrotechnical crew rig the structure's walls with more than 1,400 bullet hits, connected by wires to a firing board. All were triggered within a 40-second time period.

The atoll was the largest set ever built for a movie. Constructed in sections and assembled off the coast of Hawaii, it was comprised of eight 80-ton modules, each on a flotation unit. The set was 365 feet wide and had a deck area of 1 acre. It was highly detailed and had mechanized parts, including a massive set of gates that opened and closed.

Another important floating set was an elaborate trimaran, a three-hulled sailing vessel that could transform itself into different configurations. There were actually two versions of the boat, one for sailing and one for transformation scenes. The transforming trimaran had hidden hydraulic pumps, winches, and other equipment to raise a 30-foot telescoping boom from the deck and increase the height of the mast from 55 to 85 feet. The boat's spinnaker kite was a computer-generated image.

Also computer-generated were a hot-air balloon featured in long shots and a whale-like fish that attacks the movie's hero. Part of the creature's throat, however, was built as a practical effect. When a lever was pulled, it rose out of the water to "swallow" the actor, who was being pulled in front of the device. This live-action footage was then combined with the digital fish images, and computer-generated water was added to the scene.

Along with its digital effects, *Waterworld* featured excellent stuntwork. Its stunt professionals included Larry Rippenkroeger, a four-time world champion jet ski racer; Doug Silverstein, a national jet ski champion and water test pilot; Bob Montgomery, the inventor of the jet board; and more than 50 top stuntmen from Stunts Unlimited. They practiced for more than three-and-a-half months on location to prepare for the movie's elaborate water stunts. *See also* BLUESCREEN PROCESS; MINIATURES AND MODELS; PYROTECHNICS; STUNTS.

Further Reading
Odien, Jeff. "On the Waterfront." *Cinefex 64*, December 1995.
The Power Ski Stars in Waterworld. http://www.powerski.com/wtrwrld.html, May 1999.

Welles, Orson (1915–1985)

Orson Welles was a screenwriter, director, producer, and actor who was associated with dozens of films during his long career. In terms of special effects, his most significant work is *Citizen Kane* (1941). More than 80 percent of the film utilizes some form of trick photography, and many scenes used miniatures as well. For example, while a room of a nightclub was a full-scale interior set, its rooftop and skylight were a miniature. But more importantly, the movie introduced new cinematographic, sound, and editing techniques that were soon adopted by many others in the film industry, largely because of the unique cinematography of director of photography Gregg Toland.

Born in 1915, Welles came from a wealthy family and became involved in the theater as a boy, studying drama and staging his own plays. During a visit to Ireland after graduating from high school, he auditioned for the Gate Theater and won a starring role. The following year he returned to the United States and soon began acting there. In 1938 he began doing a dramatic radio program, "The Mercury Theatre on the Air." On Halloween of that year, Welles directed and performed in a broadcast of H.G. Wells's novel *War of the Worlds* that was so realistic it frightened people into believing that extraterrestrial aliens were actually invading the United States. The broadcast greatly increased Orson Welles's fame.

Welles had long dabbled in filmmaking, but *Citizen Kane* was his first commercial movie. He not only directed the film but cowrote the script and acted in the picture as well. He was only 26 years old when the movie was released to critical acclaim. However, despite winning an Academy Award for Best Screenplay, the film did not do well financially, nor did most of Welles's subsequent directorial efforts.

By the late 1940s, Welles had become disenchanted with Hollywood and decided to move to Europe. He acted in several films there before directing the movie *Othello*, which was released in Europe in 1952 and in the United States in 1955. Over the next several years, Welles continued to act both in other directors' movies and in his own. In the 1970s he returned to the United States, where he acted in television programs and commercials. Welles died in 1985. *See also* TOLAND, GREGG.

Further Reading
Kael, Pauline. *Raising Kane*. New York: Bantam, 1971.

Westmore, Michael (1938–)

Makeup artist Michael Westmore is best known for his work on the *Star Trek: The Next Generation* television show and the movies derived from it. He also created makeup for two other *Star Trek* shows, *Deep Space Nine* and *Voyager*. However, he has been in the makeup business his entire life, and has worked on several other important films, including *Blade Runner* (1982).

Westmore supervised makeup on *Star Trek: Insurrection* (1998), for which he created separate head and neck pieces for each of the alien beings at a reception. He also created several separate, overlapping facial pieces for a character whose face had to "stretch" onscreen. Beneath these appliances were synthetic veins. There were actually two versions of the makeup, one for before the stretching and one for after; the transition was created with a computer morphing program.

Westmore comes from a family of makeup artists. The first Westmore in the business was George Westmore (1879–1931), who in 1917 established the first motion picture makeup department, at a studio that would later become MGM. Westmore then taught makeup artistry to his six sons. All of them were employed by major studios and most garnered important film credits. For example, Michael's father Montague, or Monty (1902–1940), supervised makeup for *Gone With the Wind* (1939) and Perc (1904–1970) provided makeup for *The Hunchback of Notre Dame* (1935) and *Casablanca* (1943). Ernest, or Ern (1904–1968), worked on a variety of low-budget films, while Wally (1906–1973) did the makeup for *Dr. Jekyll and Mr. Hyde* (1932) and *War of the Worlds* (1953). Bud (1918–1973) supervised the makeup on several important films, including *The Creature from the Black Lagoon* (1954) and *The List of Adrian Messenger* (1963), and took over as head of Universal Studios' makeup department in 1945 after Jack Pierce left the position. Frank (1923–1985) not only worked with his brother Wally on the makeup for Cecil B. DeMille's *The Ten Commandments* (1956) but wrote a book about his famous family.

Michael Westmore was born in 1938. In 1961 his uncle Bud offered him an apprenticeship at Universal Studios, where he worked with makeup artist John Chambers on *The List of Adrian Messenger*. Westmore became head of the Universal makeup laboratory in 1968, but left there two years later to provide makeup to victims of accidents and birth defects. He returned to filmwork with the 1976 movie *Rocky*. His subsequent movies include *2010* (1984), *Mask* (1985), *Clan of the Cave Bear* (1986), and *Roxanne* (1987). *See also* BLADE RUNNER; CHAMBERS, JOHN; MAKEUP; MORPHING; PIERCE, JACK; *STAR TREK* MOVIES; *WAR OF THE WORLDS*.

Further Reading

Essman, Scott. "Michael Westmore: Behind the Masks." *Cinefex 68*, December 1996.
Taylor, Al. *Making a Monster*. New York: Crown, 1980.

Whale, James (1896–1957)

James Whale directed a string of horror movies during the 1930s, most notably *Frankenstein* (1931) and *The Invisible Man* (1933). Born in England in 1896, he worked as a newspaper cartoonist and an actor before becoming a set designer and then a director. Whale went to Hollywood, California, in 1930 to direct a film version of his British stageplay, *Journey's End,* and decided to remain to make more movies. In the 1940s he retired from filmmaking to become an artist. Whale died of drowning in 1957, under what the police considered mysterious circumstances.

What Dreams May Come

Released by PolyGram Films in 1998, *What Dreams May Come* won an Academy Award for its visual effects, many of which were used to create backgrounds that looked like oil paintings. To create this illusion, filmmakers employed a complicated new image-based paint animation software that attached wet or dry "brush strokes" to stationary or moving scene features. Photographs of real settings were "painted" by adding layer upon layer of these brush strokes, followed by light washes, light beams, and a final heavy texture of brush strokes. All brush strokes used by the software had been scanned into the computer using photographs of real oil paintings representing the styles of many different artists. Unlike real artwork, however, the computer paintings could be enhanced with wind and wave movements to make them seem more three-dimensional.

During postproduction, live-action footage of actors performing on a set were composited with its corresponding painted background. To make sure that the actors' images were situated properly, filmmakers collected data regarding each setting using a sophisticated new tracking system called Lidar. This system used laser-based radar technology to map landscapes and reconstruct the camera motions and camera lens characteristics used to film the scene. From this information, digital experts were able to create a 3-D computer-generated wireframe of the scene, aligned with the live-action footage via a field of orange balls that had been present during filming. Once these orange balls had served as points of reference they were digitally removed from the scenes.

It took 30 computer animators nine months of postproduction to composite all of the film's 250,000 individual elements; some of the individual composited shots had 120–150 different layers. In addition to painted live-action backgrounds, scenes included digital matte paintings created on a computer using scanned images of photographs or glass matte paintings. Live action that would be composited with the mattes was filmed in front of a greenscreen that would then be digitally removed from the shot.

The sets for these live-action performances were large. One scene was shot on a 1,200-foot-long aircraft carrier. Others were filmed in a huge hangar, where set designers had constructed a 300,000-gallon pool surrounded by several multi-story sets. A woman's house was built as a full-sized set as well as a highly detailed miniature. A ship graveyard was also an elaborate miniature. *See also* ANIMATION, COMPUTER; BLUESCREEN PROCESS; COMPOSITING; MATTE.

Further Reading

"A Different Kind of Canvas." *International Photographer*, September 1998.

Martin, Kevin H. "The Sweet Hereafter." *Cinefex* 76, January 1999.

When Worlds Collide

Released by Paramount in 1951, *When Worlds Collide* won an Academy Award for its special effects. Its producer, George Pal, worked closely with the film's special effects supervisor, Gordon Jennings, who would later win an Academy Award for his work on Pal's 1953 film *War of the Worlds*.

For *When Worlds Collide*, Pal had Jennings oversee the creation of a 4-foot-long, remote-controlled model spaceship to represent a 400-foot-long craft that was "launched" from a miniature ramp. He also ordered the construction of 6-foot-tall model buildings to represent eight blocks of New York City. Other miniature sets included a volcanic terrain and a quaking oil field.

Partially because of its elaborate miniatures, the film had a budget of $936,000, which was large at the time. Nonetheless, Pal did rely on a few inexpensive effects. For example, instead of filming a real helicopter rescue with a stuntman, Pal filmed the actor jumping from a prop helicopter. Rearscreen projection made it appear as though the helicopter was in a real setting, and a large wind machine re-created the turbulence of real helicopter blades. Similarly, for the last shot of the movie, Pal used a matte painting instead of a miniature set. Matte paintings were used for many other background shots as well. *See also* ATMOSPHERIC EFFECTS; JENNINGS, GORDON; MATTE PAINTINGS; MINIATURES AND MODELS; PAL, GEORGE; PARAMOUNT PICTURES; PROJECTION PROCESSES; *WAR OF THE WORLDS*.

Further Reading

Brosnan, John. *Movie Magic*. New York: St. Martin's Press, 1974.

Fry, Ron, and Pamela Fourzon. *The Saga of Special Effects*. Englewood Cliffs, NJ: Prentice-Hall, 1977.

Hayes, R.M. *Trick Cinematography*. Jefferson, NC: McFarland & Company, 1986.

Johnson, John. *Cheap Tricks and Class Acts*. Jefferson, NC: McFarland & Company, 1996.

White, Pearl (1899–1924)

Pearl White is representative of the actresses who performed their own stunts during the silent-film era. She was particularly famous for her starring role in *The Perils of Pauline* (1914), a movie serial that placed her character in grave jeopardy during each episode. For these adventures she galloped horses, dangled from cliffs, and performed a variety of other physical stunts. Born March 4, 1889, in Green Ridge, Missouri, White began her acting career as a child, performing in a local theater until she turned 13. At that point she joined a circus. An experienced rider, she performed horse stunts until a serious fall injured her spine. She then returned to acting, first in the theater and then in movies.

Silent-film actress Pearl White, who performed most of her own stunts. *Photofest.*

White's first lead role was in a Western, *The Life of Buffalo Bill* (1910). Four years later, because of the *Pauline* serial, she was one of the best-known actresses of her time. She subsequently did several other serials, continuing to perform their stunts herself; however, some stunts were prohibitive because of her previous spinal injury, and for these she required a stunt double. This double was always a small, slim man dressed as a woman. In addition to her serial work, White acted in Westerns, comedies, and dramas.

She made more than 100 movies, the last in 1924, before retiring in France. *See also* STUNTS.

Further Reading
Miklowitz, Gloria D. *Movie Stunts and the People Who Do Them.* New York: Harcourt Brace Jovanivich, 1980.

Whitlock, Albert

Born in London in 1915, Albert Whitlock was a special effects artist who was particularly skilled in creating matte paintings but did other special effects work as well. His first matte paintings were for the Alfred Hitchcock movie *The Birds* (1963).

Whitlock won Academy Awards for visual effects in 1974 for *Earthquake* and 1975 for *The Hindenberg.* His other movies include *The Reluctant Astronaut* (1967), *The Andromeda Strain* (1971), *Dracula* (1979), *The Blues Brothers* (1980), *Ghost Story* (1981), *Cat People* (1982), *Greystoke: The Legend of Tarzan* (1985), and *The Neverending Story II* (1990). *See also* EARTHQUAKE; THE HINDENBERG; HITCHCOCK, ALFRED; MATTE PAINTINGS.

Further Reading
O'Conner, Jane. *Magic in the Movies.* Garden City, NY: Doubleday, 1980.

Who Framed Roger Rabbit?

The 1988 movie *Who Framed Roger Rabbit?* won an Academy Award for its visual effects, which were created through a partnership between animators at Walt Disney Studios and special effects artists at Industrial Light & Magic (ILM). This partnership was necessary because the film has cartoon characters and live actors interacting with one another.

More than 1,000 optical effects were necessary to merge these two types of film images, and ILM had to develop new techniques to match color and lighting between animation and live action in each scene. ILM also invented a major special effects tool to help with their work on *Who Framed Roger Rabbit?*—a video matting system that allowed storyboard sketches to be composited with live-action footage. This moving storyboard made it possible for special effects experts to previsualize scenes, plan the live actors' movements prior to filming, and instruct the animators on character placement after each scene was shot.

The supervisor of the movie's special effects was Ken Ralston, and its director was Robert Zemeckis; three years earlier the two had worked together to make *Back to the Future*. The animation director for the film was Richard Williams, who had won a 1972 Academy Award for an animated version of *A Christmas Carol*. Zemeckis chose Williams specifically because he promised that when *Who Framed Roger Rabbit?* was finished, it would not look as though the cartoon figures had simply been pasted onto the background plates. Zemeckis disliked earlier combinations of live action and animation, such as those in *Mary Poppins* (1964) and *Pete's Dragon* (1977), specifically for this reason. *See also* ANIMATION, CEL; *BACK TO THE FUTURE* MOVIES; INDUSTRIAL LIGHT & MAGIC; *MARY POPPINS*; MATTE; PREVISUALIZATION; RALSTON, KEN; STORYBOARD; ZEMECKIS, ROBERT.

Further Reading
Duncan, Jody. "20 Years of Industrial Light & Magic." *Cinefex* 65, March 1996.

Smith, Dave. *Disney A-Z.* New York: Hyperion, 1996.

Thomas, Bob. *Disney's Art of Animation: From Mickey Mouse to* Beauty and the Beast. New York: Hyperion, 1991.

Willow

The 1988 movie *Willow* is significant because it featured the first morphing in a full-length motion picture. Morphing is a digital effect whereby a computer transforms one image into another. For *Willow,* the technique was used to show a sorceress turning from a possum into a human, with other animal forms appearing as intermediate steps. To create this effect, Industrial Light & Magic (ILM) made puppets to represent each animal, photographed them, digitized these images, and then instructed the computer to blend one image into the next. *See also* COMPUTER GRAPHICS; MORPHING.

Further Reading
Duncan, Jody. "20 Years of Industrial Light & Magic." *Cinefex* 65, March 1996.

Winston, Stan (1946–)

Stan Winston is one of the most famous makeup and creature effects artists in the film industry. He has won numerous awards, including four Academy Awards for his work on *Aliens* (1986), *Terminator 2: Judgement Day* (1991), and *Jurassic Park* (1993). His other movie credits include *The Terminator* (1984) and *The Lost World* (1997).

Born in 1946, Winston studied painting and sculpture at the University of Virginia before moving to Hollywood, California, in 1968 to become an actor. The following year, he became an apprentice in the makeup department of Walt Disney Studios. After graduating from his apprenticeship he got a job making creatures for a 1972 TV movie, *The Gargoyles,* and won an Emmy Award for his work. He won a second Emmy for the 1974 TV movie *The Autobiography of Miss Jane Pittman,* in which he made actress Cicely Tyson look as if she were 110 years old.

During the late 1970s, Winston turned from television to film and earned an Oscar nomination for his work on the 1981 movie *Heartbeeps,* which required him to make actors appear to be robots. Three years later he created another robot for *The Terminator* using not only a live actor but a full-sized animatronic puppet. He created many other sophisticated puppet monsters as well, including the alien queen in *Aliens* and the dinosaurs of *Jurassic Park*.

While working on *Jurassic Park,* Winston realized the potential of computer effects and decided to create a new company, Digital Domain, in partnership with Scott Ross, who was once chief of the effects company Industrial Light & Magic (ILM), and director James Cameron. Today Digital Domain is considered one of the leading digital special effects companies in the entertainment industry. In addition, Winston has his own makeup and creature facility, the Stan Winston Studios in Van Nuys, California, employing more than 100 artists and technicians. *See also*

ALIEN MOVIES; ANIMATRONICS; CAMERON, JAMES; INDUSTRIAL LIGHT & MAGIC; JURASSIC PARK; THE LOST WORLD; PUPPETRY; TERMINATOR 2: JUDGEMENT DAY.

Further Reading
Koltnow, Barry. "Beyond FX." Los Angeles Daily News, 24 May 1997.
Timpone, Anthony. Men, Makeup, and Monsters. New York: St. Martin's Press, 1996.

Wire Removal, Digital

Digital wire removal is the elimination, via a computer, of any wires and cables used to create a particular special effects shot. The most common reason for wire removal is wirework, also called wire flying, in which an actor is suspended on wires or cables to create the illusion of self-propelled flight or to simulate zero-gravity conditions in space. Two examples of movies that required extensive wire removal for these respective reasons were *Hook* (1991) and *Armageddon* (1998).

In order to remove wires from a scene, the footage must first be digitized and input into a computer. A digital artist then examines each shot to locate the starting and ending points of all straight wires or cables, so that the course of each line can be plotted. Once this has been accomplished, the computer is directed to sample the colors on either side of each line automatically, erasing the wire or cable by blending in the colors that appear on its left and right.

Although this process is fairly simple, it can quickly become complicated when the images behind the wires make it difficult to distinguish them from the background. This was the case with *Hook*, where wirework was done on a highly detailed set. In addition, if the cable or wire is bent, vibrating, or swinging, the computer cannot erase it automatically. Instead the digital artist must paint out the line by hand, frame by frame, again using colors from either side of the line.

It is extremely difficult to hand-paint a series of frames to make it look like continuous movement. Consequently it can take days to remove a wire from a shot. For example, for *Hook*, which had 60 wire removals representing 10,000 frames of manipulated imag-

ery, it took a team of six artists two weeks to complete the wire removal for each shot in the movie. *See also* ARMAGEDDON; HOOK.

Further Reading
Vaz, Mark Cotta. "Journey to Armageddon." Cinefex 75, October 1998.
———. "Return to Neverland." Cinefex 49, February 1992.

Wireframe

A wireframe is a computer-generated image made of interconnecting lines that appear three-dimensional—a digital framework, or skeleton, onto which muscles, skin, and other features are later added. Created with software tools, wireframes can be drawn either from scratch or using scanned real-life images as a guide. Most wireframes are complex, with their lines forming hundreds or even thousands of polygons. For example, the wireframe of a computer-generated monkey creature in *Lost in Space* (1998) had 209,000 polygons.

By "picking up," "dragging," and "dropping" various points on a wireframe, a digital effects artist can adjust the figure's shape and/or animate it. There are also programs that animate wireframes, or even figures in final form, automatically. *See also* ANIMATION, COMPUTER; LOST IN SPACE.

Further Reading
Duncan, Jody. "The Making of a Rockbuster." Cinefex 58, June 1994.

Wirework

Wirework is an effect created with wires. The most basic type is wire flying, which occurs when a performer is suspended from a wire to make it seem as though he or she is flying through the air. It is one of the oldest mechanical effects, having been used in ancient Greek theater to lower a mythical "god" down to the stage. In some cases, it is also a part of stuntwork, used in conjunction with a fall or similar event. However, modern wirework is generally safe enough for a movie's star to perform without a stunt double. For example, actor Robin Williams "flew" on wires in *Hook* (1991) and *Flubber* (1997).

The wires used to suspend today's actors are extremely strong. They are made in single-strand and multi-strand varieties, the latter of which are encased as cables. Single-strand wires range in size from 3/16 to 1/6 of an inch in thickness, while the cables used for more demanding work are approximately 1/4 of an inch thick. To provide "bounce," a thick rubberized cord, called a shock cord or bungee, might be substituted for the cable.

During the early years of filmmaking, piano wires were used for all types of wire flying. A piano wire is made from steel, tin, or a similar metal and can be as thin as .003 inches in diameter. Although it is strong, it is dangerous to use, because the weight of a person can snap it during use. Nonetheless, early filmmakers had to rely on piano wire because it was the only relatively strong wire that was thin enough to be hidden during a shot.

To facilitate a wire's concealment, filmmakers shot wirework in front of backgrounds with vertical lines, such as rooms with striped wallpaper, or painted the wire to match a solid background. For example, in making *Destination Moon* (1950), dozens of wires had to be painted to match an outer space background and minimize reflection from lights used during filming. This paint frequently wore off, so a crew member was assigned the job of regularly touching up each one using a long pole and a sponge dabbed in paint.

Once the bluescreen process was developed, it became possible to remove a wire from a shot automatically and completely. Wires no longer had to be thin, so thick cables were used instead. The cables and accompanying hardware were painted in cobalt blue and actors were flown in front of a bluescreen, so that the cable became part of a background that would later be replaced by another image during the bluescreen process.

In the early years of this process, the removal of bluescreen elements was accomplished on film via a chemical process and a device called an optical printer. Now, however, most wire removal is done digitally. Computers also make it possible to remove wires from a shot even when no bluescreen has been used.

To perform digital wire removal, a digital artist examines each shot to locate the starting and ending points of all straight wires or cables, so that the course of each line can be plotted, and directs the computer to automatically sample the colors on either side of each line and erase the wire or cable by blending in the colors that appear on its left and right.

Digital artists can also remove the equipment that accompanies a wire or cable, although in most cases this equipment can be hidden during live-action filming. The wire is attached to the actor with a harness on one end and some kind of flying device on the other. The latter is typically out of camera range, and the harness is usually worn beneath the actor's costume, which has slits to allow the wire to pass through the material.

There are many different types of harnesses, selected according to the kind of flying being performed, the build of the actor, and the personal preference of the special effects experts working on the project. Some harnesses are simple belts or a combination of belts and straps. Others are made like articles of clothing, such as pants or a body suit. All harnesses have at least one cable connection, which is a loop, hook, or snap shackle attached to some kind of metal plate, swivel, or spinner.

Two cables are necessary when a spreader bar is used during flying. A spreader bar is a piece of steel tubing with an eyebolt at either end. A cable from each side of the actor's harness, generally attached at the hip area, is run up to each eyebolt of the spreader bar, which in turn is attached to a flying rig. The spreader bar's purpose is to keep the actor balanced during flying and to prevent the cables from becoming tangled. It can also be rigged with a spinner, which makes it possible to turn the actor around with the tug of a rope.

There are many types of flying rigs from which such a system can be hung. The most basic is the flying crane, a heavy metal device built somewhat like a teeter-totter. Its ends can go up and down, it can pivot on its axis, and it can move forward or backward on wheels. The most common lengths of flying cranes used today are the 35-foot boom and the 65-foot boom, although the size ranges from 35 feet long to more than 250 feet long. The larger the crane, the more people it takes to operate it, with the minimum being three people. Most are worked manually, using counterweights to lift and lower the actor, because mechanical cranes are too noisy to be used on the set. Another common type of flying rig is the flying track, which is an I-beam mounted above the soundstage. Some flying tracks can only move the actor in two directions, either forward and back or from side to side, while others can move the actor in all four directions. As with flying cranes, tracks are usually operated manually, using some system of ropes, pulleys, and counterbalance weights.

No matter what type of rig is used, the actor's movements generally influence the type of flying that is produced. This is particularly true when the harness is attached to a spinning spreader bar, as was the case for wirework on *Superman* (1978). Just as a professional diver can create spins, rolls, and other movements by tucking legs, throwing legs back, tucking arms, throwing arms out, or doing other movements to redistribute weight, so too can an actor create similar effects while on a wire. With practice, the actor and the special effects expert manning the flying rig can work together to make the illusion of human flight extremely realistic.

Sometimes, however, a wire expert must fly an inanimate object instead of a person, which requires somewhat different techniques. First, because safety is not an issue, a piano wire or monofilament (fishing line), can be used instead of a thick cable. Second, 35- or 60-foot flying cranes are not necessary to fly small objects, so an object-flying crane is substituted. An object-flying crane is a small boom similar to the kind used to hold microphones. It usually sits on a dolly, which enables it to roll into various positions, and can pivot on its axis. Like larger cranes, the object-flying crane uses a system of pul-

leys and counterweights to move small items such as bottles and pens.

Another type of wirework is the use of trip wires to make full-scale or miniature buildings or other structures fall apart on cue. Different kinds of trip wires and trip releases produce different types of collapse, but their basic purpose is to secure an object until a manual, electrical, or pyrotechnic trigger releases it. Wires can also be used to open boxes holding debris or other devices during filming. *See also* HOOK; WIRE REMOVAL, DIGITAL.

Further Reading
McCarthy, Robert E. *Secrets of Hollywood Special Effects*. Boston: Focal Press, 1992.
Vaz, Mark Cotta. "Return to Neverland." *Cinefex 49*, February 1992.

Wise, Robert (1914–)

Director and producer Robert Wise often used special effects in his films. His works include *The Body Snatcher* (1945), *The Day the Earth Stood Still* (1951), *The Haunting* (1963), *The Andromeda Strain* (1971), *The Hindenberg* (1975), *Audrey Rose* (1977), and *Star Trek: The Motion Picture* (1979). Born on September 10, 1914, he began his movie career as an assistant film cutter for RKO Pictures in 1933. Eventually he became a film editor. His most important work in this regard was as the editor of the movie *Citizen Kane* (1941). His first chance at directing came with the 1944 horror film *The Curse of the Cat People*. The movie was well received, as were many of his subsequent works, and in the 1960s he won two Academy Awards for directing, the first for *West Side Story* (1961) and the second for *The Sound of Music* (1965). *See also* THE HINDENBERG; STAR TREK MOVIES.

The Wizard of Oz

Released by MGM in 1939 and nominated for an Academy Award, *The Wizard of Oz* is significant because it was the first major film to employ the three-color Technicolor process. The movie also featured almost every special effect known at the time: mechanical effects, miniatures, rearscreen projection, optical effects, and matte painting.

The mechanical effects in *The Wizard of Oz* include a melting witch and flying monkeys. For the former, the actress playing the witch simply stood on a hydraulically operated platform, which was then lowered beneath the floor. At the same time, dry-ice vapors were released to enhance the illusion of melting, and her costume was attached to the surrounding, non-lowered floor so that it remained in sight after her body disappeared. The flying monkeys were a more difficult mechanical effect. They were created both with miniature rubber monkeys and live actors. The live actors had small motors under their wings to make them flap, and they "flew" on thin wires suspended from a moving structure. In the case of the miniatures, extremely thin music wire not only flew the monkeys but made their wings move.

The tornado featured in the movie was also a miniature. Actually a muslin windsock, it was attached at the top to a movable steel gantry and at the bottom to a slot in the soundstage floor. Music wire running through the sock kept it from tearing as the gantry twisted it around. In addition, air hoses shot dirt around and into the windsock at its base. The fabric was porous enough to allow some of this material to escape, thereby clouding its surface. Glass panels with painted cotton pasted on them stood between the cameras and the tornado. The cotton blocked all view of the movable gantry from the final film.

The tornado scenes also included rearscreen projection. The film of the tornado was projected onto a screen behind the live actress who was trying to escape it. Similarly, film of what was inside the tornado was projected outside her window, so that she appeared to looking out at various items passing by.

One of the simplest optical effects in the film is a huge ball that moves, grows larger, and turns into the Good Witch of the North. It was created with a silver ball approximately 8 inches in diameter. The ball was mounted and filmed on a stationary neutral background. As the camera was moved closer to the object, the ball appeared to increase in size. This film was then printed in such a way that the ball appeared transparent and combined with a second film of actors reacting to a ball that wasn't really there. At the end of the scene, the ball image was faded out and replaced with a shot of the Good Witch.

Many other combination shots were used in *The Wizard of Oz,* most of which involved matte painting. Artists created backgrounds of buildings and scenery using pastels on 4-foot-wide black cardboard. Film of these paintings was then combined with live-action shots. In some cases, not only double but multiple film exposures were needed to combine all the parts. For example, film of the live-action drawbridge of the witch's castle was combined with film of a matte painting depicting its surrounding rivers and cliffs. The river's ripples of moonlight were on a third piece of film.

The Wizard of Oz also used a large number of props, sets, costumes, and makeup techniques. It took 22 weeks to film, and its final cost was $2,777,000. The tornado windsock device was responsible for $12,000 of that cost. *See also* ACCIDENTS; GILLESPIE, A. ARNOLD; MAKEUP; MATTE PAINTINGS; MECHANICAL EFFECTS; MINIATURES AND MODELS; PROJECTION PROCESSES.

Further Reading
Harmetz, Aljean. *The Making of* The Wizard of Oz. New York: Knopf, 1977.

Wonder Man

The 1945 movie *Wonder Man* won an Academy Award for its special effects. They were provided by John Fulton, who was the pioneer of photographic tricks related to the illusion of invisibility. The movie's plot concerns a man who is haunted by the ghost of his twin brother; both parts were played by the same actor, which required Fulton to use split screens as well as his standard invisibility effects. *See also* FULTON, JOHN P.; INVISIBILITY.

Wounds *See* MAKEUP.

X

The X-Files

Based on a popular television show created by Chris Carter, the 1998 movie *The X-Files* is significant because it featured advanced digital extensions to enhance live-action sets. For example, a set of a spaceship interior was enhanced with 48 digital extensions using 3-D geometry and 2-D matte paintings; 90 percent of the interior was digital rather than real. Moreover, live-action filming was deliberately staged to make the digital areas seem integrated into the real set. For example, at one point the main character, Mulder, is seen holding a pair of binoculars. These binoculars are a real prop, but when he drops them into a chasm the binoculars—and the chasm—are a computer-generated image.

Another highly advanced digital effect involved a sequence of shots showing a boy's body being slowly invaded by an alien substance. Digital effects experts first put green stickers on the actor to provide references for lining up shot elements. They then scanned, or transferred information about, the actor's face and upper body into a computer. This enabled the artists to create wireframe images of the boy's arms, legs, neck, and face. At the same time, they took photographs of the boy on the set, digitized them, and used them to paint and texture the wireframe images. Once these representations were realistic enough, the artists altered them to make it look as though the alien substance were

travelling beneath the skin. The final computer-generated images were then substituted for the live-action ones.

Many other scenes were a combination of digital effects and live-action footage. For example, in one shot of a man being blown up in a room of vending machines, each element was filmed separately. The man was shot alone in front of a greenscreen. The vending machines were also shot separately, but were not actually blown up. Instead, digital artists removed pieces of the machines frame by frame via a process called rotoscoping. The explosion was done in miniature, and its image added to the other elements during postproduction.

Similarly, a shot of ice cracking as a spaceship rises from beneath the surface was a combination of live action, miniature photography, and computer graphics. The actors were shot in front of a greenscreen. Part of the ice field was a miniature made of 2,000 carved Styrofoam blocks coated with stearic acid to make them look icy, and covered with salt and hair gel to represent both dusted and clumpy snow. The structure sat on wooden platforms rigged with pneumatic air cylinders and cables to make the model drop at certain points, thereby cracking apart the blocks. The rest of the ice field was a digital matte painting.

The X-Files also featured a spaceship ice cave made from a 150-foot-long field of real ice. Rigged to collapse in certain sections, the model was raised 8 feet from ground level so that steam hoses and nozzles for geysers, as well as basins to catch drips, could be placed underneath the surface. Air conditioning units were used to keep the set at 32 degrees.

Another ice set was a cave made of resin poured over huge sculpted forms. The resulting translucent panels were then mounted upright and backlit to make it seem as though light were filtering through them. The floor of the "cave" was covered with real shaved ice.

An alien that appeared on this set was actually a man in a costume made of a skin-tight Lycra bodysuit to which foam latex pieces were attached. The head came in several different versions, one for the ice cave scene and slightly different versions for scenes in a laboratory and a spaceship. Some of these heads had radio-controlled eyes, lips, cheeks, and brows. Operated by three puppeteers via joystick controllers, the radio-controlled mechanisms filled most of the head, so that the actor could not see outside of it and therefore had to memorize his movements. Stunt heads had cable-controlled jaws and brows, which made some limited vision possible.

The X-Files also featured a spaceship model built at 1/200 scale, which gave it a diameter of 6 feet. Constructed of aluminum with an epoxy surface, the spaceship had neon and fiberoptic lighting and was detailed in etched brass. There was also a 1/12-scale miniature ice station, built to match a full-sized set, as well as a 1/8-scale miniature office building for a pyrotechnics effect.

The office building, which stood 27 feet tall and 35 feet wide, had a vast amount of detail, including miniature desks, clocks, and books. The model was rigged with nine individual charges made with a combination of low-smoke flash powder, benzoyl peroxide, black powder, and other materials. Pneumatic cylinders ensured that the structure's floors would collapse at key points, and a propane mortar was placed in its center to add a fireball to the effect. This footage was composited with shots of a real office building in Los Angeles; a two-story-tall glass and aluminum false front was placed in front of the structure and exploded with primer cord and propane. As with the scene of the exploding vending machines, the office building shots were so well crafted that it seemed as though everything had been filmed on the live-action set and no digital compositing had been used at all. *See also* ANIMATRONICS; ANIMATION, COMPUTER; BLUESCREEN PROCESS; COMPOSITING, MAKEUP; MINIATURES AND MODELS; PYROTECHNICS.

For Further Reading

Duncan, Jody. "Hide It in Shadow, Hide It in Light." *Cinefex 74*, July 1998.

Rogers, Pauline. "Where X Meets Why." *International Photographer*, June 1998.

Simak, Steven A. *"The X-Files." Digital Magic*, August 1998.

Y

Yerkes, Bob (1932–)

Bob Yerkes is one of the oldest working stuntmen in the business. Born in 1932, he learned acrobatics at age 11 and later joined the circus. Between circus performances he did Hollywood stuntwork. He has been performing for more than 50 years and continues to do a variety of stunts, including high falls. His film credits include the *Batman* movies (1989–1997) and *Return of the Jedi* (1983). *See also* BATMAN MOVIES; STAR WARS MOVIES; STUNTS.

Further Reading
"Age Doesn't Keep Him From Taking the Plunge." *The Simi Valley Star,* 6 November 1998.

Young Sherlock Holmes

Released by Paramount Pictures in 1985, *Young Sherlock Holmes* was the first movie to include images painted directly on film using a laser guided by computer software. These images appear in a scene wherein a priest hallucinates that a figure in a stained-glass window has come to life. The figure is a knight that jumps down into a church, wields his sword at the priest, and then chases the terrified man from the building. This stained-glass character was drawn and painted using a stylus on a cathode ray tube, which is a screen that acts as an electronic canvas. Once stored in the computer, the knight was animated to move in different ways

and given its final appearance. At this point, earlier filmmakers would have filmed the moving knight directly off the computer screen. For *Young Sherlock Holmes,* however, special effects artists used a laser to scan the images of the knight directly onto the film, which greatly improved the quality of the final scene. The live-action scenes of the priest were then composited with the digital images using an optical printer.

The scanning process was an important step in the development of digital imaging. It was created by Industrial Light & Magic (ILM), a special effects studio that has been responsible for many advances in digital imaging over the years. ILM has also developed new techniques for puppetry and animatronics. In the case of *Young Sherlock Holmes,* a then relatively new method called "Go-Motion" was used to make a "harpy" puppet move. The Go-Motion system connected the puppet to a computer, so that its movements could be programmed in advance. These movements were performed in front of a bluescreen, manipulated by bluescreen rods that were later removed from the scene along with the background.

The special effects supervisor on *Young Sherlock Holmes* was Dennis Muren, who has also created special effects for such movies as *The Empire Strikes Back* (1980), *ET: The Extraterrestrial* (1982), *Indiana Jones and the Temple of Doom* (1984), *Dragonslayer*

(1981), *Jurassic Park* (1993), and *Jumanji* (1995). *See also* ANIMATION, COMPUTER; COMPUTER GRAPHICS; *DRAGONSLAYER; ET: THE EXTRATERRESTRIAL*; GO-MOTION; *INDIANA JONES* MOVIES; INDUSTRIAL LIGHT & MAGIC; *JUMANJI; JURASSIC PARK;* MUREN, DENNIS; SCANNING; *STAR WARS* MOVIES.

Further Reading

Duncan, Jody. "20 Years of Industrial Light & Magic." *Cinefex* 65, March 1996.

Smith, Thomas G. *Industrial Light & Magic: The Art of Special Effects*. New York: Ballantine Books, 1986.

Vaz, Mark Cotta, and Patricia Rose Duignan. *Industrial Light & Magic: Into the Digital Realm*. New York: Del Rey, 1996.

Z

Zemeckis, Robert (1952–)

American screenwriter and director Robert Zemeckis is known for creating popular movies that feature state-of-the-art special effects. These films include *Back to the Future I* (1989), *Back to the Future II* (1990), *Back to the Future III* (1990), *Who Framed Roger Rabbit?* (1989), *Death Becomes Her* (1992), *Forrest Gump* (1994), and *Contact* (1997).

Born in 1952, Zemeckis attended Northern Illinois University and the University of Southern California (USC) Film School, where he met fellow student and screenwriter Bob Gale. Zemeckis and Gale began writing scripts together, and in 1978 they made their first film, *I Wanna Hold Your Hand*. They then wrote the script for Steven Spielberg's *1941* (1979). This was followed by *Used Cars* (1980) and *Romancing the Stone* (1984), both of which were also directed by Zemeckis. The latter was a great success, solidly establishing his directing career. Zemeckis won an Academy Award for Best Director for his work on *Forrest Gump*. *See also* BACK TO THE FUTURE MOVIES; CONTACT; DEATH BECOMES HER; FORREST GUMP; WHO FRAMED ROGER RABBIT?

Zorro See THE MASK OF ZORRO.

APPENDIX A
Academy Award Winners and Nominees for Special Effects (1939–1998)

Special Effects

1939

The Rains Came—20th Century Fox; Photographic: E.H. Hanson; Sound: Fred Sersen.

Other Nominees

Gone With the Wind—MGM; Photographic: John R. Cosgrove; Sound: Fred Albin, and Arthur Johns.

Only Angels Have Wings—Columbia Pictures; Photographic: Roy Davidson, Sound: Edwin C. Hahn.

The Private Lives of Elizabeth and Essex—Warner Brothers; Photographic: Byron Haskin; Sound: Nathan Levinson.

Topper Takes a Trip—Roach and United Artists; Photographic: Roy Seawright.

Union Pacific—Paramount Pictures; Photographic: Farciot Edouart and Gordon Jennings; Sound: Loren Ryder.

The Wizard of Oz—MGM; Photographic: A. Arnold Gillespie; Sound: Douglas Shearer.

1940

The Thief of Bagdad—Korda and United Artists; Photographic: Lawrence Butler, Sound: Jack Whitney.

Other Nominees

The Blue Bird—20th Century Fox; Photographic: Fred Sersen; Sound: E.H. Hansen.

Boom Town—MGM; Photographic: A. Arnold Gillespie; Sound: Douglas Shearer.

The Boys from Syracuse—Universal Pictures; Photographic: John P. Fulton.

Dr. Cyclops—Paramount Pictures; Photographic: Farciot Edouart and Gordon Jennings.

Foreign Correspondent—Wanger and United Artists; Photographic: Paul Eagler; Sound: Thomas T. Moulton.

The Invisible Man Returns—Universal; Photographic: John P. Fulton; Sound: Bernard B. Brown and William Hedgecock.

The Long Voyage Home—Argosy-Wanger and United Artists; Photographic: R.T. Layton and R.O. Binger; Sound: Thomas T. Moulton.

One Million B.C.—Roach and United Artists; Photographic: Roy Seawright; Sound: Elmer Raguese.

Rebecca—Selznick and United Artists; Photographic: Jack Cosgrove; Sound: Arthur Johns.

The Sea Hawk—Warner Brothers; Photographic: Byron Haskin; Sound: Nathan Levinson.

Swiss Family Robinson—RKO Pictures; Photographic: Vernon L. Walker; Sound: John O. Aalberg.

Typhoon—Paramount Pictures; Photographic: Farciot Edouart and Gordon Jennings; Sound: Loren Ryder.

Women in War—Republic Pictures; Photographic: Howard J. Lydecker, William Bradford, and Ellis J. Thackery; Sound: Herbert Norsch.

1941

I Wanted Wings—Paramount Pictures; Photographic: Farciot Edouart and Gordon Jennings; Sound: Louis Mesenkkop.

Other Nominees

Aloma of the South Seas—Paramount Pictures; Photographic: Farciot Edouart and Gordon Jennings; Sound: Louis Mesenkop.

Flight Command—MGM; Photographic: A. Arnold Gillespie; Sound: Douglas Shearer.

The Invisible Woman—Universal; Photographic: John Fulton; Sound: John Hall.

The Sea Wolf—Warner Brothers; Photographic: Byron Haskin; Sound: Nathan Levinson.

That Hamilton Woman—Korda and United Artists; Photographic: Lawrence Butler; Sound: William H. Wilmarth.

Topper Returns—Roach and United Artists; Photographic: Roy Seawright; Sound: Elmer Raguse.

A Yank in the R.A.F.—20th Century Fox; Photographic: Fred Sersen; Sound: E.H. Hansen.

1942

Reap the Wild Wind—DeMille and Paramount Pictures; Photographic: Farciot Edouart, Gordon Jennings, and William L. Pereira; Sound: Louis Mesenkop.

Other Nominees

The Black Swan—20th Century Fox; Photographic: Fred Sersen; Sound: Roger Heman and George Leverett.

Desperate Journey—Warner Brothers; Photographic: Byron Haskin; Sound: Nathan Levinson.

Flying Tigers—Republic Pictures; Photographic: Howard Lydecker; Sound: Daniel J. Bloomberg.

Invisible Agent—Universal Pictures; Photographic: John Fulton; Sound: Bernard B. Brown.

Jungle Book—Korda and United Artists; Photographic: Lawrence Butler; Sound: William H. Wilmarth.

Mrs. Miniver—MGM; Photographic: A. Arnold Gillespie and Warren Newcombe; Sound: Douglas Shearer.

The Navy Comes Through—RKO; Photographic: Vernon L. Walker; Sound: James G. Stewart.

One of Our Aircraft Is Missing—Powell and United Artists (British); Photographic: Ronald Neame; Sound: C.C. Stevens.

Pride of the Yankees—Goldwyn and RKO; Photographic: Jack Cosgrove and Ray Binger; Sound Thomas T. Moulton.

1943

Crash Dive—20th Century Fox; Photographic: Fred Sersen; Sound: Roger Heman.

Other Nominees

Air Force—Warner Brothers; Photographic: Hans Koenekamp and Rex Wimpy.

Bombardier—RKO; Photographic: Vernon L. Walker; Sound: James G. Stewart and Roy Granville.

The North Star—Goldwyn and RKO; Photographic: Clarence Slifer and R.O. Binger; Sound: Thomas T. Moulton.

So Proudly We Hail—Paramount Pictures; Photographic: Farciot Edouart and Gordon Jennings; Sound: George Dutton.

Stand by for Action—MGM; Photographic: A. Arnold Gillespie and Donald Jahraus; Sound: Michael Steinore.

1944

Thirty Seconds over Tokyo—MGM; Photographic: A. Arnold Gillespie, Donald Jahraus, and Warren Newcombe; Sound: Douglas Shearer.

Other Nominees

The Adventures of Mark Twain—Warner Brothers; Photographic: Paul Detlefsen and John Crouse; Sound: Russell Malmgren and Harry Kusnick.

Since You Went Away—Selznick and United Artists; Photographic: John R. Cosgrove; Sound: Arthur Johns.

The Story of Dr. Wassell—Paramount Pictures; Photographic: Farciot Edouart and Gordon Jennings; Sound: George Dutton.

Wilson—20th Century Fox; Photographic: Fred Sersen; Sound: Roger Heman.

1945

Wonder Man—Goldwyn and RKO; Photographic: John Fulton; Sound: A.W. Johns.

Other Nominees

Captain Eddie—20ᵗʰ Century Fox; Photographic: Fred Sersen and Sol Halprin; Sound: Roger Heman and Harry Leonard.

Spellbound—Selznick and United Artists; Photographic: Jack Cosgrove.

They Were Expendable—MGM; Photographic: A. Arnold Gillespie, Donald Jahraus, and R.A. MacDonald; Sound: Michael Steinore.

A Thousand and One Nights—Columbia Pictures; Photographic: L.W. Butler; Sound: Ray Bomba.

1946

Blithe Spirit—Rank and United Artists (British); Visual: Thomas Howard.

Other Nominee

A Stolen Life—Warner Brothers; Visual: William McGann; Audible: Nathan Levinson.

1947

Green Dolphin Street—MGM; Visual: A. Arnold Gilespie and Warren Newcombe; Audible: Douglas Shearer and Michael Steinore.

Other Nominee:

Unconquered—Paramount Pictures; Visual: Farciot Edouart, Devereux Jennings, Gordon Jennings, Wallace Kelley, and Paul Lerpae; Audible: George Dutton.

1948

Portrait of Jennie—The Selznick Studio; Visual: Paul Eagler, J. McMillan Johnson, Russell Shearman, and Clarence Slifer; Audible; Charles Freeman and James G. Stewart.

1949

Mighty Joe Young—Cooper and RKO.

Other Nominee

Tulsa—Wanger and Eagle Lion.

1950

Destination Moon—Pal Productions and Eagle Lion.

Other Nominee

Samson and Delilah—DeMille and Paramount.

1951

When Worlds Collide—Pal Productions and Paramount Pictures.

No Other Nominees.

1952

Plymouth Adventure—MGM.

No Other Nominees.

1953

War of the Worlds—Pal Productions and Paramount Pictures.

No Other Nominees.

1954

20,000 Leagues Under the Sea—Walt Disney Studios.

Other Nominees

Them!—Warner Brothers.

Hell and High Water—20ᵗʰ Century Fox.

1955

The Bridges at Toko-Ri—Paramount Pictures.

Other Nominees

The Dam Busters—Associated British Picture Corporation Ltd., and Warner Brothers (British).

The Rains of Ranchipur—20ᵗʰ Century Fox.

1956

The Ten Commandments—DeMille and Paramount; John Fulton.

Other Nominee

Forbidden Planet—MGM; A. Arnold Gillespie, Irving Ries and Wesley C. Miller.

1957

The Enemy Below—20ᵗʰ Century Fox; Walter Rossi.

Other Nominee

The Spirit of St. Louis—Hayward-Wilder and Warner Brothers; Louis Lichtenfield.

1958

tom thumb—Galaxy Pictures and MGM; Tom Howard.

Other Nominee

Torpedo Run—MGM; A. Arnold Gillespie and Harold Humbrock.

1959

Ben-Hur—MGM; Visual: A. Arnold Gillespie and Robert MacDonald; Audible: Milo Lory.

Other Nominee
Journey to the Center of the Earth—Joseph M. Schenck Enterprises Inc., Cooga Mooga Film Productions Inc., and 20th Century Fox; Visual: L.B. Abbott, and James B. Gordon; Audible: Carl Faulkner.

1960
The Time Machine—Galaxy and MGM; Gene Warren and Tim Baar.

Other Nominee
The Last Voyage—Stone and MGM; A.J. Lohman.

1961
The Guns of Navarone—Carl Foreman Productions and Columbia Pictures; Visual: Bill Warrington; Audible: Vivian C. Greenham.

Other Nominee
The Absent-Minded Professor—Walt Disney Studios and Buena Vista Distribution Company; Robert A. Mattey and Eustace Lycett.

1962
The Longest Day—Darryl F. Zanuck Productions and 20th Century Fox; Visual: Robert MacDonald; Audible: Jacques Maumont.

Other Nominee
Mutiny on the Bounty—Arcola Productions and MGM; Visual: A. Arnold Gillespie; Audible: Milo Lory.

Special Visual Effects

1963
Cleopatra—Wanger and 20th Century Fox; Emil Kosa Jr.

Other Nominee
The Birds—Alfred Hitchcock and Universal; Ub Werks.

1964
Mary Poppins—Walt Disney Studios and Buena Vista; Peter Ellenshaw, Hamilton Luske, and Eustace Lycett.

Other Nominee
The Seven Faces of Dr. Lao—Pal Productions and MGM; Jim Danforth.

1965
Thunderball—Broccoli-Saltzman-McClory and United Artists (British); John Stears.

Other Nominee
The Greatest Story Ever Told—Stevens and United Artists; J. McMillan Johnson.

1966
Fantastic Voyage—20th Century Fox; Art Cruickshank.

Other Nominee
Hawaii—Mirisch and United Artists; Linwood G. Dunn.

1967
Doctor Doolittle—Apjac and 20th Century Fox; L.B. Abbott.

Other Nominee
Tobruk—Gibraltar-Corman and Universal Pictures; Howard A. Anderson Jr. and Albert Whitlock.

1968
2001: A Space Odyssey—Polaris and MGM; Stanley Kubrick.

Other Nominee
Ice Station Zebra—Filmways and MGM; Hal Millar and J. McMillan Johnson.

1969
Marooned—Frankovich-Sturges and Columbia Pictures; Robbie Robertson.

Other Nominee
Krakatoa, East of Java—ABC Pictures and Cinerama; Eugene Lourie and Alex Weldon.

1970
Tora! Tora! Tora!—20th Century Fox; A.D. Flowers and L.B. Abbott.

Other Nominee
Patton—20th Century Fox; Alex Weldon.

1971
Bedknobs and Broomsticks—Walt Disney Studios and Buena Vista; Alan Maley, Eustace Lycett, and Danny Lee.

Other Nominee
When Dinosaurs Ruled the Earth—Hammer Pictures and Warner Brothers; Jim Danforth and Roger Dicken.

Special Achievement Awards for Visual Effects

1972

L.B. Abbott and A.D. Flowers for *The Poseidon Adventure* (Irwin Allen and 20th Century Fox).

1973

No award given.

1974

Frank Brendel, Glen Robinson and Albert Whitlock for *Earthquake* (Universal-Mark Robson-Filmmakers Group Production and Universal Pictures).

1975

Albert Whitlock and Glen Robinson for *The Hindenberg* (Robert Wise-Filmmakers Group and Universal Pictures).

1976

Carlo Rambaldi, Glen Robinson, and Frank Van Der Veer for *King Kong* (De Laurentiis and Paramount Pictures).

L.B. Abbott, Glen Robinson, and Matthew Yuricich for *Logan's Run* (Saul David and MGM).

Visual Effects

1977

Star Wars—20th Century Fox; John Stears, John Dykstra, Richard Edlund, Grant McCune, and Robert Blalack.

Other Nominee

Close Encounters of the Third Kind— Columbia Pictures; Roy Arbogast, Douglas Trumbull, Matthew Yuricich, Gregory Jein, and Richard Yuricich.

Special Achievement Award

1978

Les Bowie, Colin Chilvers, Denys Coop, Roy Field, Derek Meddings, and Zoran Perisic for *Superman* (Dovemead Ltd., Salkind, and Warner Brothers).

Visual Effects

1979

Alien—20th Century Fox; H.R. Giger, Carlo Rambaldi, Brian Johnson, Nick Allder, and Denys Ayling.

Other Nominees

The Black Hole—Walt Disney Studios and Buena Vista; Petter Ellenshaw, Art Cruickshank, Eustace Lycett, Danny Lee, Harrison Ellenshaw, and Joe Hale.

Moonraker—United Artists; Derek Meddings, Paul Wilson, and John Evans.

1941—A-Team/Spielberg and Universal/ Columbia Pictures, William A. Fraker, A.D. Flowers, and Gregory Jein.

Star Trek: The Motion Picture—Century Associates and Paramount Pictures; Douglas Trumbull, John Dykstra, Richard Yuricich, Robert Swarthe, Dave Stewart, and Grant McCune.

Special Achievement Award

1980

Brian Johnson, Richard Edlund, Dennis Muren, and Bruce Nicholson for *The Empire Strikes Back* (Lucasfilm and 20th Century Fox).

Visual Effects

1981

Raiders of the Lost Ark—Lucasfilm and Paramount Pictures; Richard Edlund, Kit West, Bruce Nicholson, and Joe Johnston.

Other Nominee:

Dragonslayer—Barwood/Robbins and Paramount Pictures; Dennis Muren, Phil Tippett, Ken Ralston, and Brian Johnson.

1982

E.T.: The Extraterrestrial—Universal Pictures; Carlo Rambaldi, Dennis Muren, and Kenneth F. Smith.

Other Nominees

Blade Runner—Michael Deeley-Ridley Scott and The Ladd Company/Sir Run Run Shaw; Douglas Trumbull, Richard Yuricich, and David Dryer.

Poltergeist—MGM/Steven Spielberg, MGM/ United Artists; Richard Edlund, Michael Wood, and Bruce Nicholson.

Special Achievement Award

1983

Richard Edlund, Dennis Muren, Ken Ralston, and Phil Tippett for *Return of the Jedi* (Lucasfilm and 20th Century Fox).

Visual Effects

1984

Indiana Jones and the Temple of Doom— Lucasfilm and Paramount Pictures; Dennis Muren, Michael McAlister, Lorne Peterson, and George Gibbs.

Other Nominees

Ghostbusters—Columbia Pictures; Richard Edlund, John Bruno, Mark Vargo, and Chuck Gasper.

2010—Hyams and MGM; Richard Edlund, Neil Krepela, George Jensen, and Mark Stetson.

1985

Cocoon—Fox/Zanuck-Brown and 20th Century Fox; Ken Ralston, Ralph McQuarrie, Scott Farrar, and David Berry.

Other Nominees

Return to Oz—Disney/Silver Screen Partners II and Buena Vista; Will Vinton, Ian Wingrove, Zoran Perisic and Michael Lloyd.

Young Sherlock Holmes—Amblin Entertainment/Winkler/Birnbaum and Paramount Pictures; Dennis Muren, Kit West, John Ellis and David Allen.

1986

Aliens—20th Century Fox; Robert Skotak, Stan Winston, John Richardson, and Suzanne Benson.

Other Nominees

Little Shop of Horrors—Geffen Productions and Warner Brothers; Lyle Conway, Bran Ferren, and Martin Gutteridge.

Poltergeist II: The Other Side—Victor-Grais and MGM; Richard Edlund, John Bruno, Garry Waller, and William Neil.

1987

Innerspace—Warner Brothers; Dennis Muren, William George, Harley Jessup, and Kenneth Smith.

Other Nominee

Predator—20th Century Fox; Joel Hynek, Robert M. Greenberg, Richard Greenberg, and Stan Winston.

1988

Who Framed Roger Rabbit?—Amblin Entertainment, Touchstone Pictures, and Buena Vista; Arthur Schmidt.

Other Nominees

Die Hard—20th Century Fox; Frank J. Urioste and John F. Link.

Willow—Lucasfilm/Imagine Entertainment and MGM; Dennis Muren, Michael McAlister, Phil Tippett, and Chris Evans.

1989

The Abyss—20th Century Fox; John Bruno, Dennis Muren, Hoyt Yeatman, and Dennis Skotak.

Other Nominees

The Adventures of Baron Munchausen— Prominent Features & Laura Film and Columbia Pictures; Richard Conway and Kent Houston.

Back to the Future, Part III—Universal Pictures and Amblin Entertainment; Ken Ralston, Michael Lantieri, John Bell, and Steve Gawley.

Special Achievement Award

1990

Eric Brevig, Rob Bottin, Tim McGovern, and Alex Funke for *Total Recall* (Carolco and TriStar Pictures).

Visual Effects

1991

Terminator 2: Judgement Day—Carolco and TriStar Pictures; Dennis Muren, Stan Winston, Gene Warren, Jr., and Robert Skotak.

Other Nominees

Backdraft—Trilogy Entertainment/Grazer and Universal Pictures; Mikael Salomon,

Allen Hall, Clay Pinney, and Scott Farrar.

Hook—TriStar Pictures; Eric Brevig, Harley Jessup, Mark Sullivan, and Michael Lantieri.

1992

Death Becomes Her—Universal Pictures; Ken Ralston, Doug Chiang, Doug Smythe, and Tom Woodruff Jr.

Other Nominees

Alien 3—20th Century Fox; Richard Edlund, Alec Gillis, Tom Woodruff Jr., and George Gibbs.

Batman Returns—Warner Brothers; Michael Fink, Craig Barron, John Bruno, and Dennis Skotak.

1993

Jurassic Park—Universal Pictures and Amblin Entertainment; Dennis Muren, Stan Winston, Phil Tippett, and Michael Lantieri.

Other Nominees

The Nightmare before Christmas—Touchstone Pictures; Pete Kozachik, Eric Leighton, Ariel Velasco Shaw, and Gordon Baker.

Cliffhanger—TriStar Pictures and Columbia Pictures; Neil Krepela, John Richardson, John Bruno, and Pamela Easley.

1994

Forrest Gump—Paramount Pictures; Ken Ralston, George Murphy, Stephen Rosenbaum, and Allen Hall.

Other Nominees

The Mask—New Line Cinema and Dark Horse Entertainment; Scott Squires, Steve William, Tom Bertino, and John Farhat.

True Lies—20th Century Fox and Universal Pictures; John Bruno, Thomas L. Fisher, Jacques Stroweis, and Patrick McClung.

1995

Babe—Universal Pictures and Kennedy Miller Productions; Scott E. Anderson, Charles Gibson, Neal Scanlan, and John Cox.

Other Nominee

Apollo 13—Universal Pictures and Imagine Entertainment; Robert Legato, Michael Kanfer, Leslie Ekker, and Matt Sweeney.

1996

Independence Day—20th Century Fox and Centropolis Film Productions; Volker Engel, Douglas Smith, Clay Pinney, and Joseph Viskocil.

Other Nominees

Dragonheart—Universal Pictures; Scott Squires, Phil Tippett, James Straus, and Kit West.

Twister—Warner Brothers, Universal Pictures, Constant Productions, and Amblin Entertainment; Stefan Fangmeier, John Frazier, Habib Zargarpor, and Henry L. Labounta.

1997

Titanic—20th Century Fox, Paramount Pictures, and Lightstorm Entertainment; Robert Legato, Mark Lasoff, Thomas L. Fisher, and Michael Kanfer.

Other Nominees

The Lost World: Jurassic Park—Universal Pictures and Amblin Entertainment; Dennis Muren, Stan Winston, Randal M. Dutra, and Michael Lantieri.

Starship Troopers—Phil Tippett, Scott E. Anderson, Alec Gillis, and John Richardson.

1998

What Dreams May Come—Polygram Films; Joel Hynek, Nicholas Brooks, Stuart Robertson, and Kevin Mack.

Other Nominees

Armageddon—Touchstone Pictures; Richard R. Hoover, Pat McClung, and John Frazier.

Mighty Joe Young—Walt Disney Studios; Rick Baker, Hoyt Yeatman, Allen Hall, and Jim Mitchell.

Makeup

1981

An American Werewolf in London—Lycanthrope/Polygram and Universal Pictures; Rick Baker.

Other Nominee

Heartbeeps—Phillips/Universal Pictures; Stan Winston.

1982

Quest for Fire—International Cinema Corporation and 20th Century Fox; Sarah Monzani and Michele Burke.

Other Nominee

Gandhi—Indo/British Films and Columbia; Tom Smith.

1983

No award given.

1984

Amadeus—Zaentz and Orien; Paul LeBlanc and Dick Smith.

Other Nominees

Greystoke: The Legend of Tarzan, Lord of the Apes—Warner Brothers; Rick Baker and Paul Engelen.

2010—Hyams and MGM; Michael Westmore.

1985

Mask—Universal Pictures; Michael Westmore and Zoltan Elek.

Other Nominees

The Color Purple—Warner Brothers; Ken Chase.

Remo Williams: The Adventure Begins—Clark/Spiegel/Bergman and Orion; Carl Fullerton.

1986

The Fly—Brooksfilms Ltd. and 20th Century Fox; Chris Walas and Stephan Dupuis.

Other Nominees

The Clan of the Cave Bear—Warner Brothers/PSO and Warner Brothers; Michael G. Westmore and Michele Burke.

Legend—Legend Company and Universal Picutres; Rob Bottin and Peter Robb-King.

1987

Harry and the Hendersons—Universal Pictures/Amblin Entertainment; Rick Baker.

Other Nominee

Happy New Year—Columbia Pictures; Bob Laden.

1988

Beetlejuice—Geffen Film Company and Geffen/Warner Brothers; Ve Neill, Steve LaPorte, and Robert Short.

Other Nominees

Coming to America—Murphy and Paramount Pictures; Rick Baker.

Scrooged—Linson and Paramount Pictures; Tom Burman and Bari Dreiband-Burman.

1989

Driving Miss Daisy—Zanuck Company and Warner Brothers; Manlio Rocchetti, Lynn Barber, and Kevin Haney.

Other Nominees

The Adventures of Baron Munchausen—Prominent Features & Laura Film and Columbia Pictures; Maggie Weston and Fabrizio Sforza.

Dad—Universal Studios/Amblin Entertainment; Dick Smith, Ken Diaz, and Greg Nelson.

1990

Dick Tracy—Touchstone and Buena Vista; John Caglione Jr. and Doug Drexler.

Other Nominees

Cyrano de Bergerac—Hachette Premiere/Camera One and Orion Classics; Michele Burke and Jean-Pierre Eychenne.

Edward Scissorhands—20th Century Fox; Ve Neill and Stan Winston.

1991

Terminator 2: Judgement Day—Carolco and TriStar Pictures; Stan Winston and Jeff Dawn.

Other Nominees

Hook—TriStar Pictures; Christina Smith, Monty Westmore, and Greg Cannom.

Star Trek VI: The Undiscovered Country—Paramount Pictures; Michael Mills, Edward French, and Richard Snell.

1992

Bram Stoker's Dracula—Columbia Pictures, American Zoetrope, and Osiris Films; Greg Cannom, Michele Burke, and Matthew W. Mungle.

Other Nominees

Batman Returns—Warner Brothers; Ve Neill, Ronnine Specter, and Stan Winston.

Hoffa—Ve Neill, Greg Cannom, and John Blake.

1993

Mrs. Doubtfire—Blue Wolf Productions and 20th Century Fox; Greg Cannom, Ve Neill, and Yolanda Toussieng.

Other Nominees

Philadelphia—TriStar Pictures; Carl Fullerton and Alan D'Angerio.

Schindler's List—Universal Pictures/Amblin Entertainment; Christina Smith, Matthew Mungle, and Judith A. Cory.

1994

Ed Wood—Touchstone Pictures; Rick Baker, Ve Neill, and Yolanda Toussieng.

Other Nominees

Forrest Gump—Paramount Pictures; Daniel C. Striepeke, Hallie D'Amore, and Judith A. Cory.

Mary Shelley's Frankenstein—TriStar Pictures and American Zoetrope; Daniel Parker, Paul Engelen, and Carol Hemming.

1995

Braveheart—20th Century Fox, Paramount Pictures, The Ladd Company, Icon Entertainment International; Peter Frampton, Paul Pattison, and Lois Burwell.

Other Nominees

My Family, Mi Familia—American Playhouse, American Zoetrope, Majestic Film, New Line Cinema; Ken Diaz and Mark Sanchez.

Roommates—Nomura Babcock and Brown, Hollywood Pictures, Interscope Communications, PolyGram Filmed Entertainment; Greg Cannom, Bob Laden, and Colleen Callaghan.

1996

The Nutty Professor—Universal Pictures and Imagine Entertainment; Rick Baker and David LeRoy Anderson.

Other Nominees

Ghosts of Mississippi—Castle Rock Entertainment and Columbia Pictures; Matthew W. Mungle and Deborah La Mia Denaver.

Star Trek: First Contact—Paramount Pictures; Michael Westmore, Scott Wheeler, and Jake Garber.

1997

Men in Black—MacDonald-Parkes, Columbia Pictures, and Amblin Entertainment; Rick Baker and David LeRoy Anderson.

Other Nominees

Mrs. Brown—British Broadcasting Corporation (BBC); Lisa Westcott, Veronica Brebner, and Beverly Binda.

Titanic—20th Century Fox, Paramount Pictures, and Lightstorm Entertainment; Tina Earnshaw, Greg Cannom, and Simon Thompson.

1998

Elizabeth—Gramercy Pictures; Jenny Shircore.

Other Nominees

Saving Private Ryan—DreamWorks; Lois Burwell, Conor O'Sullivan, and Daniel C. Striepeke.

Shakespeare in Love—Miramax; Lisa Westcott and Veronica Brebner.

APPENDIX B
Special Effects Magazines

There are many magazines devoted to providing information about special effects businesses and techniques. The following are the most popular of those available to the general public.

American Cinematographer
P.O. Box 18089
Anaheim, CA 92817-9959
1-800-448-0145
http://www.cinematographer.com
Published monthly by the American Society of Cinematographers, this magazine concentrates on visual/digital effects.

Cinefantastique
7240 W. Roosevelt Road
Forest Park, IL 60130
708-366-5566
Published monthly, this magazine offers a wide variety of information about special effects.

Cinefex
P.O. Box 20027
Riverside, CA 92516
1-800-434-3339
circulation@cinefex.com
Published quarterly, this magazine offers the most complete information about all types of special effects used in movies. It also features photographs from major films and interviews with top special effects artists and directors.

Computer Graphics World and **Digital Magic**
918-835-3161
http://www.cgw.com
These two magazines offer information about computer graphics. *Digital Magazine* is an offshoot of *Computer Graphics World* and provides more detailed information about animation and visual effects in the entertainment industry.

Film & Video Magazine
701 Westchester Avenue
White Plains, NY 10604-3098
http://www.filmandvideomagazine.com
Published monthly, this magazine offers articles about the technical aspects of filmmaking and visual effects, not only for the movie industry but also for television production, interactive entertainment, and commercial advertising.

Make-Up Artist Magazine
P.O. Box 4316
Sunland, CA 91041-4316
http://www.makeupmag.com
Published six times a year, this magazine discusses all aspects of makeup and makeup special effects in both movies and television.

APPENDIX C
Special Effects Houses

This appendix is taken from the *Hollywood Reporter* magazine's *Blu-Book Film and TV Production Directory* section on special effects companies. Company specialties are noted in parentheses where applicable. The list should provide some idea of how many companies are involved in the special effects industry, how they are distributed geographically, and how specialized some of them are.

Computer Graphics, Digital Effects and Electronic Effects

Advanced Media Systems (Burbank, CA; Rendering services for optical and special effects companies)

Arete Image Software (Sherman Oaks, CA; High-resolution oceanographic and atmospheric graphics)

Available Light Ltd. (Burbank, CA; Rotoscoping and wire removal)

Banned from the Ranch Entertainment (Santa Monica, CA; Visual effects)

Bifrost Laserfx (West Hills, CA; 3-D animation)

Bio-Vision (San Francisco, CA; Human and Animal Motion-Capture Service)

Blue Sky Studios/VIFX (Los Angeles, CA, and Harrison, NY; Computer-generated images and visual effects)

BlueScreen LLC (Los Angeles, CA; Bluescreen)

Cinesite Digital Studios (Hollywood, CA)

Computer Café Inc. (Santa Maria, CA; 3-D Animation, Digital Compositing)

The Computer Film Company (Culver City, CA)

Cyber F/X (Montrose, CA; Laser scanning)

Digiscope (Culver City, CA; Digital visual effects)

Digital Domain (Venice, CA; Digital special effects)

Dream Quest Images (Simi Valley, CA; Digital compositing, and computer-generated imaging)

Dynacs Digital Studios (Pasadena, CA; Colorization, compositing, wire removal, and 2-D and 3-D modeling and effects)

EDS Digital Studios (Los Angeles, CA)

Encore Visual Effects (Hollywood, CA, and Santa Monica, CA; Visual effects, computer imaging, and animation)

Fantasy II Film Effects (Burbank, CA)

Film East (Marlton, NJ; Visual effects, computer-generated imaging, and motion capture)

Jim Henson Productions (Hollywood, CA)

Hollywood Digital (Hollywood, CA)

Holy Cow! Visual Effects (Los Angeles, CA)

House of Moves Motion Capture Studio (Venice, CA; 3-D motion-capture studio for animation and special effects)

Illuvatar LLC (Westminster, CA; Rendering and production support)

Industrial Light & Magic (San Rafael, CA)

Lumeni Productions Inc. (Glendale, CA; Digital and film titles, graphics, and special effects)

Matte World Digital (Novato, CA; Digital mattes, 3-D environments, and digital composites)

Metropolis Digital (San Jose, CA)

Novocom (Playa Vista, CA; Singapore; and London)

Pacific Data Images (Palo Alto, CA; 3-D character animation, visual effects)

Pacific Ocean Post (Santa Monica, CA)

Pacific Title and Art Studio (Hollywood, CA)

Pacific Title Digital (Los Angeles, CA)

Rhythm & Hues Studio (Los Angeles, CA)

Santa Barbara Studios (Santa Barbara, CA)

Soho Digital Film (Toronto, Ontario; Digital imaging and video to film)

Sony Pictures Imageworks (Culver City, CA)

Special Effects Systems (Santa Clarita, CA)

Stargate Films Inc. (Burbank, CA; Visual effects production company)

Talking Laser Company (Marina del Rey, CA; Laser effects)

Tippett Studio (Berkeley, CA)

VisionArt (Santa Monica, CA; Computer-generated imaging, digital compositing, and morphing)

Visual Concept Engineering (Sylmar, CA; 2-D and 3-D animation, compositing).

Makeup and Creature Effects

Altered Anatomy Inc. (North Hollywood, CA; Prosthetics and makeup effects)

Amalgamated Dynamics Inc. (Chatsworth, CA; Prosthetics and animatronics)

Anatomorphex (North Hollywood, CA; Special effects animatronics and action props)

Joe Blasco Makeup Center (Hollywood, CA, Los Angeles, CA, and Orlando, FL; Training, and creature and prosthetic design)

Michael Burnett Productions (Simi Valley, CA; Prosthetics)

Greg Cannom Creations (Valencia, CA; Special makeup and creature effects)

The Character Shop Inc. (Canoga Park, CA; Makeup effects and animatronics)

Creative Character Engineering (Van Nuys, CA)

Custom Color Contacts (New York, NY; Blind effects, bloody eyes, and cat eyes)

Davis Dental Supply (North Hollywood, CA; Rigid and flexible acrylics, teeth)

Direct Effects (Brooklyn, NY; Character makeup, aging, and full body suits)

Jim Henson's Creature Shop (Burbank, CA)

Image Creators Inc. (Santa Monica, CA; Prosthetic makeup and creature costumes)

The Jones Effects Studio (Santa Clarita, CA; Prosthetics, animatronics, and puppets)

S.M.G. Effects Inc. (Sun Valley, CA; Prosthetics, animatronics, creature suits)

Shapeshifter Make-Up F/X (Sun Valley, CA; Prosthetics, creatures, sculptures, and props)

Stan Winston Studio (Van Nuys, CA)

Mechanical Effects

AAFAB Engineering (La Crescenta, CA; Mechanical and atmospheric effects)

Action Jets F/X (Hollywood, CA; Radio-controlled jets, helicopters, and cars)

Amalgamated Dynamics (Chatsworth, CA; Animatronics)

ANA Special Effects (Van Nuys, CA; Flying, rain, and snow)

Anatomorphex (North Hollywood, CA; Animatronics, action props, and other mechanical effects)

Boom Boom Effects (Mission Hills, CA; Atmospheric effects)

Brazil Fabrication & Design (Los Angeles, CA; Motion control rigging)

Michael Burnett Productions (Sun Valley, CA; Mechanical creatures)

Greg Cannom Creations (Valencia, CA; Animatronic creatures and puppets)

The Character Shop (Canoga Park, CA; Robots and animatronics)

Dave's Marine Services Inc. (Long Beach, CA; Water cannons, water jets, and walk-on-water platforms)

Digital Domain (Venice, CA)

Direct Effects (Long Island City, NY; Cable control, animatronics, and pneumatics)

Effective Engineering (San Diego, CA; Mechanical and electronic effects and animatronics)

Gizmo Special Effects (Whippany, NJ; Motion-controlled custom rigs)

Jim Henson's Creature Shop (Burbank, CA Animatronics and puppets)

Hunter/Gratzner Industries, Inc. (Los Angeles, CA; Design and conceptualization of mechanical effects)

Image Creators Inc. (Santa Monica, CA; Animatronics, puppets and action props)

Industrial Light & Magic (San Rafael, CA)

JEX FX (San Rafael, CA; Custom mechanical special effects)

Lexington Scenery & Props (Sun Valley, CA; Pneumatic and hydraulic effects)

MediaMation (Torrance, CA; Motion control, motion bases, animatronics)

David Miller Studio (Van Nuys, CA; Robotic characters and mechanical puppets)

Phoenix Scale Models (El Cajon, CA; Miniatures)

Polar Technologies USA (Folsom, CA; Real snow)

Sony Pictures Imageworks (Culver City, CA)

Special Effects Unlimited Inc. (Hollywood, CA; Electronics and robotics)

Optical and/or Photographic Effects

Advanced Camera Systems (Van Nuys, CA)

Advanced Media Systems (Sherman Oaks, CA)

David Allen Productions (Burbank, CA)

Howard A. Anderson Company (Universal City, CA, and Los Angeles, CA; Optical printer service)

Available Light Ltd. (Burbank, CA)

Bifrost Laserfx (West Hills, CA)

Cablecam Systems, Ltd. (Granada Hills, CA; Repeatable Speed and Position Through Pyrotechnics)

Cinema Engineering Company (North Hollywood, CA)

Cinema Research Corporation (Hollywood, CA)

Cinesite Digital Studios (Hollywood, CA)

Digiscope (Culver City, CA; Digital visual effects)

Fantasy II Film Effects (Burbank, CA)

Bruce Fier Photography (Reseda, CA; Still Photographs for Background Plates)

Gizmo Special Effects (Whippany, NJ; Motion Control Systems and Cameras)

Richard Haas Photog Imagery Ltd. (Universal City, CA; Bluescreen work)

Holy Cow! Visual Effects (Los Angeles, CA)

International Creative Effects (Burbank, CA)

Lazarus Lighting Design (Glendale, CA; Fiberoptic special effects)

Lumeni Productions Inc. (Glendale, CA; Digital image processing and backlit effects)

Opticam Inc. (Santa Monica, CA; 35mm and 7mm film formats)

Out of the Blue (North Hollywood, CA; Visual effects)

Pacific Title & Art Studio (Hollywood, CA)

Quantel, Ltd. (Berkshire, UK, and Darien, CT; Domino: Digital Film Opticals System)

Schwartzberg & Company (Studio City, CA; Integrated Live Action and Special Effects)

Soho Digital Film (Toronto, Ontario; Digital imaging, Video to film)

Sony Pictures Imageworks (Culver City, CA)

T&T Optical Effects (Glendale, CA)

Title House Inc. (Hollywood, CA)

Todd-AO Digital Images (Hollywood, CA; High-resolution film composites; Bluescreen, redscreen, and greenscreen)

Visual Concept Engineering (Sylmar, CA; Bluescreen, motion control, and animation).

Pyrotechnics and Stunts

Advanced Fire and Rescue Services (Mission Hills, CA)

Boom Boom Effects (Mission Hills, CA)

FX Zone (Irvine, CA)

Illusions (Santa Clarita, CA)

International Creative Effects (Burbank, CA)

Special Effects Systems (Santa Clarita, CA)

Stunt Predators USA (Madison, OH)

Stunts Ability (Pine Valley, CA)

Thrillseekers Unlimited Inc. (Las Vegas, NV)

Mike Tristano & Weapons & FX (Sherman Oaks, CA)

Vision Crew Unlimited (Los Angeles, CA)

BIBLIOGRAPHY

Abbott, L.B. *Special Effects: Wire, Tape, and Rubber Band Style*. Hollywood, CA: ASC Press, 1984.

Academy Awards Web site. http://www.oscar.com.

"Age Doesn't Keep Him from Taking the Plunge." *The Simi Valley Star*, 6 November 1998.

Agel, Jerome (ed.), *The Making of Kubrick's 2001*. New York: Signet, 1968.

Archer, Steve. *Willis O'Brien: Special Effects Genius*. Jefferson, NC: McFarland & Company, 1998.

Bacon, Matt, Brian Henson, and Anthony Minghella. *No Strings Attached: The Inside Story of Jim Henson's Creature Shop*. New York: Macmillan, 1997.

Bell, Jon A., and George Maestri. *3-D Studio Special Effects*. Indianapolis: New Riders Publishing, 1994.

Bouzereau, Laurent, and Jody Duncan. Star Wars: *The Making of* Episode I: The Phantom Menace. New York: Ballantine, 1999.

Brosnan, J. *Movie Magic*. New York: St. Martin's Press, 1974.

Cadigan, Pat. *The Making of* Lost in Space. New York: HarperPrism, 1998.

Clark, Douglas. "Effects Wizard Lends *Titanic* Touch to Film." *Los Angeles Daily News*, 28 December 1997.

Cohen, Daniel. *Masters of Horror*. New York: Clarion, 1984.

"*Contact:* A New Space Odyssey." *Preview*, July-August 1997.

Cosner, Sharon. *Special Effects in Movies and Television*. New York: J. Messner, 1985.

"Creating the Special Visual Effects for *Raiders.*" http://www.smartlink.net/~deej7/sfx.htm, 1999.

Croal, N'Gai. "Maximizing the *Matrix.*" *Newsweek;* 19 April 1999.

Culhane, John. *Special Effects in the Movies*. New York: Ballantine, 1981.

Curtis, Sandra. *Zorro Unmasked*. New York: Hyperion, 1998.

De Leeuw, Ben. *Digital Cinematography*. Boston: AP Professional, 1997.

"A Different Kind of Canvas." *International Photographer*, September 1998.

"Digital Tools." *VFX/HQ*. http://vfxhq.com/tools/index.html, May 1999.

DiOrio, Carl. "The After-Effect: Slowing Follows the FX Explosion." *Hollywood Reporter*, 10 December 1997.

Dowling, Robert J. *The 1998 Hollywood Reporter Blu-Book*. Hollywood, CA: Hollywood Reporter, 1998.

Duncan, Jody. "The Beauty in the Beasts." *Cinefex 55*, August 1993.

———. "Blowing Up Baby." *Cinefex 52*, November 1992.

———. "The Ghost and Mr. Muren." *Cinefex 63*, September 1995.

———. "Gorilla Warfare." *Cinefex 62*, June 1995.

———. "Heart and Soul." *Cinefex 66*, June 1996.

———. "Hide It in Shadow, Hide It in Light." *Cinefex 74*, July 1998.

———. *The Making of* The Lost World. New York: Ballantine Books, 1997.

———. "The Making of a Rockbuster." *Cinefex 58,* June 1994.

———. *"The Nutty Professor:* Pleasingly Klump." *Cinefex 67,* September 1996.

———. "On the Shoulders of Giants." *Cinefex 70,* June 1997.

———. "Puppy Proliferation." *Cinefex 69,* 1997.

———. "A *Small Soldiers* Story." *Cinefex 75,* October 1998.

———. *"Titanic* Aftermath." *Cinefex 72,* December 1997.

———. "20 Years of Industrial Light and Magic." *Cinefex 65,* March 1996.

Ellrod, J.G. *The Stars of Hollywood Remembered.* Jefferson, NC: McFarland & Company, 1997.

Elrick, Ted. "Elemental Images." *Cinefex 70,* June 1970.

Engel, Volker, and Rachel Aberly. *The Making of* Godzilla. New York: HarperPrism, 1998.

Erdman, Terry J. "The Secrets of *Star Trek: Insurrection.*" New York: Pocket Books, 1998.

Esseman, Scott. "A Gorilla Named Joe." *Cinefex 76,* January 1999.

———. "John Chambers: Maestro of Makeup." *Cinefex 71,* September 1997.

———. "Michael Westmore: Behind the Masks." *Cinefex 68,* December 1996.

Fetrow, Alan G. *Feature Films, 1940–1949: A United States Filmography.* Jefferson, NC: McFarland & Company, 1994.

———. *Sound Films, 1927–1939: A United States Filmography.* Jefferson, NC: McFarland & Company, 1992.

Fielding, Raymond. *The Technique of Special Effects Cinematography.* Boston: Focal Press, 1985.

Fry, Ron, and Pamela Fourzon. *The Saga of Special Effects.* Englewood Cliffs, NJ: Prentice-Hall, 1977.

Gross, Edward. *The Making of the Trek Films.* New York: Image, 1992.

Harmetz, Aljean. *The Making of* The Wizard of Oz. New York: Knopf, 1997.

Hayes, R.M. *3-D Movies: A History and Filmography of Stereoscopic Cinema.* Jefferson, NC: McFarland & Company, 1998.

———. *Trick Cinematography.* Jefferson, NC: McFarland & Company, 1986.

Hines, Bill. "Techniques for In-Camera Effects." *International Photography,* December 1997.

Huffstutter, P.J. "Visual Effects Pioneer Tells How Digital Showed His Studio Who Was Boss." *Los Angeles Times,* 20 October 1997.

Hutchison, David. *Film Magic: The Art and Science of Special Effects.* New York: Prentice-Hall, 1987.

Imes, Jack. *Special Visual Effects: A Guide to Special Effects Cinematography.* New York: Van Nostrand Reinhold, 1984.

Jenson, P.M. *The Men Who Made the Monsters.* New York: Twayne, 1996.

Johnson, John. *Cheap Tricks and Class Acts.* Jefferson, NC: McFarland & Company, 1996.

Johnson, Robert K. *Francis Ford Coppola.* Boston: Twayne, 1977.

Jones, Karen R. Mars Attacks! *The Art of the Movie.* New York: Ballantine Books, 1996.

Kael, Pauline. *Raising Kane.* New York: Bantam, 1971.

Karon, Paul. "Filmmakers Pay a High Price for Techno Tricks." *Variety,* 28 September– 4 October 1998.

———. "Left Brain vs. Right: F/X Wizards Try to Conjure Equity in Pic Biz." *Variety,* 24–30 August 1998.

Katz, Ephraim. *The Film Encyclopedia.* Rev. Fred Klein and Ronald Dean Nolen. New York: HarperPerennial, 1998.

Kaufman, Debra. "Effects in the Vertical Realm." *Cinefex 54,* May 1993.

———. "Exploring *The Lost World." Digital Magic,* June 1997.

———. "Summer's CG Stars." *Digital Magic,* August 1997.

———. "Synergistic Effects." *Digital Magic,* August 1998.

Kawin, Bruce F. *How Movies Work.* Berkeley: University of California Press, 1992.

Killick, Jane, with David Chute and Charles M. Lippincott. *The Making of* Judge Dredd. New York: Hyperion, 1995.

Koltnow, Barry. "Beyond FX." *Los Angeles Daily News*, 24 May 1997.

LaBrecque, Ron. *Special Effects: Disaster at Twilight Zone*. New York: Scribner, 1998.

Laski, Beth. "High Five." *Cinescape*, May/June 1997.

Lasseter, John, and Steve Daily. Toy Story: *The Art and Making of the Animated Film*. New York: Hyperion, 1995.

Lee, Nora. "*Total Recall:* Interplanetary Thriller." *American Cinematographer*, July 1990.

Lentz, Harris M. *Obituaries in the Performing Arts, 1996: Film, Television, Radio, Theatre, Dance Music, Cartoons, and Pop Culture*. Jefferson, NC: McFarland & Company, 1997.

―――. *Obituaries in the Performing Arts 1995: Film, Television, Radio, Theatre, Dance Music, Cartoons, and Pop Culture*. Jefferson, NC: McFarland & Company, 1996.

―――. *Obituaries in the Performing Arts, 1994: Film, Television, Radio, Theatre, Dance Music, Cartoons, and Pop Culture*. Jefferson, NC: McFarland & Company, 1996.

Liebman, Roy. *From Silents to Sound: A Biographical Encyclopedia of Performers Who Made the Transition to Talking Pictures*. Jefferson, NC: McFarland & Company, 1998.

Lopez, Daviel. *Films by Genre: 775 Categories, Styles, Trends and Movements Defined, with a Filmography for Each*. Jefferson, NC: McFarland & Company, 1993.

Luskin, Jonathan. "Riders on the Storm." *Cinefex 66*, June 1966.

MacDonald, Matthew J. "Color My World." *Cinefex 76*, January 1999.

Magrid, Ron. "Effects Profiles: Power Prelude." *Hollywood Reporter*, Special Effects Special Issue; 18–24 May 1999.

―――. "Many Hands Make Martian Memories." *American Cinematographer*, July 1990.

―――. "Transparent Effects Make *Casper* a Landmark." *American Cinematographer*, December 1995.

Mallory, Michael. "Twist & Shout & Scream." *VISFX*, February 1998.

Maltin, Leonard. *The Disney Films*. New York: Bonanza Books, 1973.

―――. *Leonard Maltin's 1999 Movie and Video Guide*. New York: Signet, 1998.

Martin, Kevin H. "Close *Contact*." *Cinefex 71*, September 1997.

―――. "Kirk Out." *Cinefex 61*, March 1995.

―――. "Letting Slip the Dogs of War." *Cinefex 49*, 1992.

―――. "Life Neverlasting." *Cinefex 52*, November 1992.

―――. "Martian Chronicles." *Cinefex 77*, April 1999.

―――. "Phoenix Rising." *Cinefex 69*, March 1997.

―――. "The Sweet Hereafter." *Cinefex 76*, January 1999.

―――. "*The Truman Show:* The Unreal World." *Cinefex 75*, October 1998.

―――. "War Stories." *Cinefex 65*, March 1996.

Mason, Dave. "A Bold New 'Trek': Santa Barbara Firm Creates Digital Universe." *Ventura County Star Television Guide*, 15–21 November 1998.

Matthews, Charles. *Oscar A to Z: A Complete Guide to More Than 2400 Movies Nominated for Academy Awards*. New York: Doubleday, 1995.

McCann, Michael. "Medical Services on Set and Location." www.tmn.com/Artswire/ csa/arthazards/performing/filmmed, May 1999

―――. "Stunt Safety." Center for Safety in the Arts. http://www.tmn.com/Artswire/ csa/arthazards/performing/stunts, May 1999.

McCarthy, Robert E. *Secrets of Hollywood Special Effects*. Boston: Focal Press, 1992.

McKenzie, Alan, and Derek Ware. *Hollywood Tricks of the Trade*. New York: Gallery Books, 1986.

McNary, Dave. "Cause of Effects." *Los Angeles Daily News*, 28 September 1997.

Miklowitz, Gloria D. *Movie Stunts and the People Who Do Them*. New York: Harcourt Brace Jovanivich, 1980.

Mitchell, Jim, and Ellen Poon. "Our Favorite Martians." *Digital World*, February 1997.

Mowrey, Peter C. *Award Winning Films: A*

Viewer's Reference to 2700 Acclaimed Motion Pictures. Jefferson, NC: McFarland & Company, 1994.

Murdock, Andrew, and Rachel Aberly. *The Making of* Alien Resurrection. New York: HarperPrism, 1997.

Naha, Ed. *The Making of* Dune. New York: Berkley, 1984.

Nowlan, Robert A., and Gwendolyn Wright Nowlan. *The Films of the Eighties: A Complete, Qualitative Filmography to Over 3400 Feature-Length English Language Films, Theatrical and Video-Only, Released between January 1, 1980, and December 31, 1989*. Jefferson, NC: McFarland & Company, 1991.

Norton, Bill. "Cloning Aliens." *Cinefex 73*, March 1998.

Odien, Jeff. "On the Waterfront." *Cinefex 64*, December 1995.

Ohanian, Thomas A., and Michael E Phillips. *Digital Filmmaking*. Boston: Focal Press, 1998.

Oliviero, Jeffrey. *Motion Picture Players' Credits: Worldwide Performers of 1967 through 1980 with Filmographies of Their Entire Careers, 1905–1983*. Jefferson, NC: McFarland & Company, 1991.

"One Killed in Disney Film Stunt." AP News Report, 19 December 1995.

Painter, Jamie. "An Insider Interview with Phil Tippett." *Star Wars Insider 33*, Spring 1997.

Parkinson, David. *The Young Oxford Book of the Movies*. Oxford: Oxford University Press, 1995.

Pincus, Edward, and Steven Ascher. *The Filmmaker's Handbook*. New York: Plume, 1984.

Pourroy, Janine. "Basic Black." *Cinefex 70*, June 1997.

———. "The Game Board Jungle." *Cinefex 64*, December 1995.

———. "Split Personalities." *Cinefex 67*, September 1996.

"The Power Ski Stars in *Waterworld*." http://www.powerski.com/wtrwrld.html, May 1999.

Prokop, Tim. "Fireworks." *Cinefex 67*, September 1996.

———. "Launching Apollo." *Cinefex 63*, September 1995.

Robertson, Barbara. "Cyber Movie Stars." *Digital Magic*, January 1996.

———. "A Draconian Effort." *Digital Magic*, August 1996.

———. "Gadzooks! It's *Godzilla*." *Computer Graphics World*, July 1998.

———. "*Jumanji's* Amazing Animals." *Computer Graphics World*, January 1996.

Robertson, J.F. *The Magic of Film Editing*. Blue Ridge Summit, PA: Tab Books, 1993.

Rogers, Pauline. "*Godzilla*." *International Photographer*, May 1998.

———. "*Tomorrow Never Dies*." *International Photographer*, December 1997.

———. "Where X Meets Why." *International Photographer*, June 1998.

Ryan, Rod. *American Cinematographer Manual*. Hollywood: The ASC Press, 1993.

Sammon, Paul M. "Bug Bytes." *Cinefex 73*, March 1998.

———. *Future Noir: The Making of* Blade Runner. New York: Harper Collins, 1996.

———. "The Perigee of Apogee." *Cinefex 54*, May 1993.

Sanello, Frank. *Spielberg: The Man, the Movies, the Mythology*. Dallas, TX: Taylor Publishing, 1996.

Shannon, John. "Crash McCreery: Doing Dinosaurs and Such." *Cinefex 69*, March 1997.

Shatner, William. Star Trek *Movie Memories*. New York: Harper Collins, 1994.

Shay, Don. "Back to *Titanic*." *Cinefex 72*, December 1997.

———. "A Close Encounter with Steven Spielberg." *Cinefex 53*, February 1993.

———. "Dennis Muren: Playing It Unsafe." *Cinefex 65*, March 1996.

———. "Dick Smith: 50 Years in Makeup." *Cinefex 62*, June 1995.

———. "In the Digital Domain." *Cinefex 55*, August 1993.

———. "Mayhem over Miami." *Cinefex 59*, September 1994.

———. "Ship of Dreams." *Cinefex 72*, December 1997.

———. "30 Minutes with the Godfather of Digital Cinema." *Cinefex 65,* March 1996.

Shay, Estelle. "Company File: Pixar." *Cinefex 55,* August 1993.

Shay, Estelle. "*Dr. Doolittle:* Animals with Attitude." *Cinefex 75,* October 1998.

———. "From the Mouth of *Babe.*" *Cinefex 64,* December 1995.

———. "Michael Fink: From Fine Arts to Filmmaking." *Cinefex 66,* June 1996.

———. "Of Mice and Men." *Cinefex 73,* March 1998.

———. "Thoroughly Modern Mummy." *Cinefex 77,* April 1999.

Silberg, Jon. "*Armageddon.*" *Film & Video,* June 1998.

Simak, Steven A. "Cloning the Digital Way." *Digital Magic,* August 1997.

———. "Graphics That Sizzle!" *Digital World,* April 1997.

———. "*Lost in Space:* The Movie Camp Revamped." *Digital World*, April 1998.

———. "*The X-Files.*" *Digital Magic,* August 1998.

Smith, Dave. *Disney A–Z.* New York: Hyperion, 1996.

Smith, Thomas G. *Industrial Light and Magic: The Art of Special Effects.* New York: Ballantine Books, 1986.

Spehr, Paul C., with Gunar Lundquist. *American Film Personnel and Company Credits, 1908–1920.* Jefferson, NC: McFarland & Company, 1996.

"Spirits of the Lost Ark: Photographic Effects in *Raiders of the Lost Ark.*" http://www.smartlink.net/~deej7/sfx.htm, 1999.

Strauss, Bob. "Dogged Path to Making of *Dr. Doolittle.*" *Los Angeles Daily News*, 27 June 1998.

Stecker-Orel, Elinor. *Special Effects Photography Handbook.* Buffalo, NY: Amherst Media, 1998.

Stensvold, Mike. *In-Camera Special Effects.* Englewood Cliffs, NJ: Prentice-Hall, 1983.

Street, Rita. "The Calisto Effect." *Cinefex 69,* March 1997.

———. "The Communication of Monster-Sized Ideas through Digital Tools." *Film & Video,* May 1998.

———. *Compter Animation: A Whole New World.* Gloucester, MA: Rockport, 1998.

———. "*Dante*'s Inferno." *Cinefex 69,* March 1997.

———. "Independents Day: The State of the State of the Art in Visual Effects." *Film & Video,* May 1999.

———. "Toasting the Coast." *Cinefex 71,* September 1997.

Stuntmen and Special Effects. New York: Ripley Books, 1982.

Swinfield, Rosemarie. *Stage Makeup Step-By-Step.* White Hall, VA: Betterway Publications, 1995.

Taylor, Al. *Making a Monster.* New York: Crown, 1980.

Thomas, Bob. *Disney's Art of Animation: From Mickey Mouse to* Beauty and the Beast. New York: Hyperion, 1991.

Timpone, Anthony. *Men, Makeup, and Monsters.* New York: St. Martin's Press, 1996.

Upstill, Steven. *The Renderman Companion: A Programmers Guide to Realistic Computer Graphics.* Reading, MA: Addison Wesley, 1990.

Vaz, Mark Cotta. "Boss Film Studios: End of an Era." *Cinefex 73,* March 1998.

———. "Dredd World." *Cinefex 62,* June 1995.

———. "Freeze Frames." *Cinefex 71,* September 1997.

———. "Forever and a Knight." *Cinefex 63,* September 1995.

———. "Journey to *Armageddon.*" *Cinefex 75,* October 1998.

———. "A Knight at the Zoo." *Cinefex 51,* August 1992.

———. "*Lost in Space:* Lost in London." *Cinefex 74,* July 1998.

———. "Return to Neverland." *Cinefex 49,* February 1992.

———. "Through the Stargate." *Cinefex 61,* March 1995.

———. *Visions of* Armageddon. New York: Hyperion. 1998.

Vaz, Mark Cotta, and Shinji Hata. *From* Star Wars *to Indiana Jones: The Best of the Lucasfilm Archives.* San Francisco: Chronicle Books, 1994

Vaz, Mark Cota, and Patricia Rose Duignan. *Industrial Light & Magic: Into the Digital Realm*. New York: Del Rey, 1996.

Vaziri, Todd. "Boldly Trekking into the Digital World." *VFX/HQ*, http://vfxhq.com/spotlight98/9805b.html, May 1998.

Vincenzi, Lisa. "Digital Previsualization." *Digital Magic*, July 1997.

Wagstaff, Sean. "Buyer's Guide: After Effects Plug-Ins." *Digital World*, September 1997.

Waldman, Alan. "Bond on the Run." *Hollywood Reporter*, 19 December 1997.

White, Charlie. "It's a Horserace! The Workstation Derby." *Digital Magic*, October 1997.

Wiley, Mason, and Damien Bona. *Inside Oscar: The Unofficial History of the Academy*. New York: Ballantine Books, 1993.

Williams, David E. "Reintroducing Bond . . . James Bond." *American Cinematographer*, December 1995.

Wolff, Ellen. "SGI at 15." *Variety*, 20–26 October 1997.

Woods, Bob (ed). Star Wars Episode I: The Phantom Menace: *The Official Souvenir Magazine*. Lucasfilm Ltd., 1999.

INDEX

By John Lewis

Index

Index

Index

Index

Index

Patricia Netzley has written nonfiction for children, young adults, and adults. Her publications include *The Assassination of President Kennedy, The Importance of Queen Victoria, The Mysterious Death of Butch Cassidy, Life During the Renaissance, Encyclopedia of Social Protest Literature,* and *Encyclopedia of Environmental Literature.*